Southeast Asia

Southeast Asia

Tradition and Modernity
in the Contemporary World

Donald G. McCloud

Westview Press

BOULDER • SAN FRANCISCO • OXFORD

Copyright © 1995 by Westview Press, Inc.

Published in 1995 in the United States of America by Westview Press, Inc., 5500 Central Avenue, Boulder, Colorado 80301-2877, and in the United Kingdom by Westview Press, 12 Hid's Copse Road, Cumnor Hill, Oxford OX2 9JJ

A CIP catalog record for this book is available from the Library of Congress.
ISBN 0-8133-1897-1.—ISBN 0-8133-1896-3(pbk.)

Printed and bound in the United States of America

The paper used in this publication meets the requirements
of the American National Standard for Permanence of Paper
for Printed Library Materials Z39.48-1984.

10   9   8   7   6   5   4   3   2   1

*To Carol, who has shared with me
the experiences of Southeast Asia*

Contents

Maps and Charts

Acronyms

ABC	ASEAN Brussels Committee
AFTA	ASEAN Free Trade Agreement
ANZUS	Pacific Security Treaty
APEC	Asia-Pacific Economic Community
ASA	Association of Southeast Asia
ASEAN	Association of Southeast Asian Nations
ASPAC	Asia and South Pacific Area Council
BN	Barisan Nasional
BSPP	Burmese Socialist Program Party
CENTO	Central Treaty Organization
CGDK	Coalition Government of Democratic Kampuchea
CGI	Consultative Group on Indonesia
EAEC	East Asia Economic Caucus
EEC	European Economic Community
ESCAP	Economic and Social Commission for Asia and the Pacific
FUNCINPEC	National United Front for an Independent, Neutral, Peaceful and Co-operative Cambodia
GOLKAR	Government-controlled Functional Group (Indonesia)
GSP	Generalized System of Preferences
IGGI	Inter-Governmental Group on (or for) Indonesia
KBL	Kilusan Bagong Lipunan
KPNLF	Kampuchean People's National Liberation Front
MAPHILINDO	Malaysia, the Philippines, and Indonesia
MCA	Malayan Chinese Organization
MIC	Malayan Indian Congress
MP	Member of Parliament
NATO	North Atlantic Treaty Organization
NIC	newly industrializing country
OPEC	Organization of Petroleum Exporting Countries
PAP	People's Action Party (Singapore)

PAS	Islamic Party of Malaysia
PDI	Indonesian Democratic Party
PKI	Indonesian Communist Party
PPP	Development Unity Party (Indonesia)
PRC	People's Republic of China
PRG	Provisional Revolutionary Government
PRK	People's Republic of Kampuchea
SCCAN	Special Coordinating Committee of ASEAN Nations
SEATO	Southeast Asia Treaty Organization
UMNO	United Malays National Organization
UNCTAD	United Nations Conference on Trade and Development
UNDP	United Nations Development Program
UNTAC	United Nations Transitional Authority
VOC	Dutch East India Company
ZOPFAN	Zone of Peace, Freedom, and Neutrality

Preface

This volume is much a reflection of what I have seen and heard while working in Southeast Asia, especially in Indonesia, Malaysia, and, less frequently, Burma, Singapore, and the Philippines. These are countries where I have spent varying amounts of time over the last two decades, rarely on scholarly missions but normally as a bureaucrat—interacting with staff from government ministries and bureaus, private business-persons, lawyers, engineers, and other professionals, on occasion with university faculty members, staff from other institutions of higher education, and, also occasionally, individuals from everyday walks of life. The views—values, practices, ideas, and beliefs—from outside academia, whether the U.S. or Southeast Asian academic world, are somewhat different than those from within. Academics perhaps too frequently talk too preponderantly to one another, and the opportunity to live and work essentially outside of the academic community in Southeast Asia has given me the opportunity to see another side of the region.

Comparison of this "other side" of Southeast Asia to its academic side tends to reveal groups and individuals more conservative in views, less global in orientation, less interested in the cosmopolitan culture of the global academic community, and certainly less enthralled with things Western. This other side as a group is significantly larger than the Southeast Asian academic group and also much more reflective of the broad-based outlook of most Southeast Asians. Recently some political leaders such as Singapore's former prime minister, Lee Kuan-Yew, and Malaysia's current prime minister, Datu Seri Mahathir Mohamad, have given strong public voice to many of these views, but in reality they are simply reflecting views that a significant percentage of their peoples—both in the government and in the general population—have held for many years. The voices of Lee, Mahathir, and other public figures certainly have received great press coverage, but it is the average Singaporean, Malaysian, Thai, or Indonesian working in an office or factory who acts out and will respond to these views; they are the staple of the values and ideas reflected in neotraditionalism.

This book gives recognition to these people because they are real or "everyday" Southeast Asians in a somewhat visceral—and especially nonacademic—way. They find increasing comfort and confidence in their own modes of operations and peculiar (to Western minds) ways of doing things. They are part of a daily acting out of what it means to be Southeast Asian, or more precisely Indonesian, Singaporean, Malaysian, Thai, Burmese, Filipino, Vietnamese, Cambodian, Laotian, or Bruneian. Certainly this is not to propose that Southeast Asian academics are, somehow, not Southeast Asian; they certainly are and they play an extremely important vanguard role in defining issues which all Southeast Asians must address in the continuous molding of contemporary society. But their vanguard position means that by definition they often do not reflect the norm; particularly when they talk with other academics—they may too readily operate as part of the global academic community, which has its own language, beliefs, biases, and values. The real point is to applaud the success of all Southeast Asians in defining and protecting their own being, recognizing the value of their own cultural and historical heritage, and refusing to be pressured by outsiders into following the greatly over-glamorized West. Try as we in the West may try, it is clear that Southeast Asia is not prepared to accept the Western idea of a homogenized world culture.

The vibrancy of Southeast Asian societies is easy for anyone visiting there to sense very quickly. Many have presumed that Southeast Asia could only enter the modern world by creating a framework of Western political and social institutions. This is not true and has not been for a long time as Southeast Asia has insisted on building its own institutions and social structures. ASEAN reflects their version of regional cooperation—just one example of their particularistic approach to politics. Nine years ago, I wrote another volume, *System and Process in Southeast Asia: The Evolution of a Region* (Westview Press, 1986), which began to challenge this presumption of Western dominance. The years since the publication of *System and Process* have confirmed that Southeast Asia is well on its way to rebuilding its own unique identity. Although it will remain difficult for many of us in the West to accept or understand, the imperial age may have finally come to an end, and it is my hope that *Southeast Asia: Tradition and Modernity in the Contemporary World* helps to clarify how and why this has happened. At the same time, the emergence of this unique Southeast Asian identity is not a romanticized, panacea solution for all the many difficulties that the region faces: growth and development will continue to create real-time problems, and governments—however imbued with traditional values—as often as not will fail to provide satisfactory responses and policies. What must be understood is that the successes and the failures will be defined in Southeast Asian terms.

As with any undertaking of this magnitude, I am greatly indebted to many people for their help in completing the task. First among them are the many colleagues and friends in Southeast Asia with whom I have worked and who have shared with me some of their thoughts and hopes for the future and who have often demonstrated in the "actions speak louder than words" sense their own grasp of both the traditional and the modern in Southeast Asia. I have also appreciated the continued support of Donald E. Weatherbee from the University of South Carolina and R. William Liddle from The Ohio State University. Without doubt the greatest support has come from my good friend, colleague, and boss, William L. Flinn, who has shared with me the continuing struggle of balancing academic interests and commitments and requirements of the Midwest Universities Consortium for International Activities, Inc. (MUCIA). The opportunities that MUCIA has offered have been unique and have enabled me to work in Southeast Asia continuously for nearly twenty years. It has been through MUCIA's programs that I have had the opportunities to meet and work with such a large and diverse spectrum of Southeast Asians. More than any other, it has been the interaction with these people that has influenced the views and options in this book.

At MUCIA, a number of other people have been instrumental in preparation of this manuscript. Mrs. Gloria Mitchell has done all of the typing and word-processing through the final edits. Mrs. Patricia C. Inman and Mr. Andrew R. Shulman undertook the formatting and computer related corrections for the final draft and in preparation of the camera-ready copy. None of these tasks were simple and their willingness to give of their time and knowledge is greatly appreciated. They have made this work substantially better.

Despite the kindness and efforts of so many on my behalf, the statements of fact and opinion as well as the errors and shortcomings of this work remain my responsibility.

Donald G. McCloud
Columbus, Ohio

1

Southeast Asia in Regional and Global Contexts

Some names, like "rose," acknowledge what exists. Others, like "unicorn," create what otherwise does not exist. In between lie names that simultaneously describe and invent reality. "Southeast Asia" is one of these.[1]

Determining where Southeast Asia falls on the continuum from the rose to the unicorn is a major challenge in understanding Southeast Asia. For many Westerners, however, problems of understanding and dealing with Southeast Asia are perceptual—more a problem of looking at the rose but seeing the unicorn—and the problem is compounded because the rose is changing very rapidly whereas our image of the unicorn remains fixed.

The Southeast Asian Unicorn

Why are Western views of Southeast Asia distorted? The angle of vision for most Western observers has been determined by the prism of *Western* history. First, the fundamental worldview of many people in the West is based on the presumed superiority of Western culture. Whether derived from the European imperial experience or couched in the American Puritan ethic of moral authority, the West has readily accepted the notion that its culture and practices are the high-water mark in world civilization. In particular, worldviews of most Americans carry the notion of the United States as the pinnacle of civilization and as having a mandate from God to provide moral leadership for the rest of the world. Although other cultures such as the Chinese may be respected for their

1

past richness, their weakened position in the contemporary world as compared to most Western states is taken as fair indication that their culture is declining.

Popular Western perspectives of Southeast Asia were shaped by those involved in the region—colonialists, missionaries, and a small but vociferous group of sojourners and travelers who visited there and wrote of their experiences. Their views of the region were built on the basic Western worldview, and they reported activities that seemed to confirm that viewpoint. British, French, Dutch, and other European colonial administrators brought Weberian rational, bureaucratic organization to the region, often characterized as the "white man's burden" among indolent natives. However, this sense of moral legitimacy and obligation, a hallmark of the colonial era, stood side by side with the colonial powers' phenomenal exploitation of the region's physical and material wealth. The images of Southeast Asia, shaped in the early centuries of East-West contact, remain:

> Though the accretions of details multiplied many times, the Western image and perceptions . . . remained remarkably consistent. Ideas and stereotypes of a mysterious and marvelous region remained relatively unchanged through the centuries. . . . It seems evident that it was this stereotypical perception that sustained the growing Western interests in the region.[2]

An unfortunate but preponderant impact of the colonial period was to focus Southeast Asian history away from indigenous cultures and politics and toward Western involvement, thus establishing the view that little of political or economic importance had transpired in Southeast Asia before the arrival of the Europeans. Histories of Southeast Asia from 1500 to 1940 are largely elitist records of colonial conquests, governors, policies, and economic developments, with the "natives" depicted as recipients of colonial largesse in the form of occasional educational, health, or other reforms.

By the nineteenth century, Europeans, although not rejecting their claims to superiority based on the Christian religion, came to view "science and especially technology as the most objective and unassailable measure of their own civilization's past achievement and present worth. In science and technology, their superiority was readily demonstrable, and their advantages over other peoples grew at an ever increasing pace."[3] Even after World War II, despite Allied rhetoric about self-determination and independence, a primary goal for many leaders was to reestablish colonial administrations in Southeast Asia, perhaps with an evolutionary program leading toward some type of semi-independence or commonwealth status. For example, a British plan promised to help

Burma attain, "as fully and completely as may be possible . . . [the] high position of Dominion status—a position to which [the British] would not lightly admit outside people without full consideration of the character of their Government."[4] At the time (1941), British newspapers carried letters suggesting that the Burmese were unfit for early self-rule. As a result, the Western world has held the deeply ingrained perception that Southeast Asians are incapable of defining or managing their own affairs.

The Christian missionary movement similarly reinforced these perceptions. Missionaries were, by definition, bringing the—obviously superior—message of Christianity to an uninformed populace. From the very earliest years of colonial expansion, Europeans "viewed their Christian faith . . . as the key source of their distinctiveness from and superiority to non-Western peoples."[5] Americans were less aggressive in the development of a colonial empire but equally zealous in missionary work. Missionaries brought stories and pictures of poor and dependent natives waiting to be saved with the message of Christianity to countless church meetings throughout the United States and Europe as part of fund-raising ventures. The missionary ideal of carrying the Christian message to the weak, downtrodden, and poor was a natural extension of the belief that the West was blessed by God and chosen for this very mission. The missionary attack on behalf of Christianity required that local religion and culture be denigrated or rejected. The consistent message of deprivation among these poor, Southeast Asian souls (who could be "saved" with a small donation from each parishioner) deeply reinforced the image of unequal status for the region and, by implication and extension, meant that it was not necessary to understand local cultures because they were about to change—be Christianized—in any case.

Since early information coming to the West was largely obtained from the reports and writings of colonialists and missionaries, many unicorn-like perceptions of Southeast Asia became and remain firmly established in Western thought. Even the burgeoning tourism industry has not expanded understanding of the region and may, in fact, have contributed to the continuation of stereotypical images. Mention of Thailand, Indonesia, or the Philippines, for example, often brings to mind an exotic tropical paradise of palm trees, beautiful ocean beaches, and costumed dancers or mysterious and fearful jungles with poisonous snakes, deadly upas trees, and endless swamps inhabited by savages and headhunters. Monkeys, temples, volcanoes, and terraced rice fields are sometimes added to this travel-poster image, but names other than Bali, Manila, Singapore, and perhaps Bangkok are difficult to recall and impossible to locate on a map. The issues confronting tourists—air travel or cruise-ship schedules, the number of stars used to rank the quality of hotels, the endless shopping emporia, and even the traditional dance program performed at the hotel dinner theater—offer scant hope of conveying the realities of life and culture in Southeast Asia. A region so different from home cannot be understood without serious effort to transcend enigmatic stereotypes.

In the years following World War II, Western perceptions of Southeast Asia have also been distorted by a worldview dominated by cold war competition with the Soviet Union and by a subvariable of the cold war—development assistance or foreign aid—which reinforced the Western view that the states of Southeast Asia were not only incapable of acting at the global political level but that they required Western assistance (and, not infrequently, manipulation) to survive at the regional or national level. This unequal view has perpetuated a contemporary version of the colonial unicorn—a region and peoples incapable of making their own decisions and certainly unable to participate equally in the modern world. The bipolar mentality of the decades following World War II (characterized by the phrase, "You are either with us or against us; no compromise or middle ground is possible") diminished the necessity of understanding the particular and local issues confronting the states in Southeast Asia. Although Americans were proud of their role in the Philippines, where U.S. colonial policies had led to independence and democracy following the acquisition of the Philippines from the Spanish, the United States readily compromised the interests of independence in the face of European demands to return to their Southeast Asian colonies in the hope of ensuring that the European states would maintain their anticommunist policies. From that point to the present, particularly including the period of the Vietnam War, U.S. policies toward Southeast Asia have consistently been shaped by political factors at the global level with little consideration or understanding of their impact at the regional or state level.

In many respects Vietnam was the arena in which global politics (the domino theory framed the nature of the bipolar conflict there) ran amok because of the lack of understanding of local conditions; however, the experience there did little to educate the American people to the realities of Vietnam or Southeast Asia. Decades of misunderstanding and perceptions based on an image of Southeast Asia as a tropical paradise populated with somewhat lazy and less than competent natives came face-to-face with bamboo spikes, tiger cages, and death for young soldiers in the jungle foliage of Vietnam. More important, the tenacity and patience, aggressiveness and skill, commitment and purpose of the North Vietnamese found no parallel in Western mythology about Southeast Asia. For Americans, who think of themselves as mentors of freedom and nationalism, the traumatic experience of Vietnam may have been analogous to the rejection felt earlier by the colonial powers. Vietnam became the site of the collapse of the broader U.S. policy of containing communism in Asia, but most Americans were unable to grasp sufficiently the political implications of this conflict and were thus unable to judge whether the United States should have intervened in the first place or withdrawn when it did. Ultimately, Americans will remember the Vietnam War for its impact on U.S. domestic politics, not because it altered perceptions of the region or the course of U.S. foreign policy in Asia.

The final barrier to improved understanding of Southeast Asia is the growing Western concept of an evolving world culture, which most define as American consumer culture spread throughout the world. World culture is perhaps a secular extension of the Christian missionary concept of reshaping the world's peoples in the Christian image. In a facile leap of logic, proponents of this view argue that such symbols of the United States as blue jeans, rock music, and McDonald's hamburgers, so readily accepted by youth around the world—including those in Southeast Asia—signify that Western (i.e., American) values are being adopted throughout the world. Some have tried to argue both sides of the issue: "The very idea of becoming Westernized will lose meaning as we think of the more generalized concept of a world culture;" but at the same time, "national cultures are much too distinctive, even in long-industrialized countries, to justify the fear of a single, homogenized modern culture enveloping all of mankind."[6] Even those who study Southeast Asia have emphasized the disintegration of an idealized—if not romanticized—view of traditional societies, evoking images of peace, harmony, and quiet stability based on communal village life and mutual social welfare in the face of intruding Western values of individualism, consumerism, and other trappings of the modern world. Ironically, it is our very limited understanding of regions such as Southeast Asia and our lack of appreciation of the cultural resilience of peoples there—which grow out of a general lack of understanding—that enable us to make the world–culture generalization.

Southeast Asia itself has added to this Western confusion and misperception. The region's diversity is legend, making generalization and summary difficult at best and certain to highlight as many exceptions as to confirm regularity in economics, culture, politics, and life. The precolonial state system in Southeast Asia did not lend itself to enhancing regional cooperation and exchange, and the subsequent colonial period increased the isolation within the region by linking respective colonies more tightly to European metropoles than to neighboring economic and political centers within the region.

Much of the early rhetoric of independence and state development was couched in Western terminology. Most early nationalist leaders were trained in Europe, and many were more comfortable in the colonial metropoles than in their own capital cities, let alone in hinterland villages and rural areas. Under such leadership, it should be no surprise that most Southeast Asian states sought to emulate the Western model state by creating parliaments and other political institutions in mirror images of those in Europe or the United States. Western technical advice and technology were widely sought and utilized.

Once independence became a reality, however, the situation began to change. The glamor and anticipation of independence quickly gave way to recognition of the innumerable and intractable problems that few political leaders could solve. Frustrations increased and many early policy prescriptions advocated by early leaders failed. The vast majority of second-generation leaders were trained at home, products of the national educational process and fully imbued with the nationalist ideals of their newly independent states; at times they translated those ideals into a hostility toward foreign—particularly Western—ideas and values. This increasingly nationalist focus is still taking shape in many Southeast Asian states, and it finds expression in many forms: greater economic independence and assertiveness, renewed religious fervor, rejection of the use of English or other foreign languages, adaptation and adjustment of Western political structures to local conditions, and restatements of the value of traditional cultural norms.

Western stereotypes sustain the perceptions that Southeast Asia cannot be a competent part of the global political system, but, more important, they demonstrate the West's failure to measure accurately the vigor of anticolonialism, growing nationalism, and other radical sentiments, as well as the resilience of cultural traditions there. Western images belie a region that is rich in historical and cultural traditions; complex social structures; vigorous political, economic, and cultural growth and that is increasingly confident in its prominent place within global politics. The lack of sensitivity to Southeast Asia's social and political environment has left the governments of Western Europe and the United States with inadequate knowledge of how to formulate policies that would strength-en local political dynamics. Just as the moral certitude of the "white man's burden" proved insufficient for the reassertion of colonialism, so the moral verve and simplicity of saving people from communism collapsed in the face of the complexities of the Vietnamese revolution.

Lack of comprehension throughout the Western world may be part of a larger inability to grasp the contemporary realities of global interrela-tionships; what transpires in Malaysia (or Botswana or Chile) has little obvious impact on day-to-day life in Europe or in the United States. Also, Western stereotypes are expressed in terms of unilinear relationships: Imperialism was the outward extension of Western control over subject peoples, and the missionary movement was similarly singular in directional flow. The cold war relationships between superpowers and newly independent states were also largely unidirectional. Western ideological underpinnings of innate superiority coupled with nearly 500 years of proactive world expansion, domination, and leadership have etched in the Western mind a set of hierarchical rankings for all of the world's peoples. This relational perspective has left the West unprepared to deal with Southeast Asia on an equal footing.

There is also constant pressure to focus on issues and concerns closer to home: For Europeans, there are the struggles in the evolution of the European Common Market; for Americans, pressing domestic political issues always take precedent over foreign policy and international relations, except for occasional war ventures. The size of the United States, particularly the vastness of its Middle West, sustains a certain insulation from the outside world. Although quantities of consumer items are imported from Asia to these Middle Western areas, a sense of stability remains that is not influenced by the external world. The price of a Toyota (or blue jeans or tennis shoes) may rise at any time, but the price is still fixed in dollars, and for all intents and purposes the Toyota seems just like the domestic Chevrolet. The connection between life, politics, and productivity in the rest of the world and general U.S. well-being has not been made by most middle-income Americans. Ultimately, the average citizen, whether in Great Britain or the United States or France, is not cognizant of the economic realities of a highly integrated global economy.

Nevertheless, signals from Southeast Asia are clear. The West is now in danger of falling two generations behind in its perceptions of Southeast Asia. Not only are the platitudes and generalizations of the colonial and missionary eras no longer valid, but our thinking from the days of the cold war—envisioning a largely dependent Southeast Asia patiently waiting for guidance from the United States or Europe—is equally bankrupt. The message, which continues to gain strength and find clarity of voice, is unmistakable: The region is prepared to stand, and is capable of standing, on its own, and Americans as well as other Westerners should recognize the terms and conditions implied in this independence when shaping their interactions with Southeast Asia. The widely popular term the *Pacific Century* may be too glib, but in the coming decades Asia in general and Southeast Asia in particular will probably demonstrate the greatest growth of any region in the world. A parallel expansion in Western understanding of Southeast Asia must take place if conflict is to be minimized and relations are to be expanded usefully.

Region of Divisions

The boundaries of Southeast Asia are relatively easy to delineate. The region can be outlined by extending a line from the eastern tip of China to the northern coast of Australia, from there to the southern tip of India, and finally from India back to the first point in China. The area within this triangle—the Indo-Pacific Peninsula, the Indonesian archipelago, and the Philippine archipelago—constitutes Southeast Asia. There are, however, exclusions within this triangle. For example, Hainan Island is usually included as a part of China. Papua New Guinea, under Australian control for many years, is also not generally considered part of Southeast Asia, although it has increasingly developed an Asian focus since attaining independence. Sri Lanka (Ceylon) and, to a lesser extent, Bangladesh, although geographically close and economically and politically similar to Southeast Asia, are generally linked to South Asia because of their cultural and geographic proximity to India. Even the inclusion of the Philippines as a part of Southeast Asia has sometimes been challenged because, despite geographic and ethnic similarities to the region, the intensive Spanish and U.S. colonial impact on the Philippines has diluted its regional cultural affinities.

The region, then, includes Burma, Thailand, Laos, Cambodia, Vietnam, Indonesia, the Philippines, Singapore, Malaysia, and Brunei (see Map 1.1). In addition to their geographic proximity, these countries are similar, although not identical, in tropical monsoon ecology. With the exception of Thailand, which avoided direct colonial control and thus never lost its independence, independent governments reemerged in Southeast Asia only following World War II. At independence, all were underdeveloped economically but extremely sophisticated culturally. Prior to the colonial period, Southeast Asia had been part of a world trading system that linked China to the Middle East and Europe; as a crossroads in this system, the region experienced various forms of cultural and religious penetration from Hinduism, Buddhism, Islam, and Christianity. Because these commonalities mask diverse and complex political, cultural, and economic patterns, an understanding of Southeast Asia must begin with balancing these often divergent and overlapping characteristics.

Much of the diversity of Southeast Asia is rooted in its geographic fragmentation. Not only is the area that encompasses Southeast Asia large, but there is a natural division between the area attached to the

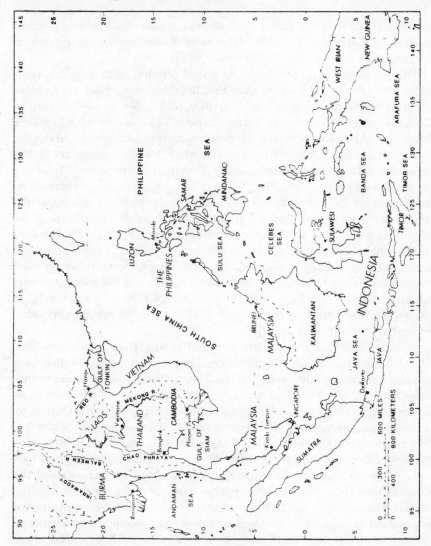

MAP 1.1 From Ashok K. Dutt, *Southeast Asia: Realm of Contrasts*, 3d rev. ed. (Boulder, CO: Westview Press, 1985), p. 3. Used by permission.

Asian landmass (called mainland Southeast Asia) and the insular portion of Southeast Asia. Burma, Thailand, Laos, Cambodia, and Vietnam are located on the Indo-Pacific Peninsula, which extends directly southward from China. The archipelagic countries include Indonesia, the Philippines, Singapore, Brunei, and Malaysia. Although the inclusion of Malaysia in this group can be disputed because it is, in part, attached to the mainland, its historical, cultural, ethnic, religious, economic, and political links to Sumatra and the other islands of the archipelago suggest that Malaysia fits more precisely with that group.

This division within Southeast Asia is also found in its religious base. Most of the mainland countries are Buddhist, although there are resident enclaves of Hindu, Muslim, and Christian minorities, as well as various Chinese religions such as Taoism and Confucianism. Archipelagic Southeast Asia, by contrast, is predominantly Muslim in Malaysia, Brunei, and Indonesia, with a substantial Muslim minority in the southern part of the predominantly Christian Philippines. There are exceptions to these generalizations, including the Hindu population on the island of Bali in Indonesia, the Buddhists in Singapore, and the Buddhists and Hindu Indians in Malaysia. Further complicating the religious picture is the plethora of animistic, mystical, and other traditional belief systems, which, in intertwining with the major religions, have given the region a syncretic religious disposition. Although such religions as Islam have large numbers of devout and doctrinally correct adherents, many of the Muslims in Southeast Asia, particularly in Indonesia, also continue to practice a wide range of mystic and other non-Islamic rituals and beliefs.

Ethnic subdivisions reflect the geographic and religious subdivisions. The Islamic archipelago is inhabited largely by Malayo-Polynesian peoples commonly known as Malays. Their common ethnic background, however, has not prevented great cultural and linguistic diversity from developing among various Malay subgroups throughout the archipelago. In Indonesia alone, there are approximately 25 major languages and 250 or more dialects. On the mainland there are four major ethnic groups—the Sino-Tibetan group, which includes the Burmese and Karens as well as Chinese; the Austroasiatic group, including the Vietnamese and the Khmer; the Thai, also including the Laos and the Shans; and the Malayo-Polynesians, including mostly Chams. These four major population groups make up the nucleus of the contemporary Southeast Asian countries, but there are numerous subdivisions within these groups, some of which are ethnically related (e.g., the Annamese of Indochina and the Mon-Khmer of Thailand). More than 150 distinct ethnic groups are found in mainland Southeast Asia. Throughout much of the region are mountain peoples and other small ethnic groupings, many of whom inhabited the region before the arrival of the current principal ethnic groups but who were pushed into the more remote areas as the present inhabitants arrived. Inhabiting the northern part of mainland Southeast Asia in particular are mountain peoples, such as the Meos, who are relative newcomers to the region. The size of these groups has declined substantially as they have been absorbed into the dominant groups. Debates are ongoing concerning the migration patterns and movements of peoples into Southeast Asia, an area the great historian D.G.E. Hall described as a veritable "chaos of races and languages."[7]

Nonethnic factors also divide the peoples of Southeast Asia. The intersections of these factors with the ethnic and geographic patterns already noted have created a mosaic of inlaid and overlaid loyalties, belief systems, and communications patterns. For example, in terms of domicile and agricultural practices, people can be divided into upland and lowland groups. Upland peoples generally practice dryland agriculture, and the lowland peoples generally practice irrigated cultivation. Wet-rice cultivation, which requires sophisticated systems of water management and regulation and returns a significantly higher-volume product (compared to unirrigated production areas) from each unit of land, was tied closely to the evolution of many of the great land-based kingdoms of traditional Southeast Asia. During various historical periods, lowland peoples have been divided into agricultural and commercial or agricultural and seafaring populations. Seafaring groups, historically dependent upon the regional and world trading systems, monopolized the Southeast Asian segment of these systems and were able to amass great wealth and establish strong political units based on their control. These economic divisions provided the basis for the development of several strikingly different types of political units in Southeast Asia.

Southeast Asia in Its Historical Context

Although for centuries the region has been recognized in political and geographic terms by kings, writers, merchants, and travelers, the term *Southeast Asia* (also South East Asia and South-East Asia) is relatively new in Western political thought. Occasionally used by European, especially German, writers in the late nineteenth century, it was first brought to general prominence with the British establishment of a Southeast Asian military command during World War II—one of the first attempts to bring together the previously fragmented colonial perspectives of the British, Dutch, French, and Americans.

Southeast Asian ethnocentric views, as well as political and economic divisions, established during the colonial era and perpetuated by Christian missionaries ever since have made it very difficult for Western-ers to perceive or accept the region as a viable unit. Acceptance of the concept of a regional unit has been made more difficult by social and cultural complexities and by the paucity of available data for historical analysis. In recent years the regional concept has been further obscured by Western scholars, particularly international relations theorists who have applied culturally biased models and theories of regional systems to their analyses of contemporary realities in Southeast Asia. One concerned scholar noted that "Southeast Asia, as a conventional term, has become increasingly the property of university area specialists," thus possibly limiting and obscuring intellectual "horizons through an over-obsession with a geographical convention."[8]

Yet even prior to the colonial period, the region was recognized with some clarity by Chinese, Arabic, Egyptian, and even Greek and Roman writers. Southeast Asia appears on Ptolemy's map (dated about A.D. 150) as the *Chryse Chersonesos*, a large peninsula and islands dividing the Indian Ocean and the China Sea (*Magnus Sinus* in Latin). Functional recognition was based on the role Southeast Asian states played in the international trading systems. The Chinese provided for Southeast Asians, as for other barbarians in the theoretical worldview of the Middle Kingdom, by dividing outlying regions according to the points of the compass and in terms of distance. They used the generic term *Nanyang* to refer to the region of the Southern Seas and, by the third century B.C., employed the term *K'un lun* as a referent for islands or states in that region. The latter term designated volcanic lands endowed with marvelous and potent powers and also denoted ocean-going peoples engaged in international trade. The Chinese later divided the region into Burma, Laos, and Annam while maintaining a distinct set of relationships for the rest of Southeast Asia. The Japanese referred to Southeast Asia as *Nan yo*. The early Arabic term *qumr*, used as a reference for Southeast Asia, was later replaced by *waq-waq*, which evolved to include all of the little-known area from Madagascar to Japan. The confusion of Madagascar with the islands of Southeast Asia may be related to the fact that by the very early centuries of the Christian era, Malay sailors frequently traveled there, leaving a cultural imprint that masked the geographic distance. The term *Zabag* also was used by the Arabs to refer to Southeast Asia, and the Indians called the region *Suvarnadvipa*.

By the end of the seventh century A.D., Arab navigators were sailing regularly to Southeast Asia. The region was also known to the Greeks and Romans. International trade by sea occurred frequently by the end of the second century A.D., although sea routes through Southeast Asia may have been active as early as the middle of the third century B.C., when land routes across Central Asia and India were blocked. Although its geographic limits and location were obscure, Southeast Asia was recognized as a mysterious region that produced spices and other exotic products and that was populated by skilled and courageous seafarers.

Implicit in this latter point is that the Southeast Asians themselves were active in the transshipment of cargo in the early centuries A.D. They traveled as far west as Madagascar in such numbers and with such frequency that early geographers and navigators often thought of Madagascar as a part of Southeast Asia. By the thirteenth century, the Malacca Strait was recognized as one of the most significant links in the world trading system. Thus, from the earliest times, Southeast Asia was an integral part of the evolving world trading system, providing valuable commodities and fulfilling vital functions in linking the Asian and Middle Eastern segments of the system.

Southeast Asia's close association with, if not dependence on, international trade has continued into the modern era. Historically, when overland caravan routes from China through Central Asia to Europe were open, sea routes and, concurrently, the welfare of Southeast Asia declined; conversely, when caravan routes were closed, the region flourished economically and politically. Europeans recognized Southeast Asia's importance when they sought to establish monopoly control of regional production and trade through colonial expansion.

Southeast Asia in the Western Lexicon

Domination by colonial writers and intellectuals over a period of three hundred years ending only with World War II fragmented Southeast Asia as a cultural, political, and economic unit as much as did political domination of the region. Whereas colonial administrators and European businesspeople emasculated indigenous political and economic systems, the nationalist perceptions of British, Dutch, and French writers ensured that regional history was characterized as an appendage of European history and that little comparative regional study across colonial boundaries was undertaken: "Unlike the giant monolithic civilizations of India and China, Southeast Asia in the Western conception was a fragmented region of islands, kingdoms and cultures . . . a relative *terra incognita*, a region enveloped in mystery."[9] Ironically, however, it was also during the colonial period that details of Southeast Asia's cultural richness became known to the world. The rediscovery and repair of great religious monuments at places such as Angkor in Cambodia and Prambanan and Borobudur in Indonesia, the early recording of the sociology of peasant society, and reports of linguistic and cultural aspects of Southeast Asian societies by early European scholars provided a foundation for contemporary understanding of the region. This discovery and recovery of some of its antiquarian landscape laid the foundation for Western reassessment of the region's culture, history, and level of civilization.

Following World War II, Southeast Asia was viewed with varying degrees of uncertainty within the scholarly community. Debates concerning its validity as an independent region were weighed down by the mass of Chinese and Indian cultural imprints. Nevertheless, as bits of history have been uncovered, the concept of Southeast Asia as an entity that is unique in its regional and global contexts has been strengthened. The process has been evolutionary. Some have argued that, in fact, Southeast Asia existed culturally only as a colonial annex of India.[10] For example, an organization called the All-India Kamboja Association still exists; it claims that Indians founded the "overseas" Kamboja and that "fraternal relations have existed between the Kamboja or India and the Cambodians since the time of the Mahabharata when Rana Sudarshan Kamboj and his followers had established 'blood bonds' between the two countries."[11] These views were later restated as a theory of cultural extension and adaptation in which Southeast Asia developed a civilization of its own, although one of Indian parentage. Most current views accept the belief that indigenous culture, although strengthened through selective borrowings from India and China, was independently responsible for the evolution of Southeast Asian history.

Thus, despite a continued lack of data and the presence of diversity and contradictions, the region has increasingly been accepted as a unit. Southeast Asia may not lend itself to political analysis as Western theorists would have it, but by the early 1970s it had become clear that the region was very much its own master—despite the continued interest of and intrusion by global powers. In the modern era the region has emerged as part of a global system predicated on Western international law, which is markedly different from the law of traditional Southeast Asia. International relations within the region since independence have constituted a history of adjustment and accommodation to this system.

The impetus for this regional self-assertion has come, as it had to, from within Southeast Asia, and it has not occurred without misdirection and false starts. Early political thinking was dominated by Western values and views, few of which proved viable for Southeast Asian political institutions. Early political leaders often attempted to play prominent roles on the global political stage rather than focusing on building viable states at home. Following independence, a period of adjustment was necessary to allow the states of Southeast Asia to discard the political, economic, and even cultural residue of the colonial era and to form their own political, economic, and cultural values and, over time, shape their institutions. Foreshadowing this process, Ann Ruth Willner described the "neotraditionalization" of political leadership in the following terms: "Traditional, indigenous elements of belief and behavior become reinvigorated within the modern organizations . . . increasing the influence of indigenous and particularistic rather than modern, rational criteria on the way in which public officials fulfill their prescribed roles."[12] The reemergence of traditional values can be criticized as impeding the development of "rational" (i.e., Western) behavior, but these values have offered an alternative to Western ideologies by providing structural models for the organization of the state and explaining the behavior of political leaders and bureaucrats.

The concept of neotraditionalization underlines the importance of accepting the Weberian concept that rationalism exists in all cultures but that "cultures have rationalized different areas of life in terms of different ultimate values and ends."[13] Above all, we cannot gain an understanding of the political evolution of Southeast Asia by applying models that carry a preference for Western rationalism. It is clear that restating political and social behavior in terms that are meaningful within the indigenous cultural context is imperative for the growth and functioning of local institutions. The impact of traditional political philosophy and practice on contemporary state and regional politics has rarely been considered by Western scholars, yet it is increasingly evident that the states of Southeast Asia are defining their own approaches to both domestic and international politics and that much of the substance of these definitions is drawn from the traditional cultural and political heritage of the region itself.

The term *traditional* may connote qualities of timelessness and static social structures and behavior. Southeast Asian history demonstrates that in that region, nothing could be further from the truth. The region has always been a hotbed of change, often stimulated by external forces but also intermingled with local values and practices in ways that have added to the vibrancy of sociopolitical structures. The temptation remains, nevertheless, to assume a "time-frozen" model of the traditional state and to ascribe uniform structures and behavior to all places and times in traditional Southeast Asia. Although a model can enable us to better arrange and organize information about early Southeast Asia, reality in the region's history is dominated by a continuum of traditional practices drawn from previous experiences and fitted to present circumstances (whenever that present happened to be). Transformed to fit the contemporary present and bereft of dominating external forces such as colonial authorities, traditional values, practices, and understandings now form a fertile base of knowledge and perceptions for interpreting how relationships should be ordered.

Regional politics have been subject to this same process. Early attempts to form regional associations were singularly unsuccessful because (1) they were largely created by external powers, for example, the Southeast Asia Treaty Organization (SEATO), which had only two regional members—Thailand and the Philippines—and six nonregional state members, or (2) there was too much suspicion among key state leaders, as in several ill-fated attempts at regional cooperation such as MAPHILINDO (Malaysia, the Philippines, and Indonesia) and the Association of Southeast Asia (ASA), which included Malaysia, the Philippines, and Thailand.

The most successful venture in regional cooperation has been the Association of Southeast Asian Nations (ASEAN), founded by five regional states—Indonesia, Malaysia, Singapore, Thailand, and the Philippines. Yet even regional cooperation and organization have not followed Western prescriptions or models. Rejecting theoretical goals of regional integration that are so strongly supported in the West, members of ASEAN structured the organization to facilitate the accomplishment of *national* goals and objectives. Further, ASEAN has frequently been criticized by Western scholars and policymakers for its lack of concrete achievements. Yet as regional states have come to see regional cooperation in terms of their own national interests, support for ASEAN has grown. Only when Indonesia, the largest country in the region, saw that regional events had a direct bearing on its own national development did it give strong support to regional cooperation through organizations such as ASEAN. Thailand has always sought a strong regional structure as a counterweight to its U.S. alliance, whereas Malaysia has looked for regional support as Britain has expanded its European relationships at the expense of its Commonwealth. Singapore has sought regional cooperation to stabilize its regional economic role, and the Philippines has used regional linkages to strengthen its Asian self-image.

A Conceptual Framework for Understanding Southeast Asia

Western scholars have attempted to capture the Southeast Asian view of a political unit or system by focusing on a "subordinate state system" in Asia that consists of three "fields"—South Asia, Southeast Asia, and China. Although one study suggested that weakness and tendencies toward disintegration were among the more important and predominant features of the system, the author concluded that "for all states but India and China, the Subordinate System is the primary, if not exclusive, framework for their foreign policy."[14] Another author recognized the complexities of Southeast Asia as "not one system, but a series of overlapping groups of states interacting in the political, economic, or military issue areas" and viewed ASEAN as the most institutionalized political system in Southeast Asia.[15] Others have attempted to integrate the Southeast Asian subsystem with the global system by focusing on security issues and on the region's strategic position within global politics.[16]

That Southeast Asia is a regional unit can best be shown by applying concepts of a political system, including the principal systems vocabulary (e.g., actors, boundaries, environment, and interaction), to a regional analysis. The systems model provides an organizing framework for comparing patterns in foreign policy behavior and regional interaction within and among the traditional and contemporary systems of Southeast Asia and also helps to clarify elements of historical continuity.

The systems framework is ideal for regional analyses because it allows for shifts in the level of analysis above and below the regional unit. The value of shifting from the regional unit upward to the global system or downward to the actor (state) or substate level is seen in an understanding of the linkages among various systems and subsystems. For example, knowing the relationship between governors and the governed is essential in understanding state behavior. At the same time, however, state behavior in traditional Southeast Asia was also conditioned by relationships with China, India, and other states external to the regional system. The interrelatedness of these levels can be conceptualized in a systems model. Within the boundaries of the system, specified parts—states, or actors—exhibit certain behaviors that are sustained and repeated over time, and these actors will interact with one another and also perhaps with external systems or actors outside the immediate system. The systems framework also provides for interaction between individual systems that exist in unequal or subordinate relationships to other independent systems. Key distinctions among political systems, or within the same system at different times, can be made on the basis of modernity, distribution or political skills and resources, patterns of cleavage and cohesion, severity of conflict, and the institutional use of power. Finally, the theoretical construct of the system may force the definition of political characters into forms at variance with reality unless care is taken to give the particular full consideration.

The use of a systems framework can, however, lead to the premature conclusion that such a system actually exists. This is an important issue in the case of Southeast Asia because some analysts still reject the idea that the region constitutes any type of homogeneous unit. A second concern is that the systems framework can create perceptions that a system is moving toward some ideal and perhaps highly integrated form based on Western models and theories of political organization and processes. A third concern is that the systems framework will lead to an overstated perception of uniformity, regularity, stability, and harmony when reality provides ample illustrations of fragmentation, antithesis, dispute, disruption, and cacophony. Hence the systems framework is applied rather cautiously here to avoid these problems. Although the system in question is not presented as static (i.e., change is accepted as constant), tendencies toward disintegration are treated as being similar to integrative tendencies to the extent that both explain the functioning of the system. No value judgment is attached to either of these extremes. The focus is on the subsystem, or region, as the principal area for discussing Southeast Asia, whereas the global system constitutes the environment.

The application of this analytical framework to two historical periods—the precolonial era and the contemporary, post–World War II era—shows the evolution of neotraditional values from the former to the current period. The analysis focuses on a discrete regional unit functioning, with varying degrees of efficiency, in a general environment of global and extraregional states. Although their forms and practices were very different from those of their Western counterparts, large political units—traditional states—have existed in Southeast Asia at least since the beginning of the Christian era. Scattered throughout the region, many of these states have been lost to recorded history; a few, however, are sufficiently well-known to allow some generalizations to be made about the nature of such units in traditional Southeast Asia. The traditional state is analyzed by constructing a model to clarify the social relationships that exist between government and the mass of society. Such a model also reveals strengths and weaknesses of traditional states as the principal actors in the regional system. This model state is based in part on archaeological and other historical sources and in part on extrapolations from contemporary anthropological and social science data, as many social practices in the region's rural villages differ little today from those of the last millennium.

A secondary focus of analysis is the adaptation of traditional Southeast Asian states to a global system increasingly shaped by principles of European international law, given that those states' experiences with and understandings of international politics are grounded in another, more traditional system of interstate relations. The concept of two competing systems—the traditional Asian system of international politics and the Western system as manifested by the intruding colonial powers—provides insight into the reasons for the successful penetration of Southeast Asia by the European powers and also clarifies unique characteristics of traditional Southeast Asia. Elements of the traditional system have important explanatory value in regard to contemporary politics, and the process of the neotraditionalization of political leadership is extended to political institutions and other activities in order to explain much of the current activity at both the national and regional system levels.

Following a relatively brief period during the immediate post-independence years, when some Southeast Asian political leaders sought vigorously to reshape the global system, a more stabile regional system emerged. This system has increasingly shown many of the traditional, indigenous elements of bureaucratic politics. It has become clear that Southeast Asia—from its political leaders to its general populace—is a product of the totality of its history and cultural experiences. The colonial experience did not erase the past for Southeast Asians; the colonial period did introduce new structures and practices, but although this experience may have obscured their past and temporarily deflected Southeast Asians, it did not stop them from evolving a modern system based on their indigenous cultural and political heritage. Anything Southeast Asians may have absorbed from the colonial experience or from the West in general has been conditioned and legitimized by their own cultural and historical perceptions and experiences. Similarly, anything Southeast Asians now absorb from the West will be adapted and absorbed into the local milieu only after it is conditioned by these same experiences. By definition, this process has been one of interpretation of Western principles through indigenous eyes. In the realm of regional and international politics, Western patterns of behavior have also been adopted, but those in the West must understand that adoption more correctly means adaptation—the selective filtering by a particular people of features of external belief, behavior, and organization that make sense in terms of their previous experiences and traditional practices. Southeast Asia is not in the process of being absorbed into a world culture; rather, it is absorbing, as it always has, those features of its external environment that will better enable it to cope with the modern world as locally perceived.

NOTES

1. Donald K. Emmerson, "Southeast Asia: What's in a Name?" *Journal of Southeast Asian Studies* 15 (March 1984), p. 1.

2. Victor R. Savage, *Western Impressions of Nature and Landscape in Southeast Asia* (Singapore: Singapore University Press, 1984), p. 323.

3. Michael Adas, *Machines as the Measure of Men; Science, Technology, and Ideologies of Western Dominance* (Ithaca: Cornell University Press, 1989), p. 134.

4.   John F. Cady, *A History of Modern Burma* (Ithaca: Cornell University Press, 1958), p. 431, quoting the official statement issued November 4, 1941, by the British secretary of state for India, Leopold S. Amery.

5.   Adas, *Machines as the Measure of Men*, p. 22.

6.   Lucian W. Pye, *Asian Power and Politics, The Cultural Dimensions of Authority* (Cambridge: Belknap Press of Harvard University Press, 1985), pp. 2, 12.

7.   D.G.E. Hall, *A History of South-East Asia* (New York: St. Martin's Press, 1968), p. 5.

8.   Michael Leifer, "Trends in Regional Association in Southeast Asia," *Asian Studies* 2 (August 1964), p. 198.

9.   Savage, *Western Impressions*, pp. 323–32.

10.   K. M. Panikker, R. Mookeriji, and R. C. Majumbar were among the protagonists of this view. See Hall, *A History of South-East Asia*, p. 16.

11.   B. R. Chatterji, "A Current Tradition Among the Kamboja or North India Relating to the Khmers of Cambodia," *Artibus Asiae* 24 (1961), pp. 253–254.

12.   Ann Ruth Willner, "The Neotraditional Accommodation to Political Independence: The Case of Indonesia," in *Cases in Comparative Politics*, edited by Lucian Pye (Boston: Little, Brown, 1970), pp. 242–244.

13.   Andreas E. Buss, "Introduction," in *Max Weber in Asian Studies*, edited by Andreas E. Buss (Leiden: E. J. Brill, 1985), p. 4.

14.   Michael Brecher, *The New States of Asia* (London: Oxford University Press, 1963), p. 105.

15.   Sheldon W. Simon, "East Asia," in *World Politics*, edited by James N. Rosenau, Kenneth Thompson, and Gavin Boyd (New York: Free Press, 1976), pp. 528–551.

16.   S. Chawla, Melvin Gurtov, and A. G. Marsat, eds., *Southeast Asia Under the New Balance of Power* (New York: Praeger Publishers, 1974); Lim Joo-jock, *Geo-Strategy and the South China Sea Basin* (Singapore: University of Singapore Press, 1979); and Wu Yuan-li, *The Strategic Land Ridge: Peking's Relations with Thailand, Malaysia, Singapore and Indonesia* (Stanford: Hoover Institution Press, 1975).

2

An Overview of
Early Southeast Asia

In this chapter I summarize the early history of Southeast Asia, illustrating some of the region's major historical features and providing an overview of its general political, economic, and cultural evolution. Even today, knowledge of Southeast Asian history is expanding at a rapid rate because of increased anthropological and archaeological interest, particularly among local Southeast Asian scholars. Although new studies are pushing further into the past, our understanding of the region's history prior to A.D. 800 is still sketchy, and our knowledge of the region before A.D. 200 is obscure and fragmentary. However, as more and more historical data have become available, additional evidence has emerged to support an interpretive history of Southeast Asia as a unit. From the earliest records, Southeast Asian growth and development have been inextricably linked to external stimulation in economic as well as cultural terms.

It is difficult to select a point of departure for an overview of the interstate history of Southeast Asia. Funan, recognized as one of the oldest regional states, enters the historical records—primarily through Chinese sources—as early as the second century A.D., and Ptolemy's *Geographia* provides additional place names thought to have been located in Southeast Asia in even earlier times. Recent archaeological work in southern Thailand just north of the Malaysian border at Satingpra has revealed the presence of complex irrigation works also dating from the second century A.D., but little is known of the political structures that may have existed there.[1] The soundness of the sources reporting the existence of Funan and other kingdoms as single political entities is not beyond question. Archaeological records give evidence of very early societies, but so little is known about their political organization that it is presumed that most were essentially kinship groups. As knowledge is expanded, the records of political organizations within these societies may be discovered.

Early Southeast Asian States

Funan was established in Indochina sometime during the first or second century A.D.; the precise date of its founding remains uncertain. However, it is known that early Funan leaders capitalized on growing maritime trade from China to the Middle East and Europe. At the time of Funan's founding, major sea routes still followed the coastline because navigational skills and vessels were too primitive for direct transoceanic travel. As the volume of coastal trade grew, the barrier of the Malay Peninsula remained the terminus for the first westward segment of the trade route leaving China. Funan's port city of Oc-eo prospered because it was located approximately halfway between southern China and the Malay Peninsula, had a safe harbor, and with its excellent agricultural hinterland already stabilized and unified by earlier Funan leaders, was a good site for reprovisioning. Capitalizing on its strategic location, Funan applied additional revenues derived from maritime traffic to further expand its inland control of rice-producing territories. Funan also appears to have increased its agricultural productivity by draining mangrove swamps and introducing irrigated agriculture.

The political organization process extended over several centuries, proceeding from kinship groups led by a variety of chieftains and elders. These groups increased limited kinship capacities for common action through various combinations of skillful leadership and expanding resources, which were necessary to congeal fragmented populations into larger units resembling what today might be thought of as confederations. Third-century A.D. Chinese records refer to Funan's many vassal states that had previously had their own chiefs.[2]

The identity of Funan's earliest rulers is unknown, but we know from Chinese sources that during the latter part of the second century Hun P'an-huang, a descendant of the original ruler, expanded his control by stimulating strife among local leaders, using his army to bring order, and installing his sons as governors of the conquered areas. Funan continued to expand through the fifth century A.D., at which time international trade shifted away from Funan toward the Strait of Malacca. As shipbuilding and navigational skills evolved, coastal sailing routes were replaced by direct routes across the South China Sea, thus reducing revenues from entrepôt activities. This decline in trade revenue forced Funan's leaders to develop a broader agricultural base and stimulated a parallel adoption of Hindu trappings of state, which provided the stronger legitimizing paraphernalia, ritual, and legal codes required by an agrarian state. By the end of the sixth century, Funan was bereft of a major source of income from international trade. Despite its turn to a more extensive irrigated agriculture, it was weakened and divided by the Chams, who took control of the Mekong Delta, and the Khmers, who controlled the expanding agricultural area around Tonle Sap in modern-day Cambodia.

Funan's history provides perspective on several factors in the ebb and flow of the commercial political economy of Southeast Asia prior to the colonial period. International commercial trade was critical in shaping regional history because it provided the source of and mechanism for accumulation of capital beyond that which was extractable from domestic agricultural production. State organization and power became stronger when an agricultural chiefdom was able to gain increased economic resources through international trade. There was also a close inverse relationship between the well-being of the leading maritime states of Southeast Asia and stability and peace along overland caravan routes through Central Asia. As early as the fourth century B.C., after Alexander the Great had conquered much of the Middle East, there emerged an "age of ascendancy of the overland route over the sea route, of the pack animal over the ship."[3] Toward the end of the third century B.C., however, land routes were blocked by the Parthians, and trade shifted to the sea routes through Southeast Asia. In the early centuries of the Christian era, overland routes—as arduous as they were—again became preferable to the extremely problematic sea routes from China through Southeast Asia to India and the Middle East before reaching the Mediterranean and Europe. Nevertheless, the Romans built a canal to the Red Sea that served the sea routes until the end of the sixth century A.D. When land routes were not accessible, sea-lanes through Southeast Asia were used, and the increased revenues from this international trade system ensured the rise and sustained the power of many regional states.

Some states are known to have been contemporaries of Funan. For example, the state of Langkasuka on the northeastern coast of the Malay Peninsula was located at the point at which most of the international trade moved overland across the isthmus. The Kra Isthmus, farther north, was also used for overland transshipping, but because of the lack of agricultural support there it was less important than Langkasuka. This state, like Funan, developed in part because of international commerce; also like Funan it suffered when shipping was developed sufficiently to allow the use of the deep-water routes through the Strait of Malacca, bypassing Langkasuka.

At least two other states are thought to have existed on either side of Funan—Dvaravati to the west in present-day Thailand and Burma, and Champa in the central regions of present-day Vietnam. Champa may have previously been known as Lin-yi, which according to Chinese records was established in A.D. 192. Much of what is known about Lin-yi comes from Chinese descriptions of its attempts at territorial expansion, especially into lands previously controlled by the Chinese themselves.

The early political history of the area comprising present-day Thailand remains obscure. Dvaravati, the first empire to have consolidated much of central Thailand, appears to have been formed in the seventh century but was unsuccessful in its attempts to expand from the lower Menam River to the fringes of the Tenasserim range on the west and southward into the Malay Peninsula. Dvaravati may have been active in the transisthmus portage near Kra, but if this was the case increased revenues from trade did not appear to aid Dvaravati's expansion, as had been the case for Funan. Nevertheless, as a result of its long history of contacts with Sri Lanka (Ceylon), Dvaravati may have been one of the first sites of Hinduism and Hindu cultural practices in Southeast Asia.

The Pyu peoples of Burma may also have been organized into a state in competition with Funan. Although the accepted founding date of Srikshetra, the capital of the Pyu kingdom, is A.D. 638, earlier records indicate that trade groups traveled up the Irrawaddy to meet caravan traders en route to and from China. It is unlikely that such complex trading linkages could have been maintained without some effective governmental control.

Little is known of the states in Southeast Asia's archipelago during the early centuries of the Christian era. The first records are inscriptions from Kalimantan and from Java near Jakarta dated approximately A.D. 400 or later. Presumably, there was little impetus for state formation until the international shipping routes shifted southward (although a lack of records may be the limiting factor in this case).

Funan declined when its geographic location as the last major stopping point on the coastal route between Canton and the portage across the Malay Peninsula diminished in importance because shipbuilding and navigational skills had progressed sufficiently to enable traders to travel directly through the Strait of Malacca. Records of such travel are found in the diaries of Fa-Hsien, a Chinese Buddhist who visited India by way of the Strait in the early fifth century A.D.[4] After this time, Chinese records of tributary states also contain many references to Javanese and Sumatran emissaries, whereas most earlier recorded tributary missions from Southeast Asian states had been from Funan.

Maritime or Commercial Kingdoms

The longer-term impact of this shift in the trade routes away from the coastal route and directly through the Strait of Malacca was seen in the rise of new and larger maritime kingdoms in the archipelago around the Strait. The first of these kingdoms appears to have been Śrīvijaya, located at Palembang in Sumatra. The shift of power did not simply proceed directly from Funan to Śrīvijaya. Other states—such as Langkasuka in Malaya, Dvaravati in Thailand, and Champa in Vietnam—as well as numerous smaller consolidated political units of the Pyu and Mon peoples in Burma and petty states around the Kra Isthmus were contemporaries of Funan, whereas the state of Mělayu and the port state of Tan-t'o-li preceded Śrīvijaya in the archipelago. However, Śrīvijaya apparently succeeded in controlling maritime commercial traffic in the archipelago, establishing an extensive empire in the process. Śrīvijaya is thought to have controlled the Strait of Malacca from the seventh through the twelfth centuries A.D.

Although questions remain concerning both the duration of Śrīvijaya's ascendancy and the geographic extent of its authority, available evidence suggests that it followed a specific political and economic form based on its relationship to the international trade routes. Śrīvijaya has been described as a purely maritime kingdom with virtually no hinterland and as having relied on Malay sea nomads as the major source of its power.[5] Śrīvijaya may have been an imperial kingdom or a more loosely structured confederation or alliance system or perhaps an organization of vassal trading ports under the center at Palembang. As with earlier Funan, Śrīvijaya received its revenues from passing trade. In return, the state controlled piracy in the Strait (much of the Śrīvijayan navy may have been composed of pirates who had been subjugated or bribed) and provided harbor facilities for shipbuilding and repair, warehousing, and trading. But Śrīvijaya's power was not constant. Wolters, in researching Chinese records, has shown that during certain periods Śrīvijaya was the only archipelagic state to send tribute to China, whereas at other times missions arrived from many states or ports of the archipelago. He has theorized that when Śrīvijaya alone sent tribute, its power and control were sufficient to stop others from doing so. When other emissaries arrived, Śrīvijaya must have been weaker.[6]

Śrīvijaya's preoccupation with the maritime world has led most scholars to assume that it had only limited contact with peoples living inland from Palembang and had no political control over its hinterland. Kenneth Hall has suggested that, in fact, substantial trade and communication occurred between the port city of Palembang and the inland villages of Sumatra. He has argued that Śrīvijaya "developed continuing 'treaty' relationships with different groups of people who would have owed each other nothing. Trade transactions became social strategy; reciprocity between representative chiefs of the various peoples became the basis of continued prosperity."[7]

John Cady argued that Śrīvijaya, although based at the mouth of the Palembang River (South Sumatra), extended over the northeastern half of Sumatra, all of coastal Malaya, and smaller portions of Java and Borneo.[8] One of the few descriptions of Śrīvijaya comes from a Buddhist monk, I-tsing (A.D. 635–713), following his return from India: "After a month we come to the country of Mĕlayu, which has now become Bhoga [Palembang of Śrīvijaya]; there are many states under it."[9] Another Chinese writer, Chau Ju-kua, described Śrīvijaya as a "country lying in the ocean and controlling the straits through which the foreigners' sea and land traffic in either direction must pass."[10] Still other Chinese sources list Śrīvijayan traders in Canton, and Śrīvijayan ambassadors made regular appearances at the Chinese imperial court from A.D. 960 until 1178, when several Javanese missions appeared to ask for Chinese aid against Śrīvijayan oppression. A few statements about Śrīvijaya are found in Arab references to that country's spectacular military strength.

The lack of fine-arts and archaeological records from Śrīvijaya as compared with the Khmer Empire, for example, may have been the result of limited cultural values and neglect resulting from intense economic interests. Others have argued that such records could have been destroyed in the raids by Chola in 1025.[11] The use of wood and bricks for buildings (instead of volcanic rock widely available in Java and elsewhere) could also explain the lack of enduring structures.[12] Still others, focusing on the lack of supporting archaeological evidence to confirm historical or chronicle records, have suggested that Śrīvijaya may have been a minor kingdom that existed for less than a hundred years after its founding in A.D. 650, even though its name continued to appear in Chinese records, because "the same name might have been borne by one or two later and equally short-lived" kingdoms.[13] The paucity of archaeological evidence may also be explained by the corresponding lack of information on the coastal and riverine configurations of the east coast of Sumatra during the first millennium A.D.[14]

As a trading center (or group of centers), Śrīvijaya resembled the later Malacca in that many of its laws and resources worked to encourage trade; virtually all available sources mention the state in connection with some phase of international trade. Although Chinese records describe important Buddhist activities there, little archaeological evidence indicates that rulers of Śrīvijaya developed the more permanent cultural artifacts.

There may have been no necessity for Śrīvijaya to transform itself into an inland agricultural kingdom, as Funan had; thus, it may simply have never developed either the population base or the politico-cultural status system that produced most of the inscriptions, monuments, and temples found in other kingdoms.

Elsewhere in archipelago Southeast Asia, interisland and international commerce offered a constant stimulus to growth, as exemplified by the many entrepôt city-states that flourished in places such as Ternate, Malacca, Bandjarmasin, Makasar, Palembang, Bantam, Cheribon, and Aceh. The states that developed as commercial kingdoms were often little more than confederations of competing city-states held together by the use of force from another strong center. As the spice trade developed, for example, a state such as Ternate in the eastern archipelago of present-day Indonesia emphasized spice production to the point that it had to import food, buying most of its rice from Java.[15] At certain times in history, a single city-state was able to monopolize this trade while competing centers languished for lack of strong leadership, organization, and trade revenues; lack of demand for their commodities; or poor geographic position on the maritime trade routes.

One city-state for which information is widely available is Malacca, the last great entrepôt city-state of Southeast Asia's precolonial period. Until the beginning of the fifteenth century, Malacca was little more than an obscure fishing village on the Malay Peninsula, probably part of an insignificant, subsistence-oriented, river-delta kingdom. Legend has it that a Sumatran prince named Paramaswera was driven from Palembang to Singapore (then known as Tumasik) and eventually to Malacca. Two factors helped to elevate Malacca as an entrepôt center over a relatively short period: China's need for an ocean trade route because the caravan routes had been closed, and India's desire for a safe route through the Strait of Malacca in order to compete with the Thai-controlled portage across the Kra Isthmus.

Malacca's commercial growth began in direct competition with Majapahit on Java and Ayudhya in Siam, both of which had strong trading and commercial interests. A Chinese naval fleet appeared in Southeast Asia in 1403, however, and Malacca's future was secured. The Chinese fleet had been dispatched to the region to protect the ocean routes for international trade because Tamerlane had closed the caravan routes to the Middle East; however, the fleet also provided immediate protection for Malacca's expansion without risk of attack by Ayudhya or Majapahit. In a bid to secure the eastbound commercial traffic from India and the Middle East, Paramaswera also transformed Malacca into an Islamic port.

A unique feature of Malacca and similar city-states was the extent of their dependence on trade: A preponderance of the local population was foreign, the proportion of Malays was small, and there was virtually no indigenous middle class. The government not only maintained a safe harbor but also offered low customs fees, repair facilities, warehouse facilities, and other conveniences in order to attract international shipping merchants. Entrepôt centers such as Malacca depended on international trade for their very existence; consequently, resources were allocated to maintain and expand commerce at the neglect of local society. There was little indigenous cultural development, as was possible in the wet-rice kingdoms. Malacca became the greatest of these entrepôt centers, truly the crossroads of Asia; as such, it was the first target for control by Europeans when they entered Southeast Asia.

Land-Based Agricultural Kingdoms

The mainland agricultural successor to Funan and Chenla was the Khmer Empire, a different type of kingdom that was based not on control of international trade routes but on a firm agricultural foundation. As capabilities in seamanship grew, allowing ships to navigate directly from China to the Strait of Malacca, Funan's entrepôt importance declined. As a consequence, Funan drew ever increasing shares of its revenues from agricultural production, turned inward, expanded its irrigation system, and added Hindu rituals to its court and kingship in an attempt to strengthen its legitimacy with the rural agricultural peasantry.[16] Funan was not entirely successful in this attempt at transformation and was eventually destroyed. Its eastern regions were annexed to another state—Chenla—and the western areas were conquered by Mons and divided into numerous fiefdoms. The Khmer subsequently inherited much of Funan's territory and its complex irrigation system, which controlled the flow of monsoon rains by using grass dams to hold water in natural basins. The Khmer also used Hindu rituals to support their kings' claims to the throne.

At the founding of Angkor in A.D. 802, Jayavarman II used a Brahman to perform magic ceremonies to protect Cambodia from foreign invaders, especially the Javanese. In another ceremony, the Brahman was to fix a curse on all future usurpers.[17] Archaeological evidence indicates that Jayavarman had built a pyramid-temple, Krus Preah Aram Rong Chen—the first of its kind in Cambodia to be linked to the worship of the royal linga (a phallus symbol of the Hindu god Siva, as well as the representation of the king as the center of the world) and the devaraja (god-king). Thus Jayavarman was thought by some to have transformed the long-standing concept of Siva-linga worship by linking it directly to the king himself, creating the concept of a god-king. At the same time, however, an ambiguous dichotomy was maintained in such a way that the god-king concept could be supplanted by elements of ancestral worship that were more readily comprehended and accepted by the peasant masses. The essence of god embodied in the king was symbolized in the linga, which was thought to have been received by the king from Siva through the intercession of a Brahman. The meaning of the cult of the devaraja has been widely debated; Hermann Kulke, for example, has argued that Jayavarman was not consecrated as god-king but that the god Siva, as "god who is king," was called to protect Cambodia and especially its king.[18]

The ancestral link was critical, especially for the peasant masses, inasmuch as the "central temple-mountain undoubtedly represented less the Semeru than the symbol of the abode of their ancestors, radiating their force of protection over all the realm."[19] The belief in supernatural powers, recognition that ancestors and spirits regularly intervened in earthly events, and concepts of the king as exemplar of his social order became bound together so that the king appeared to be a deity. However, the emphasis was not on the deity of the king but on his exalted position, which made him an intermediary to gods and ancestors because "ancestors alone were the source of 'life-power' and were thus comparable to the gods," whereas the king was not a source of "life-power" but more the "bearer and transmitter of that power."[20]

As the Khmer civilization developed, its agriculture and water management techniques became increasingly complex. For example, by A.D. 889 an artificial lake had been constructed by diverting the course of the Siemreap River. The lake measured 1,800 by 7,000 meters and provided water for cities and monasteries as well as irrigation.[21] The high point of Khmer hydraulic development came around A.D. 1000, during the reign of Suryavarman I, who constructed:

> a marvelous system of waterways, basins, channels, and fountains [in his capital]. These basins, sometimes lined with brick, are separated at intervals by embankments, but are connected . . . by conduits to permit the passage of water. Other basins—more than a thousand at Angkor alone . . . depend on rain-water . . . [and] are arranged in plans throughout the city. . . . Every sanctuary had its own basin.[22]

Key in this development were the stability of the population and the necessary sociopolitical structures to ensure smooth operation of the irrigation systems. Nevertheless, the paddy systems, as well as the political units of traditional Southeast Asia, did not display the rigid authoritarianism of "oriental despotism," a concept that stresses the regulatory needs of irrigated agriculture and the development of authoritarian political structures to ensure that such regulation is maintained. The social stability and organization did allow the mobilization of resources for cultural and religious developments, of which Angkor Wat—the greatest monument of Khmer civilization—is an example.

There is an unsubstantiated link between the decline of Funan and the rise of Śailendra rulers in Java. Both events took place at about the same time—early in the seventh century—and both kings held dynastic titles meaning "king of the mountain." It has been hypothesized that the great Śailendra dynasty ruler Sanjaya was descended from the exiled princes of Funan. Śailendra power—like that of earlier Funan and its successor, the Khmer Empire—was based on agricultural production and the control of enough human resources to maintain that production. A magnificent reminder of the potential of these controlled resources was the construction of the Borobudur temple in central Java.

The Śailendras also had rather broad regional interests. It appears that Jayavarman II of the Khmer Empire was installed on the throne with Śailendra assistance. There are also records of Śailendra attacks on Ligor in A.D. 775 and on the Cham capital in A.D. 782. Perhaps most significant is the Śailendra's increasing interest in international maritime commerce, which brought them into conflict with Śrīvijaya. By the ninth century, Śailendra rule over Śrīvijaya had been established, perhaps through royal marriages.

Śailendra rulers are known to have governed Mataram in central and east Java after A.D. 732. During this time, Indian cultural, philosophic, and religious influences were absorbed throughout Java—first through Mayhayana Buddhism and later through Hinduism. Mataram was an inland agricultural kingdom that used its resource and labor bases to produce the finest Javanese architecture, which is exhibited in temple construction that is still evident throughout much of central Java. These temples, built as royal tombs, provide a glimpse into the life of early eighth-century Java: "Gods and Bodhisattva kings were everywhere similarly represented; the Brahman priests were bearded, mustachioed foreigners; the monks and hermits were . . . Javanese."[23] Other details give evidence of hairstyles, dress, jewelry, royal accoutrements, chariots, tools and utensils, furniture, and games. By the end of the ninth century, Mataram had shifted from Buddhism to Hinduism, but vigorous temple construction continued in central Java; the Prambanan complex remains the best example. In the early tenth century, the capital of Mataram was moved to east Java, where the present-day Balinese Siva-Buddha had its origins.

At about the time of Mataram's decline in Java, a kingdom known as Pagan arose in Burma, built as the result of an alliance between the Burmese and the Mons. The Burmese, given their great affinity for spirits and superstitions, were culturally less sophisticated than the Mons but provided military and political leadership. Buddhism flourished under Mon instruction and pervaded the legal and educational systems. The *sangha*—the collectivity of Buddhist monks—gained great influence, although spirit worship never died out. In the traditional Buddhist kingdoms, religion was linked to kingship in the "karmic concept of 'merit' [Thai: bun; Pali: punnya]. . . . If the king possessed sufficient merit, his kingdom would be peaceful, orderly, and prosperous and the religion of the Buddha would flourish there."[24] Eventually, the monasteries, temples, and other Buddhist centers claimed too much of Pagan's productive capacity, and the kingdom declined:

> Although the *sangha* gave Pagan its culture and "soul," and initially contributed to its economic development, it inadvertently destroyed the state's subsequent basis for survival. Since the wealth that had made Pagan was now in the hands of the *sangha* as well as the artisan class, the state could no longer maintain its armies nor the loyalty of its aristocracy.[25]

Other factors may have caused royal revenues to decline, including dynastic decay, secular elite disloyalty and competition, and institutional changes; it has also been argued that many of the land parcels thought to have been assigned to the *sangha* were "communal lands or royal lands which the tenants misrepresented . . . in order to avoid paying taxes."[26] Pagan was not destroyed, however, until Kublai Khan invaded Burma in 1287.

As the Khmer Empire weakened, the Thais developed an independent cultural and political identity in the central regions of mainland Southeast Asia. Multiple centers of political power appear to have existed in the Menam Basin until, following the Mongol invasions during the period 1253–1293, a Thai garrison commander led a revolt against Khmer overlords and established a new kingdom at Sukhothai. Sukhothai's rulers were strong enough to resist Khmer attempts at conquest and were wise enough to send tribute to the Mongols in Beijing, thereby avoiding the vengeance aimed at Pagan. By 1350, however, the Thai political center of gravity shifted southward to Ayudhya, eclipsing both Sukhothai and the kingdom of Chiengmai to the north.

Confucian Bureaucratic Kingdoms

The northern regions of Vietnam—Tonkin and Annam—were unique in Southeast Asia because they were controlled by the Chinese from approximately 200 B.C. until A.D. 900. Throughout most of this period, Vietnam was administered as a province of China. Yet despite ten centuries of Chinese domination and cultural penetration, Vietnam survived as an entity that was distinct in culture and driven to protect its independence and its identity.

Early in the tenth century (A.D. 939), in the wake of the collapse of T'ang China, the Vietnamese gained their independence. Independent Vietnam immediately faced threats not only from China to the north but also from the Hindu Cham kingdom to the south. Eventually, however, Vietnam gained strength and moved aggressively against the Chams. After Vietnam's independence, Indian Buddhism expanded somewhat at the local level as a result of suspicions directed against Chinese Buddhists, but the political relationship between Hinduism and kingship never developed in Vietnam as it had elsewhere in Southeast Asia. Although it maintained its independence from China, Vietnam modeled its kingship and administrative structures on those of the Chinese state.

Vietnamese expansion southward became slow but constant, beginning with the Li dynasty around A.D. 1009. The first historical record of this southward movement came in 1069 when the Cham kingdom was defeated and was forced to cede two northern provinces to Vietnam.[27] This occurrence marked the beginning of five hundred years of southward pressure by the Vietnamese until the Cham kingdom disappeared from Chinese records in 1543.

As Vietnamese strength was consolidated along the eastern coast of Indochina, present-day Laos and Cambodia became buffers between the Thais to the west and the Vietnamese to the east. The three centuries between the mid-1500s and the arrival of the French in the mid-1800s were turbulent times in Vietnam as palace coups and dynastic rivalries alternated with military moves against the Cambodians or the Laotians. This period was significant for Southeast Asian history because of the emergence of a pattern of southward movement by Vietnamese peasants who were fleeing the instability of dynastic conflicts, wars, and religious persecution but were followed by certain annexation by the Vietnamese government.[28] Until their movements were stopped by the French, these migrating farmers were often encouraged by the court and supported by the army.[29]

The Vietnamese borrowed many Chinese characteristics, but—as was true in other Southeast Asian cultures—they were selective and adaptive in molding a distinctive culture of their own. Although some Chinese social institutions, such as marriage rituals and dress, were simply imposed upon the Vietnamese, an indigenous core of Vietnamese culture—although altered by the long experience with the Chinese—survived. The Chinese also strengthened Vietnam's infrastructure by building new roads and bridges and introduced new agricultural techniques—notably, the iron plow. The Vietnamese became the strongest cultural group in Indochina, overtaking the Chams by the sixteenth century and challenging the Khmers and the Laotians until they were inhibited by the French after 1860. The adoption of the more sophisticated Chinese management techniques may have given the Vietnamese the strength to ward off Chinese domination.

The Ebb and Flow of Historical Development

The historical development of Southeast Asian states took place with a certain rhythmic ebb and flow based on factors as diverse as the movement of international trade-goods through the region, the emergence of charismatic leaders, local geographic and physical resources, and the availability of culturally strengthening religious and philosophical ideas from India and China. These external factors were not only accommodated within the region but provided much of the stimulus for the region's dynamism and growth. The region's openness, which was the source of this dynamism, was also the source of its demise as Southeast Asia was unprepared to effectively counter the penetration by the Europeans beginning in the 1500s. (For a clear view of the history of Southeast Asia prior to the arrival of the Europeans, see Chart 2.1.)

When the Europeans first arrived, Malacca was the principal commercial center in the area of the Strait of Malacca, which left Sumatra under the control of petty states except at the northern tip, where Aceh was gaining stature. Java was under the control of Majapahit, whose power was being increasingly limited by the emergence of many small, northern coastal principalities that had adopted Islam. Somewhat later, the Thai kingdom of Ayudhya was destroyed by the Burmese, and the Chakri dynasty (centered at present-day Bangkok) arose; Burma was ruled by the Konbaung dynasty. Laos, first united in the fourteenth century, was again divided into three kingdoms centered in Vientiane, Luang Prabang, and Champassak. Cambodia, which had been in decline since the days of the Khmer Empire, was ruled by Ang Doung but acknowledged the suzerainty of both the Thai Chakri kingdom and Vietnam. Vietnam, following its wars of succession, had been reunified under Emperor Gia Long for fewer than fifty years when the French began to extend their control. Finally, the Philippines, although perhaps influenced intermittent-

CHART 2.1 Timeline for Southeast Asian History

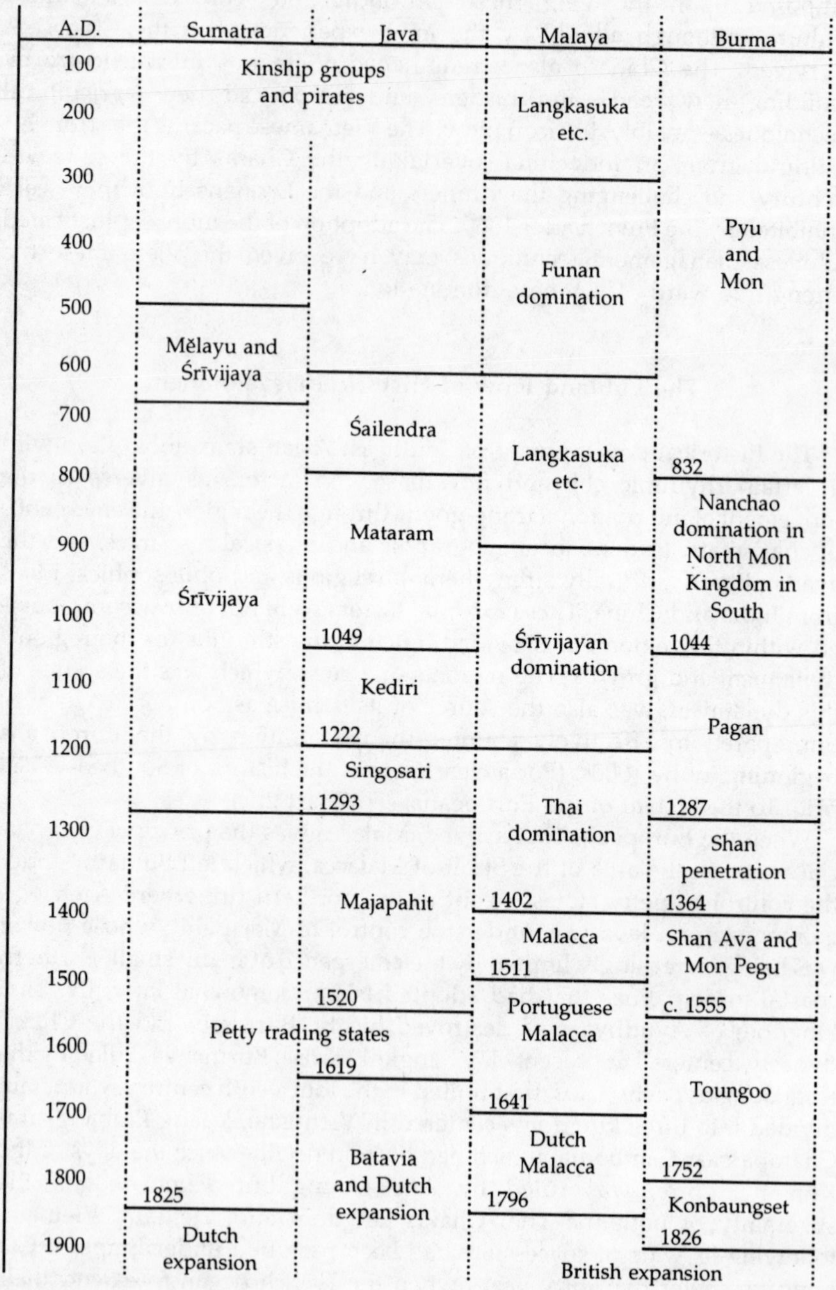

A.D.	Sumatra	Java	Malaya	Burma
100	Kinship groups and pirates			
200			Langkasuka etc.	
300				
400			Funan domination	Pyu and Mon
500	Mĕlayu and Śrīvijaya			
600				
700		Śailendra		
800	Śrīvijaya		Langkasuka etc.	832 — Nanchao domination in North Mon Kingdom in South
900		Mataram		
1000		1049	Śrīvijayan domination	1044
1100		Kediri		Pagan
1200		1222 — Singosari — 1293	Thai domination	1287
1300				Shan penetration
1400		Majapahit	1402 — Malacca — 1511	1364 — Shan Ava and Mon Pegu
1500		1520	Portuguese Malacca	c. 1555
1600	Petty trading states — 1619			Toungoo
1700			1641 — Dutch Malacca	
1800	1825	Batavia and Dutch expansion	1796	1752 — Konbaungset — 1826
1900	Dutch expansion		British expansion	

(continues)

CHART 2.1 (*continued*)

Thailand	Laos	Cambodia	Vietnam	Philippines
Dvaravati	Cham domination			Kinship groups and pirates
		Funan		
Funan domination			Champa and Annam	
		Chenla		
		802		
Haripunjaya and Dvaravati	Angkor domination			Śrīvijayan influence
			939	
Angkor domination		Angkor	Champa and Nam Viet or Dai Viet	
1238	Thai penetration			
Sukhothai etc.				
1350	1353			
		1432		Majapahit influence
			1471	
Ayudhya	Lan Xang	Post Angkor	Kingdom of Annam	
				1571
			1673	
	1712		Trinh and Nguyen	Spanish colony
1782	Three Kingdoms		1802	
Chakri		1863	Nguyen	1898
	1893	French expansion		U.S. rule

ly by Śrīvijaya and Majapahit, had not developed recognizable state political units before the Spanish arrived at Manila in 1571.

The details of Southeast Asian history are still surfacing. New information is being uncovered about known states, and new discoveries are being made about previously unknown states. The dates of the beginnings of political organization and state formation are being pushed back. What emerges from this historical overview is an understanding of Southeast Asia as a region that has prospered despite its geographic fragmentation and ethnic diversity. Drawing upon the great cultures of India and China, Southeast Asia formed a cultural and historical unit that contained unique social, economic, and political structures but had close linkages to India, China, and the historical world system.

NOTES

1. Janice Stargardt, "Hydraulic Works and South East Asian Polities," in *Southeast Asia in the 9th to 14th Centuries*, edited by David G. Marr and A. C. Milner (Singapore: Institute of Southeast Asian Studies, 1986), p. 24.

2. O. W. Wolters, "Khmer 'Hinduism' in the Seventh Century," in *Early South East Asia: Essays in Archaeology, History, and Historical Geography*, edited by R. B. Smith and W. Watson (London: Oxford University Press, 1979), p. 428.

3. Joseph Desomogyi, *A History of Oriental Trade* (Hildesheim: Georg Olms Verlagsbuch-Handling, 1968), p. 24.

4. Fa-Hsien, "A Record of the Buddhist Countries," translated by Li Yung-hsi (Peking: Chinese Buddhist Association, 1957), pp. 87-90, in *The World of Southeast Asia*, edited by Harry J. Benda and John A. Larkin (New York: Harper & Row, 1967), pp. 3–5.

5. O. W. Wolters, *The Fall of Śrīvijaya in Malay History* (Ithaca: Cornell University Press, 1971), pp. 1–7.

6. O. W. Wolters, *Early Indonesian Commerce: A Study of the Origins of Śrīvijaya* (Ithaca: Cornell University Press, 1967), pp. 229–253.

7. Kenneth R. Hall, "State and Statecraft in Early Śrīvijaya," in *Explorations in Early Southeast Asian History*, edited by Kenneth R. Hall and John K. Whitmore (Ann Arbor: Michigan Papers on South and Southeast Asia, no. 11, 1976), p. 93.

8. John F. Cady, *Southeast Asia: Its Historical Development* (New York: McGraw-Hill, 1964), p. 69.

9. I-tsing, "A Record of the Buddhist Religion as Practiced in India and the Malay Archipelago," translated by J. Takakusu, in Benda and Larkin, *The World of Southeast Asia*, pp. 5–6.

10. Chau Ju-kua, *His Work on the Chinese and Arab Trade in the Twelfth and Thirteenth Centuries, entitled Chu-fan-chi*, translated by F. Firth and V. Rockhill (Taipei: Literature House, Ltd., 1965; reprint of a 1911 St. Petersburg edition), p. 62.

11. D.G.E. Hall, *A History of South-East Asia*, (New York: St. Martin's Press, 1968), p. 56.

12. Satyawate Subiman, "The History and Art of Śrīvijaya," in *The Art of Śrīvijaya*, edited by M.C. Subhadradis Diskul (Paris and Kuala Lumpur: UNESCO and Oxford University Press, 1980), p. 11.

13. Bennet Bronson, "The Archaeology of Sumatra and the Problem of Śrīvijaya," in Smith and Watson, *Early South East Asia*, p. 403.

14. See John N. Miksic, "Archaeology and Palaeogeography in the Straits of Malacca," in *Economic Exchange and Social Interaction in Southeast Asia: Perspectives from Prehistory, History and Ethnography* (Ann Arbor: Michigan Papers on South and Southeast Asia, no. 13, 1977), pp. 155-157; O. W. Wolters, "Landfall on the Palembang Coast in Medieval Times," *Indonesia*, no. 20 (October 1975), pp. 1–58.

15. D.J.M. Tate, *The Making of South-East Asia*, vol. 1, *The European Conquest*, (London: Oxford University Press, 1979), p. 55.

16. Kenneth R. Hall, "The 'Indianization' of Funan: An Economic History of Southeast Asia's First State," *Journal of Southeast Asian Studies* 13 (March 1982), pp. 104–105.

17. Lawrence Palmer Briggs, *The Ancient Khmer Empire*. Transactions of the American Philosophical Society (Philadelphia: American Philosophical Society, 1951), p. 89.

18. Hermann Kulke, *The Devaraja Cult*, translated from German by I. W. Mabbett (Cornell: Southeast Asia Program, Data Paper no. 108, 1978), p. 37.

19. Nidhi Aeusrivongse, "The *Devaraja* Cult and Khmer Kingship in Angkor," in Hall and Whitmore, *Explorations in Early Southeast Asian History*, p. 126.

20. *Ibid.*

21. Briggs, *The Ancient Khmer Empire*, p. 106.

22. *Ibid.*, p. 165.

23. Cady, *Southeast Asia*, p. 77.

24. Lorraine Gesick, "The Rise and Fall of King Taksin: A Drama of Buddhist Kingship," in *Centers, Symbols, and Hierarchies: Essays on the Classical States of Southeast Asia*, edited by Lorraine Gesick (New Haven: Yale University Southeast Asian Studies, Monograph Series, no. 26, 1983), p. 89.

25. Michael Aung-Thwin, "Kingship, the *Sangha*, and Society in Pagan," in Hall and Whitmore, *Explorations in Early Southeast Asian History*, pp. 234–235.

26. Victor B. Lieberman, "The Political Significance of Religious Wealth in Burmese History: Some Further Thoughts," *Journal of Asian Studies* 39 (August 1980), p. 768.

27. Jerry M. Silverman, "Historic National Rivalries and Interstate Conflict in Mainland Southeast Asia," in *Conflict and Stability in Southeast Asia*, edited by Mark W. Zacher and R. Stephen Milne (Garden City, N.Y.: Anchor Books, 1974), p. 55.

28. Gerald C. Hickey, *Village in Vietnam* (New Haven: Yale University Press, 1964), p. 6.

29. Ronald Provencher, *Mainland Southeast Asia: An Anthropological Perspective* (Pacific Palisades, Calif.: Goodyear Publishing Company, 1975), p. 41.

3

Bases for Political Community in Traditional Southeast Asia

To understand the structures of traditional Southeast Asian states, we must also understand the social organization underlying them. There has been a concerted effort among Southeast Asian scholars to learn "more about the character and persistence of indigenous value systems, about the changing nature of the relationship between political center and periphery, and about how ordinary people perceived and experienced their world."[1] Unfortunately, few records have been found that provide data on the historical structure of rural communities in Southeast Asia. Historians must glean fragmentary information from traditional histories written in the sixteenth and seventeenth centuries, from surviving temple carvings, from diaries of early—mostly Chinese—travelers, and from descriptions provided by Portuguese and other European writers and later colonial administrators.

Another hindrance to understanding Southeast Asia's traditional social base is that most formal histories have been concerned with matters of state as embodied in activities of kings and courts. Information about villages and peasant populations is available primarily in recent work of sociologists, anthropologists, and economists who, moreover, have recognized that change within the village community has taken place very slowly. Much of the material gathered in the twentieth century— much of it since 1945—describes traditional patterns of village organization, behavior, and needs. This material, although modern, can be used to construct a model of village social structures because few changes occurred within those structures until very recent times: "As early as the fourth millennium B.C. in parts of mainland Southeast Asia . . . [were found] the established competencies and disciplines required to sustain a settled existence not markedly different than [that] encountered in rural villages today."[2]

What follows, then, is a composite picture of traditional village society drawn from contemporary literature. The village community was essential in the formation and development of the traditional Southeast Asian state. Although the picture of the village presented here cannot be historical, it is a substantive composite based on the records that exist today.

The Village Community

Robert Redfield noted four characteristics of village communities that apply here: The village community is distinctive in terms of both its inhabitants and its geographic locale; it is small enough that its members can all know each other; it is homogeneous so that activities, roles, and states of mind are well understood, accepted, and slow to change; and it is self-sufficient, providing for nearly all of the activities and needs of its members.[3] Traditional Southeast Asian society was divided into two groups—the village sphere and the court sphere. At times, as much as one-third of the village peasant population may have been slaves, although the distinction between slaves and peasants appears to have been slight. In Burma, the master-slave relationship, as understood in the West in the seventeenth and eighteenth centuries, never existed, but various bonded relationships were common in which an individual could, voluntarily or involuntarily, be tied to the state, the church, or another individual in a legally contracted sense.[4] In Cambodia, the concept of slaves was obscured because many commoners were "slaves" of the gods and "property" of the temple, a condition not yet fully understood.[5] In Vietnam, the law code of the fifteenth century distinguished levels among the lower classes—freemen, those in bond, slaves, and those in servitude to the state.[6]

The court group included not only the aristocracy but also artisans, clerics, warriors, wealthy merchants, businesspeople—many of whom were foreigners—and others who supported governmental structures. The two segments of society were linked by both an overall metaphysical worldview and common perceptions of the individual's role within that world. The result was a socioeconomic system that maximized village autonomy while providing it with a modicum of security against temporal threats—thieves and invaders—and assuring a harmonious relationship with the supernatural. Although the functional part of this court-village relationship—basic protection—was important, it was the ritualized relationship with the supernatural that provided legitimacy through the metaphysical view of the world aggrandized variously with Hindu, Buddhist, or Islamic terminologies. Traditionally, Western perceptions have focused on the urban centers, as John McAlister and Paul Mus have noted: "The authentic life of the country has been that of its villages. However, the representatives of the French tended to think of Viet Nam in terms of urban centers."[7]

The bulk of the peasant population of traditional Southeast Asia resided in village communities. The village comprised not only dwellings (including courtyards, gardens, and religious and community buildings) but also agricultural lands—in production and fallow—grazing lands, and certain forest areas used for fuel cutting or hunting. The village was a closed community in that most members were blood relatives—of greater or lesser degree, depending on the overall size of the village—and outsiders were seldom accepted permanently. The village was also defined by its *adat*, or customary law unique to each village, being "unwritten and derived from 'historical' memory, which serves to define not only the relations between segments of the village but the village itself."[8] Foreigners did reside in some villages but retained low social status and were subject to discrimination, including having to pay certain taxes apparently not levied against native residents.[9]

Traditional villages varied in size and form. In some areas, they were walled enclosures; in others, they constituted numerous scattered hamlets in which only a few families lived. But in general,

> Villages [had] two basic designs, the linear and the cluster. The former [were] found along water-courses, roads or pathways; the latter [became] established around some focal point such as a source of water, temple, or the homes of original settlers or village leaders. Many villages [were] composed of discrete hamlets, separated from one another by their fields; more rarely individual houses may [have been] separated from their nearest neighbors in a scattered formation.[10]

In addition, site selection was determined by a variety of factors such as topography, material convenience, proximity to kin, social distinctions, availability of fresh water, strategic defensibility, stream transport, privacy, and supernatural beliefs about auspicious directions and forces, as well as by the village economic base.

As the center of economic and social life, the village developed basic patterns of organization that not only governed day-to-day activities but also had a major impact on the general community. The village was a corporate unit that maintained clear definitions of citizenship based on kinship, or occasionally, ritual admission. It regulated agricultural activities primarily through the control of land and land use and imposed discipline either directly through enforcement of judgments by elders or indirectly through social sanctions. Nonagricultural economic activities, home-industry production, day and wage labor, and some social services were primarily supplements to basic agricultural activities.

The origins of the corporate village are obscure. Some have argued that it evolved as part of the communal nature of peasant society,[11] whereas others have viewed it as a component of the evolution of complex political structures, perhaps as a unit for taxation.[12] The village as a self-contained social unit experienced extreme pressure in the twentieth century when colonial policies increasingly drew villagers into the cash economy and made them more dependent on colonial administrators or other outsiders for welfare support. Previously, the social mores of the village had withstood nearly every outside influence: "After a millennium of Sinization . . . Chinese culture had not penetrated into the masses of the Vietnamese."[13] The ability of the village community to maintain its basic organization, and the tenacity of its controlling social powers despite many diffuse influences from without, qualify it as a logical beginning for an analysis of social organization.

Corporate Governance

Beyond such principles as common language, geographic proximity, and ethnic similarities, it was the social linkages of the peasant societies that provided the basis for state organization, as well as the ultimate limits on the development of states within the region. According to Anthony Reid and Lance Castles, "The village community forms the basic unit of social organization, of land management, and of conflict resolution. Whether we look at the Batak huta, or the Gaukang community of Bone . . . it is the little community with which we must begin an analysis of the historical rise of states."[14]

Basic governance at the village level was conducted by the council, known variously as the village council, council of elders, or council of notables. Its composition differed, but it was essentially made up of everyone who had influence in the community. Some villages drew representation from each ethnic or descent group; others included all villagers over a certain age (such as sixty years), and wealthy individuals were sometimes able to purchase titles that enabled them to sit on the council. In some villages individuals were elected or otherwise selected for the council based on their past demonstrations of wisdom or other prowess. At other times, representatives of the central government who lived in the village also participated in the council; in Vietnam, any degree-holders not engaged in mandarinal careers participated in the council.

Village governance has often been represented as consensual and democratic. Such Indonesian concepts as *mufakat* and *musyawarah* as well as *gotong-royong* have been highly politicized and romanticized. The village management system did depend upon general consensus, but it was a consensus shaped by village power groups and imposed on the rest of the village by the very requirement of consensus. It was nearly impossible to disagree with the village leadership, given the internal pressures to conform and the clearly defined relative positions of knowledge and authority of each member of the village group. Village democracy, such as it may have been, never approached the Western concept of majority rule and "one person, one vote." There may have been room for expressing differing views, but once these views had been heard—usually in private—and decisions had been made, consensus and conformity were automatic. Understanding how this traditional village-level consensus building and management operated is essential for understanding how contemporary governments—at the national level—function. This top-down model of decisionmaking and consensus management is widely used today throughout Southeast Asia.

The central government rarely reached directly into the village. In some regions, village chiefs held appointments as government agents. In Vietnam, the *tong* was an administrative office linked to a group of villages, and its responsibility was to "collect taxes and to induct military draftees."[15] In practice, *tongs* became the messengers, brokers, and mediators poised between the two worlds of the government and the village.

The Economic Base

Historically, as the populace in Southeast Asia moved from gathering and hunting to a more sedentary existence, stabile village communities emerged. Modes of agricultural production influenced these village structures and their concomitant stability. In areas where slash-and-burn agriculture was practiced—where fields were defoliated through the cutting of brush and burning of the residue on the field to add nutrients—villages moved every few years to be close to new fields while previously used fields were left fallow. Fallow periods varied with general soil and ecological conditions and, more important, with population pressure. Reports show that some fields were not ready for recultivation after a period of twenty years; more recently in northern

Thailand, however, fallow periods have lasted from three to ten years, although the original foliage had not returned and soil fertility had declined to the extent that only a single cropping cycle could be supported.[16]

The ecological balance of slash-and-burn agriculture is such that it will only sustain sparse populations. Estimates of sustainable population for this form of agriculture vary from twenty to fifty persons per square kilometer, with variations attributable to natural ecological differences and to the use of different agricultural techniques in different areas. Population growth stimulated by colonial improvements in health care had very negative impacts on slash-and-burn agricultural areas, although such growth was not an acute problem prior to the colonial period.

Locational stability of slash-and-burn villages varied throughout the region. Some groups were nomadic, moving all of their belongings with them while traveling over wide areas, whereas others maintained permanent communities in which nonproductive members resided. Still other villages were permanent and maintained extensive agricultural lands, only a portion of which were under cultivation at any one time. The size of any particular slash-and-burn village was related to the amount and productivity of available agricultural lands, and permanence was often a function of the value of the village location for purposes of marketing, religion, or transportation.

Among more stabile or permanent villages in Southeast Asia, most depended on some form of flooding or irrigation to provide soil nutrients that slash-and-burn farming obtained through the fallow and burning process. In certain areas, principally broad floodplains of primary and secondary river systems, unrestricted floodwaters provided rejuvenating nutrients for soils, and rice seed was sown in a broadcast manner. Irrigation was not controlled, as it was on mountainside terraces, but monsoon weather and flooding were sufficiently regular to allow for stabile agricultural production and the evolution of a sedentary agricultural existence.

Controlled flow irrigation, the most intensive form of agricultural production, ranged from simple dikes built to retain floodwaters to the complex and highly interdependent water-distribution systems of paddy fields or terraced hillsides with reservoirs or streams flowing from above. This type of agriculture not only provided the highest yield potentials for rice but also increased the possibilities for multiple crop cycles because water was more readily and predictably available.

In relatively stable production areas, villages took on greater permanence, particularly if they were able to fulfill secondary functions astride major waterways or roads or if they were hosts for some type of religious temple or monastic complex. Whether physical structures of the village followed more common patterns of centrally clustered households and common buildings or the linear pattern with buildings strung along rivers, roadways, or irrigation canals, each villager's personal relationships resembled a series of mutually inclusive, concentric circles beginning with the immediate family and extending outward from genealogical clan and ethnic bases to territorial groupings. The last circle in this case would connote the outside world beyond the perimeter of the village.[17]

Areas that supported advanced agricultural technologies corresponded roughly to those in which larger and more complex political organizations developed. Such parallel developments were undoubtedly mutually reinforcing. Household manufacturing of all types of commodities for everyday living included food products, simple household and agricultural tools and utensils, and specialized services. Peddler trade—that is, the continual buying and selling of commodities while traveling from market to market—was sufficient to satisfy village needs but did not foster the development of a local, middle-class commercial or merchant population. Peddler trade in Southeast Asia, as in the rest of Asia, was complex, "mak[ing] use of very sophisticated organizational forms such as commenda, bottomry, partnerships and combined credit and transfer transactions by means of bills of exchange."[18] The result was a village unit, "slightly above subsistence and somewhat below self-sufficiency, [that] neither called for state support nor encouraged undue state depredation,"[19] that saw only a small outflow of surplus food and occasional corvée labor for tax purposes, as well as a minimal exchange of goods with external peoples.

The social distance between agricultural and commercial functions was great. Peasant agriculturalists comprised the bulk of the village population, whereas economic contact with the outside world occurred largely through the market. Local markets had a distinct and separate physical location near, but not usually in, the village and often at convenient intersections of roads leading to several villages; their operators and inhabitants were generally excluded from the village group. The fact that traders were not part of the village structure is made clear by the Javanese word for trader, *dagang*, which also means "foreigner" or "wanderer." The market was a cultural unit separate from the village with a "status in the wider society [that] has been ambiguous at best, pariah-like at worst."[20] Local peddlers, as well as Chinese who had settled in Southeast Asia, traveled between China and Southeast Asia, with so little capital that they often had to be indentured to cover the price of passage. Peddlers traveled overland when possible, but their movements were governed by the monsoon, as well as by the cycle of acquiring goods at one end of the trade route to be sold at the other.

As in many peasant societies, the market's physical location as separate from the village was symbolic of the fact that the market was outside the scope of the complex social relationships and obligations of the village itself. Merchants and peddlers from outside the village—particularly those from different ethnic groups—held a social distance that freed them from the village's generalized rules of generosity, fair play, and deference of personal gain in favor of the community good; they could act outside these village norms precisely because they were different. Also villagers were able to act differently toward merchants because the merchants were outsiders. To the extent that village life was predicated on social harmony and reciprocity and the market was based on regulated conflict or negotiation, of necessity the two were separate and distant systems operating next to each other and needing each other but not blending in any way.

Some evidence suggests that early governments preferred to deal with foreign merchants and discriminated against native merchants: "Malays conceptualized riches in political terms. Rich Malays became powerful Malays and the Raja therefore sought not only to enhance his own fortune but to prevent the accumulation of wealth on the part of his Malay subjects."[21] Whether such policies were planned proactively to discourage the accumulation of wealth by potential competitors remains speculative, but the cumulative impact of negative sanctions from the government and distrust and discrimination by villagers served to create a very strong social stigma against commercial activities among most Southeast Asians. The social implications of this separation between the village and the market, particularly when compounded by ethnic differences, are important for understanding the social and ethnic differentiations extant today throughout Southeast Asia, where commerce as a career or profession does not appeal to the local population and remains in the hands of the Chinese, Indians, or other outsiders.

Nevertheless, markets were essential for village life; they provided the point of entry and exchange between the village and the outside world. Although undoubtedly larger than the common village market, the Banten market in West Java as portrayed in Dutch reports (c. 1596) provides a glimpse of the market's complexity and variety of provisions: (1) sellers of sugar and honey, (2) sellers of beans, (3) sellers of bamboo, (4) sellers of knives, spears, and sabres, (5) sellers of cloth for men, (6) sellers of cloth for women, (7) booths for spices and drugs, (8) booths in which Bengalis and Gujeratis sell ironworks and small manufactures, (9) booths for the Chinese, (10) meat stalls, (11) fish stalls, (12) fruit market, (13) vegetable market, (14) pepper market, (15) ayun and leek market, (16) rice market, (17) jewelers stall, and (18) poultry market.[22] Markets varied in size and volume, but most of the commodities and provisions listed here would have been available in some quantity at every market.

Landholding and Land Use

Landholding was closely related to the mode of village production. Slash-and-burn agricultural villages held greater areas of land than did wet-rice villages that supported populations of comparable size. In most cases, villages held "ownership" of the land, and use of the lands was determined by complex social and economic relationships within the village. Even in those cases in which parcels of land were held by individuals, villages frequently placed restrictions on disposal of the land. Western concepts of landownership and private property were not recognizable in any type of village in Southeast Asia.

Robert Whyte has identified four types of landholders in the Asian village: (1) individuals who held blocks of land of such size that they could not handle them alone and therefore rented some portion, usually on a sharecropping basis; (2) individuals who held blocks of land that they could farm but only with additional hired labor at planting and harvesting time; (3) individuals who farmed their own land and some sharecropped land, usually one to five acres, but were unable to generate a stabile surplus; and (4) landless or almost landless laborers who depended primarily on wage employment.[23] This last class was small in the traditional village but grew significantly during the colonial period as internal village dynamics were disrupted by external forces, particularly where land was expropriated for plantation crops or where farmers were required to grow a specific crop which might not have required additional labor. Today, it is likely that the first two groups have increased their hold on the land, whereas many in the third—and previously largest—group have entered the landless class.

Other factors were important in determining patterns of landholding. For example, the most important lands were the rice lands; other productive lands—whether they supported secondary crops, grazing lands, fish ponds, or forests for harvesting foods or fuel—were considered less desirable. Distribution of communally held lands of these types was determined by status, right, or heredity. Communal lands were further divided between those over whom the sultan or other nonvillage officials exercised control and those which were controlled by the village. Family lands were also divided between these two categories and were maintained to protect ancestral ritual obligations, as well as to ensure continued productive land use. The village as a unit, however, exercised considerable weight in determining how available lands could be distributed or redistributed.

Kinship and Communal Relationships

An integral part of village self-sufficiency was the traditional emphasis on communalism, which reached beyond common labor on communal lands. Undoubtedly enhanced by the complexities of wet-rice cultivation, in which the success of many people depended on the work of others and on the sharing of resources such as water, corporate action eventually permeated all of village life. Village cooperation was probably attributable largely to the strong influences of headmen and to the intense pressures of closed village society. The *slamatan* feast as practiced in Java symbolized communal forces within the village such that "friends, neighbors, fellow workers, relatives . . . all [were] bound, by virtue of their commensality, into a defined social group pledged to mutual support and cooperation."[24] Similarly, in Vietnam the communal meal was essential for confirming status and was provided for the entire village by wealthy villagers or others who saved for years to accumulate the wherewithal to undertake this important communal obligation. Communal obligations were so extensive that landed peasant farmers were expected to hire day laborers at planting and harvest times even if the farmers could do the work alone. The communal nature of village life, established through the social and economic interdependence among villagers, became so pervasive that it found expression in many village religious practices.

In traditional Southeast Asia, as now, kinship probably formed the basis for interpersonal relationships and strong communal links. Gerald Hickey found that as recently as the late 1950s, nearly three-quarters of Vietnamese village households were made up of blood relatives.[25] Kinship provided security of the familiar, as well as links between the world of the living and the supernatural world of the dead and the unborn.[26] The Balinese extended kinship concepts include the supernatural, as implied by the term *kaiket*—which means tied to an array of people, places, things, organizations, temples, interpersonal duties, and obligations, as well as to the very earth on which the individual was born.[27] This view of humankind as only one of many components rather than the master of the environment—so pervasive in traditional Southeast Asian culture—is anathema to Western thought, which has stressed individualism, freedom of action, and manipulation of the environment.

Kinship bonds reinforced the village's closed nature and parochial worldview. Robert Wessing has shown how the closed kinship system was maintained in three hamlets in Banten in western Java.[28] Men and women sought marriage partners in "opposing" directions: Women from Cibeo, for example, married men from Cikeusik, whereas men from

Cibeo tended to marry women from Cikartawana. A similar pattern of out-marriage operated in Cikeusik and Cikartawana. In actuality, outsiders did enter the system in order to preserve a male-female balance, but the system was maintained within the village hierarchy.

Kinship bonds not only made it difficult for outsiders to become part of the village but, when extended to ethnic group levels, they also provided (and still do provide) the greatest extent of community to which most Southeast Asians ascribed. Kinship was sometimes extended to a large ethnic group, as occurred among the Bataks of north and central Sumatra; for instance, there was "a consciousness of themselves as a people and a genealogical system, [as] the descendants of their epony-mous ancestor Si Raja Batak . . . [although] seeing Batakdom as one huge family had to await the conditions of colonial rule. . . . In any case there was never the remotest question of political action at the all-Batak level."[29]

Custom and Law

Customary law represented the sum of traditions, current practices, and taboos governing behaviors in the village community. It was not a codified set of regulations but a continuously evolving set of standards and norms specifying acceptable limits for all types of relationships and situations. Particularly important to village structure was the syncretic nature of its customary law. In this connection, two traits of Southeast Asian society—its flexible capacity to absorb outside influences and the continual mutation of custom and habit—can be grouped together. Customary law differed from village to village and changed within the same village over time; however, it provided a further measure of village autonomy. There is a Vietnamese saying that the law of the emperor yields to the customs of the village.[30] It was also true that customary law had the ability to absorb new influences while maintaining a high degree of continuity with the past. Customary law encompassed all of the rules, customs, and beliefs that defined acceptable behavior within the village. It constituted the single most important control over village members, governing the family, the fields, and virtually all aspects of village life—with the result that radically new concepts associated with Hinduism, Buddhism, and Islam were accepted once they had been rationalized in terms of customary law. Customary law was seldom written but was generally passed orally from generation to generation through the village power structure—the council of elders. It was easily adaptable to a new consensus within the village but was rigid when change lacked the support of a consensus.

Mysticism and Worldview

Another important feature of village life was its emphasis on harmony, drawn in part from the communal rather than individualistic social organization of the village but also linked to the concept of the human being's relationship to nature:

> Seen as an ecosystem, man is no longer the measure of all things nor the master of nature. He is bound intimately to the grain [rice] he would grow, for without his sensitive observation of wilting and flourishing, these plants might have dwindled to extinction. Like the haiku poets who converse with a still pond, they [village farmers] believe that man, properly trained, develops sensitivity to the voices of plants, and plants can hear men's entreaties.[31]

The concept of harmony with nature was extended to include harmony with the cosmic whole. Cosmic power existed in all entities. Balance and harmony had to be maintained because the cosmos was regarded not "as the undifferentiated sum of the entities but rather as the unity of various categories of entities in differing degrees of opposition to each other."[32] Cosmic harmony was maintained through orientation of village buildings and temples using numerology, the points of the compass, and nearby natural landmarks that were believed to be residences of forces of evil. Evidence of geomancy, defined by Paul Wheatley as the "analysis of the morphological and spatial expressions of *chi'i* [cosmic breath] in the surface features of the earth" similar to expressions found in Chinese belief systems,[33] has also been found in Vietnam and elsewhere in Southeast Asia. These patterns, "in addition to placating spirits . . . enable the individual to interpret the portents of nature and thereby so orient himself toward his physical surroundings as to attract favorable cosmological influences."[34] In describing Sundanese society, Wessing has noted that

> a major feature of the Sundanese belief system is the conviction that life is influenced by various supernatural forces, both beneficent and deleterious. It is important therefore in the conduct of daily affairs to determine where the positive and negative influences are located since these forces are not stationary. . . . If a Sundanese wants to conduct some business in a given place he must ask in which direction his objective is located relative to himself. He then consults his *paririmbon* [divining books] in order to find out where the evil influence is located on that particular day. If the evil is located in a direction other than the one he must take, he may set out directly toward his goal. Should his goal and the evil coincide, however, it would be best not to go at all. If one must go then it is best to start by

heading in the direction opposite to the one in which the evil influence is located and only later curve toward one's objective.[35]

The Socio-Political Foundations of Village and State

It is the interplay of these variables of village life—an agricultural economy in juxtaposition with commercial, market, or peddler activities; communal interdependence and the social pressures of a closed system; the intuitive aspects of law and behavior that embodied generations of behaviors and beliefs; and the preoccupation with natural and cosmological harmony—that provided the basis for the evolution of political units approximately equivalent to the state. The maintenance of harmony or balance in all things found expression at three levels in traditional Southeast Asia—the village, the state, and the universe. But it was the village level upon which the others rested: "At the very foundation of Vietnamese society, the rice fields have throughout history supplied this society with a reason for being. The fields have provided the basis for a stable social structure, a discipline for work, and a rhythm of communal celebrations—in short, a contract between the society itself, the soil and the sky."[36]

Although village social structures varied from place to place as well as over time, traditional villages had several common characteristics. First, kinship, particularly at the family level and to some degree at the extended family level, was a major force in social organization. Next, most of the labor or productivity of the village was agricultural; therefore handicrafts, peddling, and other trades were of secondary importance and status and were often handled in transitory fashion by outsiders. Additionally, the sense of communal cooperation that extended beyond the immediate family became an important means of attaining common goals and meeting local needs. Finally, this communalism enveloped or produced a set of cultural values and mores in which individualism was met with suspicion, whereas commitment to and sacrifice for the common good were held in higher esteem. As with so many elements of traditional village society, this sense of communalism, which places greater value on the interest of the community against those of the individual, has important political significance in contemporary Southeast Asia.

Kinship and Ethnic Groups

Above the village level, the common base for political organization within early Southeast Asian society was the kinship group, which often provided a measure of geographic continuity as well. Isolated groups were able to coalesce into larger groups by extending the kinship bond for a common cause, such as meeting an external threat. These extended ethnic groupings were often ad hoc or task-specific and tended to revert to smaller or more local organizations when the common problem was eliminated. Neither kinship groups nor ethnic groups represented intermediate or transition stages in state formation, and in some situations, both groups seem to have inhibited state building. Nevertheless, the kinship group was a key management unit for much of the geographic area of Southeast Asia throughout much of its history. State structures and interstate relations in traditional Southeast Asia can be comprehended if we envision the region as being divided among rather amorphous kinship groups rather than clearly demarcated in terms of geographic segments or discrete political units.

Records of Batak and Minangkabau societies, although not written until early in the colonial era, provide a glimpse into the common core of Southeast Asian societies at the beginning of the Christian era or earlier. The clan or ethnic group was the widest grouping to which individuals gave allegiance. Beyond that level, common language, customary law, and extended ethnic ties made cooperation possible for some adjudicatory as well as religious or other ceremonial purposes and occasionally for common defense against external threats. But interclan warfare and strife were more common than was interclan cooperation, and they tended to reinforce the fragmentation that limited state building. In the Toba-Batak areas, for example, no clearly defined political unit above the village or kinship group level ever developed. Bataks had a strong genealogical sense of themselves as a people; the concepts of clans and related subclan or extended clan units were widely recognized, but these ethnic and genealogical ties were rarely translated into political linkages. There were numerous examples of institutions organized above village and clan levels, including judicial structures, market organizations, and land and water management groups. Even the famous Singamangaraja, despite the god-king title, "was not a major factor in the Batak political system in normal times though it became so in the final stages of the destruction of that system by the Dutch."[37] Contradicting the generally held view that the Singamangaraja was a royal political dynasty, Lance Castles has concluded that

> the Bataks of the interior, left to their own devices, were able to solve their problems without the need of a central authority. . . . Certainly there was constant rivalry and frequent disputes leading to wars. But the ferocity of the wars was limited by tabus, and resources for arbitration were abundant. The small scale of external trade meant that no chief or community could

make the monopolization of it a basis of power. The notion that the clan owned the land was very strongly entrenched. Only rarely did one clan displace another from a territory it had occupied. There was thus no room for the state or ruler as an outsider demanding part of the produce of the tiller.[38]

There are no instances in which the entire Batak populace or even one of its major genealogical or dialectal divisions acted as a political unit, even in the face of external threat.

The same is true for another Sumatran people, the Minangkabau, for whom the concept of the Minangkabau world was nearly global—as in "Western world" or "modern world"—although it did not have political connotations. Minangkabau clan groups often included place names, although these referred not to territorial units but rather to kinship groups or lineages of several extended families following matrilineal ties. Local village units—which did have contiguous territorial bases—were sometimes federated into larger units, but even these did not adopt practices common to states. For example, revenues were raised and retained at the village level. As with Bataks, Minangkabau also had other coalition groups above the village level that exercised some control over one or more aspects of social organization. The recipients of formal titles and great respect but carrying little effective authority were the chiefs, or distinguished elders: the king of customary law, the king of religion, and the king of the world. The role of these "kings" is not fully understood, but they appear to have been judicial more than political figures, even though they made rather grand claims about their powers.[39]

Still other areas relied on informal kinship groups rather than highly developed centralized political systems. In present-day Bali, the extended kin group, called *dodia*, provides a strong focus for the individual as part of a "highly corporate group of people who are convinced, with whatever reason, that they are all descendants of one common ancestor."[40] Much of the present-day Philippines appears to have adopted similar sociopolitical practices. Until the beginning of the colonial era in that country, the primary political units were probably small ethnic or kin groups (with some territorial connotations) headed by respected elders or chiefs. At the time of the Spanish arrival, the largest of these communities consisted of approximately one hundred families, usually linked by blood; moreover, although multiple groups might have been mixed throughout the same geographic area, the several chiefs were considered equals, and each kinship acted independently.[41] There is little evidence that larger, integrated political units functioned in the Philippines. Although Cebu, Manila, and Vigan developed communities with larger populations than most local clans, "only in Manila did the barangay chief have attributes resembling those of a monarchial ruler."[42] Evidence is sketchy, but Bennet Bronson has shown that in Thailand before the rise of Dvaravati (about A.D. 600) there may have existed at most a "group of smallish states or proto-states in a formative stage of political development."[43] These were probably clan or kinship groups.

The reason these peoples were slow to develop stronger governmental structures above the local level is not known. Their widespread irrigated agriculture systems would seem to have made authoritarian political organization likely. Their weak political organization did not necessarily leave them vulnerable; in fact, they may have actually reinforced their own isolation by not creating a weak state apparatus that could have been dominated from the outside. The few export products of these areas may have held little attraction, given—at least in the case of the Bataks—a predilection for cannibalism. The great Sumatran states in early history were maritime states such as Śrīvijaya, which seemingly had little interest in maintaining control of its own hinterland.

Societies such as these did not proceed in social organization beyond "networking," in which marriage played a role in creating links among villages, but the "closeness or openness of the mesh, the range or scope of the network, the kinds of human interests served by the relationships . . . [and] the stability of the relationships" became measures of both the expanse and the limits of larger political organization.[44] Lucy Mair has argued that state formation could take place in such kinship networks when "privileged kin groups are able to command the services of followers through whom they can impose their will on the rest of the people,"[45] whereas Malcolm Webb has maintained that "chiefdoms apparently represent the natural, inevitable end product, the natural culmination of the agricultural revolution."[46]

The transition from village-level kinship groups to larger political units was not simultaneous or linear throughout all parts of Southeast Asia. There is evidence that as Islam moved into the Philippines, new concepts of kingship emerged with it. But in general, the underlying pressure toward state organization arose from the need at the village level for some superior form of protection and organization. In Trengganu on the Malay Peninsula, there was a community "defined by religion and culture as much as by political ties . . . [having] no single capital, no fixed boundaries, and no encompassing administrative network."[47] It was not a state by Western definition, yet it had many of the attributes of loyalty and support that even some modern Southeast Asian states lack. The kind of state or nation building in which people recognize their commonality to the exclusion of all outsiders and, on the basis of that recognition, act to form a political organization to protect their values, way of life, or other unique attributes of their society did not occur in traditional Southeast Asia. The creation of a higher, more remote authority that controlled significantly expanded reserves of human resources met the needs for protection from the bandits of the everyday world and from the spirits and evil forces of the supernatural world, but the government could not break through kinship and local loyalties and refocus them on a nation. This local focus for political community, coupled with the embodiment of sovereignty in the person of a king rather than in the institutions of a state, meant traditional states of Southeast Asia were very fragile units at best.

NOTES

1. Ruth T. McVey, "Introduction," in *Southeast Asian Transitions: Approaches Through Social History*, edited by Ruth T. McVey (New Haven: Yale University Press, 1978), p. 3.

2. See Stanley O'Connor's review of R. B. Smith and W. Watson, *Early South East Asia: Essays in Archaeology, History and Historical Geography* (London: Oxford University Press, 1979), in the *Journal of Southeast Asian History* 15 (1981).

3. Robert Redfield, *The Little Community* (Chicago: University of Chicago Press, 1960), p. 4.

4. Michael Aung-Thwin, "Hierarchy and Order in Pre-Colonial Burma," *Journal of Southeast Asian Studies* 15 (September 1984), pp. 226–232.

5. J. M. Jacob, "Pre-Angkor Cambodia: Evidence from the Inscriptions in Khmer Concerning the Common People and Their Environment," in Smith and Watson, *Early South East Asia*, p. 423.

6. John K. Whitmore, "Societal Organization and Confucian Thought in Vietnam," *Journal of Southeast Asian Studies* 15 (September 1984), p. 302.

7. John T. McAlister and Paul Mus, *The Vietnamese and Their Revolution* (New York: Harper & Row, 1970), p. 44.

8. John S. Lansing, *Evil in the Morning of the World—Phenomenological Approaches to a Balinese Community* (Ann Arbor: Michigan Papers on South and Southeast Asia, no. 6, 1974), p. 2.

9. Antoinette M. Barrett Jones, *Early Tenth Century Java from the Inscriptions* (Dordrecht, Holland: Forsi Publications, 1984), pp. 24–25.

10. Robert O. Whyte, *The Asian Village* (Singapore: Institute of Southeast Asian Studies, 1976), p. 13.

11. James C. Scott, *The Moral Economy of the Peasant: Rebellion and Subsistence in Southeast Asia* (New Haven: Yale University Press, 1976), pp. 57–150.

12. Samuel L. Popkin, *The Rational Peasant: The Political Economy of Rural Society in Vietnam* (Berkeley: University of California Press, 1979), p. 39.

13. Joseph Buttinger, *The Smaller Dragon* (New York: Praeger Publishers, 1958), p. 108.

14. "Introduction," in *Pre-Colonial State Systems in Southeast Asia*, edited by Anthony Reid and Lance Castles (Kuala Lumpur: Malaysian Branch of the Royal Asiatic Society, Monograph no. 6, 1975), p. iii.

15. Truong Buu Lam, *New Lamps for Old, The Transformation of the Vietnamese Administrative Elite* (Singapore: Maruzen Asia, 1982), pp. 19–20.

16. Lucien M. Hanks, *Rice and Man: Agricultural Ecology in Southeast Asia* (Chicago: Aldine-Atherton, 1972), p. 23.

17. Koentjaraningrat, "The Village in Indonesia Today," in *Villages in Indonesia*, edited by Koentjaraningrat (Ithaca: Cornell University Press, 1967), p. 389.

18. Niels Steensgaard, *Carracks, Caravans and Companies: The Structural Crisis in European-Asian Trade in the Early 17th Century* (Copenhagen: Scandinavian Institute of Asian Studies, Monograph Series, no. 17, 1973), p. 30.

19. Truong Buu Lam, *New Lamps for Old*, p. 20.

20. Clifford Geertz, *Peddlers and Princes: Social Development and Economic Change in Two Indonesian Towns* (Chicago: University of Chicago Press, 1963), p. 44.

21. A. C. Milner, *Kerajaan: Malay Political Culture on the Eve of Colonial Rule* (Tucson: University of Arizona Press, 1982), p. 28.

22. G. P. Rouffaer and J. W. Ijzerman (eds.), *De eerste schipvaart der Nederlanders naar Oest-Indie onder Cornelis de Houtman, 1595–1597* (The Hague, 1915), cited in *Brides of the Sea: Port Cities of Asia from the 16th–20th Centuries*, edited by Frank Broeze (Honolulu: University of Hawaii Press, 1989), pp. 70–71.

23. Whyte, *The Asian Village*, pp. 33–34.

24. Clifford Geertz, *Religion in Java* (New York: Free Press, 1964), p. 11.

25. Gerald C. Hickey, *Village in Vietnam* (New Haven: Yale University Press, 1964), p. 93.

26. Robert Wessing, "Life in the Cosmic Village: Cognitive Models in Sundanese Life," in *Art, Ritual and Society in Indonesia*, edited by E. M. Bruner and J. O. Becker (Athens: Ohio University Papers in International Studies, Southeast Asia Series, no. 53, 1977), p. 116.

27. Lansing, *Evil in the Morning of the World*, p. 1.

28. See Wessing, "Life in the Cosmic Village," p. 114, which draws on two earlier studies of Sundanese society: N.J.C. Geise, *Badujs en Moslims in Lebak Parahiang* (Leiden: Zuid Banten, 1952), n.p. and Louis Berthe, "Aines et Cadets L'alliance et la Hierarchie chez les Baduj," *L'Homme* 3–4 (1965), pp. 189–223.

29. Lance Castles, "Statelessness and Stateforming Tendencies Among the Batak Before Colonial Rule," in Reid and Castles, *Pre-Colonial State Systems*, p. 68.

30. John Adams and Nancy Hancock, "Land and Economy in Traditional Vietnam," *Journal of Southeast Asian Studies*, 1 (September 1970), p. 92.

31. Hanks, *Rice and Man*, p. 23.

32. Wessing, "Life in the Cosmic Village," p. 1021.

33. Paul Wheatley, *The Pivot of the Four Quarters* (Edinburgh and Chicago: Edinburgh University Press and Aldine Publishing Co., 1971), p. 459.

34. Hickey, *Village in Vietnam*, p. 40.

35. Wessing, "Life in the Cosmic Village," pp. 103–104.

36. McAlister and Mus, *The Vietnamese and Their Revolution*, p. 46.

37. Castles, "Statelessness and Stateforming Tendencies," in Reid and Castles, *Pre-Colonial State Systems*, p. 74.

38. Ibid., pp. 75–76.

39. Christine Dobbin, "The Exercise of Authority in Minangkabau in the Late Eighteenth Century," in Reid and Castles, *Pre-Colonial State Systems*, pp. 77–89.

40. Hildred Geertz and Clifford Geertz, *Kinship in Bali* (Chicago: University of Chicago Press, 1975), p. 5.

41. D.J.M. Tate, *The Making of Modern South-East Asia*, vol. 1, *The European Conquest* (London: Oxford University Press, 1979), p. 335.

42. *Ibid.*

43. Bennet Bronson, "The Late Prehistory and Early History of Central Thailand," in Smith and Watson, *Early South East Asia*, p. 326.

44. Robert Redfield, *Peasant Society and Culture* (Chicago: University of Chicago Press, 1956), p. 34.

45. Lucy Mair, *Primitive Government* (Baltimore: Penguin Books, 1962), p. 13.

46. Malcolm C. Webb, "The Flag Follows Trade," in *Ancient Civilization and Trade*, edited by Jeremy A. Sabloff and Clifford C. Lamberg-Karlovsky (Albuquerque: University of New Mexico Press, 1975), p. 168.

47. Heather Sutherland, "The Taming of the Trengganu Elite," in McVey, *Southeast Asian Transitions*, p. 36.

4

State Formation and Development in Early Southeast Asia

If Southeast Asian states did not evolve through social and cultural processes in which the governed joined together in a social contract with the governors to achieve a greater common good, how were states created there? Some have argued that Indian princes conquered the region and established states. Another, perhaps more likely theory is that economic change, brought about by increased international trade routed through the region, gave rise to a need for greater political organization. Trade did offer creative leaders access to additional economic resources that could be used to expand their domains. Yet the presence or the possibility of trade did not automatically give rise to greater state organization. Some Sumatran ethnic groups, for example, lived in areas with high levels of commercial traffic but never developed state structures. Other states developed great power and controlled vast territory but did not participate extensively in international commercial trade.

The Nascent State

If we remember that the term *state* should be applied cautiously in early Southeast Asia, it is best to envision numerous enclaves of peoples living under the leadership and authority of an individual who may have been little more than first among equals. Claims to leadership may have been derived from the individual's moral authority, wisdom, or age or equally from the person's skills as a warrior or protector of the group, demonstrated magical prowess or cosmic power, or charismatic influences.

Although it was geographically proximate, the group itself may have been little more than several loosely connected villages joined by common ethnic bonds. Other linking features, in addition to geographic proximity and kinship, included similar productive activities (rice farming or fishing, for example), fresh-water sources, and from time to time the need for protection from external threats. Differentiation and role responsibilities may have existed but were not highly structured, and decisionmaking for the extended group was probably performed by a council of elders—a structure used widely in Southeast Asia, with membership determined variously but usually including representation for each local ethnic or descent group. In some instances, the council of elders retained the right to choose a chief or ruler and was regarded as the voice of the people.

Leadership was necessary for group decisionmaking purposes and was always present, but occasionally a petty chieftain, with purposes broader than management of the status quo emerged as the prime leader. O.W. Wolters described early Southeast Asian leaders in terms of their prowess, saying that a leader's "spiritual identity and capacity for leadership were established when his fellows could recognize his endowment and knew that being associated with him was to their advantage not only because his entourage could expect to enjoy material rewards but also, perhaps, because their own spiritual substance would participate in and share his."[1] These early leaders gave political shape to local kinship units that were based on tribe or clan loyalty. Over time and in specific situations, these local units were able to extend authority beyond the immediate locale and establish a regional power center. In a very few cases regional centers expanded to an even more far-reaching imperial level.[2] The reasons these stages were reached in some places and not others remain in doubt:

> The success of the society would depend upon the exact balance of favorable circumstances beyond its control to a much greater extent than is true for states, with their greater capacity for unified and innovative policy making. . . . The transition from chiefdom to state therefore represents a complete transformation in the bases of social control . . . [so that] the point in the archaeological record at which one begins to refer to evolving polities as "states" (without qualification) is not, perhaps, solely a semantic issue.[3]

Embodied with some measure of authority and buttressed with a few ceremonial practices, such groupings accounted for many more incipient or nascent states than the one hundred states making up Southeast Asia as reported by a Chinese envoy in the year 231. Some of these numerous chiefdoms found means to grow, extending their authority over wider geographic areas and increasing the complexity of their organizations. This local polity provided the staple of political organization through the first millennium of the Christian era, as true imperial kingdoms do not appear to have evolved until the latter part of the millennium.

Early Southeast Asian states had tenuous institutional bases and often crumbled when a leader left or a challenge to authority arrived. What gave one leader or one locale an advantage over others in the evolution process? Two conditions were necessary for the evolution of larger, more complex state structures. Exceptional leadership was important, but it was not sufficient. A second requirement was the accumulation of excess resources—beyond the subsistence base—to finance the increasingly complex structures of the evolving state. The way these resources came to be accumulated shaped both the character of the state and its ability to ensure that excess resources were available reliably and consistently over time. Two economic activities—agricultural production and international trade—were the primary means for generating these surpluses.

Military force was also key in the establishment of many early states. Petty, competing chieftains—divided among themselves—were conquered individually, and sons, relatives, or other trusted allies were placed as leaders of the conquered political units. Yet the use of substantial military force required strong leadership and available surplus economic resources. Malcolm Webb has pointed to difficulties in making the transition from kinship group–incipient state to full-fledged state.

> The full emergence of the state would appear to require eventually the final overthrow of a previously existing traditional system of authority, social controls, and resource allocation whose inelasticity and whose decentralized and localized organization would indeed have very largely inhibited even the initial concentration of power and resources. . . . Despite the areas of continuity, or seeming continuity, between advanced tribal and incipient state systems of governance, the shift from the former to the latter entails a basic and total alteration in the manner in which the authority of the leadership is ultimately enforced and upheld.[4]

The convergence of these factors—leadership, excess economic resources, and human resources—shaped the fortunes of the evolving nascent state. The excess economic resources provided the means to acquire additional human resources that could be used to extend political authority. In a compounding process, new human resources enabled the state to claim further territory and other resources. Transition periods, which may have extended over generations, were highly instable because of the widespread use of force in maintaining both economic control and political authority.

Paul Wheatley has emphasized the political, religious, and social elements of the nascent state, pointing out that "with Hinduism came the concept of divine kingship, a political device especially attractive to village chieftains in situations in which the egalitarian solidarity of the tribal society was proving incapable of extending authority to validate the power required for institutionalization of supra-village rule."[5] Elsewhere, Wheatley drew this view to the core of culture, arguing that people whose religion holds that "human order was brought into being at the creation" (as opposed to revelation) tended to model the earth as a "reduced version of the cosmos" and that, in the process, "kingdoms, capitals, temples, and shrines" became physical symbols of the cosmos.[6] Wheatley perceived this as a cultural transition at a specific point in society's development—not necessarily related, but also not in opposition, to economic models of Asian political development.

These organizational patterns were common throughout Southeast Asia—patterns that represented aggregates of minor kingdoms that covered much of the region's landscape. Scattered between these kingdoms were sparsely populated areas that lacked political centers of gravity, such as parts of Sumatra and the Philippines. These small, minimally connected states accounted for the continual shifting of power centers; with the necessary combination of additional economic resources and skillful political leadership, any nascent state could have ascended to the top ranks of the regional powers.

Agricultural Kingdoms

Increased agricultural production that was sufficient to provide surplus resources appears to have required the development of irrigation techniques for rice production. In the second millennium A.D., agricultural kingdoms based on export commodities such as cloves and pepper are known to have developed, but earlier agricultural kingdoms were based primarily on rice production.

Free-Fall Catchment Irrigation

A prototype of this form of irrigation, the upland agricultural kingdom, developed in mountainous regions of Bali, Java, Luzon, and elsewhere. Highly complex irrigation systems were created in mountainside catchments, taking advantage of highly fertile volcanic soils and plentiful rainfall while controlling natural runoff areas and water flow to intensify agricultural production, especially rice production. Kingdoms based on upland rice production appeared in larger river basins, such as the Mekong or the Irrawaddy, and also in the smaller Solo and Brantas basins of Java. These kingdoms developed highly sophisticated societies, including complex infrastructure of roads and waterworks, important rituals, art forms, and temple construction—all supported by advanced techniques of irrigated agriculture. In such wet-rice farming systems, stability, organization, cooperation, and control were imperative: "Supply and control of water [was] . . . the key factor; not merely the gross quantity of water, but its quality, in terms of the fertilizing substances [as well as] the timing of the flow."[7]

Other Hydraulic Systems

Recent archaeological research by Janice Stargardt and others has shown that similar evolutionary hydraulic development was possible in areas in which natural conditions were less hospitable for irrigation.

The Satingpra hydraulic works . . . were in origin a discontinuous set of village works of very limited extent. For every ancient settlement which succeeded in providing itself with water for irrigation as well as domestic needs, there were several others that achieved only a lower degree of environmental control and practiced bare subsistence forms of unirrigated agriculture. Nevertheless, the technology acquired by some villages through the practice of small-scale hydraulic works was in time to become a valuable instrument in transforming the natural aquatic levels . . . and converting low agricultural yields into substantial and reliable surpluses.[8]

Excavations at Satingpra, located in southern Thailand just north of the present-day border with Malaysia, have shown the "regular construction of hydraulic works of different kinds and on widely differing scales— village tanks and field channels; short, medium and long-distance canals; cattle ponds, great royal reservoirs, temple and stupa tanks; moats both sacred and secular, functional and ritual."[9] Importantly, Satingpra was not located along a great river delta nor in a commonly recognized area of high agricultural production. The durability of its hydraulic system was not based on the power or stature of the state but was "deeply rooted in the local econom[y] and serviced by village-level social institutions."[10] Harry Benda, who also formed a model for the basic structure of Southeast Asian political units, noted that small, poorly integrated territorial units covered much of the region but that inland-agrarian or despotic hydraulic kingdoms emerged from these loosely formed units.[11]

These states focused largely on agriculture to the exclusion of international commerce as the principal source of state revenues, and they tended to be somewhat introverted, with the court elite strongly emphasizing religious rituals as such practices related to cycles of agricultural production. The epitome of this form of state was the Khmer Empire, located in the Mekong region of present-day Cambodia.

Commercial Kingdoms

International trade and commerce offered a second avenue by which nascent states could develop the resources needed to finance further growth and expansion. Opportunities for participation in international trade were not assured for any group and often depended on factors, such as location or the presence of a good harbor, largely beyond the control of the local groups. There were three primary ways local nascent states could become involved in the trade system: as predators, as servicing agents, or as participants. Predatory activities included piracy as well as extractions, such as taxes and tolls or protection payments, whereas servicing activities included portage, safe harbor, and reprovisioning. Participation included commodity production and serving as an entrepôt.

Predatory: Piracy and Protection

Predatory activities were the most common way local chiefs interacted with the international trade system because these activities required little organization and control. Predatory involvement with international trade was widespread and became an important first step in accumulating excess resources required for more sophisticated state development. The transition from pirate lair to nascent state to major kingdom may have required several generations and a certain amount of luck in the form of competent leadership and optimum location, but it was possible to achieve. Importantly, such transitions moved in both directions, as some highly developed kingdoms disintegrated into numerous scattered pirate strongholds.

Piracy has a long history in Southeast Asia. It is almost a natural "reciprocal" of the weak state structures—in those widespread areas and times when state leadership was weak, disintegrating, or nonexistent, piracy was a natural practice and source of revenue for petty leaders. The geography of the archipelago—thousands of small islands with mangrove swamps and scattered river deltas—provided ideal locations for pirate bases. In addition, all shipping was forced to navigate through such narrow passages as the Strait of Malacca or the Sunda Strait, which made tracking and trapping merchant ships a simple task. At various times, the Kra Isthmus at the northern end of the Malay Peninsula was used for portage; despite the arduous and time-consuming nature of overland transshipment, it was a way to avoid pirate attacks in the Malacca Strait.

Pirates were so prevalent and so numerous that merchant vessels usually traveled in convoys, and many merchant ships carried soldiers, cannons, and other defensive weapons. Weak state structures, particularly the inability of the state to effectively extend control throughout its realm, left pirates free to practice their trade. For example, especially in the archipelago:

> Malays moved from trade to "piracy" with apparent ease. . . . The people of the East Coast of Sumatra had once been "addicted to piracy," but when new opportunities arose they became "entirely addicted to commercial pursuits." . . . The rulers of the great Sumatran state of Aru . . . shifted their attention from trade to "plunder" in the early fifteenth century. The Temenggong of Johore, who was described as the "chief pirate" in the Singapore region, turned rapidly to "legitimate trade" when the opportunity offered itself.[12]

Little removed from piracy was payment of protection for safe passage through the sea lanes or for general safety while in port. The presence of hundreds of transient foreigners at all of the major Southeast Asian commercial centers provided nearly unlimited opportunities for extraction of payments in port as well as at sea.

Predatory: Taxes and Tolls

Extraction of taxes and tolls on the movements of goods and peoples offered another simple means of intervening in international or intra-regional trade. Virtually every area and every nascent state participated to some degree in regional commerce through its local markets, which provided items not manufactured or produced locally. Although the more complex aspects of commercial activity were dependent upon strategic location along the trade routes, the collecting of taxes and tolls was an option for nearly every petty chieftain.

Among nascent states located along the many waterways, a chieftain—having established control over the mouth or main trunks of a river system—could sustain his position by exacting taxes, tolls, and other levees for goods and persons moving on the waterway, thereby generating revenues for state building. In the rough, densely vegetated terrain of much of Southeast Asia, river systems offered the best and frequently the only method of reaching inland areas. Each river valley also offered a protected enclosure in which to organize a state. Many early kingdoms were located away from major waterways, but smaller rivers and tributary systems offered ideal locations. Most areas were largely self-sufficient in food production and were active in international trade and exchange only to the extent of filling needs that could not be met internally. In referring to the natural drainage basins of intermountain water systems as self-contained geographic units, Bennet Bronson hypothesized that control of a river artery or of one or more major tributaries provided opportunities to develop the "lord-subordinate" relationships needed to expand kinship ties into political units by providing revenues from controlled commercial and other river traffic. These revenues constituted the critical economic surplus needed for expansion.[13]

Service and Support: Provisioning, Safe Harbor, Portage, and Transshipment

Especially during the early centuries of the Christian era, when shipping lanes followed the coast, many localities fortunate enough to have substantial harbors or river inlets provided protection from storms or pirates as well as provisions and fresh water for merchant vessels as they moved from China along the coast of Vietnam to Malaya and on to India. There was also substantial portage activity at the narrow Kra Isthmus on the Malay Peninsula, and the state of Langkasuka is known to have controlled and prospered from this overland transport system. However, as ships developed and were able to sail on direct line and away from coastlines, states such as Langkasuka lost important sources of revenue and declined.

Early in the Christian era Satingpra, with its network of canals, may have been another important portage across the Malay Peninsula. Although little is known of Satingpra's actual history, in general, when international trade routes offered potential for resource accumulation, some states became entirely dependent on the flow of international trade. The geography of these kingdoms was not so much riparian as characterized by "facing coastal lowlands linked together by their own ships across a common stretch of sea."[14]

Participation: Cash-Crop Commodity Production
for International Commerce

Southeast Asia was the production area for many products that entered the international commercial system. Not only did early Southeast Asian states try to control the flow of international trade in an entrepôt sense; but they also produced agricultural, forest, and other products for the system. Prior to the fourteenth century A.D., Southeast Asian commodities in the international commercial network were primarily gathered products such as camphor, birds' nests, perfumes, pearls, aromatic woods, and gold; after that time, however, cultivated crops such as pepper, nutmeg, cloves, and rice commanded greater portions of the trade, and rice remained within the region to feed growing urban populations. Product lists varied from time to time and port to port but generally included pepper, rice, timber, camphor, tin, benzoin, spices, resins, precious metals, pearls, tortoiseshell, foodstuffs, deer hides, silk, cotton, sugar, and medicines. The state often controlled export production—Burmese kings, for example, maintained a monopoly over export commodities such as ivory, silver, amber, rubies, and sapphires. Slave trade—which provided labor for pepper, spice, and other plantations; supplied troops for military service; and provided crews for sailing and rowing ships—was an important economic activity, especially in Makasar and Sulu.[15]

By the fourteenth century, local involvement in production for international trade had increased significantly. Pepper, spices, sandalwood, and certain hardwoods were grown in quantity specifically for international commercial trade. Production of export commodities became so lucrative that some states and regions completely neglected the production of basic foodstuffs and were forced to import even rice for local consumption. For example, virtually all of Ternate's productive land was committed to cloves. Similarly, nutmeg and mace production for export dominated Banda, and sandalwood became the primary product of Timor. Increasing direct participation in international commercial activities may have been stimulated by the eastward expansion of Muslim kingdoms or perhaps by the Ming Dynasty's renewed commercial interests in China after 1368.

Participation: Entrepôt

Particularly in the archipelago, both interisland and international trade stimulated the growth of competing entrepôt centers, which, because of the lack of interest in the hinterland, became almost city-states. The external economic impetus of the international trade routes was important in making the transition from kinship network to state. As entrepreneurial opportunities appeared, particular kinship groups acquired and controlled surplus resources; as a result, reciprocal exchange was supplanted by a system of allocation of surpluses in order to accomplish the greater goals of nascent states. These maritime commercial kingdoms were of necessity outward-looking and cosmopolitan, given their close links to the international trading system. These riparian or coastal kingdoms did not follow the hydraulic despotism model because of their predominant interest in international commerce and because of the presence of "a more cosmopolitan population composed of traders and merchants of various, including indigenous, races, an urban, trading bourgeoisie with substantial financial resources and, consequently, very likely possessing some degree at least of 'countervailing' political power."[16]

The maritime-agricultural divisions were not mutually exclusive. For instance, it is known that Funan evolved toward the inland-agricultural model as maritime traffic began to bypass its ports. Most Javanese kingdoms exported rice for intraregional commerce, and some were strong competitors for international trade. Ports such as Barus in Sumatra provided camphor and benzoin produced in the inland mountains and highlands which were under the control of Batak hill dwellers who were distinct and separate from the Malay peoples governing Barus itself.[17] Even Śrīvijaya may have had more interest in agricultural production, at least for commercial purposes, than scholars have previously believed. Thus, in the evolution of the nascent state, "agrarian and maritime proclivities should be viewed as complementary features of intraregional cohesion and regional integration rather than as 'internally' and 'externally' oriented divergent forces."[18]

State Formation

The precise manner in which kingship evolved, and how it acquired much of its ritual as well as administrative character, remains unclear. Even the emergence of kingship did not necessarily signal the rise of the territorial state. Early theorists focused on Indian and Chinese cultural penetration in the region. Some asserted that India or China or both had controlled the region; a less extreme view was put forward by G. Coedès, who argued that Indochina developed a "civilization of its own . . . of Indian parentage [except for Vietnam], which even when it achieved political independence remained an offshoot of Chinese civilization."[19] But even in Vietnam, where Indian Buddhism was influential through the eleventh century and Chinese Buddhism—which grew in influence from the ninth century on—penetrated much of society,[20] an independent culture developed. Recently, more emphasis has been given to the role of indigenous cultural forces, with the resulting argument that Southeast Asians borrowed only those Indian and Chinese cultural traits that complemented and could be adapted to the indigenous system.

The adoption of Indian or Chinese culture took place over extended periods in conjunction with the evolution of states. The rise of the state was a two-step process in which the relationship between cities and the hinterland was at first "a contrast between these indigenous scattered communities and cosmopolitan trading centers thronged with expatriates and with local people who, by virtue of living there, had in large measure cut themselves off from their own society."[21] The second step, the integration of cities and the hinterland, took place under different circumstances but was essentially led by the political and urban centers in search of resources—human resources or commodities or both. Paul Wheatley has pointed out that the adoption of Hinduism, early urbanization, and primitive state building were all linked:

> These changes were reflected morphologically in the conversion of the chief's hut into a palace, the spirit-house into a temple, the spirit-stone into a *linga* that was to become the palladium of the state, and the boundary spirits into the Lokapalas presiding over the cardinal directions. In other words, the village community had become the city-state, the whole process signifying a transformation from culture to civilization.[22]

A three-step series, or cycle, documented for Burma[23] can be loosely applied to all of Southeast Asia. At the beginning of each cycle, political power and economic control were scattered among local, fortified towns and hamlets ruled by hereditary chieftains, recognized as individuals of prowess. Hermann Kulke has called this the *nuclear area*, whereas others have labeled it the substate or prestate level because of its limited territory, lack of bureaucratic structure, and dependence on the personality and ability of the particular leader. I refer to this early phase of state formation as the *nascent state*. The second phase began with the rise of a charismatic leader who, using military skill and a band of loyal followers, consolidated authority and built a centralized polity complete with capital, court, rudimentary administrative structures, and military forces. Kulke has labeled these *early kingdoms*, and most scholars agree that at this point the structure was sufficiently strong to be defined as a state, although its internal structures—such as bureaucracy and the military—remained poorly defined. At the peak, or third, level of the cycle was the *imperial kingdom*, which was differentiated from the early kingdom in several ways. First, it represented the forcible unification of two or more areas of formerly independent kingdoms. It relied on a centralized bureaucracy, and it maintained firm control over, and had legitimate access to, all of its regions. Additionally, it elevated ritual to a more sophisticated and complex level as "new temples became the magico-political centre of the empire and the cosmos [and] the imperial kings themselves became directly associated with the divine power of these centres." Finally, infrastructure associated with religious buildings and temples extended to all local and regional areas and included roads and rest houses, providing both a network for pilgrims, traders, and other travelers and access to the farthest reaches of the kingdom for government officials.[24]

History also provides ample evidence, however, that within a few generations these states—even the imperial kingdoms—became vulnerable to disintegration. The courts remained vulnerable to factionalism, fratricide, and other intrigue. Once central leadership had weakened, administrative control broke down and military strength diminished. Outlying regional tributary states then declared their independence, furthering decentralization and fragmentation. Forces of localism returned until another charismatic leader came forward—from the original center or perhaps from a former vassal—and the cycle began again.

State Organization

The main pressure underlying state formation—the villages' needs for protection from outside forces—required centrally controlled human resources. This centralization process established a resource and labor pool that expanded the capacities of the system. Yet the resulting kingdoms were fragile and often disintegrated as readily as they had formed. The process was evolutionary but by no means linear and was "characterized by a 'multiplicity' of local political centres and shifting loyalties of their leaders, particularly at the periphery of the system."[25] A chief may have capitalized on an alliance of friendship, kinship, marriage, or conquest to knit together a state that fragmented upon the chief's demise. In applying these concepts to Funan, Kenneth Hall argued that international commercial patterns induced Funan's chieftains to "mediate these initial commercial transactions as the instigators and organizers of Funan's port."[26] Subsequently, early chieftains established a "higher economic order, possessing a dual economic base, which was supportive of a more sophisticated level of political integration than was previously true." In the end, one ruler of Funan, Hun P'an-huang, was able to subordinate "local chiefs to his authority as well as that of his successors," thereby creating a more permanent human resource base.[27]

The Southeast Asian state did not approach the classic model of oriental despotism.[28] The irrigation systems in Cambodia, Java, and parts of Vietnam met three basic economic criteria of the model, including very specific divisions of labor, intensified techniques of cultivation, and cooperation on a large scale. At the same time, however, the traditional states never fulfilled the necessary "managerial functions" of maintaining "critical hydraulic works" or controlling "major nonhydraulic industrial enterprises."[29] This level of organization was not attained in traditional Southeast Asia despite the sophistication of construction and of water systems, as in Cambodia.

The traditional state was not a concrete or fixed territorial unit but instead was structured in several concentric zones around the nucleus of the capital, a centripetal phenomenon in state authority called the "galactic polity."[30] In many senses, the capital *was* the state, and its power radiated from the center to the periphery. The extent of power in a functional sense varied greatly over time and may not have been extremely important to the state in any case: "The centre was less a political powerhouse than a paradigm, exemplar, and manifestation of the idea of divine perfection. The classical *negara* [state] was, because of its structure, oriented towards spectacle and ceremony, and the king, because of his role, [was] immobilized by ritual."[31]

The state's orientation toward the capital city did not change with the coming of Islam, in which *madina* expresses the nearly identical concept of "the city as religious centre, administrative capital and economic pivot for a society, state or kingdom."[32] Moreover, the state was not "constructed of bureaucratic hierarchies . . . [but] was a collection of revenue-producing regions, which its ruler allocated to individual members of the elite, who were linked to each other by personal ties and derived their status from royal recognition."[33]

Beyond the nucleus were secondary or closely held village settlements, which included villagers who farmed royal lands. More distant yet was the strategic zone in which villages were sometimes stockaded. At the farthest extension of the kingdom were the conquered or foreign areas. The maritime kingdom was also divided into several zones: the nucleus of the dominant city-state and its immediate coastal areas, the extended coastal regions under continuous control of the kingdom, farther coastal-regions or port cities under irregular control, and the hinterland which was only sporadically under state control.

The lack of rigid structure lent a quality of 'survivability' to traditional states. For example, when Ayudhya (Thailand) was destroyed in 1767, there was no long-lasting disruption of Thai political history; indeed, the only new elements at the beginning of the Bangkok period "were the dynasty and the construction of the capital city."[34] Moreover, and important for understanding contemporary politics, vassal states or ethnic groups did not give up their local identities but maintained a quasi-autonomous status.

Loyalty and Legitimacy

The organized system of state control was usually based on patrimonial relationships between the king and his retainers. Territorial subdivisions were delegated to royal families in return for specific services, but loyalty was a continuing concern. Loyalty to the king may generally have been consensual at the center of the kingdom, but it was mediated by power at the periphery. To ensure that obligations were carried out, minor princes or their families were usually retained at the central court. Royal genealogies were also important means by which numerous and extended kinship groups were bound to the court, thus "mobilizing political support through emphasizing a ramifying network of kinship."[35] Oaths of all kinds—including calling on the gods and promising heinous fates to those who broke such oaths—were issued by kings and Brahmans. Malay seafarers, who were essential for the stability of the great maritime kingdoms, were noted for their loyalty, but they were also fickle and were capable of reverting to piracy whenever a king's power waned. When the sultanate of Johore was left without an heir in the seventeenth century, most of its seafarers (*orang laut*) moved to the former Śrīvijayan ruler at Palembang.[36]

Loyalty among villagers was also tenuous. Many discoveries have been made of inscriptions exhorting pride in "this country called Arimaddana" or "this country called Pagan" in an attempt to supersede village and kinship loyalties. Yet local loyalties were never really broken because in the view from below, individual peasant villagers gave loyalty first to an immediate chief, then upward through regional divisions, and finally to the king through primary ministers and retainers of state.[37] Vietnam, however, had a history of popular mobilization for defense against the Chinese from as early as A.D. 974.[38]

The traditional political system was basically extractive in nature. Western concepts of social welfare and governmental responsibility for the needs of the people (beyond protection) were not part of the traditional polity. Ministers, as well as lower officials and staff, did not perceive themselves as public servants; nor did they see providing for peoples' welfare as a government responsibility. Traditional political philosophers admonished kings to show concern for the people, as when Sultan Mansur Shah admonished his son, Raja Radin: "Upon you is laid the duty of faithfully cherishing those who are subject to you and of liberally forgiving any offenses they may commit."[39] In fact, the state primarily served the needs of the king and his court, and the peasants had few expectations that specific services would be forthcoming from the state.

Sources of Legitimacy

Functional Legitimacy. The state's functional legitimacy was based on the need for stability in the kingdom, which ensured protection so village life could continue largely uninterrupted. The king drew upon corvée labor to provide for such services as road and dam building. When banditry or foreign military incursions occurred, or when the king and his court intervened too frequently—seeking corvée labor or military support or levying too many taxes—legitimacy was lost and peasants drifted away. In 1725 and again in 1773, the Vietnamese court revised the population registers used for taxation, military service, and corvée labor, a move many villagers opposed: "Many people became agitated . . . and fled . . . and [the government] ordered the old registers to be used."[40] A regime of slightly benign neglect—which allowed the villages to operate in an unfettered way—was nearly ideal, but with too much neglect, bandits returned and the roads decayed—both traditional signs of the weakening and decline of authority. Functional legitimacy was often supported by the use of force; however, legitimacy itself was not bestowed on the basis of force, power, or material wealth but on qualities of spiritual greatness.

Externally Derived Ritual. It is well-known that most Southeast Asian kingdoms borrowed heavily from Hindu political traditions to strengthen the perceived power of the state. Ceremonial practices linked to the fertility of the soil provided an ideal and important bond between king and peasant. Concepts of the king as an earthly representative or interlocutor between the gods and people further strengthened the king's position. Recognition by and participation in the Chinese tributary system with its highly ritualized exchange practices also served as an important source of legitimacy for Southeast Asian kingdoms. Moreover, Vietnam borrowed very heavily from Chinese court practices. Finally, Islam became an important legitimizing force, particularly in the archipelago and in commercial kingdoms.

Cosmology and Harmony. Traditional states were not popular—that is, their governments were not derived from the will or consent of the population. It was necessary, then, to find some means of securing tacit acceptance, if not consent. Force or coercion created some acceptance and apathy and poor communication further eased the burden of state control, but this was not sufficient to sustain the state indefinitely. The common solution was to provide the king with legitimacy based on supernatural justification—a divine right developed to its highest level through borrowed Hindu political concepts that linked the state to the universe and the king to the gods.

The court's legitimacy was established through its role as intermediary between the village and the supernatural and temporal representative of the cosmos. For example, the capital city was usually located near the kingdom's geographic center. In Brahmanical terms, the universe revolved around Mount Meru, the city of the gods. Mount Meru's axis was important in ordering all Hinduized societies, but even in the sinicized Vietnamese system, "the term 'Dragon's Belly' (*Long-do*) became synonymous with the capital city; it connoted the realm's spiritual center of gravity."[41] The capital city was analogous to Meru; thus the king was intimately linked to the gods in a symbolic king-god merger that rationalized the peasants' position in a servant-master relationship. The circle was completed as the king, interceding with the gods, linked his sovereignty to the soil and fertility, returning the full mystic force of nature to the village. The village was associated with the capital—and thus the universe—in concentric circles radiating from the capital in terms of geomancy and the points of the compass. Harmony was to be found in this world through imitation of the macrocosmic universe, and each segment of society was placed in the larger framework of the cosmos and metaphysical thought.

In the Southeast Asian mind, harmony and balance hold a significance with which few Westerners can identify. Orientation, the physical as well as metaphysical locale of the individual vis-à-vis the natural and supernatural worlds, was bound up in the relationships of village-individual and kingdom-king. If any segment of these relationships was out of place, all was lost. Lack of kingship was equated with anarchy.[42] The Balinese developed locational concepts of self and place more intensely than most other groups, but this sense of identity is found throughout Southeast Asia:

> One of the most important words in the Balinese vocabulary is *kaiket* (Indonesian *terikat*), which means literally "to be tied." The Balinese are "tied" from birth to a bewildering variety of obligations, duties, organizations, temples, places, people and things. It is this fact which distinguishes them, not merely as being Balinese, but as being human. According to some Balinese, the severest social sanction, worse than death or incarceration, is banishment, for it affects not only this life but the whole orientation of the soul or spirit . . . .[43]

This sense of place and identity greatly reinforced the king's legitimacy among a people who might otherwise have been inclined to establish other forms of government.

The metaphysical view of the world—indeed, of life or existence itself—subordinated the state to the larger pattern of the cosmos. The cosmological significance of all of life was based on five principles.

1. Reality was a function of the imitation of a celestial archetype.
2. Reality was conferred through participation in the symbolism of the center; that is, cities, temples, and houses became real by the fact of being assimilated with the center of the world.
3. Every act that had a definite meaning—hunting, fishing, farming, games, war, sex—in some way participated in the sacred; hence, profane activities were those that had no mythical meaning.[44]
4. The parallelism between the macrocosmos and the microcosmos necessitated the practice of ritual ceremonies in order to maintain harmony between the world of the gods and the world of humans.
5. The techniques of orientation necessary to define sacred territory within the continuum of profane space involved an emphasis on the cardinal compass directions.[45]

Three aspects of this metaphysical view are particularly important for understanding traditional society: (1) The state was a microcosmic version of the macrocosmic universe; (2) mysticism and magic were used to explain the supernatural and animism worlds; and (3) the desire for continuity of past and present, particularly the link to ancestors, brought together the gods of the macrocosm and the spirits, mysticism, and magic of the microcosm.

Manipulation of symbols—primarily spiritual, mystical, or magical trappings—linked the king and the court to the supernatural. The adaptation of successive titles for the king—maharajah from Indian political thought and sultan from Middle Eastern Islamic thought—strengthened his authority and power. In addition, continual rewriting of histories served important purposes of connecting the current king to previously recognized great kings and, through birth or lineage, to one or another of the gods.

Actual objects and symbols of magical or supernatural power surrounded the person of the king. For instance, according to stone inscriptions, Jayavarman II of Khmer selected "a brahman named Hiranyadama, skilled in magic science . . . to perform a ceremony that would make it impossible . . . to pay allegiance to Java."[46] In Malaya, the royal regalia—which included swords, knives, lances, drums, flutes, pipes, betel boxes, jewels, scepters, seals of state, and umbrellas—was said to have been protected by a "death-striking" electrical charge of divine power.[47] In Burma and elsewhere, white elephants were treasured as magical symbols of good fortune; they also exemplified the syncretic belief in Buddhism, animism, magic, and astrology.[48] Hinduization took place because many leaders saw Hindu rituals as representing more sophisticated justifications or sanctifications of their position.

Mysticism and magic engulfed both village and court. A striking example of the use of mysticism was found in traditional dance: The highly costumed and choreographically complex dances were used for incantations and spirit liberation, welfare and fertility rites, or direct communication with the gods. In Vietnam, the emperor assigned a guardian spirit to each new settlement—in effect, a symbolic bond between the village and the emperor.[49] Burmese concern for spirits (*nats*), of which there are thirty-seven principals representing ghosts and spirits of departed heroes, governed all traditional interactions not only between the village and the court but also between humans and the environment. Criminal punishments frequently relied on some mystical control over bodily functions and pain. The court's most powerful source of magic was the king's regalia, possession of which was often sufficient to justify a usurper's claim to the throne. So pervasive were mysticism and magic that they could not be supplanted by even a force as strong as Islam:

> Beginning their invocations with the orthodox preface: "In the name of God, the merciful, the compassionate," and ending them with an appeal to the Creed: "There is no god but God, and Muhammad is the Apostle of God," many Southeast Asian Moslems are conscious of no impropriety in addressing the intervening matter to a string of Hindu Divinities, Demons, Ghosts and Nature Spirits, with a few Angels and Prophets thrown in, as the occasion may require.[50]

Although the pervasive nature of magic and mysticism in the Southeast Asian worldview may be difficult to comprehend, these concepts were fundamental to the organizational beliefs of traditional society in that region.

Continuity of past and present was apparent at all levels of traditional society. In Java, Clifford Geertz described "a pious respect for the dead plus a lively awareness of the necessity of being on good terms with one's deceased father and mother"—not outright ancestor worship but indicative of an "active past" permeating the present.[51] In Cambodia, sanctuaries "indicate that a pyramid-temple could be devoted, at least in part, to the cult of ancestor-worship."[52] An obvious example of the desire to maintain continuity was the alteration of folktales to incorporate a usurper king into accepted genealogies. Traditional Javanese histories, such as the *Pararaton*, were occasionally rewritten to eliminate competing lines to the throne or to establish new lines to the past for the present ruler. They were also rewritten to adjust the cultural past to the present, as was seen when earlier Hindu wordings were replaced by Buddhist phrases.

The Vietnamese, although not following the essentially Hindu concepts, developed similar cosmological roles for the emperor as the "Son of Heaven." The capital was considered a "repository of benevolent supernatural influences," and the emperor, as the patron of agriculture, "performed a plowing ritual with a gilded plow every spring" to ensure fertility for the cropping cycle.[53] Moreover, Vietnamese village autonomy was similar to that of villages elsewhere in Southeast Asia, and it required a similar type of state structure.

Problems of Legitimacy

A critical weakness of legitimacy was its focus on the king's person rather than on the institutions of kingship or the state. For the modern Western state, "the essence of the concept was always its impersonal nature; the state was never to be wholly identified with the individuals holding power. In the European tradition, the state broke the personal identification of the older notion of sovereignty."[54] Although the transition from personalized to institutionalized sovereignty was not evenly successful throughout Europe, it did take place. In traditional Southeast Asia, there was no evidence that such a transition had begun by the time of the intervention of the European powers.

Ritual was important in both defining and limiting the king's power. First, kings represented the only link between the temporal realm and the cosmos, so the power ascribed to the king's person was enormous. The connection to the cosmos, however, limited the action and decisional latitude of the king, who "had to conduct himself in an exemplary way in order that society as a whole might benefit from the omnipotent goodness of Heaven and be protected from the incalculably bad consequences of Heaven's wrath."[55] Thus, important aspects of power were derived externally—that is, beyond the control of people:

> Power that is generated by the performance of correct rituals lacks any precision of purpose. The person who carries out the rituals can be held accountable only for the general state of affairs. . . . The connection between cause and effect is not close enough . . . to think about power as being in the service of policies guided by national choice.[56]

Thus, Asian concepts of power were separated from one's responsibility for acts associated with the use of power in a fatalist perception of forces beyond any human control.

Among the court elite, kinship ties were less effective in maintaining harmony than they were among villagers. Blood relations were important in aristocratic society, and many positions were hereditary, but the "communal interdependence" that sustained the village socioeconomic subsistence systems was replaced by expediency and the desire for riches and power: "Kin relationships helped people to identify who could be considered royalty and who might be enlisted in the king's supporting circle, but kinship in and of itself was no guarantee of loyalty," and, as often happened, "kin who were on losing sides or otherwise incurred the king's disfavor could find themselves [and their families] reduced from royalty to slavery."[57] The struggle within elite ranks was often marked by intrigue that countermanded blood relations. Upward struggle, as well as threats from below, were constant, and power was the key to court success. Law was of little use without the ability to apply the necessary force. Burma may have been a partial exception to this predominance of power, inasmuch as the Burmese Book of Law carried strong religious sanctions against the unrestrained abuse of power, but John Cady also noted that "old Burma was a shut-in state which maintained no windows to the outside world capable of providing . . . a more progressive outlook. . . . Burma's kings were too absorbed in crushing potential rivals, in waging predatory warfare . . . in collecting white elephants, and building pagodas to concern themselves with governmental reforms."[58] Yet power was tenuous at best, as was indicated by the vague rules of succession, and the king's position was assured only as long as he was able to maintain sufficient power.

Legitimacy and Limitations of Authority

Nevertheless, kings were required to perform minimal but necessary political functions. For example, within the limits of available power, the king dealt with foreign affairs—which frequently included fighting wars. The system provided a degree of protection from the vagaries of lawlessness: The presence of bandits was one of the first signs indicating that a king's power was on the decline. Minimal service tasks—road building and maintenance, for example—fell to the king, and the decline of a ruler's effectiveness was signaled by poor maintenance of the road system.[59] In the final analysis, the king's principal responsibilities were to maintain order and ensure that the village society could function with a minimum of outside interference.

Concepts of legitimacy were designed to support claims of a dominant and all-powerful king and to specify submission of the realm to the king. Little nation building could take place under these concepts. In a passage in the *Malay Annals*, written about A.D. 1500, King Sri Tri Buana agreed to a covenant that limited his authority over the realm—suggesting some sort of a contract between the governor and the governed.[60] Whether the *Malay Annals* could have become a Southeast Asian Magna Carta can never be known because the Portuguese soon ended Malacca's independence.

Bureaucratic Structures and Functions

Bureaucratic structures were based on a metaphysical concept of the state. As late as the 1890s, Thailand—at that time the most advanced state in the region—still designated its principal ministers to represent the four cardinal points of the compass, with additional ministers given responsibility for the royal court (capital city), fields, and treasury. All royalty and officials were ranked "according to genealogical proximity to the monarch," beginning with the heir apparent, who was "Lord of the Eastern [front] House," whereas other sons were ordered as southern, western, or northern princes, in that order. The chief queen, who ranked below the princes, was the southern queen, followed by the western, northern, and eastern queens. The eastern queen, who was unmarried and was "reserved" for the heir apparent, was also called the Princess of the Solitary Post. Four chief ministers and numerous subordinate ministers were usually present, most of whom had senior status over ranking military officers except in time of war. This group constituted "higher officialdom" and resided at court.[61]

The minister who was responsible for a geographic quadrant of the kingdom accepted responsibility for administrative, regulatory, judicial, and governmental functions there. The minister also played a role in the metaphysical structure of the kingdom, linking the peasantry to the king and, ultimately, to the divine or universal. Divine prescriptions for harmony throughout the realm, as well as between heaven and earth, had a more practical meaning at the ministerial level: in order for the kingdom to prosper (i.e., for agricultural production in the form of wet-rice cultivation to succeed), the minister had to ensure that the village community fulfilled its designated role so that water would be properly available and applied, transplanting and cultivation could be carried out appropriately, and people would be available for harvest. The minister did not direct these activities, although in Angkor and other agricultural kingdoms the waterworks reached a level of complexity that required central control. A central Javanese inscription from the eighth century lists official titles for village-level functionaries who managed irrigation works.[62] In northern Thailand, authority below the ministers was divided on a decimal system "in groups of ten, with a hierarchy of officials controlling groups of ten, fifty, a hundred, thousand, and ten thousand."[63]

A minister's first responsibility was to ensure a stabile environment in which the complex agricultural production system could operate. In other words, public order had to be maintained and the activities of thieves, bandits, and foreign invaders curtailed. The second court responsibility was to ensure that the metaphysical world was equally well-ordered, so each peasant—permeated with a belief system heavily laden with fatalism and the expectation that the best life was obtained through social harmony and the status quo at the expense of individual freedom and growth—could see and receive, through the vehicle of the minister and the king, some assurance of the greater purposes of life. Temple and stupa construction and the lavishing of support and offerings on temples already in existence were meant to confirm that there were life and meaning beyond the rice paddy and to soften the likely prescriptions of fate. Road systems connecting various temple complexes provided much of the kingdom's infrastructure.

Such symbols and infrastructure also required that the ministers gather resources. Taxes were gathered in cash, in kind, and in the form of corvée labor for construction as well as military service. Transportation taxes—particularly river tolls—village taxes, and head taxes were common. Imported and exported commodities were taxed at a rate of 5 to 15 percent and were usually collected in kind, making the state a major marketing competitor. In Burma, a household tax was levied on each village unit "apportioned roughly according to ability to pay . . . not a levy on property or an income tax as such."[64]

Within the court, other officials served the necessary functions of administration. Virtually every court had a chief priest, who often doubled as the primary adviser to the king and in many cases was the king's teacher prior to his ascension. Such advisers, who were usually very close to the king and who controlled the mystical rituals, exercised great power and influence in the kingdom. Maritime kingdoms required several specialized officials, such as the powerful harbor master who was in charge of admitting the ships and checking all cargo, and special judges to hear complaints from foreign merchants.[65] Many individuals who received titles carried out no functions but formed a part of the king's retinue.

When Sultan Mahmud Shah came to the throne in Malacca, his new appointments included a minister for commerce and a chief minister (who were to sit opposite one another in the audience hall), a treasurer, several ministers of state, a chief herald, a mystic to cast curses, a chief admiral, and several nonspecific title holders. Malacca was a maritime kingdom, and three of these appointees had specifically commercial assignments: The minister of commerce was in charge of the harbor and the movement of goods through the harbor; the treasurer had overall responsibility for the revenues of the kingdom, which were derived mostly from commerce; and the admiral controlled sea traffic through the Strait of Malacca, keeping the seas free of pirates and ensuring that all ships stopped at Malacca. In addition, there were numerous mystical, ceremonial, and honorary appointments.

Vietnam did not follow the Hindu constructs of state but instead adopted Confucian bureaucratic structures from China. The Vietnamese bureaucracy and kingship were separate entities, and bureaucrats were selected by examination after they had studied Confucian writings. Yet despite this systematic and rational approach to government office holding, the traditional state in Vietnam represented a "largely passive style of authoritarianism, which stressed moral example rather than more dynamic goals."[66] The Vietnamese bureaucratic system developed not so much a strong problem-solving elite as a highly compartmentalized elitist structure that, as elsewhere in Southeast Asia, gave great importance to the autonomy and isolation of the village.

Neither the Vietnamese bureaucratic system nor the few known instances of ministers being appointed to functionally defined positions (as in Malacca or Trengganu) signaled a movement toward Western (Weberian) rational bureaucratic structures in traditional Southeast Asia.[67] In a study of commercial and political development in Aceh, Anthony Reid concluded that a rational system did not appear to be on the horizon: "The apparent arbitrariness of such exactions from merchants, and the total dependence of officials on royal favor, does not suggest any substantial development towards professionalism of the bureaucracy."[68] The state systems remained highly personalized in administration and dependent on the mystical for legitimization, yet considering the environmental demands of the time these systems appear to have functioned effectively—expressing the rational values of the political culture.

Leadership and Administration

Traditional leadership worked within a narrow framework; indeed, there was little room for dynamic political initiatives of the type expected from contemporary governments. Theoretical legal restrictions on a monarch's power rarely inhibited his authority, especially within the governmental structures and among his retainers; more important, the king's ability to impose his authority over the village was limited, and in many dry-farming areas particularly, villagers simply left if a ruler became too oppressive. Even in the commercial sectors,

> effective administration was not via a centrally managed bureaucratic structure, but through the ruler's exercise of patronage and reciprocal relations with the elite. Relations between the centre and component parts of the state, which were inherently fragile and fluctuating, were held in balance by the ruler's individual strength and wisdom, which determined his power.[69]

In Burma and throughout much of Southeast Asia, the court was governed by the Code of Manu. Law was adopted from Indian legal thought, but these concepts were blended with indigenous philosophy, producing a set of "rules of conduct that *ought* to be observed by reason of social condition."[70] In Vietnam, the legal code was shaped by that of Han China, although there are known references to an ancient law code in Au Lac territory well before the Han takeover of Vietnam in 111 B.C. In A.D. 1042 Emperor Ly Thai Tong issued the *Hinh Thu*, or *Book of Punishments*, for Vietnam.[71] The Vietnamese public law code was strongly influenced by Buddhist thought, which had a humanizing impact, and by Confucian thought, which was reflected in the many detailed prescriptions for the role of public officials; it also reflected a strong interest in protecting as well as regulating private interests.[72]

Although the quasi-feudal organization of most states stifled growth of government activities beyond those determined by basic social organization and needs, law codes were specific and well-defined. Court systems and structures varied, but punishments for individual crimes were often precisely specified, including banishment, fines, tattooing on the face or body, and caning with a light or a heavy stick. Torture was officially sanctioned, and the *Le Code* in Vietnam, for example, limited its use to three times for each detainee.[73] The death penalty was mandated for a wide range of crimes, particularly treason or suspected treason, but it was not used as capriciously as might be expected under absolute rule. The appeal process usually required personal review by the king or emperor.

Administration was organized within a system of land distribution such that each subregion was relatively autonomous except for taxes and services owed superiors. Administrative divisions evolved into complex systems of appanage lands, *bengkok* (villages usually assigned to support high government officials or monasteries), free villages, and crown domains—all of which formed a "hierarchical line of separate self-sufficient and highly autonomous units of power."[74] This autonomy was reflected in a conversation between Tun Perak, an administrator, and Sri Amarat, a herald of the Malay king, in which Tun Perak stated, "As for the business of us who administer territory, what concern is that of yours? For territory is territory even if it is only the size of a coconut shell. What we think should be done we do, for the Ruler is not concerned with the difficulties we administrators encounter; he only takes account of the good results we achieve."[75]

The hierarchy of administrative power reflected basic social principles that allowed the lower units to operate with minimal interference. At the same time, official and unofficial channels existed for communication between the village and the court. Official channels included royal officials, some of whom may have resided in the village, and landed nobility. Informal channels included religious authorities, reports from tax collectors, and direct contact between the village—particularly its elders—and the court.[76]

At times, wealthy merchants (*orang kaya* in Malaya or *thutes* in Burma) became so powerful that they controlled the political system. Merchants were not part of the royal elite, although some were usurpers, and they were not even indigenous peoples. They did, however, often hold appointed positions within government, especially in the maritime kingdoms. In a system that gave primacy to personal wealth and that had few institutional counterbalances, the potential for corruption and influence buying was enormous: "These merchants proved to be a force capable of righting any imbalance in the exercise of power. . . . When they were ignored or abused, they lent their assistance to a rival. . . . When they were courted, they responded favorably and contributed toward a successful working relationship with the ruler."[77] The arbitrariness of politics could also work against these wealthy merchants, as it did in Aceh in 1589 when the new sultan executed many of the politically powerful merchants, took their possessions, and strictly regulated those who remained.[78]

Evolution of the Traditional Southeast Asian State

State formation throughout traditional Southeast Asia was uneven. States did not evolve in all parts of the region, and where there were states, many were poorly organized. The state was overlaid on the village community. Although some states controlled considerable resources from maritime trade or agricultural production, they did not dominate the village community. In fact, the reverse was the case: The state developed in response to the peasants' need for organization and harmony because "the concern . . . was not tyranny but disorder; the 'abuse' of power was not reflected by autocracy but by chaos."[79] Harmony in traditional Southeast Asian culture was manifested at three levels: at the village level, where people existed in harmony with the ecosystem and managed (not manipulated) that system for agricultural production; at the societal level, where the state controlled banditry (or piracy) and maintained social stability; and at the level of the universe, where the king ensured harmony with the gods on behalf of the entire society.

Tension always existed between the village (given its desire for harmony) and the court (with its predilection for hierarchy). Following its independence from China, the Vietnamese court at first tried to draw all Vietnamese together both culturally and politically by employing many Vietnamese traditions, such as moving the capital city to its ancient third-century-B.C. site. In time, however, various Confucian traditions reemerged, and the Vietnamese court lost contact with its people.[80]

Elsewhere, traditional states were variously effective in fulfilling their roles of maintaining earthly and cosmic harmony, meeting the requirements of early Southeast Asian society, and responding to the commercial needs of the international trading system. The state was an institutionally fragile entity, relying on the personal capabilities of its king to mobilize limited available resources. This fragile state had sufficient capacity to maintain the independence and integrity of the Southeast Asian region for nearly two millennia, but it was not capable of withstanding the challenge of the Europeans.

NOTES

1. O. W. Wolters, "Culture, History and Region in Southeast Asian Perspectives," in *ASEAN: Identity, Development and Culture*, edited by R. P. Anand and Purificacion V. Quisumbing (Quezon City and Honolulu: University of the Philippines Law Center and the East-West Center, Culture Learning Institute, 1981), p. 5.

2. Hermann Kulke, "The Early and the Imperial Kingdom in Southeast Asian History," in *Southeast Asia in the 9th to 14th Centuries*, edited by David G. Marr and A. C. Milner (Singapore: Institute of Southeast Asian Studies, 1986), p. 5.

3. Malcolm C. Webb, "The Flag Follows Trade: An Essay on the Necessary Interaction of Military and Commercial Factors in State Formation," in *Ancient Civilization and Trade*, edited by Jeremy A. Sabloff and Clifford C. Lamberg-Karlovsky (Albuquerque: University of New Mexico Press, 1975), pp. 164–165.

4. *Ibid.*, p. 157.

5. Paul Wheatley, "Urban Genesis in Mainland South East Asia," in *Early South East Asia: Essays in Archaeology, History and Historical Geography*, edited by R. B. Smith and W. Watson (London: Oxford University Press, 1979), p. 295.

6. Paul Wheatley, *The Pivot of the Four Quarters* (Edinburgh and Chicago: Edinburgh University Press and Aldine Publishing Co., 1971), pp. 416–417.

7. Clifford Geertz, *Agricultural Involution: The Process of Ecological Change in Indonesia* (Berkeley: University of California Press, 1966), p. 31.

8. Janice Stargardt, "Hydraulic Works and Southeast Asian Polities," in Marr and Milner, *Southeast Asia in the 9th to 14th Centuries*, p. 24.

9. *Ibid.*, p. 30.

10. *Ibid.*, p. 33.

11. Harry J. Benda, "The Structure of Southeast Asian History: Some Preliminary Observations," in *Man, State and Society in Contemporary Southeast Asia*, edited by Robert O. Tilman (New York: Praeger Publishers, 1969), pp. 24–25.

12. A. C. Milner, *Kerajaan: Malay Political Culture on the Eve of Colonial Rule* (Tucson: University of Arizona Press, 1982), p. 20.

13. Bennet Bronson, "Exchange at the Upstream and Downstream Ends: Notes Toward a Functional Model of the Coastal State in Southeast Asia," in *Economic Exchange and Social Interaction in Southeast Asia*, edited by Karl L. Hutter (Ann Arbor: Michigan Papers on South and Southeast Asia, no. 13, 1977), pp. 39–52.

14. Charles A. Fisher, "Geographical Continuity and Political Change in Southeast Asia," in *Conflict and Stability in Southeast Asia*, edited by Mark W. Zacher and R. Stephen Milne (Garden City, N.Y.: Anchor Books, 1974), p. 9.

15. James Francis Warren, "Trade, Slave Raiding and State Formation in the Sulu Sultanate in the Nineteenth Century," in *The Southeast Asian Port and Polity; Rise and Demise*, edited by J. Kathirithamby-Wells and John Villers (Singapore: Singapore University Press, 1990), pp. 187–211.

16. Benda, "The Structure of Southeast Asian History," in Tilman, *Man, State and Society*, p. 25.

17. Jane Drakard, *A Malay Frontier: Unity and Duality in a Sumatran Kingdom* (Ithaca: Cornell Southeast Asia Program, 1990), pp. 13–15.

18. J. Kathirithamby-Wells, "Introduction," in Kathirithamby-Wells and Villers, *The Southeast Asian Port and Polity*, p. 3.

19. G. Coedès, *The Making of South East Asia* (Berkeley: University of California Press, 1969), p. 218.

20. Gerald C. Hickey, *Village in Vietnam* (New Haven: Yale University Press, 1964), pp. 4–5.

21. I. W. Mabbett, "The Indianization of Southeast Asia: Reflections on the Prehistoric Sources," *Journal of Southeast Asian Studies* 8 (March 1977), pp. 13–14.

22. Wheatley, "Urban Genesis in Mainland South East Asia," in Smith and Watson, *Early South East Asia*, pp. 296–297.

23. Michael Aung-Thwin, "The Role of *Sasana* Reform in Burmese History: Economic Dimensions of a Religious Purification," *Journal of Asian Studies* 38 (August 1979), p. 673.

24. Kulke, "The Early and the Imperial Kingdom in Southeast Asian History," in Marr and Milner, *Southeast Asia in the 9th to 14th Centuries*, pp. 11–16.

25. *Ibid.*, p. 7.

26. Kenneth R. Hall, "The 'Indianization' of Funan: An Economic History of Southeast Asia's First State," *Journal of Southeast Asian Studies*, 13 (March 1982), pp. 85–86.

27. *Ibid.*, p. 91.

28. Karl A. Wittfogel, *Oriental Despotism: A Comparative Study of Total Power* (New Haven: Yale University Press, 1957), p. 22.

29. *Ibid.*, p. 48.

30. Stanley J. Tambiah, "The Galactic Polity: The Structure of Traditional Kingdoms in Southeast Asia," *Annals of the New York Academy of Sciences* 293 (1977), pp. 69–97.

31. Jan Wisseman-Christie, "Negara, Mandala, and Despotic State: Images of Early Java," in Marr and Milner, *Southeast Asia in the 9th to 14th Centuries*, p. 69.

32. J. Kathirithamby-Wells, "The Islamic City: Melaka to Jogjakarta, c. 1500–1800," *Modern Asian Studies* 20 (1986), p. 333.

33. Heather Sutherland, "The Taming of the Trengganu Elite," in *Southeast Asian Transitions: Approaches Through Social History*, edited by Ruth T. McVey (New Haven: Yale University Press, 1978), p. 34.

34. Klaus Wenk, *The Restoration of Thailand Under Rama I, 1782–1809*, translated by Greeley Stahl (Tucson: University of Arizona Press, 1968), p. 122.

35. A. Thomas Kirsch, "Kinship, Genealogical Claims, and Societal Integration in Ancient Khmer Society: An Interpretation," in *Southeast Asian History and Historiography: Essays Presented to D.G.E. Hall*, edited by C. W. Cowan and O. W. Wolters (Ithaca: Cornell University Press, 1976), p. 201.

36. James D. Tracy, "Introduction," in *The Political Economy of Merchant Empires*, edited by James D. Tracy (Cambridge: Cambridge University Press, 1991), p. 16.

37. Virginia Matheson, "Concepts of State in the Tuhfat Al-Hafis," in *Pre-Colonial State Systems in Southeast Asia*, edited by Anthony Reid and Lance Castles (Kuala Lumpur: Malaysian Branch of the Royal Asiatic Society, Monograph no. 6, 1975), p. 16.

38. Keith W. Taylor, *The Birth of Vietnam* (Berkeley: University of California Press, 1983), p. 287.

39. *Sĕjarah Mĕlayu*, or *Malay Annals*, translated by C. C. Brown (London: Oxford University Press, 1970), p. 103.

40. Ta Van Tai, *The Vietnamese Tradition of Human Rights* (Berkeley: Institute of East Asian Studies, 1988), p. 52.

41. Taylor, *The Birth of Vietnam*, p. 253.

42. Milner, *Kerajaan*, p. 104.

43. John S. Lansing, *Evil in the Morning of the World—Phenomenological Approaches to a Balinese Community* (Ann Arbor: Michigan Papers on South and Southeast Asia, no. 6, 1974), p. 1.

44. Mircea Eliade, *The Myth of the Eternal Return, or Cosmos and History*, translated from French by Willard R. Trask (Princeton, N.J.: Princeton University Press, 1954), pp. 5, 27–28.

45. Wheatley, *The Pivot of the Four Quarters*, p. 418.

46. Lawrence Palmer Briggs, *The Ancient Khmer Empire*. Transactions of the American Philosophical Society (Philadelphia: American Philosophical Society, 1951), p. 89.

47. Walter William Skeat, *Malay Magic, Being an Introduction to the Folklore and Popular Religion of the Malay Peninsula* (New York: Dover Publications, 1967; first published in London by Macmillan, 1900), p. 24.

48. Hla Pe, "Burmese Attitudes to Plants and Animals," in *Natural Symbols in South East Asia*, edited by G. B. Milner (London: School of Oriental and African Studies, 1978), p. 102.

49. Hickey, *Village in Vietnam*, p. 6.

50. Skeat, *Malay Magic*, pp. xiii–xiv.

51. Clifford Geertz, *Religion in Java* (New York: Free Press, 1964), p. 76.

52. Briggs, *The Ancient Khmer Empire*, p. 133.

53. David J. Steinberg, ed., with David K. Wyatt, John R.W. Smail, Alexander Woodside, William R. Roff, and David P. Chandler, *In Search of Southeast Asia: A Modern History* (New York: Praeger Publishers, 1971), pp. 68, 70.

54. J. P. Nettl, "The State as a Conceptual Variable," *World Politics* 20 (July 1968), p. 575.

55. Lucian W. Pye, *Asian Power and Politics, the Cultural Dimensions of Authority* (Cambridge: Belknap Press of Harvard University Press, 1985), p. 39.

56. *Ibid.*, p. 40.

57. May Ebihara, "Societal Organization in Sixteenth and Seventeenth Century Cambodia," *Journal of Southeast Asian Studies* 15 (September 1984), p. 283.

58. John F. Cady, *A History of Modern Burma* (Ithaca: Cornell University Press, 1958), pp. 6, 11.

59. Christine Dobbin, "The Exercise of Authority in Minangkabau in the Late Eighteenth Century," in Reid and Castles, *Pre-Colonial State Systems*, p. 79.

60. *Malay Annals*, pp. 15–17.

61. Michael Aung-Thwin, "Hierarchy and Order in Pre-Colonial Burma," *Journal of Southeast Asian Studies* 15 (September 1984), p. 225.

62. Stargardt, "Hydraulic Works," p. 35, citing N. van Setten van der Meer, *Sawah Cultivation in Ancient Java, Aspects of Development During the Indo-Javanese Period, Fifth to Fifteenth Centuries* (Canberra: Oriental Monograph Series, Australian National University Press, 1979).

63. David K. Wyatt, "Laws and Social Order in Early Thailand: An Introduction to the *Mangraisat*," *Journal of Southeast Asian Studies* 15 (September 1984), p. 247.

64. Cady, *A History of Modern Burma*, p. 20.

65. J. Kennedy, *History of Malaya, 1400–1959* (New York: St. Martin's Press, 1967), p. 8.

66. Steinberg, *In Search of Southeast Asia*, p. 68.

67. Max Weber, *The Theory of Social and Economic Organization*, translated by A. M. Henderson and Talcott Parsons, edited with an introduction by Talcott Parsons (New York: Free Press, 1964), pp. 324–407.

68. Anthony Reid, "Trade and the Problem of Royal Power in Aceh," in Reid and Castles, *Pre-Colonial State Systems*, p. 51.

69. Kathirithamby-Wells, "Introduction," in Kathirithamby-Wells and Villers, *Southeast Asian Port and Polity*, p. 4.

70. M. B. Hooker, "The Indian Derived Texts of Southeast Asia," *Journal of Asian Studies* 37 (February 1978), p. 201.

71. Nguyen Ngoc Huy and Ta Van Tai, *The Le Code; Law in Traditional Vietnam, A Comparative Sino-Vietnamese Legal Study with Historical-Juridical Analysis and Annotations*, vol. 1 (Athens: Ohio University Press, 1987), pp. 4–5.

72. Ta Van Tai, *The Vietnamese Tradition of Human Rights*, p. 42.

73. Nguyen Ngoc Huy and Ta Van Tai, *The Le Code*, p. 279.

74. Soemarsaid Moertono, *State and Statecraft: A Study of the Later Mataram Period, Sixteenth to Nineteenth Centuries* (Ithaca: Cornell University, Modern Indonesia Project, 1958), pp. 104, 110, 117–118: also, Aung-Thwin, "Hierarchy and Order in Pre-Colonial Burma," p. 224.

75. *Malay Annals*, p. 57.

76. J. G. de Casparis, "Some Notes on Relations Between Central and Local Government in Ancient Java," in Marr and Milner, *Southeast Asia in the 9th to 14th Centuries*, pp. 51–52.

77. Leonard Y. Andaya, "The Structure of Power in Seventeenth Century Johore," in Reid and Castles, *Pre-Colonial State Systems*, pp. 48–49.

78. Reid, "Trade and the Problem of Royal Power," in Reid and Castles, *Pre-Colonial State Systems*, pp. 48–49.

79. Michael Aung-Thwin, "Divinity, Spirit, and Human: Conceptions of Classical Burmese Kingship," in *Centers, Symbols, and Hierarchies: Essays on the Classical States of Southeast Asia* (New Haven: Yale University, Southeast Asia Studies, Monograph Series no. 26, 1983), p. 74.

80. Taylor, *The Birth of Vietnam*, p. 270.

5

The Interstate System in Precolonial Southeast Asia

Prior to the sixteenth century, the political and economic system that spanned the distance from China to Europe was constructed of a series of loosely connected and largely autonomous subsystems. Communication—except for commerce—was intermittent, but subordinate systems such as Southeast Asia borrowed extensively from the East Asian, South Asian, and Middle Eastern subsystems. For example, Ottoman links to the Islamic kingdoms of Southeast Asia, although important, were largely restricted to religious exchanges and occasional advice on matters of state. Southeast Asia had great latitude for autonomous action, and it drew strength from China, India, and other subsystems for its own systemic development.

Within the system of traditional Southeast Asia, power, defined as the level of available military force, was the determining factor in interstate relations. Although no codified system of international law had been developed and the regional states followed practices similar to those adopted in India and, to a lesser extent, China, patterns of interaction were regularized through ritual and repetition and—especially in the regulation of trade and maritime traffic—were sophisticated and clearly defined, although the ruler's whims could have a strong effect. The principal functions of the state were (1) control of conflict, (2) resource management as population densities increased, (3) management of growing domestic commerce, and (4) management of international trade.

Foreign policy was the "sole prerogative of the king,"[1] and its two most general objectives were the aggrandizement of the king and the court in order to reinforce the king's claim to domestic legitimacy and the attainment of greater wealth for the kingdom so the preeminent position of the king in his realm could be bolstered further.[2] Thus, interstate politics were carried out to enhance the state's domestic political philosophy. The state's dichotomous village and court social structures, with broadly different purposes and constituencies, had an important impact on foreign policy.

The economic base of the kingdom also had a direct effect on foreign policy. Commercial kingdoms established and maintained monopoly control of various products from their hinterland or elsewhere for international trade and also sought a monopoly over entrepôt services for their area. The land-based agricultural kingdoms, however—which sought to enrich the royal house; to demonstrate the righteousness, sanctity, and legitimacy of the kingship through proper religious activities; and to emulate, where possible, the perception that the kingship was the "center of the world"—sought to control human resources and territory through imperial adventures. Both maritime and agricultural kingdoms tried to monopolize their environments, the commercial kingdom in an effort to control the wealth flowing through the region and the land-based kingdom in an effort to control human resources. This propensity for monopoly severely limited the options of each state for dealing with its environment and with other states.

The power resources of the kingdom, however, defined the limits of its foreign policy. Although China sometimes mediated regional conflict, as in 1403 when a fleet under the command of Admiral Yin Ching intervened to protect Malacca from Thai invasion, there was little recourse beyond the state's capacities to use its available power for control, protection, or expansion. Such a regional political system, with basic interaction framed largely in the use of force, could achieve a modicum of balance or equilibrium only if a group of states developed comparable military capabilities or when technological limits defined the geographical limits of the empire. There was no institutional structure to maintain the balance, a condition that gave the system an inherent instability that was magnified by the institutional weakness and the concomitant internal instability of the states themselves, leaving little likelihood that a balance of power could be sustained.

The interstate system of traditional Southeast Asia can be divided functionally into cultural, religious, economic, political, diplomatic, and military subsystems. Although these subsystems overlapped in operational senses, a separate discussion of each clarifies the analysis of the ways in which they shaped regional politics.

Cultural and Religious Subsystems

Religion and custom were critical elements of power within the state and linked the village and the court in an all-subsuming metaphysical view of the world. They also played very important roles in sustaining patterns of interstate conduct. Concepts of sovereignty were bound up in the belief that the sovereign was a direct link to the gods. As a group, then, the court elite was set apart from the populace, and the blood ties among royal leaders (and indirectly to the gods) were important in maintaining regional stability. As sovereignty was linked to blood, the elite found opportunities for contact and communication through marriage and through the common maintenance of royal genealogical links to the supernatural when no direct heir to the throne remained.

Records of contacts are few, but it is known that in the early ninth century a Khmer prince spent his childhood in Java.[3] Other royal exchanges probably took place as well and cultural interchange appears to have been frequent. For instance, similar corruptions in the Javanese and in the later Khmer forms of the nagari script (an alphabet originally from North India) suggest that it reached Cambodia by way of Java, and there are records of various kings contributing to the support or building of Buddhist or Hindu temples in neighboring kingdoms. Records of contact between Muslim kingdoms of Southeast Asia and the Ottoman Empire are extensive, but they primarily involved religious exchange and teaching rather than the political structure of kingship.

Although blood relationships and religious interchanges may have led to some measure of interstate cooperation, two additional factors served to reinforce divisions. First, as kingship evolved, the concept of the god-king became stronger. The exact meaning of this concept is not yet fully understood, with most disagreement focusing on the *degree* of godliness embedded in the king. Variations range from the view that the king himself was a god to the more limited concept suggesting that "the king had vassals but no overlord."[4] The supernatural concept of kingship was balanced with local spirits, gods, and ancestor worship and—as with most of the cultural borrowings in Southeast Asia—was adapted with little difficulty. Whatever its degree of embodiment of supernatural power, the god-king concept was important in the interstate system because of the inseparability of the king and the state. The perception of the state as the center of the world was elemental to the system of interstate politics because this philosophy provided, in theory, that only one prime state could exist, although lesser states with vassal or tributary status were recognized. Thus a multistate system of sovereign and, theoretically, equal states did not develop in Southeast Asia. Although the theoretical never approached reality, the prime state model limited the possibilities for interstate cooperation and alliances because there were no equals with which to cooperate.

Economic Subsystem

As a goal of foreign policy, material enrichment was promoted by whatever means were available. Maritime kingdoms employed impressive naval forces to control trade because they sought power to control the flow of traffic through the Strait of Malacca, the primary water route for the China-to-Europe trade. These kingdoms also controlled trade by providing harbor facilities and other attractions for merchant fleets. Major entrepôt trade centers had the effect of controlling nearby lesser kingdoms because merchants sought the larger markets at major centers. Another important strategy among commercial kingdoms involved the monopoly of interisland trade. Naval force was used to coerce smaller kingdoms to transship produce through the dominant entrepôt center and to prevent them from setting up independent trade centers.

Another facet of trade control was the maintenance of security along the main shipping routes. Pirates, which were common throughout Southeast Asia, found easy refuge among the many small islands scattered throughout the archipelago. In addition, the distinction between smaller kingdoms and large pirate lairs was more a matter of conjecture than of fact. So blurred was the distinction between pirates and legitimate kingdoms that the members of the naval forces used by the maritime kingdoms could, in times of breakdown of authority, become pirates. The burden of patrolling the sea lanes fell on the major commercial kingdoms, and their success or failure had a direct impact on their revenues.

The land-based kingdoms—although primarily interested in agriculture, especially rice production—controlled foreign trade and exchange through their power over passage on the major river systems. Some kingdoms, such as Ayudhya and Mataram, played dual roles as both maritime commercial and agricultural kingdoms. Export commodities (e.g., rice, spices, minerals, precious metals, and lumber) were controlled by the state, having been gathered domestically as tax payments. Not only trade routes but commodity trading itself was handled by the state, and exchanges were carried out at the state-to-state level or between state officials and merchants from China, India, or the Middle East.

Much of the wealth gained through commodity trading was used for religious purposes linked to the legitimization of the state, particularly among agricultural kingdoms. Consecration of temples, donations of lands to sustain monasteries, construction of new temple complexes, and pilgrimages to India and later to Mecca were among the court religious activities that filled a basic redistributive need in these nonmarket economies. In Burma, however, the flow of wealth to the religious community is thought to have eventually contributed to the decline of the state,[5] and during the late Angkor period of the Khmer Empire, "all of the Cambodian peasantry was in the service of the gods."[6]

Wealth, an important measure of political legitimacy, was both an outcome and a prerogative of political power: "There was no effective distinction between official and personal revenue."[7] The *Malay Annals* records Sultan Mahmud Shah as having said, "If the Sul-Fan Muda has but the sword of kingship, he will have gold as well. That is to say, where there is sovereignty there is gold."[8] The ability of the king to lavish gifts on his clients and retainers was very important in maintaining sovereignty; conversely, the loss of wealth had grave consequences. The sultan of Perak—although Perak was never an extremely wealthy trading center—fell from power in part because his chief supporters acquired more wealth than the sultan himself.[9]

Political and Diplomatic Subsystems

The political philosophy of the state, based on the metaphysical view of the kingdom as a microcosmic version of the universe, left little room for the development of a set of relationships that presumed the existence of more than one state. Although in reality there were always many states, and although these states dealt with each other regularly, the dealings could not be routinized. To have made them routine would have threatened the legitimacy of the states because the concept of multiple sovereign states enjoying domain over specific territories and interacting as equals was eclipsed by the concept of a universal sovereign.

Based on this political philosophy, traditional states established interstate relations based on tributary or overlord-vassal relationships, using a system somewhat like that of China. The close proximity of many of these Southeast Asian states, however, afforded opportunities to assert these relationships more directly. Although this system offered a means of regulating relationships between states and minimized conflict and war, its unequal, hierarchical structure encouraged manipulation, conspiracy, and unending challenges to the status quo as coalitions of vassals sought to break the extant structure. On the other hand, given the Southeast Asian understanding of the nature of the state and its relationship to its environment, tributary relations were inherently more stable than the situation in which two states of equal power existed side by side. Since the system provided no theoretical underpinnings with which to make this situation acceptable, the inevitable result was that rivalry and conflict dominated relations between these states until one was subordinated to the other.

The exchange of ambassadors and diplomatic missions on a permanent basis was not common, and most capital cities had no facilities for receiving them. When envoys or emissaries were sent from one kingdom to another, they were usually met at a frontier point or a port city and rarely traveled to the capital city. The standard mode for diplomatic communication was a type of courier system, using exchanges of letters. For instance, the *Malay Annals* contains an exchange in which the raja of Pahang sent a letter of "friendship" to Siam; however, the foreign minister of Siam rejected the letter, asking that it be rewritten to express "obeisance" to Siam. This was done—reluctantly, and the letter was accepted.[10] Letters were also commonly used in exchanges between China and the states of Southeast Asia.

Such exchanges of letters may also have been accompanied by tributes. Tributes from Southeast Asia to the Chinese Imperial Court have been widely recognized, but a similar custom also operated within the region, as when "incessant border warfare and threats of warfare may have led the Burmese king to pay tribute to Cambodia."[11] Cambodia, under the weak predecessors of Jayavarman VII, also paid tribute to Champa. At another time Pagan, having conquered Thalon, left it largely intact to be used as a tributary link to the international maritime trade.[12] It is important, however, not to overstress the subordinate status associated with tributes because the Asian system at all levels had the capacity to ignore the implications of inferiority while emphasizing its benefits in the exchange of wealth. For example, the sultanate of Trengganu paid tribute to Siam until the end of the eighteenth century. The British, applying European legal concepts of suzerainty, sought authority over Trengganu through cession from Siam, failing to recognize that tributary status could "mean anything from friendship to total subordination, and one of the central characteristics of Southeast Asian state relationships was the constant reinterpretation of such ties, reflecting the waxing and waning of relative power."[13]

Political contacts in traditional Southeast Asia in an age of slow communications were intermittent and were almost certainly a function of geographic distance. Unilateral imperialistic action was the most common pattern of interstate action, and force was the diplomatic tool employed: "A built-in expansive tendency [was] the most important of all qualities pertaining to the definition of the state."[14] Neighboring states were almost continually under threat of or threatening attack, and the effective border between any two neighbors was established at the point at which their opposing power met in equilibrium. Common reasons for military action included expanding the territory, increasing the pool of available human resources, or controlling economic resources. Violence or the threat of violence was also the principal means of enforcement of authority in the kingdom.

The prevalence of the use of force did not mean relations between people and states were not governed by law or that law did not exist. Law codes were developed in Vietnam before its incorporation into China in 111 B.C.[15] Throughout Southeast Asia, legal systems were borrowed from Indian models and adapted to local conditions. Precise law and regulations were developed in the maritime kingdoms. Most of these kingdoms enforced detailed regulations on weights and measures as well as other commercial relations governing both local and foreign merchants.[16]

Several factors within the social context might explain why, despite the sophisticated development of legal systems, violence remained so important in interstate relations. First, the metaphysical view of the kingdom justified its expansion over the maximum territory because the kingdom, as the center and controller of the universe, did not theoretically comprehend other universal centers or kingdoms. Second, the mobility of some segments of the peasant population limited potential revenues from domestic taxes, thus making plunder more attractive. Finally, the political geography of Southeast Asia, with its numerous minor river-delta societies, offered many targets for imperialism, as well as a multitude of nascent power centers from which imperialism could emerge. For all of these reasons, war remained the arbiter of many interstate disputes and the most common form of interstate action.

The use of force was, in one important sense, an extension of political legitimacy. The cosmological concepts on which kingship was based left little room for development of a stabile system of equal and sovereign states. The extension of power and use of force worked to establish an unequal system of dominant and vassal states. Although the state's legitimacy was, in part, ethnically and culturally based, its territorial extent was determined by its ability to extend its power through force. Boundaries were not established at fixed geographic points but fluctuated along the frontier between two states. As capabilities for using force changed over time, affecting equilibrium, so, too, was the boundary affected. Distinct borders between states may have been accepted in principle, but in reality boundaries were expansive frontier areas over which no state had effective control, making them more akin to buffer zones than clearly demarcated lines. Frontier areas were beyond the permanent control of any government, and the resettlement of loyal peasants—encouraged by the availability of land—at these frontiers was one technique used to bring them under control. Power, measured in available military force, was critical in holding the state together, but it "faded into insignificance with distance from the capital; otherwise the autonomy of local chiefs was nearly complete, and whether the effective boundaries of a major state encompassed a certain area depended on ties of blood and marriage, calculations of alliance, and force of arms."[17]

Inexact boundary concepts were legitimized through the Indian concept of *mandala*,[18] which in its Indian form connoted an alliance system; in Southeast Asia, however, the term referred to a "circle of kings" in which "one king, identified with divine and universal authority and defined as the conqueror, claimed personal hegemony over the others, who in theory were bound to be his obedient allies and vassals."[19] The *mandala* of any kingdom reflected several levels of reality, the first level being that territory over which the kingdom exercised continuous authority. At the second level were those principalities, city-states, and other centers of power that were subordinate participants and contributors in the tribute system. The third level included those power centers whose submission was maintained largely in the minds and poems of the court chroniclers; only occasionally, and in conjunction with the threat or use of force, did they actually submit to the center.

The fluid nature of this system meant that kingdoms rose and declined frequently. Intrigue at court was common, as when the sultan of Ternate was poisoned by a daughter of the sultan of Bachan in a plot by the rulers of Tidore, Jailolo, and Bachan. Early Portuguese records from the years 1512 to 1535 indicate that numerous incumbents, claimants, heirs, and pretenders to the thrones of Ternate and Tidore died from poisoning or in other suspicious circumstances.[20] Sacking and razing capital cities of nearby kingdoms were done to break the terminal from which power was extended. But once the equilibrium had been broken, there was no assurance that the victor could sustain power throughout the conquered territory. When sustained control was not possible, plunder and retreat were common. The establishment of a vassal state through the installation of a pretender in place of the defeated king was also a common alternative.

The overlord-vassal system of interstate organization was a direct consequence of imperial action. Such maritime kingdoms as Śrīvijaya were conglomerates or confederations of previously independent entrepôt centers scattered along the Strait of Malacca. In Śrīvijaya's case, the confederation was established and maintained by its navy, and each additional port city brought under Śrīvijayan vassalage augmented that navy. But such systems had limited permanence and clearly depended on the power of the center for their continued existence. For example, the Khmer Empire owed allegiance to Java prior to A.D. 800, but Java was unable to maintain its position after A.D. 802.[21] Likewise, at various times the Khmer Empire demanded allegiance from Champa, Annam,

Chenla, Louvo, and parts of the Malay Peninsula. Overlord-vassal systems were established and maintained by the power of the leading state for the benefit of that state and were reinforced by blood bonds to the throne of conquered states. If the power of the leading state waned, or if a new king came to power in the center, its imperial organization also diminished.

Temporary alliances and confederations were common, but few developed deep or lasting links among kingdoms beyond their expedient or immediate utility. Most alliance systems performed specific defensive tasks or met immediate goals. Lawrence Briggs noted several references over a long period of time to a confederation of Mon kingdoms in the Mekong-Menam and Irrawaddy-Sittang valleys, which appeared to have been a mutual association—perhaps a defensive alliance against the Khmer Empire or Burma.[22] Ternate and Hitu (on the northern coast of Ambon) concluded a friendship agreement when Zainal Abidin, sultan of Ternate, met the Hitu chief on his return from Java in 1501; however, Ternate later used this agreement as a claim to the island of Ambon. Had Southeast Asian kingdoms been more practiced in cooperation, they might have united to defeat the first European arrivals. This did not happen, however, precisely because of the lack of systemic conventions for such mutual cooperation.

Other cooperative but disjointed ventures were recorded. For example, not only did Jayavarman II of Khmer live in Java for a time, but he was installed on the Khmer throne by the Javanese army. Almost immediately thereafter, however, hostile relations between the two countries resumed. Also, during the eleventh century, Kediri (eastern Java) and Śrīvijaya tacitly agreed on exclusive trading spheres within the archipelago, but Kediri demonstrated the limits to such an agreement by refusing to aid Śrīvijaya in fighting the Chola raids. In 1495 Zainal Abidin went to Java (Giri) to study Islam and "most probably had also studied the organization and administration of the Javanese courts."[23] Such cooperation was expedient and short-term, and little in Southeast Asia's systemic context suggests that interstate cooperation was a valued goal. Because sovereignty was personal rather than institutional in nature, "foreign relations lacked continuity of obligation, extending from one king to his successor,"[24] and the instability of the system increased with the constant need for building, rebuilding, and anticipating changes in relationships.

Military Subsystem and War

One assurance of the continued stability of kingship and kingdom was the possession of loyal military forces. Only a sketchy picture of military capabilities in traditional Southeast Asia can be presented. The system was rife with conflict, and war was often bloody, with heavy loss of life in actual combat and further loss as defeated soldiers often committed suicide rather than be taken captive. The principle of "stand fast until the last man drops" was not given undue credence, however, and escape from combat into the rough jungle terrain was a widely accepted strategy, even for the bravest warriors. Moreover, ritual war, in which a battle was planned for an appointed hour and continued—at a rather leisurely pace and from safe distances—until one side retired from the field, was common in Southeast Asia.[25] Also recognized was the idea of righteous war,[26] although plunder was usually a sufficient reason for war, as was the case when the Javanese raided Ligor, Champa, and Tonkin six times during a thirty-five-year period. This is not to say that wars were not devastating and destructive: Much of the population and local agricultural resources were often carried away, and entire villages, towns, and crop areas were sometimes destroyed—as occurred when the Burmese decimated Ayudhya.

Mysticism and magic, as in all areas of traditional Southeast Asian life, were important in the preparations for and execution of war. Dreams forewarned leaders and warriors of impending ill fates. Shells, animal teeth, and pieces of iron or copper were worn as amulets or war talismans to ward off evil spirits. Auspicious days were selected for battle—the first day of the new moon was thought to be a particularly good choice. The route leading to the battle site was prepared with small sacrifices, and all natural phenomena along the way were examined for signs of bad omens. Even the actions of villagers who remained at home were strictly proscribed; for example, women were forbidden to sew because a pricked finger would signify the certain wounding of their husbands.[27]

Naval Forces

Shipbuilding and naval activity were common in all of the kingdoms of Southeast Asia, particularly in the archipelago. Shipbuilding was also widespread in the Mekong and was long-standing and common in all of the region's major river deltas.[28] The maritime kingdoms of Southeast Asia "built, owned, and operated ocean-going ships of respectable size" as early as the first centuries of the Christian era.[29]

Early Southeast Asian ships are often thought to have been similar to Chinese junks, but evidence suggests otherwise. Pierre-Ives Manguin noted that six of these ships were large enough to carry 500 to 1,000 people and a cargo of 250 to 1,000 tons; they used no iron in fastenings, utilized two or more layers of planks in the hulls, required dual quarter rudders for steering gear, and used multiple masts with no outrigging.[30] The origin of these ships is obscure, but Chinese sources date them as early as the third century A.D. Ships were constructed from several layers of thick planks held together with pegs and cords made from coconut fiber. No nails were used. The largest ships required at least six or seven feet of water, were more than sixty meters in length, and used sails because they could not be navigated with oars alone. The sixteenth-century Portuguese writer Gaspar Correia observed: "Because she was very tall . . . our people did not dare board her and our firing did not hurt her at all, for she had four super-imposed layers of planks, and our biggest cannon would not penetrate more than two."[31]

The naval capacities of Southeast Asian states were considerable. Chau Ju-kua, the Chinese scholar, has provided a description of the development of naval skills in Śrīvijaya:

> This country in older times . . . used an iron chain as a barrier to keep the pirates of other countries in check. . . . If a merchant ship passes by without entering, their boats go forth to make a combined attack, and all are ready to die in the attempt. This is why the country is a great shipping center.[32]

In addition, a stone engraving tells of a Cambodian fleet of 700 ships sent against Annam in A.D. 1128.[33] At sea in 1577, the Portuguese met an Acehenese fleet consisting of 115 to 150 ships and carrying approximately 10,000 troops and state-of-the-art artillery.[34]

Maritime states did not so much create large navies as co-opt the sea peoples of the area, many of whom may have been pirates and others of whom were sailors from vassal states, in an effort to gather enough strength to counter any remaining competing threats. These naval forces, then, constituted the primary mechanism for maintaining the state's commercial position, not only by controlling pirates but also by subduing other competing entrepôt centers and forcing transient shipping into harbor. The discipline, trustworthiness, and dependability of these forces varied greatly depending on their loyalty and commitment to the ruler under whom they fought.

Distinctions among legal commerce, monopoly, breakdowns in monopoly control, and simple piracy were difficult to perceive. By the fifth century the Strait of Malacca was so dangerous that trade moved through the Sunda Strait at a greatly reduced flow and traveled along the western coast of Sumatra. The fear of such danger seems to have been well justified:

> When the vessels sail to the west sea . . . the natives are quite at ease, but on their return voyage the crew have to put up arrow shelters and curtains, and

sharpen their weapons. . . . Two or three hundred boats of the pirates would come silently and fight for several days. It would be fortunate if the traveller could meet a fair wind; otherwise the crew would be butchered and the merchandise would be looted.[35]

Tactics in naval warfare remained primitive. The primary naval strategy was to bring opposing barges alongside one another, where the conflict was completed in hand-to-hand combat. Southeast Asian navies did not develop the mobile tactic of deploying ships to take advantage of speed and maneuverability. Battle rams, too, were apparently seldom used.[36] Although armaments equal to those known and used by the Europeans were available, they were not in general use, perhaps because of the lack of sufficient sources of metal with which to manufacture them.

Land Forces

Practices for maintaining armies varied over time and throughout the region. Soldiers were not professionals, and most members of village populations held some military service obligation when called upon. Some Islamic kingdoms used slaves as warriors, although not in the numbers common in the Middle East.[37] The system was indirect and in some respects feudal. Ministers of state with administrative responsibilities for given areas were required to organize residents from those areas for military service. Chou Ta-kuan, a Chinese writer who visited Cambodia in A.D. 1296, described the army as "both naked and barefooted. . . . In the right hand they hold the lance; in the left, the buckler. . . . And [they] have neither bows nor arrows, neither ballistas nor cannon, neither armor-plate nor helmets. All the people were obliged to fight . . . but have neither tactics nor strategy."[38] H. G. Wales, however, has described the Burmese and Siamese armies as being organized to include wing groups on either side of the main unit, as well as advance- and rear-guard groups. Army divisions were composed of infantry, with elephant support groups and cavalry used for reconnaissance. Tactics included surprise attacks, night attacks, guerrilla warfare, false retreat, blockades, and siege, as well as frontal attacks.[39]

Anthony Reid compiled figures that show standing armies ranging from a royal guard of 3,000 troops in Pasai (about A.D. 1518), 40,000 troops in Aceh (A.D. 1620), 30,000 troops available in Turban "within 24 hours," to 100,000 troops available "within 4 leagues of Malacca" (A.D. 1510).[40] Neighboring states, free-lance seafarers, and warriors from regions with no organized states provided mercenary support for regional military forces. For example, Bugis seafarers intervened in northern Malaya for nearly a century to protect or defeat kings in Perak and

Kedah.[41] Raids on other areas were often designed to take slaves for military purposes, and armies, although massive, usually left the acquisition of equipment and provisions to the individual. There were, however, cases in which the king provided the arms and collected them at the end of the campaign.

Military equipment described by most sources was more advanced than that described by Chou Ta-kuan. Most mainland kingdoms employed trained war elephants. General military equipment included lances, bows and arrows (sometimes poisoned), darts, and crossbows that were large enough to be effective against elephants. The degree of sophistication in weaponry is captured in this description of a pistol crossbow: "The grip might have been from a modern handgun with mortised wooden bow support, [and] the longitudinal channel . . . [combines] bronze and wood components."[42] A study of early Indian weaponry, which was similar to that used in Southeast Asia, lists swords, daggers, clubs, spears, pikes, thunderbolts, axes, bows and arrows, and shields used for protection.[43] The Ottoman Empire provided expert gunsmiths to Islamic rulers in Southeast Asia.[44]

Fortification and Defense

Although some cities were protected by moats and brick walls, Anthony Reid has noted that most cities—even capital cities—were not well fortified, having only walls or, in times of war, hastily erected bamboo stockades. He pointed out that human resources, not territory nor even cities themselves, were essential in sustaining kingship.[45] Barbara Andaya, who cites the same principle within the context of Johore, indicated that "Admiral Verhoeven offered to build a fort for Sultan Alauddin" but he "refused, saying that . . . he and his subjects could always flee upriver."[46] She further noted that small islands were not thought to be acceptable locations for capital cities because they did not provide room for escape.[47] The resilience these kingdoms gained by their willingness to abandon specific terrain is shown by the fact that "only a few months after the Dutch reported 'the complete destruction' of Johore Lama in 1673 and a large booty and numerous prisoners taken, a Johore fleet appeared at the mouth of the Jambi River and threatened the 'victorious' Jambi."[48] Not until European fortifications began to appear were permanent walled enclosures emphasized, as at Kedah: "Though this castle has such a miserable appearance in the eyes of the Europeans, yet it is sufficient to keep the nations here about in awe, merely because it looks European."[49] As late as 1620, the capital of Aceh had no walls, and only one stone fortification is known to have been built in the Philippines prior to the arrival of the Spanish.

Extraregional Powers

Different viewpoints about the role of indigenous peoples in state building are vital for an understanding of Southeast Asian culture, but they also obscure an important aspect of the interstate system—the impact of major external powers. Michael Brecher, although writing about contemporary Southeast Asia, defined the Chinese and Indian impacts as "the presence of relatively powerful peripheral states" whose power gave them "de facto membership" in the system.[50] Historically, too, this view may well describe a situation in which autochthonous factors were dominant, and India and China interacted in the region but as participants in the global trading system. The Ottoman Empire was also in regular contact with the Islamic kingdoms of Southeast Asia, providing leadership in Islamic thought as well as occasional material support to these kingdoms.

One area of diplomacy most kingdoms of Southeast Asia maintained meticulously throughout their history involved relations with India and China. In many respects excluding the village setting, the Southeast Asian system was remarkably open in its dealings with foreigners. For purposes of interstate commerce, Malay was accepted as the lingua franca throughout the archipelago by the Arabs, Chinese, and later the Europeans, as well as by all indigenous merchants. O. W. Wolters noted that Śrīvijaya's goal was to cultivate good trade relations with India and China while attempting to dominate or monopolize the Southeast Asian trade routes in order "to protect a privileged trading system."[51] Ayudhya's regular tributes to China prevented the kingdom from being destroyed during the invasion by Kublai Khan, and Malacca converted to Islam in order to attract Indian merchants.

There were opportunities and mechanisms for states to establish contacts and develop cooperative ventures; however, these ventures did not, and probably could not, flower within the traditional Southeast Asian context. With the exception of Vietnam, much of the interest in India was apparently cultural, although commercial relations were also important. Southeast Asian states looked to India for religious and philosophical doctrines believed to be superior to their own; these doctrines were adopted and blended with indigenous thought and belief structures. In Vietnam alone, the mandarin system of bureaucratic organization and practice was adopted.

Both India and China made contributions to the political legitimacy of Southeast Asian kingdoms but in markedly different ways. Whereas Southeast Asia's kings made use of Hindu rituals and metaphysics, recognition by the Chinese emperor was valuable for enhancing claims to the throne because the emperor provided letters and seals acknowledging authority. The Chinese emperor, by conferring military titles and other honors on Southeast Asian kings, intervened directly to influence the stature of states in the region.

Later, after the arrival of Islam, Mecca became central to religious, cultural, and political development, particularly in the archipelago. Islam spread through Southeast Asia from west to east, and Aceh—on the western tip of Sumatra—became an essential link between the region and Middle Eastern Islam. Pilgrims traveling to Mecca used Aceh as their point of departure, and some remained in Aceh for extended periods to study Islam. Aceh not only hosted numerous Muslim scholars from the Middle East but also received several embassies from Mecca, the first in 1683.

Commerce and trade were additional areas in which India and China played important roles. Southeast Asian ports offered safe harbor in the international maritime route from China to India. Later, Southeast Asians became active and competitive producers of commodities, such as pepper, for the international market. India provided pepper to China in the early centuries of the Christian era, but by A.D. 800 Sumatran pepper, although inferior, had supplanted Indian varieties in the China market because of its comparatively lower cost. Trading interests with a number of Indian kingdoms, particularly those on the northeast coast of India, might have influenced organized patterns of interaction.

Tributary missions to Imperial China seem to have contradicted the "center of the world" concept of the Southeast Asian states, but potential economic returns and (at certain periods in history) the added security provided by the Chinese navy more than countered the potential humiliation of playing the tributary role. Although written records are few, it is equally likely that Southeast Asian potentates were able to rationalize away any perceived inferior status as easily as the Chinese accentuated that status.

Cases of military intervention by Indians have been recorded, such as the Chola raids on Śrīvijaya during the eleventh century, but India seems to have rarely been feared for its military might. China offered a somewhat different case. Chinese armies controlled Vietnam for nearly ten centuries, until 939 A.D. and Mongol armies occupied part of mainland Southeast Asia in the late thirteenth and early fourteenth centuries, reaching as far as Java in 1292. There is little doubt that the presence of a Chinese navy prompted indigenous kingdoms to send their missions to China to save them from the wrath of the Chinese. The Chinese presence also gave smaller kingdoms a powerful ally against harassment by other Southeast Asian kingdoms: Malacca, for example, was protected from Thai intervention. Moreover, trading interests with China also surely stimulated the desire for good relations.

Patterns of interstate relations among the traditional kingdoms might thus be characterized as unilateral actions. Although other patterns (such as essentially forced allegiance or mutual alliance) were found, they were the exception rather than the rule. China and India held the interest of the larger Southeast Asian states for commercial reasons, whereas weaker states looked particularly to China for protection from their stronger neighbors.

Characteristics of the System

The interstate system, as well as the structure of the states supporting that system, in traditional Southeast Asia has been described in necessarily broad terms built upon bits of information gathered from various historical situations. This broad level of discussion has provided useful generalizations that help to clarify the historical context of the region. Of course, there were differences between the villages in Vietnam and those in Java or between the kingdoms of the second century and those of the fifteenth century. But the detailed studies on which this work is based have also uncovered sufficient substance to allow and support these generalizations. The principal characteristics of this regional system can be summarized in terms of four components: weak institutions, weak interactions, limited regional recognition, and patterns of dependence on extraregional powers.

Institutional Strength

The key to the fragile nature of the system was a corresponding fragility in its primary actor—the traditional state. No state built a mass political base, nor is there significant evidence of movement in that direction. The personalized nature of political leadership and its reliance on metaphysical and religious sources of legitimacy seemed to ensure that the gap between the people and the government would remain wide. The coming of Islam did not significantly change this situation. In one of the last Southeast Asian states to give way to colonial domination, Trengganu on the Malay Peninsula, the sultan introduced some reforms (courts, police, and written law) and created some functionally oriented governmental positions that were filled on the basis of merit. But more basic government reforms were rejected because they were likely to bring religious contamination (following the ways of infidels) whereas others would have infringed on the sultan's personal financial status.[52]

From another perspective, this lack of institutional strength meant that the state did not exist—except in its embodiment in the king. Kings were transitory, and the state remained in a permanent condition of dependence on the personality of the king and on minimal bureaucratic organization. In addition, because the state offered little in the way of amenities or services to the people living within its borders, little sense of loyalty or commitment was established to entice their support for the institutions of the state. Although bonds within the village, links to kinship groups, or even the natural draw of a birthplace engulfed in spirits and supernatural meaning could attract an individual to stay, the state could not. The consequence was a state structured in such a way that resources were only sporadically and inefficiently mobilized, and the authority of the government remained limited, even within its own territory.

System Interaction

The internal weakness of actors carried over into the interstate system. A critical factor was the lack of rationale for developing a multistate system. Stated simply, the problem arose because claims of legitimacy, which were developed for domestic purposes in line with Hindu mythology, made the state the center of the world—of which there could be but one. To the extent that other states were recognized, they were located hierarchically on the periphery and in a lesser or lower position with respect to the center.

In the interstate context, the embodiment of the state in the person of the king reinforced a centrist perspective of the state, which meant that boundaries were poorly defined. Although the myth that claimed that all lands should be controlled by the ruler did not match reality, it did preclude the development of a clearly defined set of boundaries among states. In the absence of a rationale for fixed boundaries, power and its extension to the frontier became the only means of establishing limits. The theoretical construct of the state as the center of the world did make it possible to envision several concentric levels of control moving progressively farther from the center, but there was no theoretical or practical end to these circles. This moving frontier was a "means of gauging and aligning the international equilibrium."[53]

What followed from this type of claim to legitimacy was a system constructed of tributary and vassal states rather than a multistate system of theoretically equal governments. The inherent inequality of the system meant that little could be accomplished among states on an equal footing, not even mutually beneficial actions. With little room for mutual agreement, patterns of interstate cooperation failed to develop, and violence remained the principal means for resolving disputes.

Violence was also an important tool for state development. Territorial expansion for the control of human resources and maritime expansion to control sea lanes and commerce were the most common mechanisms for enhancing the state. Raids of plunder between "legally" constituted states were also frequent, with booty including not only gold and gems but slaves as well.

The low level of institutional development and the high incidence of violence meant that general lawlessness and banditry were commonplace. Without doubt, the single most important function of the state was to protect the village from bandits. However, piracy was the most rampant form of lawlessness throughout the region, and pirates preyed on coastal communities as well as on local shipping and international trade routes. The state co-opted when possible and fought when necessary to bring pirates and thieves under control or to drive them from the region.

System Recognition

Systems theorists point to the recognition of membership as one of the critical ingredients for the development of an effective system. By implication, in an interstate system member states should recognize themselves as being different from states in the external environment. Although the many terms the Chinese, Indians, and Arabs applied to Southeast Asia suggest external recognition of the region as a discrete unit, there is little evidence that the state leaders in that region understood themselves within this context.

Examples such as intermarriage among Southeast Asian royalty suggest some such recognition of regional identity, and such marriages increased after the coming of Islam. Local kingdoms may have spread Islam more aggressively in response to Christian missionary activities of the Portuguese and Spanish,[54] indicating the beginnings of a sense of regional community, at least in the archipelago. Islam, therefore, may have had a unifying effect on the region, although this theory may be more a result of better information than of a true change in behavior. These states also appear to have understood the unique position of China vis-à-vis the collectivity of states in Southeast Asia. However, the very open, commercial nature of much of the interaction and communication in traditional Southeast Asia, as well as its propensity for absorbing external values and cultural traits, tended to obscure the development of a separate identity.

This weak self-identity had particular importance at the time of the first arrival of the Europeans. The characterization is hypothetical, but had Southeast Asian state leaders developed a stronger sense of self-identity, the states of the region may have been able to recognize more clearly the systemic nature of the threat presented by the Portuguese and even more intensely by the Dutch. The fact that this recognition did not develop and, indeed, could not have developed in traditional Southeast Asia was a key weakness of the traditional system.

System Dependence

A fourth characteristic of the traditional interstate system was its dependence on actors external to the system, especially China and India. In an economic sense, the interstate system was largely dependent on the maritime trade routes from China to Europe. There is a clear correlation between well-being in Southeast Asia and the functioning of this international trading system: "It was the voyage from Indonesia to China alone which made possible the creation of entrepôt centres."[55] At those times when China repudiated interest in trade or when trade followed overland caravan routes, Southeast Asia suffered. The relative transport costs of the caravan routes compared with the sea routes never favored the maritime routes through Southeast Asia.[56]

Traditional Southeast Asia reached its peak when the maritime trade routes flourished and the states used their wealth to give expression to Buddhist and Hindu concepts. At this time, dependence on India seems to have been mostly intellectual in nature, as political and religious thought was shaped primarily by philosophies of Indian origin. However, these philosophies also set real limits on the capabilities of the interstate system. By contrast and with the exception of Vietnam, Southeast Asian dependence on China was primarily economic and secondarily military or political. Moreover, whereas Southeast Asia had long been accustomed to adopting otherwise transient external ideas and practices, and despite the fact that by the early 1600s as many as 5,000 Europeans were in the service of Asian rulers,[57] the Southeast Asian system was unable to engender sufficient changes to counter the European challenge.

Nevertheless, although the traditional Southeast Asian system was dependent on or subordinate to the Chinese and Indian systems for much of its cultural well-being and was reliant on the global trading system for much of its economic well-being, these dependencies should not be considered apart from the context of a growing and active regional system. This interdependence continued over long periods of time, as much because it was useful to Southeast Asians themselves as because it was imposed by Chinese or Indian power. The record of conflict with Indian and Chinese military forces was by no means one of unmitigated success for the outsiders, and there is little indication that Southeast

Asians knowingly conceded to the superiority of these forces. Traditional Southeast Asia cannot be perceived as an open area for the inevitable political collision between the greater forces of China and India.

The concept of dependence must be kept in perspective, and the traditional system of Southeast Asia stood on its own. It was weak and, by contemporary standards, had many deficiencies; yet it prospered over a period of approximately two thousand years. Moreover, all of the regional subsystems—the Chinese system, the Southeast Asian system, the Indian system, the Middle Eastern system, the Mediterranean system, and the European system—were dependent on each other from at least the beginning of the Christian era. Although the notion of global interdependence is a modern phenomenon, the interaction of these traditional regional systems suggests that the concept of interdependence is not new. This historical interdependence was limited by lack of knowledge and by the undeveloped technological capacities of the time, but it was constant until the regional systems were destroyed by European imperial expansion and monopoly control.

NOTES

1. David A. Wilson, "Thailand," in *Governments and Politics of Southeast Asia,* edited by George McT. Kahin (Ithaca: Cornell University Press, 1964), p. 8.

2. O. W. Wolters, *The Fall of Śrīvijaya in Malay History* (Ithaca: Cornell University Press, 1971), p. 98.

3. Lawrence Palmer Briggs, *The Ancient Khmer Empire.* Transactions of the American Philosophical Society (Philadelphia: American Philosophical Society, 1951), pp. 108, 148.

4. Nidhi Aeusrivongse, "The *Devaraja* Cult and Khmer Kingship at Angkor," in *Explorations in Early Southeast Asian History: The Origins of Southeast Asian Statecraft,* edited by Kenneth R. Hall and John K. Whitmore (Ann Arbor: Michigan Papers on South and Southeast Asia, no. 11, 1976), p. 110.

5. Michael Aung-Thwin, "Kingship, the *Sangha,* and Society in Pagan," in Hall and Whitmore, *Explorations in Early Southeast Asian History,* pp. 214–219.

6. Louis Finot "Les grandes epoques de l'Indochine," *Bulletin de l'Academie du Var* (Toulon, 1935), pp. 77–78, cited in Briggs, *The Ancient Khmer Empire,* p. 261.

7. Heather Sutherland, "The Taming of the Trengganu Elite," in *Southeast Asian Transitions: Approaches Through Social History,* edited by Ruth T. McVey (New Haven: Yale University Press, 1978), p. 35.

8. *The Malay Annals,* translated by C. C. Brown (London: Oxford University Press, 1970), p. 182.

9. Barbara Watson Andaya, "The Nature of the State in Eighteenth Century Perak," in *Pre-Colonial State Systems in Southeast Asia,* edited by Anthony Reid and Lance Castles (Kuala Lumpur: Malaysian Branch of the Royal Asiatic Society, Monograph no. 6, 1975), p. 26.

10. *The Malay Annals*, p. 190.

11. Briggs, *The Ancient Khmer Empire*, p. 217.

12. Aung-Thwin, "Kingship, the *Sangha*, and Society in Pagan," in Hall and Whitmore, *Explorations in Early Southeast Asian History*, p. 231.

13. Sutherland, "The Taming of the Trengganu Elite," in McVey, *Southeast Asian Transitions*, p. 35.

14. Bennet Bronson, "The Late Prehistory and Early History of Central Thailand," in *Early South East Asia: Essays in Archaeology, History and Historical Geography*, edited by R. B. Smith and A. C. Milner (London: Oxford University Press, 1979), p. 326.

15. Nguyen Ngoc Huy and Ta Van Tai, *The Le Code: Law in Traditional Vietnam, A Comparative Sino-Vietnamese Legal Study with Historical Juridical Analysis and Annotations*, vol. 1 (Athens: Ohio University Press, 1987), pp. 4–5.

16. Sir Richard Winstedt and P. E. de Josselin de Jong, "The Maritime Laws of Malacca," *Journal of the Malaysian Branch of the Royal Asiatic Society* 99 (August 1956), pp. 22–59.

17. Sutherland, "The Taming of the Trengganu Elite," in McVey, *Southeast Asian Transitions*, p. 35.

18. John W. Spellman, *Political Theory of Ancient India: A Study of Kingship from the Earliest Times to Circa A.D. 300* (London: Oxford University Press, 1964), pp. 156–158.

19. O. W. Wolters, "Culture, History, and Region in Southeast Asian Perspectives," in *ASEAN: Identity, Development and Culture*, edited by R. P. Anand and Purification V. Quisumbing (Quezon City and Honolulu: University of the Philippines Law Center and the East-West Center, Culture Learning Institute, 1981), p. 9. See also Soemarsaid Moertono, *State and Statecraft in Old Java: A Study of the Later Mataram Period, Sixteenth to Nineteenth Centuries* (Ithaca: Cornell University, Modern Indonesia Project, 1958), p. 71.

20. Paramita R. Abdurachman, "'Niachila Pokaraga'; A Sad Story of a Moluccan Queen," *Modern Asian Studies* 22 (1988).

21. Briggs, *The Ancient Khmer Empire*, pp. 88–89.

22. *Ibid.*, p. 159.

23. Abdurachman, "A Sad Story of a Moluccan Queen," p. 575.

24. John F. Cady, *A History of Modern Burma* (Ithaca: Cornell University Press, 1958), p. 19.

25. Christine Dobbin, "The Exercise of Authority in Minangkabau in the Late 18th Century," in Reid and Castles, *Pre-Colonial State Systems*, p. 83.

26. Aung-Thwin, "Kingship, the *Sangha*, and Society in Pagan," in Hall and Whitmore, *Explorations in Early Southeast Asian History*, p. 231.

27. H. G. Quaritch Wales, *Ancient South-East Asian Warfare* (London: Bernard Quaritch, 1952), pp. 4–11.

28. Paul Johnstone, *The Sea-craft of Prehistory* (Cambridge, Mass.: Harvard University Press, 1980).

29. Pierre-Yves Manguin, "The Southeast Asian Ship: An Historical Approach," *Journal of Southeast Asian Studies* 11 (September 1980), p. 267.

30. *Ibid.*, p. 276.

31. Cited in *Ibid.*, p. 267.

32. Chau Ju-kua, *His Work on the Chinese and Arab Trade in the Twelfth and Thirteenth Centuries, Entitled Chu-fan-chi,* translated by F. Hirth and W. Rockhill (Taipei: Literature House, 1965; reprint of the 1911 St. Petersburg edition), pp. 60, 62.

33. Briggs, *The Ancient Khmer Empire,* p. 190.

34. I. A. MacGregor, "A Sea Flight Near Singapore in the 1570s," *Journal of the Malaysian Branch of the Royal Asiatic Society* 29 (1956), p. 12.

35. Hsu Yun-Ts'iao, "Singapore in the Remote Past," *Journal of the Malaysian Branch of the Royal Asiatic Society* 45 (1973), p. 2.

36. Wales, *Ancient South-East Asian Warfare,* p. 110.

37. Geoffrey Parker, "Europe and the Wider World, 1500–1750," in *The Political Economy of Merchant Empires: State Power and World Trade, 1350–1750* edited by James D. Tracy (Cambridge: Cambridge University Press, 1991), pp. 171–172.

38. Briggs, *The Ancient Khmer Empire,* p. 249.

39. Wales, *Ancient South-East Asian Warfare,* pp. 160, 165–169.

40. Anthony Reid, "The Structure of Cities in Southeast Asia, Fifteenth to Seventeenth Centuries," *Journal of Southeast Asian Studies* 11 (September 1980), p. 329.

41. Virginia Matheson, "Concepts of State in the Tuhfat Al-Nafis," and Andaya, "The Nature of the State in Eighteenth Century Perak," in Reid and Castles, *Pre-Colonial State Systems,* pp. 12–21, 22–35.

42. E. Morton Grosser, "A Further Note on the Chou Dynasty Pistol-Crossbow," *Artibus Asiae* 23 (1960), p. 210.

43. K. Krishna Murthy, "Weapons of War in the Sculptures of Nagarjuna-konda," *Artibus Asiae* 28 (1966), pp. 211–218.

44. Michael Adas (ed.), *Islamic and European Expansion: The Forging of a Global Order* (Philadelphia: Temple University Press, 1993), p. 113.

45. Reid, "The Structure of Cities in Southeast Asia," p. 243.

46. Barbara W. Andaya, "The Structure of Power in Seventeenth Century Johor," in Reid and Castles, *Pre-Colonial State Systems,* p. 3, n. 12.

47. *Ibid.,* pp. 3–4.

48. *Ibid.,* p. 7, citing KA-1185, OB1674, Missive from Governor Bort of Malacca to Batavia, 21 December 1673, file 636. KA denotes the colonial archives of the General State Archives in The Hague.

49. M. Osbeck, *A Voyage to China and the East Indies* (London: n.p., 1771), pp. 217–218, cited in Dianne Lewis, "Kedah—The Development of a Malay State in the Eighteenth and Nineteenth Centuries," in Reid and Castles, *Pre-Colonial State Systems,* p. 39.

50. Michael Brecher, *The New States of Asia* (London: Oxford University Press, 1963), p. 159.

51. O. W. Wolters, *Early Indonesian Commerce: A Study of the Origins of Śrīvijaya* (Ithaca: Cornell University Press, 1967), p. 241.

52. Sutherland, "The Taming of the Trengganu Elite," in McVey, *Southeast Asian Transitions,* p. 49.

53. Robert L. Solomon, "Boundary Concepts and Practices in Southeast Asia," *World Politics* 23 (October 1970), p. 15.

54. Bertram Schrieke, *Indonesian Sociological Studies*, Part Two (The Hague: W. van Hoeve Publishers, 1957), pp. 235–237.

55. Wolters, *Early Indonesian Commerce*, p. 32.

56. Russell R. Manard, "Transport Costs and Long-Range Trade, 1300–1800," in Tracy, *The Political Economy of Merchant Empires*, p. 249.

57. Parker, "Europe and the Wider World," in Tracy, *The Political Economy of Merchant Empires*, p. 177.

6

Colonial Interlopers and System Disjunction

Europeans arrived in Southeast Asia with little fanfare. Although their presence was not commonplace, there were other visitors and travelers from Europe in various cities in China and Southeast Asia both before and after Marco Polo's trip there in 1292–1293, and at least one traveler visited the kingdom of Majapahit in Java. Southeast Asian commercial cities were open to foreign merchants, and the arrival of a new group was generally accepted or even welcomed as an expansion of opportunities for trade. The use of force was so commonplace that when the Portuguese first attacked Malacca, the latter's local competitor trading states—seeking to strengthen their positions by weakening Malacca—supported the Portuguese. The Chinese navy had retired from the region more than a century earlier, and although united action by local Southeast Asian states could have mustered sufficient capacity to repel the Europeans, there was no underlying or systemic rationale for organizing a regional force to challenge the Portuguese and later colonial interlopers.

European Intrusion and Systemic Change

Europeans came to Southeast Asia with a mix of objectives and strategies designed to enhance commercial power and spread Christianity. The strategies of the colonial regimes changed frequently, and at times major objectives of the colonial metropole changed as well. Although actions were often couched in Christian or other moral terms, the economic significance of the colonial policies cannot be overstated. For example, despite the high costs and enormous potential for total loss of any specific fleet, the rewards were such that by 1518 "the spice trade produced . . . some 39 percent [of royal income in Portugal], which was more than the Crown's income from metropolitan Portugal."[1] Three colonial powers—the Portuguese, Dutch, and British—stand out: the Portuguese because they initiated colonial interventions and control and the Dutch and British because their strategies had longer-term impacts on the regional system. From the time of the voyage of Pedro Alvares Cabral in March 1500, it was clear that the Portuguese and Europeans meant to dominate the trading system and that "the period of unarmed trading was over in the Indian Ocean."[2]

The Portuguese

Southeast Asians did not realize the Portuguese were pursuing two goals that would inextricably alter the indigenous system. Motivated by their animosity toward Islam, the Portuguese linked their aim of securing monopoly control of the commercial spice trade with the religious goal of arresting the expansion of Islam. These goals became intertwined because by the sixteenth century, most active traders in the South and Southeast Asian sections of the international trading system were Muslim. The Portuguese plan for control was not a unified strategy, and decisions were taken in the field without approval or agreement from Lisbon. After the Portuguese had extended their position around Africa and through India, it became apparent that achieving either of their primary goals would necessitate expansion into Southeast Asia.

European knowledge of Asia, particularly Southeast Asia, was fragmentary at the beginning of the sixteenth century. However, European and especially Portuguese navigational skills and equipment were improving rapidly, and the Portuguese extended the range of their commercial ventures in stages. By the latter part of the fifteenth century, Portuguese sailors had rounded the Cape of Good Hope, and they reached India (Malabar) just before the close of the century. Once they were established in Goa in 1510, the move to Southeast Asia at Malacca was the next logical step in the Portuguese quest to stop the eastward diffusion of Islam and to control the flow of spices and other commodities on the westward route to Europe. By the early 1600s, galleons weighing up to 2,000 tons were being built for the Asian routes.

The defeat of Malacca did not alter the basic interstate system of sixteenth-century Southeast Asia. Malacca may have been past its zenith as an entrepôt center, but several other trading states and kingdoms— notably Aceh, Demak, Ternate, Johore, and Mataram on Java—were strengthened by the shift of commerce away from Malacca. The Portuguese had some success in controlling the spice trade to Europe, although they were unsuccessful in maintaining monopoly control because they were unable to control all of the producers, particularly Aceh and the Javanese and Eastern archipelago kingdoms. Individual traders also circumvented Portuguese control, and by the 1550s supplies of black pepper were again plentiful in Alexandria and Italy.[3] The Portuguese secured their position in Malacca with the assistance of disgruntled merchants, but they had neither the human resources nor the diplomatic skill to assert the monopoly control they had sought. And they were not successful in their missionary efforts to spread Christianity or to curtail the spread of Islam.

In the religious competition between Islam and Christianity, the Southeast Asians, especially those in the archipelago, recognized the adversarial situation. The Portuguese introduced the region to the previously European and Middle Eastern conflict between the two religions, but Islam was actually strengthened by the intrusion of the Portuguese because it became a rallying symbol against them. Arab and Indian merchants, many of whom were also Muslim, were well acquainted with the Portuguese goals from their experiences in South Asia. They were anxious to block Portuguese influence and control but were unable to translate these desires into political force. Although Islam arrived in Southeast Asia at least several centuries before the major European push for Christianity, it had been slow to penetrate inland until after "the decline of the Maritime states, [when] many of their citizens migrated to the territory of Mataram and other inland areas," thus greatly expediting the Islamization of the countryside.[4]

The Portuguese also maintained contacts with Thailand, Burma, Vietnam, and Cambodia and on several occasions tried to form alliances with Java, but their focus from the base at Malacca was largely on spice production in the Moluccas. Meanwhile, most commercial interests in the region were flexible enough to bypass Portuguese control. During the sixteenth century, spice production spread to many new areas in Southeast Asia. Although Portuguese vassals (or allies) such as Tidore were required to give their entire spice production to the Portuguese, in fact the Tidorese simply resorted to smuggling and to black-market sales of the crops. Other trading centers expanded rapidly to accept the overflow of merchants leaving Portuguese-controlled Malacca. Aceh in particular benefited from the shift of Muslim merchants leaving Malacca and looking for new bases.

Although the Portuguese penetrated the Southeast Asian system, they became only one more new competitor in the existing system of political and commercial power. Their inability to dominate the system resulted from their limited human resources, poor management and organization skills, and meager financial resources. Their strategy was to establish a fort and a warehouse at each port while relying on naval forces to direct local shipping into port. In order for this strategy to be successful, large numbers of sailors and soldiers, as well as colonial administrators, were needed; without them, discipline broke down. Portuguese-led piracy and other forms of adventurism became common. The Portuguese nevertheless demonstrated that the Southeast Asian system was vulnerable to outsiders who brought sufficient force and manipulated the "rules" of the system to their advantage. The Portuguese did not attain all of their goals, but the Dutch who followed were more successful.

The Dutch

News and information about Portuguese activities could not be kept secret, and in 1595–1596 a Dutchman, Jan Huygen van Linschoten, published three books—including a navigational guide—on his experiences in Portuguese possessions in Asia.[5] By the time the Dutch arrived in Southeast Asia, the Portuguese fanaticism for Christian missionary activities, more than their economic intervention, had caused them to be vigorously hated. Southeast Asians, who still saw no basic threat to their system, welcomed the Dutch, hoping they could counter the Portuguese; they did so, although as late as the early 1700s some Portuguese influence remained in Cambodia in addition to their control of Timor.

The arrival of the Dutch, who at first were in league with the English, was hastened by the closing of the port at Lisbon to Dutch merchants in 1594; hence, sources of pepper and spices the Dutch had distributed through northern Europe were cut off. The Dutch were initially content to adapt to customary trading practices within the regional system, and their early successful expeditions, which focused on commerce, created good profits as well as goodwill among the Bandanese, Ambonese, and others. The Acehenese were more suspicious of Dutch intrusions, but they sent two ambassadors to the Netherlands to gain a better understanding of Europe.

In the early seventeenth century, the Dutch consolidated their commercial houses under the Dutch or United East India Company (VOC) and concentrated on both monopoly regional control and elimination of Portuguese influences. The VOC was empowered to "act in behalf of the States General of the Netherlands and to exercise *all the rights of sovereignty.*"[6] However, at first the Dutch found it advantageous to follow standard commercial practices in the regional system by trading throughout Sumatra, where the sultans acted as intermediaries to the pepper growers. In the Moluccas, which were already politically and economically disrupted by the Portuguese and the Spanish, the Dutch found an opening when Ternate sought their protection. A similar agreement with Ambon put the Dutch in a very strong position in the eastern archipelago. They also established a fort at Sunda Kalapa—sometimes called Jakarta—situated in the territorial buffer zone between the kingdoms of Mataram, whose power was centered in east Java, and Bantam whose power was centered in west Java.[7]

Early in the seventeenth century the VOC, led by the aggressive Governor-General Jan Pieterzoon Coen, established a new southern sea route to Southeast Asia, initially to avoid Portuguese forts and strongholds along the coast of Africa. The Dutch could not dislodge the Portuguese from Mozambique, so the value of following the African coast after rounding the Cape of Good Hope was minimized. It later became known that making use of the prevailing westerly wind patterns south of the Cape could take Dutch ships directly to the Indonesian archipelago in a shorter time and under better conditions in terms of heat, hurricanes, and dependable winds.[8] This navigational strategy—establishing a southern route to Southeast Asia—had a great impact on Dutch thinking with respect to the shaping of its empire.

As the Dutch focused more intently on Southeast Asia, Coen and others recognized the shortcomings of the Portuguese strategy of controlling the flow of trade from fortified port cities. Smuggling and overproduction would always reduce the likely profit. Thereafter, the Dutch embarked upon a two-pronged strategy: first, to gain control of trade within Southeast Asia or between Southeast Asia and China, India, or Syria; and second, to control the local commodity crop and production areas to the greatest extent possible. The Batavia base was secured with the defeat of a large army from Mataram in 1629, and the Dutch poised for "the first decisive step towards the formation of a new empire, commercial at the outset like Śrīvijaya and Malacca, but gradually becoming predominantly territorial; yet not in the true line of succession to either since the centre of control lay thousands of miles away."[9] Not only was the control center far away, but the rules that governed Dutch conduct in Southeast Asia were also at odds with those of the extant system. The Dutch strategy ultimately led to the destruction of the traditional Southeast Asian political and economic systems.

The Dutch captured Malacca in 1641, and by the 1650s the Portuguese had been effectively eliminated as a regional force. The Dutch extended their influence to Ayudhya, assisting the Siamese against both the Cambodians and Patani, after which they established a "factory of solid brick construction" there.[10] They tried, with limited success, to extend their contacts throughout Indochina, where they met strong competition from the English.

In effect, the VOC became a new actor in the traditional Southeast Asian system. Within the context of that system, the VOC had enormous resources at its disposal, and it had been granted the power "to dispense justice, to employ and direct the use of troops, to conclude alliances with native princes, and to conduct diplomatic and commercial relations generally."[11] At the same time, it experienced few of the limitations common among indigenous states: It had no general constituency to satisfy, as its shareholders received their dividends irregularly and they came from capital funds; even the company directors had little control because of the time required for communications.

The Dutch move to displace the Portuguese in Southeast Asia was initiated largely for economic reasons grounded in inter-European commerce. However, political goals within Southeast Asia almost immediately evolved in support of these European economic and commercial goals. From the time of the formation of the VOC in 1602 through the period of direct government control after 1798, the Dutch progressively deepened their penetration of Indonesian social and economic activity and expanded their geographic control. During this period, more than 1,770 ships made 4,789 voyages to Asia—a greater number of voyages than any other European power including the British.[12]

Sometimes unwittingly, the Dutch introduced, social, economic, and political changes that fundamentally altered Southeast Asia. For example, under Dutch protection, the role of itinerant Chinese in the economy greatly expanded. Economic exploitation of agriculture reached highly intensive levels under the cultivation system, which theoretically required that farmers plant government-specified crops on one-fifth of their land. In reality, much higher percentages were often taken. Such intensive exploitation required that the "authoritarian content of native society be not only maintained but considerably increased."[13] Even after the Dutch gave up their monopoly control and introduced private capital (after 1877), compulsory labor was still required, substantial taxes were due periodically, and credit at reasonable rates was not available. The continually stronger economic position of the Chinese and the new European entrepreneurs further increased the exploitation and disruption of Indonesian society. In some ways the Dutch colonial government sought to protect that society from external penetration and exploitation; failing that, its disjointed social, economic, and political policies maximized status and rewards for a few while stripping the remainder of society of all but the barest essentials.

The British

The British were late in developing major colonial interests in Southeast Asia. They had cooperated with the Dutch in early challenges to the Portuguese but later refocused most of their resources on developing India. Not until the late eighteenth century were the British, working from their secure Indian base, able to challenge and eventually supplant Dutch control. The Dutch had tried to monopolize not only the China-to-Europe trade but the inter-Asian trade as well. But it was the British, using private capital and vessels, who were able to dominate this inter-Asian trade: "Whereas the Dutch Empire had operated from within Indonesia and had been essentially monopolistic in its character and objectives, that of Britain was based on the enormous resources of the Indian subcontinent and finally functioned virtually on a free-trade basis."[14] This free-trade system, which was based in Singapore, harked back in some respects to the traditional entrepôt centers of Śrīvijaya (Palembang) and Malacca, although, more important, it was initially managed by the British and later by local Chinese—not by indigenous entrepreneurs.

British territorial acquisitions in Southeast Asia followed their general economic activity. Penang, an island off the west coast of Malaya, was acquired from the sultan of Kedah in 1786. Singapore, acquired from the Dutch in 1824, evolved as a leading entrepôt center during the remainder of the nineteenth century and became the regional base for British colonial free trade. Control of the coastal regions of Burma came in 1826, following a war precipitated by Burmese military activity in India; upper Burma was not annexed until 1886 as the British responded to fears of renewed French activities. The Malay states of Singapore's hinterland held little interest until instability there threatened tin production, much of which was exported through Singapore. Britain developed a protectorate system for four tin-mining states—Larut, Selangor, Sungai Ujong, and Perak. These were followed by similar agreements with Negri Sembilan (1888), Pahang (1888), and Johore (1895). Four other states—Kedah, Perlis, Kelantan, and Trengganu—were acquired from Thailand by treaty in 1909.

Along with other colonial empires, the British introduced social, economic, and political changes that left the fabric of indigenous society threadbare. Indigenous political leadership was undermined or destroyed. Foreign ethnic groups and local minority groups were given preferential treatment, particularly in the economic sphere. In Burma, the British took steps to introduce some measure of self-rule, but in Malaya there was little political development prior to World War II. British capital investment was substantial but was highly specialized and largely extractive. The net result, as elsewhere, was the creation of a social system that could not survive without the paternal hand of the British colonial government. The social disjunction that followed the collapse of the British regime in Burma and Malaya was severe, although economic disruption was less catastrophic in postindependence Malaysia because British economic interests were not disturbed after independence.

Other Colonial Powers in Southeast Asia

A second group of states—Spain, France, the United States, and Japan—also played roles in the colonial period, but these roles were less systemic and were more limited in the territory under their control or the duration of that control. Importantly, although these countries' policies disrupted the social and economic structure of the territory they controlled, their activities did not directly alter the regional system, as did the Portuguese, Dutch, and British. Japan is an exception to this because it did bring an end to the colonial European system while imposing its own brief colonial rule. But the traditional Southeast Asian system had already been destroyed before the Japanese intervention, and Japanese colonial control was too short-lived to influence the new system. In a broader sense, however, the Japanese contributed to the reassertion of independence by stimulating the growth of nationalism in Southeast Asia.

The Spanish

Establishment of Spanish control in the Philippines took more than forty years to complete following Magellan's visit there in 1521. Blocked by the Portuguese, the Spanish traveled to Southeast Asia by way of Mexico and the Pacific, and a successful colony was not established until 1565 after four expeditions had failed. With only a very few Spaniards and some local allies, the Spanish were still able to unify the Philippines, although complete pacification and unification began with the Spanish missionary effort. The Filipinos seem to have been culturally amenable to outside influences. In those areas in which Islam had arrived ahead of the Spaniards, missionaries had little success. Elsewhere in the Philippines, Christianity, the Spanish language, and other cultural traits were more readily adopted than was the case in any other Southeast Asian area. Moreover, the Spanish cultural impact was intense and spread into social services and education, although pacification did not occur in some areas in the north until the nineteenth century and the conflict with the Muslims of Mindanao was never completely settled.

The Portuguese and later the Dutch prevented Spanish influence from extending into other parts of Southeast Asia. The Spanish tried to establish direct trade links between Manila and China and Japan, but this proved difficult; moreover, the strongest Spanish commercial ties were developed between Manila and New Spain (Mexico), which left the inter-Asian trade in the hands of the Chinese or other Europeans. Spanish galleons brought gold and silver to Manila to exchange for silks, rugs, cotton, spices, and aromatic woods. This trade continued until the Spanish lost Mexico, after which Manila reoriented its trade to accept non-Spanish shipping. Manila's role as a trading center declined throughout the nineteenth century, particularly as more ports were opened in China.

From the beginning, the Spanish had put Filipinos in positions of responsibility, if not authority. They relied heavily on local troops to complete the conquest of the islands. They created a Filipino constabulary and continued to use local chiefs and elders in the colonial administration and also created a Filipino clergy. These groups became the foundation for the elite that led the Filipino nationalist movement—the earliest and most sophisticated such movement in Southeast Asia, despite the previous lack of political organization and experience there.

The French

The French movement into Indochina was not as direct as either the Portuguese or the Dutch intrusions into Southeast Asia. The initial French focus was on missionary activities, and their first target for a base was Ayudhya. There, French Catholic missionaries encouraged political linkages between King Narai and France, but Narai died in 1688 before the agreements could be fully implemented. French interest in Southeast Asia receded to low-level missionary activities through most of the next century, although a small group was instrumental in returning the Nguyen dynasty to power following the Tay-son rebellions.

Ostensibly, concerns about the persecution of Christians and the harassment of missionaries prompted the French to intervene in Vietnam during the 1830s. Their initial foothold around Saigon was not secured until 1863, and the French did not develop a plan for economic exploitation until later, when all of Indochina had come under their control.

The French, having established control in Vietnam, found it necessary to take control in Laos and Cambodia to block further Thai penetration. In both Laos and Cambodia the French employed some Laotian and Cambodian officials in the colonial administration but brought in large numbers of Vietnamese to handle upper-level bureaucratic functions. Colonial control was relatively brief in these two countries; it began in Cambodia in 1864 and in Laos in 1904.

The highest levels of colonial administration in Vietnam were controlled by the French colonial officials, and although the monarchy was left in place, all acts had to be approved by the French resident superieur. The French continued to place more emphasis on Vietnam, and they used most of the revenues obtained from Laos and Cambodia for programs in Vietnam. The period of colonial domination was insufficient to settle the many ethnic, dynastic, and other conflicts that had traditionally dominated life in these countries.

The United States

The U.S. acquisition of the Philippines, which was taken from Spain following the Spanish-American War in 1898, constituted the last introduction of a Western power to the region. From the beginning, U.S. policies seemed to give credence to the goal of Philippine independence; plans for that independence were first formalized by U.S. congressional actions in 1916 and again in 1934. There were signs of a Philippine nationalist movement as early as 1815, and it became stronger during the 1840s and 1850s when Filipinos widely criticized the Spanish clergy for racial bigotry. The image of championing freedom and independence fit nicely into U.S. mythology, but at the same time, economic policies were enacted to ensure continued Filipino dependence on the United States regardless of the country's political status.

The Japanese

The destruction of the European colonial system was accomplished in a time and fashion that could not have been imagined, let alone predicted. The Japanese success was a spectacular stimulant for anti-Western sentiment, and nationalist feelings throughout Southeast Asia were strengthened by the call of "Asia for the Asiatics." The Japanese presence deeply stirred nationalist sentiments in places such as Java and Burma and challenged both the older intelligentsia and the "semi-militarized" younger generation to become political forces.[15] Thailand was in a unique position to somewhat limit Japanese penetration during World War II, but as the hard realities of war and defeat became evident, its relationship with Japan cooled. As World War II unfolded and the U.S. military challenge increased, the harsh extractive policies of the Japanese in the region, as well as their brutality and insensitivity, soon turned people against them; yet Southeast Asians—to the surprise of many Westerners—did not look to the colonial powers for assistance.

The Japanese also stimulated strongly negative racial feelings, especially among indigenous ethnic groups and against local Chinese and Indians. This was especially true in Malaya but was also the case in Burma and Indonesia. Although Southeast Asians were aligned on both sides in the global conflict, the underlying goal was to not assist the Japanese or the old colonial powers but to advance local national interests. The expectation that somehow Southeast Asians owed European colonial powers a measure of loyalty seems a bit ludicrous today. The Europeans had done little to engender such loyalty and, at the hands of the Japanese, had "suffered far more than a military defeat; indeed, they lost the prestige and aura of invincibility."[16]

The period of Japan's intervention in Southeast Asia was brief, and its goals were dictated by a war that quickly became a losing proposition. However, whereas from the beginning of its colonial venture Japan may have sought to establish a colonial regime similar to that of the displaced Europeans, the immediate needs for support of the war required a degree and type of human and resource mobilization in Southeast Asia that had not previously been experienced. And as the war progressively worsened, Japan moved to politicize the growing nationalist elements in the region. But events quickly overtook the Japanese colonial empire in Southeast Asia, and with the collapse of Japanese authority Southeast Asia had its first opportunity in more than 400 years to function as a regional system free of external domination.

The Southeast Asian Response

The Portuguese incursion into Southeast Asia represented the first meeting of two radically different interstate systems. Whereas Europeans and Southeast Asians had participated in separate, semiautonomous but loosely linked subsystems, each of which in turn transported goods from east to west toward Europe, the autonomy and isolation of each subsystem—which were assured by the difficulty of long-distance travel—meant that each developed its own traditions or was free to choose from external practices and structures in the process of evolutionary growth and development. Although Europeans had visited Southeast Asia as individual, itinerant travelers, the Portuguese intrusion in 1508 represented the beginning of an entirely different level of contact in that they and all subsequent European interlopers maintained the specific objective of eliminating other autonomous subsystems by creating a global monopoly system. In essence, the Portuguese and other later

Europeans and Southeast Asians were playing the international game with different rules.

Southeast Asian states responded to the Portuguese in terms of their own perspectives on interstate behavior and expected the Portuguese to apply similar perspectives. For example, Sultan Mahmud—who believed that the Portuguese attack on Malacca would follow the traditional pattern of sack, plunder, and abandon—retired from the conflict, expecting to return after the Portuguese had departed, which they did not. The sultan could hardly have understood that these European merchants had major political goals for the region in order to buttress their economic strategies. Furthermore, weaker states such as Tidore in the Moluccas, which followed traditional patterns of behavior, were willing to align with the Portuguese against their stronger regional rivals (e.g., Ternate), not recognizing that the Portuguese intended to totally control spice production. Other states—including Johore, Aceh, and Mataram—attacked the Portuguese at Malacca and at other strongholds in the Moluccas more than fifteen times during the sixteenth century but were unable to create an alliance that had sufficient strength to dislodge them. Only twice were these attacks coordinated, as the traditional interstate system had provided few precedents for alliances and coordinated action.

The regional system, in fact, proved capable of absorbing the Portuguese, but the remaining indigenous states—although in some respects stronger than Malacca—did not adapt in a way that would have allowed them to counter further European intrusions. Islam was consolidated in the archipelago, but despite a common religious philosophy, the indigenous states still found it difficult to cooperate with each other. From the Portuguese they inherited new military techniques, wider use of firearms and cannons, and ways to alter sailing vessels for military purposes; yet they did not fully capitalize on these new technologies because "in Asia, unlike Europe, there was no connection at all between science and technics, which meant that scientific results were not tested by experimental technology."[17] More critical still, Southeast Asians failed to make the organizational changes at either the state level or the level of the regional system that could have led to different regional responses; simply put, they were unable to make common cause against the Europeans.

Perhaps it was the indigenous propensity for looking past reality to rationalize away the European successes which prevented the Southeast Asians from recognizing the threat to their system. For example, in the *Babad Tanah Jawi* (*Chronicle of Java*) the chronicler explained that the army of Mataram had been defeated because King Agung sent his traitorous General Mandureja to attack Batavia; therefore when Mandureja was killed, the Dutch were actually fulfilling Agung's plan. In any case, it was said, Agung had sufficient magical power to destroy the Dutch at any time.[18] Curiously, the Dutch may have enhanced this view when, following their defeat of Mataram's army, they determined that it would be less costly to make peace with Mataram than to fight another war. The ambassadors from Batavia, with their gifts, were recorded in the *Babad* as recognizing the overlordship of Mataram.[19] Despite such complacency, by the end of the seventeenth century traditional Southeast Asian states were meeting new actors that had more resources, better organization, singleness of purpose, and an overriding determination to ignore, undermine, or monopolize the region's traditional system. The reality of that system was that the claims of indigenous states "were often absolute but their capabilities were usually feeble, and colonial forces at nearly every stage possessed superior strength and organizational ability."[20]

Colonial Impact on the Regional System

The traditional Southeast Asian system proved incapable of responding effectively against the penetration of European power. It was not that the traditional states had insufficient power in a military sense, although the heavy European ships and advanced armaments proved decisive against the lighter Asian vessels. But more critically, the individual states lacked the hierarchical authority structures that would have allowed them to respond quickly, nor did they recognize the arrival of the Europeans as a system-level threat until it was too late. The Ottoman government provided expert gun makers for some Islamic rulers in Sumatra to assist in their defense against the Europeans;[21] however, following the Ottoman defeat at Diu in 1538, local Muslim rulers throughout South and Southeast Asia were left to their own devices. Despite the receipt of more than 2,000 artillery pieces from Ottoman and European sources, "firearms never fully replaced . . . war elephants as the front line of defense among Southeast Asian kingdoms."[22]

There are several reasons for the failure of the indigenous system to respond effectively. First, the Southeast Asian system was weak in terms of its systemic relationships, particularly the inability of regional states to develop and sustain cooperative interactions. This inability to cooperate was reinforced by a high degree of ethnic separation among the states and by Hindu political philosophies of state structures that inhibited the evolution of a multistate system. Furthermore, the regional states had only a weakly defined sense of themselves as an exclusive grouping. Historically, they had recognized threats from the Chinese and the Indians, but even these threats rarely stimulated joint military defense.

The openness of the region made the arrival of new groups of foreigners commonplace; moreover, early European arrivals, who also lacked the capacities to alter the system, tended to adapt to the existing system. Further, when traditional institutions and practices were insufficient to meet the European challenge, local innovations, changes, and the adaptations of European methods were very slow and were often insufficient to counter more effectively deployed European power. Finally, although the Southeast Asian states recognized the religious challenge posed by the Portuguese, their economic actions were familiar and nonthreatening in terms of the standard systemic behavior of "acquiring tribute and booty."[23] Although the Portuguese were quick to use their naval power, the "display of power was in the last instance a factor of rather limited import for the thousands-of-miles-long trade routes [and] became one thread more in the fabric of the international exchange of goods."[24] The Portuguese did profit handsomely from their Asian intervention but only because they were able to transfer products out of the system and back to Europe.

It was the Dutch who first seriously disrupted the traditional regional system. They were successful because their military power, which had initially been employed against the Portuguese and the Spanish, later became an important tool against the indigenous states. Dutch military power was not only superior to that of the Portuguese, it was also more effectively organized. The chief aim of the new VOC was to consolidate Dutch power in such a way as to counter the Portuguese more effectively: "Portuguese power was typically medieval" in that there was no distinction between civil and military administration, and colonial stations and forts were managed by a conglomeration of nobles, military adventurers, mercenaries, and others with little lasting loyalty to the state.[25] After 1610, with the creation of the governor-generalship, the Dutch achieved a centralized authority and decisionmaking power superior to that of the Portuguese.

Although the Dutch gave support to Christian missionary activities, they did not have the fanatical approach of the Portuguese and concentrated more directly on economic control—an endeavor local states seemed completely unable to check even when economic disputes became overtly political. The typical sequence of the transition to Dutch control began with a contract, usually a monopoly purchase agreement for spice production, between the Dutch and the sultan or regent of a particular island or state. The sultan frequently signed the agreement under duress, either because Dutch warships were anchored in the harbor or because the sultan feared the power of another local potentate and needed Dutch protection and assistance. The contract price for the commodity was always significantly lower than its market value, and local traders and producers invariably turned to smuggling and black-market sales of the crop. The Europeans generally failed to recognize or care that most of the spice islands were net food importers; the heavy spice production in the Moluccas had made them dependent on rice produced in Java, and the commodity exchange between the two countries was vigorous because it provided economic advantages to both. When the Dutch interrupted this commodity exchange, the traditional states had to use cash for food imports, but the low contract price for spices meant less food and an effective decline in the standard of living.

The results of these unequal economic relationships became increasingly political under the Dutch because they had sufficient military power to act, whereas the Portuguese had not. Many Southeast Asian states continued to seek protection from a European ally—most commonly the Dutch, rather than seeking security arrangements among themselves against the Europeans. The Dutch exploited this very effectively. The essence of the Dutch perspective is summarized in a letter by Coen, then governor-general of the VOC, in which he spoke of the nutmeg monopoly contract with the Banda Islands: "The contracts have been violated so many times that one cannot hope for anything certain from that nation unless it be once and for all brought under control by warfare."[26]

The power of the VOC made it an actor with capabilities previously unknown in Southeast Asia. The Portuguese had used greater striking power and better navigational techniques to gain the upper hand in Malacca and elsewhere, but the Dutch added organizational improvements and unity of purpose which allowed them to outstrip the local states still further. The VOC's charter gave the company sovereign authority as though it were a state, leading J. C. van Leur to observe that corporations such as the Dutch VOC represented "national political creations . . . characteristic of the growing strength of the northwestern European states at the time."[27] The company, operating thousands of miles from its board of directors and without the inhibitions of a conservative agriculturally based mass constituency, was a potent new force in the regional system.

The VOC did not adapt or fit into the locally operating regional system; in fact, it moved to fragment the traditional system in order to fit the remaining pieces into the European system. The company operated virtually without limitation except for that of available power. The Dutch rejected the sanctity of state sovereignty in favor of the primacy of conquest and refused to acknowledge legitimate economic interests or needs in their drive for monopoly control.

Having established themselves as the most powerful actor in archipelagic Southeast Asia, the Dutch soon recognized that attaining monopoly control of the Asia-to-Europe spice trade was probably impossible. More important, the spice trade could not generate enough profits to support the growing Dutch regional establishment. It soon became evident to Governor-General Coen that control of actual commodity production as well as inter-Asian trade was the solution. Thus, in the second half of the seventeenth century, the Dutch took two steps that, while greatly increasing Dutch revenues, significantly advanced the demise of traditional Southeast Asian structures. First, they intervened in the Java-to-China trade and in other intraregional commercial routes, replacing local shippers with Dutch carriers. Second, they moved to control commodity production by, for example, destroying all of the clove trees on northern Maluku and Huamoal while generally impoverishing local populations throughout the archipelago with polices of buying spices cheaply and selling rice dearly. By decimating the indigenous economic system, the Dutch further ensured the fragmentation of political power, especially in the archipelago. As with the Portuguese, however, the Dutch seemed to reach the limit of their managerial capacities without creating new political forms or unity in the area.

During the eighteenth, nineteenth, and early twentieth centuries, Southeast Asia was pulled even farther from its traditional systemic economic framework. Such external events as the opening of the Suez Canal and the development of the steamship were critical in wedding Southeast Asia to the evolving global economic system. Materials such as tin and rubber replaced spices as the principal commodities sent from the region to the industrializing world, and Southeast Asia itself became more important as a market for basic consumer goods.

Within the region, the British took preeminent control of the Southeast Asian economy. Although the Dutch built an empire on Java and the other islands under their control and exploited that empire as fully as possible for their own purposes, they were unable to match the free-trade system fostered by the British from Penang and later Singapore. Banking and investment became important in the region as industrialization began during the nineteenth century.

By the end of the nineteenth century, nearly every component of the regional economic system was controlled by Europeans or their Chinese or Indian surrogates. Important indigenous merchant groups and shipping interests had largely disappeared. In traditional Southeast Asian states, the commercial sector of the economy was very closely linked to the political system, and external domination of the economic sector only ensured the demise of the political sector. "Where there is gold," said the *Babad Tanah Jawi*, "there is sovereignty." When the gold disappeared, sovereignty fell as well. Although the European interlopers often used the local leaders to control the population while assigning a European adviser to direct decisionmaking, the people recognized that the power, as well as the gold, now resided with the Europeans.

Conclusion

In this chapter I have focused on the movement of European colonial powers into Southeast Asia, primarily into the archipelago, where the spice trade first attracted them. The extension of colonial authority on the mainland was at first less intense but no less destructive of the social, political, and economic fabric of the states there. The Japanese colonial venture prior to World War II—its "Greater East Asian Co-Prosperity Sphere"—brought the Western colonial period to an end; although the human disruption and suffering during that time were acute, there was little further disruption of the indigenous system itself. The Japanese interregnum also provided a brief and not entirely positive stimulus for national independence.

The legacy of the colonial experience was one born out of the paranoia of a conquering force that acted as much from fear and lack of understanding as from a strategic plan. European interventions effectively destroyed the traditional interstate system of Southeast Asia in several steps. First, the Southeast Asian segment of the China-to-Europe trading system was disrupted, and the indigenous political leaders and merchants were strangled by the monopolistic economic practices of the Europeans. Then, having lost much of their economic base, the political elites were further undermined, and the state system eventually collapsed as authority was secunded to Europeans—even when indigenous leaders continued to hold title and office. Third, the socioeconomic integrity of the subsistence agricultural sector—at first only minimally affected by changes in the international commercial sphere—was penetrated through the introduction of forced cultivation, plantation agriculture, privatization of land, and other colonial production and social policies. Fourth, the colonial powers introduced and established alien groups, notably Chinese and Indians, in positions of economic power. And finally, the colonial powers furthered the overall regional economic and political fragmentation by developing intense economic dependencies on the respective colonial metropoles while cutting off virtually all contact with other regional centers.

At the same time, the colonial era introduced many Western concepts and practices, most in imperfect or fragmented form. Most prominent were governmental and military institutions based on Western rational concepts. Yet Western historical and social underpinnings of political culture, necessary for the effective adoption of these institutions and practices, were precisely what the colonial era failed to transmit and probably could not have transmitted. Southeast Asians could adopt the forms of Western government, but their substance and practice required that these foreign institutions adapt to local norms and understandings. The extractive preoccupations of both traditional Southeast Asian and colonial governments provided poor preparation for such concepts as public service in government.

This, then, is the legacy the former colonies inherited at independence. Moreover, the former colonies emerged again at independence into a global politico-economic system that would no longer tolerate idiosyncratic practices among its regional subsystems. In the time since independence, much of the colonial heritage has been shed, at times slowly and painfully. But the emergent regional system, although—as in the past—adapting certain external elements from the colonial experience and elsewhere, has gained confidence from the recognition that it has a cultural, political, and economic heritage of its own that will ensure a regional identity that is unique within the global system.

NOTES

1. M. N. Pearson, "Merchants and States," in *The Political Economy of Merchant Empires*, edited by James D. Tracy (Cambridge: Cambridge University Press, 1991), p. 77.

2. K. N. Chaudhuri, *Trade and Civilization in the Indian Ocean: An Economic History from the Rise of Islam to 1750* (Cambridge: Cambridge University Press), p. 68.

3. *Ibid.*, p. 75.

4. S. Soebardi and C. P. Woodcroft-Lee, "Islam in Indonesia," in *The Crescent in the East*, edited by Raphael Isreali (London: Curzon Press, 1982), p. 181.

5. J. R. Bruijn, F. S. Gaastra, and I. Schoffer, *Dutch-Asiatic Shipping in the 17th and 18th Centuries*, vol. 1 (The Hague: Martinus Nijhoff, 1987), p. 59. This three-volume work provides a detailed record of outbound shipping (volume 2) and homeward-bound shipping (volume 3) with an introductory summary and description (volume 1).

6. Bernard H.M. Vlekke, *Nusantara: A History of Indonesia* (The Hague: W. van Hoeve, 1965), p. 199 (emphasis added).

7. *Ibid.*, p. 130.

8. Bruijn, Gaastra, and Schoffer, *Dutch-Asiatic Shipping*, pp. 59, 70.

9. D.G.E. Hall, *A History of South-East Asia* (New York: St. Martin's Press, 1968), p. 331.

10. John F. Cady, *Southeast Asia: Its Historical Development*, (New York: McGraw-Hill, 1964), p. 213.

11. *Ibid.*, p. 215.

12. Bruijn, Gaastra, and Schoffer, *Dutch-Asiatic Shipping*, pp. 95–96.

13. George McT. Kahin, *Nationalism and Revolution in Indonesia* (Ithaca: Cornell University Press, 1952), p. 13.

14. Cady, *Southeast Asia*, p. 304.

15. Benedict R. O'C. Anderson, "Japan: The Light of Asia," in *Southeast Asia in World War II: Four Essays*, edited by Josef Silverstein (New Haven: Yale University, Southeast Asia Studies Monograph Series no. 7, 1966), p. 31.

16. Jon M. Reinhardt, *Foreign Policy and National Integration: The Case of Indonesia* (New Haven: Yale University, Southeast Asian Studies Monograph no. 17, 1971), p. 28.

17. M.A.P. Meilink-Roelofsz, *Asian Trade and European Influence* (The Hague: Martinus Nijhoff, 1962), p. 9.

18. Vlekke, *Nusantara*, p. 147.

19. *Ibid.*, p. 153.

20. Ruth T. McVey, "Introduction," in *Southeast Asian Transitions: Approaches Through Social History*, edited by Ruth T. McVey (New Haven: Yale University Press, 1978), pp. 12–13.

21. Michael Adas (ed.), *Islamic and European Expansion: The Forging of a Global Order* (Philadelphia: Temple University Press, 1993), p. 113.

22. Geoffrey Parker, "Europe and the Wider World, 1500–1750," in Tracy, *The Political Economy of Merchant Empires*, p. 168.

23. J. C. van Leur, *Indonesian Trade and Society* (The Hague: W. van Hoeve, 1955), pp. 170.

24. *Ibid.*, p. 164–165.

25. *Ibid.*, p. 181.

26. *Ibid.*, p. 183, citing T. H. Colenbrander and W. P. Coolhaas (ed.), *Jan Pieterzoon Coen: Bescheiden omtrent zijn befrijf in Indie* [Jan Pieterszoon Coen: Documents Concerning His Activities in the Indies], vol. 4 (The Hague: n.p., 1919–1953), p. 134.

27. *Ibid.*, p. 177.

7

Traditional Values in Western Cloth: The State at Independence

In the early twentieth century, hostility toward Western colonial domination in Southeast Asia began to surface. Fueled in part by increasingly destructive colonial exploitation and its concomitant social disruption, this hostility was vented circumspectly by small groups of intellectuals. Islamic and Buddhist religious revivals stimulated a more general awakening of anticolonial feelings throughout Asia, and Japan's defeat of Russia in 1905 diminished the sense of European superiority. Hostile feelings resulted in early expressions of nationalism; however, in some areas nationalist feelings were slow to coalesce, inhibited by centuries-old ethnic and religious divisions and by poor communication. Also, little in the experiences from either the traditional or the colonial period conditioned Southeast Asians for participation in a Western-model state.

Bases for Political Community

The desire to be free of colonial masters became widespread in Burma, Vietnam, the Philippines, and Indonesia, creating a common goal that sustained the nationalist independence movements in the face of colonial repression. This goal gave nationalist movements sufficient strength to survive the Japanese interregnum, but proindependence forces also used the war years to strengthen their positions—with some belated help from the Japanese—in preparing to confront directly the returning colonial powers at the end of World War II. With the close of the colonial period and the arrival of independence, however, numerous divisions and contradictions surfaced, often to the detriment of national development.

When the colonial powers retired, the common enemy that had united most local peoples disappeared, and latent animosities and suspicions resurfaced in national and regional politics. Concomitantly, the colonial managerial expertise that had been lost left serious deficiencies to be filled by individuals whose primary experiences had been as opposition or revolutionary politicians or fighters. Dorothy Guyot has pointed out that in Burma "the sudden elimination of the British so racked the prevailing role system as to create new and conflicting definitions of ethnic self for both Burmese and Karens."[1] Moreover, colonial divisions and boundaries, which often cut across traditional kinship and ethnic groups in ways that made little sense for the development of national identities, became boundaries for the newly independent states. Official borders divided common groups as often as they brought them together because Europeans had "ignored local factors and introduced extraneous political considerations and alien concepts in the determination of colonial boundaries."[2]

Few newly independent states were built on geographically and ethnically homogeneous populations. On the contrary, the geographic units inherited from colonial powers had little historical rationale, except that the newly independent states liberated specific lands and peoples from colonial exploitation. To the extent that traditional cultural and ethnic division crisscrossed or subdivided new national boundaries, development of national identity and national cohesion was seriously inhibited because no evolutionary process had been possible to allow ethnic or kinship identity to make the transition to a national identity. These crisscrossed loyalties continue to make political cohesion difficult. Because cultural and ethnic groups overlap so randomly and ethnic identity is so deeply felt, no single group has been able to completely impose its identity on the state. Nor have any governments been completely successful in creating a new national identity specifically focused on the state and apart from old ethnic and kinship group identities.

Ethnicity and National Identity

Opposition to colonial authority smoothed over many deep-seated differences among various factions in early movements toward independence; after independence the growth of nationalism slowed and fragmented. Throughout the region, most traditional limitations on the sense of political community remained muted but intact. Ethnic, geographic, religious, and economic divisions inhibited feelings of commonality among most peoples. The concepts of national identity that did emerge remained heavily couched in ethnic feelings, and smaller, minority ethnic groups sometimes strongly opposed independence. The fact that these smaller ethnic groups fought with colonial armies against independence movements led by different, larger ethnic groups is indicative of the animosity that existed among some groups, who viewed the colonial authorities as protectors against discrimination or repression by major ethnic groups that sought to control any independent government.

Even in those areas that had an ethnic core within the new states—the Burmese in southern Burma, the Vietnamese in north and central Vietnam, and the Javanese in central and east Java of Indonesia—there had been no evolutionary development of a national consciousness linked to a political elite or a set of political institutions. The complex historical experiences that forged national identities among peoples in other parts of the world did not take place in Southeast Asia because the traditional political elite, which might have led the region toward a "crystallization" of national consciousness, was emasculated or eliminated by the colonial powers.[3] *Bahasa Indonesia*, a lingua franca based on local Malay dialects and formed as a regional commercial language over several centuries but belonging to no major ethnic group, was essential for Indonesia's national integrity because it muted interethnic fears that state unity might have accompanied the adoption of, for example, Javanese as the national language.[4] Burmese is spoken by approximately two-thirds of the population of Burma, whereas Karen, Chin, and Kachin are spoken by the remaining third, who have resisted adopting the official Burmese. In the Philippines the official language, *Tagalog*, is spoken by about one-quarter of the population, and others speak several mutually unintelligible Malayo–Polynesian languages. Neither Burma nor the Philippines have been successful in creating national languages.[5]

Although language provides a unifying force in Indonesia, the cultural dominance of the Javanese—which reflects their political dominance—still severely strains interethnic relations, and it remains unclear whether a sense of Indonesian identity has emerged since independence. Ethnic animosities between core groups and minority ethnic groups were insulated during the colonial era but they endured because there were few opportunities under colonial administration for these groups to work together and to know each other. Yet the corpus of values and practices that made up "national" identity for the core group seemed like oppression to minority groups. Further, in Malaysia there were few nationalist tendencies prior to World War II.

Thailand is an exception because its independence was not destroyed through colonial intervention; at the same time, however, it did not experience even the limited growth of national consciousness that resulted from opposition to colonial authority. Vietnam, despite deep ideological divisions between communist and noncommunist groups, may also be an exception given that its sense of nationalism, "deep-rooted in the xenophobia of the people, arose from recognition of the difference between being Vietnamese and not being Chinese, French, or American."[6] Thus in a simple way, and recognizing that many colloquial feelings remain for the Vietnamese as for those in other parts of Southeast Asia, "every Vietnamese is a nationalist whatever his politics, social status, or education." Nationalism and national identity require common differentiation on ethnic, historical, ideological, or other bases between peoples within a nation-state and all others; Southeast Asian differentiation, with roots that are millennia old, remains focused on substate ethnic units.

The Village Sphere

The traditional political system, of which the village sphere was the core, functioned more or less effectively for a thousand years or more because it met basic needs for the society's largest group—the village peasant population. Above the village level, the traditional political system was weak; it was focused more on ritual and status than on achievement and was subject to considerable manipulation and exploitation. Moreover, the philosophical division between village peasant society, which was largely animist, and the court—whether Hindu, Buddhist, or Muslim—was great. Particularly in Vietnam, the Confucian court evolved views widely divergent from those of the village, whereas the latter remained closer to the norm of peasant culture elsewhere in Southeast Asia.

Whether conceptualized in group-cooperative terms[7] or as rational individual initiative,[8] the village's carefully delineated norms provided for the social welfare of its members. The resilience and self-sufficiency of the village, albeit at a near subsistence level, created few demands for services from a central authority. The village's external needs—protection, a modicum of trade and supplies, and a metaphysical rationale for life itself—were provided, at a cost, by the state. The traditional sociopolitical structures thus created, although based on mystic and supernatural views of power, provided an internally coherent system for sustaining village autonomy.

When the internal balance of the system was broken, however, its inherent weaknesses—lack of identity, lack of goal orientation, lack of decisionmaking—made economic exploitation and political domination simple matters. Colonial authorities manipulated, bribed, or otherwise co-opted everyone—from kings to village chiefs—in an effort to achieve colonial production goals. The position and authority of village chiefs were actually strengthened in an attempt to increase the level of extraction from village production for the colonial enterprise, but traditional structural social balances of reciprocity and mutual support were shattered as resources were siphoned out of the village. This economic manipulation was profitable for the colonial powers but devastating for the village, destroying its interlocking social and economic welfare systems. For example, in Cochin China under the French, widespread land alienation reduced two-thirds of the farm population to tenancy,[9] whereas in the 1850s Dutch policies resulted in famine in east and central Java.[10] Most devastating to village society were the disjunction and disruption of the set of social norms and balanced economic structures that, although consuming most of the productive output within the village itself, had enabled the village population to sustain its members for more than a millennium.[11]

Colonial intrusions disrupted the structures of village authority, generally strengthening authority in the legal context while weakening its socioeconomic responsibilities to the community. Colonial political disruption, which introduced the forms and the means to increase the state's authority, and pervasive economic penetration, which extracted ever larger percentages of production at below market prices, of Southeast Asia's traditional sociopolitical structures impoverished entire regions, changed population patterns, and undermined social relations. Colonial policymakers undoubtedly understood little of the socioeconomic reciprocity that had sustained the village for generations, primarily because Western philosophy, with its greater focus on individual initiative, left no frame of reference for comprehending the intricately woven social relationships of the Southeast Asian village.

Despite the coming of independence, the village could not fully resume its traditionally autonomous economic position, nor could it sustain its role as the primary social welfare unit for the rural populace. In essence, the colonial powers broke the continuity of the traditional state and society and provided no philosophical or ideological "whole" in its place. By manipulating production goals for the village, they had destroyed the historical balance among the government, the individual, the land, and social welfare. By the time independent states reemerged following World War II, the global system had changed to such an extent that a return to the state forms of precolonial Southeast Asia could not have been successful. Unfortunately, the village population had neither the skills nor the resources to deal with change of the magnitude required; prior to World War II, for example, rural people in Thailand and the Philippines were the only rural groups who received state-sponsored secular education.[12]

The Urban Elite

Education, which may have helped to develop common bonds among Southeast Asians through the three hundred years of colonial domination, under most colonial regimes was reserved for only a very small percentage of the indigenous populace. For many individuals in this elite group the educational experience awakened their nationalist pride and their desire for independence but also separated them from the masses of their own peoples. In Malaysia, "During the early 1950s and 1960s, the elites who engaged in working out [political] bargains . . . had much in common. Most . . . had an English-medium education and were quite Westernized in values and deportment."[13] Many sought Western education as a means of escaping the poverty of rural areas, but in the process they also lost contact with the concerns of their potential constituencies. Particularly under first-generation leaders, the nationalism that developed was an urban, educated, and largely Westernized phenomenon that inspired relatively little support among the masses of rural, uneducated, and poor peoples because it addressed few of the economic and social problems of the village.

The first-generation national elites, true to their Western educational values, led their states to independence, and many adopted various forms of parliamentary democracy. Vietnam, although it did not espouse liberal democratic theory, paradoxically adopted an equally Western but also communist model. However, as the mass base was unable to cope with the rigorous demands of political participation, the elite responded by "drawing all political resources to the top."[14] The timing of this process varied throughout the region but generally followed a pattern of transition from parliamentary government to charismatic leadership to bureaucratic-military government; however, the elites were drawn from a shrinking political base, and leaders with lesser and differing political goals were blocked or eliminated. It appeared that this small, elite group in many respects recreated the symbolic form of government of the precolonial era.

Slowly these states began to exhibit structural characteristics drawn from the indigenous, traditional systems. The social dichotomy between the court and peasant spheres of the traditional era was replicated in the contemporary period in the division between the urban-Westernized sphere and a still largely traditional and rural peasant sphere. The new states were urban-oriented, especially in relation to the capital city—not unlike the kingdoms of the traditional era. But the new elites could not remanifest the metaphysical and mystical nature of traditional govern-ment and often had more in common with former colonial elites than with their rural peasant constituencies: "Elite members tend to look outward for their behavioral models and their guiding values."[15] The new urban elites did not and could not lay claim to the Indianized concepts of authority and legitimacy because "Western education and ideas had undermined indigenous ones," and these new leaders, who did not have traditional claims to rule, "were not interested in restoring the old ideological system."[16] Yet at the same time, they were unable to define a national alternative that met the needs for a modern nation-state until second-generation leaders began to express indigenous values in order to distinguish the Southeast Asian state (in a modern Indonesian, Burmese, or other form) from alien, purely Western models and to draw in the mass of still highly traditional peasants.

From the beginning, the political leadership that emerged in these systems—even when democratic institutions functioned—was not representative in a popular sense but was paternalistic.

> Post colonial experience has, if anything, enhanced the attractiveness of strong, paternalistic rule. The Westernized elite holds a virtual monopoly on the education, technical skills, and experience necessary to run a modern state. Furthermore, the traditional masses for the most part look to the Westernized elites with their knowledge and organizational skills for leadership. It is not a question of the educated elites usurping the role of traditional leaders; popular acceptance of, and deference to, the Westernized elites—particularly civil servants—is the rule rather than the exception.[17]

Paternalism in the political and social arenas was a hallmark of traditional society and of the traditional political system at both the local village and state levels, and it shows no signs of diminishing in the contemporary system. Authority in precolonial Southeast Asia was absolute, but it was mitigated by the obligations of persons in power to take care of and assure the welfare of those dependent upon them. In this way the powerful were to use—almost to share—their power, authority, and position by taking care of those dependents as well as of the self.

Elite communication with the mass peasant base, although enhanced with traditional symbols and practices, is limited. The dichotomy remains, with Western-educated technocrats at the reins of government in a system defined by a population—not unlike that of the traditional era—that does not actively participate in politics and places only broad limits on the use of power. Contemporary second-generation political elites, with few exceptions, have not violated traditional prescriptions, and even in Vietnam, where ideology provides for mass participation, power, which "traditionally has been more personal than public, more symbolic than utilitarian, more reserved than purposeful, and above all more a matter of status than of programs and activity,"[18] has essentially accrued to the party elite.

The factor that differed so greatly from the traditional system was the inability of the village to reestablish its traditional socioeconomic isolation and its autonomous, sustainable subsistence. Too much disruption had occurred—land alienation was widespread, wage labor in major urban centers had drawn workers out of the villages, crop and production patterns had changed, communication and information had penetrated even the remotest villages, and village authorities and leaders had been sanctioned by the state rather than by the village itself. At the same time, the rural populace had insufficient resources, skills, leadership, and access to the new national political system to bring needed changes. Moreover, the primary traditional political responses of the village— apathy and acquiescence—remained prominent. Thus, the traditional village environment was transformed from one of secure self-sufficiency to one of a steady social decline and increasing poverty.

Legitimacy and National Cohesion

National cohesion remained difficult to establish because of the lack of political community and the ad hoc geographic nature of these states. Diverse ethnic and religious groups brought together under colonial authority frequently attempted to reassert their individual identities once colonial powers had departed. Political loyalties remained focused on the local clan or ethnic levels. In the traditional state, these minority groups would not have presented a significant problem, especially if they were located on the geographic fringes of the kingdom. In fact, their separate ethnic identities would have been assured through vassal-status relationships with the political center. The concept of political loyalty to the state, having neither traditional precedent nor colonial model, has been difficult to develop and impossible to sustain.

For the new state, however, established on the Western concept of complete sovereignty within its borders, such divisiveness and lack of control were unacceptable. The state was defined within the Western political context of sovereignty, territory, authority, and representation; however, the reality more closely resembled a reemergence of local political concepts in which sovereignty and territory existed relative to available power, authority was focused on personal leadership at the center of the state, and representation in a popular sense found little support.

A degree of national cohesion developed during the revolutionary struggles, when the urgency of conflict allowed the subordination of differences. However, the mythology or ideology of national independence was built on unobtainable promises of economic well-being, nearly utopian social development, and highly romanticized political independence. The failure of states to meet these expectations fed ethnic suspicions that surfaced during the postindependence years as the enormity of each state's economic and social needs and lack of political capacity became apparent.

Much of the confusion in the rhetoric of independence resulted from the gap that existed between the peasant population and the urban nationalist elite. The village, although its social fabric had been damaged by the colonial experience, retained its position as the primary locus of loyalty for the bulk of the Southeast Asian population,[19] and the parochial and uneducated villagers maintained many of their traditional values and goals.[20] Above the village level, the clan or ethnic group also remained intact as a focal point for self-identity and loyalty. Tenuous though the traditional, mythical Hindu link between court and village had been, its philosophical underpinnings had been broadly understood and accepted, and the contemporary elite—Western-educated and urban-oriented as it was—developed no such bond with the village population. The goals and aspirations of this elite group were heavily influenced by its members' educations and adopted cultural worldviews; however, they were unable to transform these aspirations into meaningful programs and policies to solve the pressing needs of the rural village population and thus were unable to deliver most of the promises of independence. At the same time, the needs of the village population, which had been unable to reestablish its previous self-sufficiency, were real and massive—they included landlessness, unemployment and underemployment, poor marketing systems, poor infrastructure, poor or nonexistent health care facilities, poor or nonexistent schools, inadequate housing, and an almost total breakdown of the philosophical underpinning of society. The elite, still captive in its own political culture, could not devise or implement the problem-solving, achievement-oriented policies that were needed to address the problems of rural poverty and disjunction. Moreover, it had little interest in doing so, given the social distance between the elite and the village.

The social and political gap that existed between the village and the political elite became increasingly obvious after independence as the new governments defined and implemented policies designed to turn the rhetoric of independence into reality. But this rhetoric—which employed such concepts as democracy, social welfare, political parties, elections, parliament, public services, and education—often confused rather than enlightened the population because the concepts had little meaning in either the traditional or the colonial experience. Political representation—in which a vote implied a link between the official and the electorate, and the official accepted a measure of responsibility for his or her constituents—had no precedent in Southeast Asia.[21] The concepts of Western democracy that were articulated by the elites could not provide a rationale for operating the newly independent states until and unless these concepts became understood, agreed upon, and adapted in a system in which a balance of responsibilities and obligations in a social contract met the basic needs of the people. The new states of Southeast Asia obtained sovereign status but could not implement the practical policies or develop the national cohesion needed to support that status.

The State at Independence

The newly independent states were successors to colonial territories conquered and constructed over a period of three centuries in pursuit of a wide range of economic, religious, and strategic goals essentially established in Europe. In some cases this process joined peoples who had not previously been part of one political unit, whereas in other instances single peoples were divided across arbitrary colonial boundaries. The new states of Indonesia, Malaysia, Singapore, and the Philippines had no historical precedent as political units, notwithstanding the eloquence of certain traditional histories and chronicles that implied otherwise. Indonesia and Malaysia were combinations of a number of previously independent or autonomous chiefdoms, sultanates, kingdoms, and peoples. Burma, Thailand, Cambodia, Laos, and Vietnam, however—although having long historical traditions as independent polities—found that their postindependence boundaries included ethnic groups that would previously have been vassals. Few minority ethnic groups were prepared to give up their separate identities to a state that had an uncertain future and was dominated by larger ethnic groups that historically had tread very heavily on minority groups.

The colonial powers broke down the traditional system but were unable to introduce an effective alternative. Initially, they attacked the central authority of the state. In some cases the king, sultan, or chief and his court were physically eliminated and replaced by a colonial governor. In other cases, rulers remained in place but were controlled by colonial advisers. The effect was the same—local officials were no longer subject to traditional social restraints because authority was buttressed by external colonial powers. The reciprocity of the traditional system allowed the state to function sufficiently well to meet the needs of its constituencies. No such reciprocity was established between the elite and the village community in the postindependence period.

Colonial authorities introduced more effective uses of coercion than had been common in the traditional system. Their policies and decisions were planned to expand profits for the metropole, and colonial administrators showed little concern or understanding of the sociopolitical systems under their control. However, the colonial experience also did much to reinforce the traditional view that "government was the center of all life, that its officials were the elite of all society, that its authority was omnipotent, and that there should be no limits to the concerns or interests of those in power."[22] Under the aegis of colonial powers, new and far more efficient governmental practices were introduced, particularly regarding the extraction of resources. Few practices were introduced that would have led to the development of popular government.

Postindependence government leaders faced nearly impossible tasks regarding education and mobilization if, indeed, they were to stimulate and sustain mass participation in political processes. For the most part, mass participation was ultimately rejected in favor of a more traditional, center-oriented, bureaucratic style of government that, in fact, was sanctioned by both the traditional and the colonial systems. Yet the foundation of the traditional system—the village's self-contained autonomy—proved impossible to reestablish. First, the internal socioeconomic relationships that had bound the village population together for millennia had been broken by the economic penetration of the colonial system. Second, the world had changed fundamentally, and the precolonial social model was not viable for life in the twentieth century. By the time of independence, peasant societies throughout Southeast Asia were in need of assistance from proactive governments capable of implementing social and economic reforms that were in tune with contemporary rural needs. No governments met this challenge during the early postindependence years.

The dichotomy of Southeast Asian society had not changed during the transition from the traditional period to the colonial period, and it had also not changed by the start of the contemporary period. At the macro level, continuity was maintained in the layering of the governmental structures on top of the societal base, as contrasted with the polity in which governmental structures grow from within society itself. Even in Thailand, the governmental reforms of 1932 and earlier essentially made the bureaucracy "the inheritor of royal authority" and ensured the "continuation of the bureaucratic system under its own leaders—senior military officers and civilian officials—rather than under kings and princes."[23] Elsewhere, as in Brunei, "indigenous structural forms persist into the present" but now include many added features; furthermore, the addition of new forms has been accompanied by an "extensive transfer of content from the old forms to the new forms."[24] As a result, authority has continued to be derived from above, reinforced by the strong traditional propensity for personalized authority and bureaucratic management.

The traditional polity, although mystical in its legitimacy, was bureaucratic in form, and the colonial regimes used effective force and bureaucratic control to dispense with or coerce required legitimacy. Governments at independence, however, combined the more effective techniques of the colonial regimes with some traditional forms of legitimacy (also adding the verbiage of contemporary national concepts of legitimacy)—the product being a refined bureaucratic governmental structure. Interpersonal as well as political and bureaucratic relationships continue to be defined in terms of superior-inferior status couched in paternalism. Despite the inherent inequalities in these relationships, their reciprocal linkages offer channels for communication as well as potential mutual benefit. Although such relationships may be uncomfortable for Westerners, they are normal and not necessarily dysfunctional within the Southeast Asian context. The combination of paternalism and dependency contributes to a very strong sense of belonging that makes the very concept of "opposition politics" difficult to express: "In-group feelings [can be] so strong that whenever significant opposition elements want to challenge existing authorities legitimately, they seek dependency under what they hope will be a sympathetic paternalistic authority."[25]

Bureaucracy and the Bureaucratic Polity

Bureaucracy has been variously defined but is generally identified as pertaining to institutions made up of public officials; it sometimes focuses on the higher levels of policymakers and at other times on the lowest-level village workers.[26] Max Weber described nine characteristics associated with the "pure type" of bureaucratic administration.

1. Administrators are personally free and are subject to authority only in the sphere of official obligations.
2. Officers are organized in a clearly defined hierarchy.
3. Each office has defined competences and legal responsibility.
4. Offices are filled by free contractual relationships.
5. Officer selection is on the basis of technical competence, and officers are appointed, not elected.
6. Remuneration is fixed on a graded scale, and rights of termination are protected.

7. The duties of office are the primary occupation of the incumbent, and the office constitutes a career position.
8. Officers work without ownership of the means of administration and without appropriation of appointed positions.
9. Officers are subject to systematic discipline and control.[27]

The bureaucratic polity has been distinguished from other types of polities "by the degree to which national decisionmaking is insulated from social and political forces outside the highest elite echelons of the capital city."[28] In addition, Fred Riggs has noted that this type of polity is distinguished by the fact that the bureaucracy is not under the effective control of any extrabureaucratic institutions.[29]

Southeast Asian governments have achieved a level of institutional insulation by relying on traditional power capacities that were strengthened by colonial techniques, as well as on the inertia of their populations. Factors such as popular deference to authority, reinforced by the educational advantage of the bureaucratic elite, further enhanced the position of the bureaucracy in the political system. In addition, Southeast Asian bureaucrats have been more concerned with protecting and promoting their own values—such as social status, hierarchical authority structures, and personal leadership and patronage—than with rational Western administration. Bureaucratic control has been a protector of the status quo in government and society, satisfying by various means most of the aspiring elites, as well as confirming the peasants' mostly negative traditional expectations of typical government behavior. However, Southeast Asian bureaucratic administration has not followed Weber's pure form in several critical respects.

1. Administrators have not been free from outside authority, as patron-client relations have been and remain critical in gaining and keeping positions.
2. The hierarchy of offices has had little impact on performance, and responsibilities have frequently not been defined.
3. Patron-client, ethnic, clan, or other relational links to authority are important entreés for many officials because few have clearly defined areas of competence and responsibility.
4. Offices have often been filled with political appointees and relatives of high officials.
5. Remuneration may be fixed, but it has often been so low that officers are forced to take additional jobs.

6. The traditional expectation that wealth accrues to the officeholder as a right of office and by virtue of holding the position has reinforced corrupt practices.

7. Duties of office may or may not be the primary occupation, although the individual may well remain in the bureaucracy for all of his or her working life.

8. Patron-client or personal authority may influence or determine whether individuals have "extraordinary access" to the means of administration, while ownership per se may not be an issue.

9. Officers have seldom been disciplined and can often use their contacts and influence to circumvent regulations and control.

The processes of neotraditionalization at first created forms and procedures of bureaucratic organization and behavior less Weberian than Southeast Asian in character. It may appear that the failure of Weberian prescriptions foreshadowed bureaucratic collapse, and for some period that appeared possible: "Lack of system is the central fact of life about today's society and politics in Vietnam. Ever since the French left, Vietnam has suffered from a serious shortage of technically trained civil servants . . . [with the resulting] insufficient managerial capacity that has perpetuated the anarchic condition of South Vietnam."[30]

As time has moved forward, this propensity for Southeast Asian neotraditional behavior has become pervasive and solidified not only in the bureaucracy and in other political institutions but throughout the political culture. Although many Westerners may still be tempted to perceive this neotraditionalization process as backsliding or moving away from the modern, the opposite is true. Neotraditionalization represents the restatement of basic values, drawn from the indigenous history and captured in its cultural milieu, in a contemporary context, which is the only way Southeast Asian society can modernize. It is important to recognize these values and the processes that follow from them as representing what is contemporary for Southeast Asia. Values cannot be adopted wholesale from without, as the failure of Western political processes has so clearly indicated. These values are modern in that they enable these peoples and societies to function, more or less efficiently, in the contemporary world; at the same time, they are traditional in that they are drawn from the historical experiences summarized in the extant culture of the region. Whether they can provide the foundation for efficient government remains in question. But whether they satisfy Western definitions of modernity is less relevant than the fact that the restatement of neotraditional values provides at last a consensual basis on which to build Southeast Asian society and the polities therein.

Structure and Function in the Bureaucratic System

The structures of the state were among the most obvious legacies of the colonial experience. Traditional structures of kingdoms, based on mythology and cosmology, were replaced by functional ministries typical of most European states. Thailand began this replacement process in the nineteenth century, well ahead of others. Other traditional states, such as Aceh, adopted bureaucratic structures based on functional notions but continued "arbitrariness of such exactions from merchants, and the total dependence of officials on royal favor"[31] meant that a transition to rational bureaucratic forms had not generally taken place in Southeast Asia at the time of the colonial penetration.

The term *functional bureaucratic structures* is misleading. It is well-known that particularly in developing countries, while bureaucracies have adopted Western or Weberian structures, forms, and labels, "the cultural environment determines the kind of administrative behavior that actually exists."[32] As a result of traditional cultural characteristics such as deference to authority, the propensity toward form and status over substance, and certain forms of nepotism—combined with poor training and limited or nonexistent supplies and support systems—these bureaucracies often became refuges for underemployed officials rather than becoming functional governmental structures.[33] The fact that functional form did not automatically assure functionality in operation is evidenced in the continued propensity to emphasize form over substance or performance, which has remained enormously debilitating in governmental management. In many ways, the bureaucracy has been a reflection of society at large, which is still controlled by "a host of traditional-type organizations which are part social, part political, and part religious . . . [and are] largely unsuited for national development, being unlimited rather than specifically defined, with generalized, diffuse interests and obligations."[34]

These bureaucracies became highly politicized in both the appointment-promotion and decisionmaking processes, which eroded public confidence in the civil service (or, more correctly, confirmed the public's traditional lack of confidence in the government) and weakened the government's already weak claims to legitimacy. Moreover, concepts such as corruption are universally understood as improper and unacceptable; however, activities that fall under the rubric of corruption may vary: "Improper conduct, and not necessarily or even usually the use of status for private material benefit, was what suggested . . . violating the taboos of his status."[35] Bureaucratic weaknesses were initially more acute in foreign affairs than in other fields: Knowledge and experience were scant, little information was provided by the unpracticed foreign service staff that was sent abroad, policy positions and personal convictions were often blurred, and officials were highly sensitive to any foreign pressure. Most new states opened full embassies in only a few selected states and were forced by lack of staff or funds to accredit their representatives in more than one state.[36] However, over time, ministries that dealt with the conservative rural population—especially ministries of the interior, public works, and sometimes religion—began to reflect their connections to that population, in the process becoming central regarding neotraditionalization. Even when Western institutional forms were overtly adopted, their functioning was governed by indigenous interpretations of purpose and action.

The bureaucratic nature of government in contemporary Southeast Asia is indicative of the coming together, or the reemergence and blending, of traditional and contemporary political thought and structures. Southeast Asian regimes have retained elements of traditional, charismatic, or personalistic rule as exemplified in particular by the early leadership styles of U Nu, Sukarno, and Sihanouk. Although the governments of Burma, Indonesia, and Cambodia under their leadership were perhaps not as personalistic as the traditional kingdoms and sultanates, their leadership styles brought many traditional behavior patterns to the fore. The ultimate downfall of each of these leaders signaled not so much the demise of traditional values in the political arena as the rise of bureaucratic polities that gave further expression to many of these same traditional values. Another clear demonstration of the rise of the bureaucratic polity has been the management system that has been evolving in Vietnam since the death of Ho Chi Minh. It is the bureaucratic maintenance of state power this system has engendered that defines the contemporary polity in Southeast Asia.

Military-Bureaucratic Systems

Early experimentations with democratic governmental forms—even when led by leaders such as Sukarno, who offered a charismatic personality with a blend of neotraditional hierarchy and contemporary populism—were unsuccessful in shaping politically cohesive polities in the face of the pressures toward fragmentation emanating from ethnic, economic, cultural, and religious cleavages. As the consensus derived from personal leadership dissipated, alternatives had to be found. Early civilian political leadership was discredited because it came to represent cultural and economic indecision and inaction and to symbolize the intrusion of Western values, models, and policy prescriptions—however modestly advocated—into systems still dominated by the substantively tradition-bound political culture. Some states showed a propensity for the military to move toward an alliance with the civilian bureaucracy. In Thailand, Burma, Cambodia, and Indonesia, the military intervened directly in the political system, largely because there were few alternatives short of revolution:

> Doubt, division, and opportunism among elites often accompany alterations of national institutions in the absence of an overriding imperative, and . . . the resulting illegitimacy and instability of the government increase the risk of interventions by military officers in the interest of stability, law, and order.[37]

At the same time, the military has lacked the necessary human resources and expertise to manage the government alone. Given the generally highly politicized nature of civilian bureaucracies, the transfer of allegiance from a charismatic leader to a military authority figure has been easily accomplished.

Indeed, some writers have noted an almost inevitable trend during the fixed span of time in which disillusionment with civilian leadership sets in and some type of military coup follows.[38] Perhaps the most common theme among analysts of military intervention in Third World states has been the argument that such intervention is caused by the inability of the civilian politicians to govern. However, equally critical has been the inability of the governed to define a new set of expectations for the political system; traditional views of government as manipulative, self-serving, and extractive remain pervasive, whereas concepts of public service languish among both government officials and the public.

The concept of the military as an interventionist agent or as an aberration of normal civilian politics may grow largely out of the biases of Western writers, who frequently perceive democratic political models as ideal types toward which all civilizations strive. J. Stephen Hoadley has argued that military interventions do not take place when governments are "led by a cohesive group of purposeful civilian elite," but that the breakdown among civilian politicians of "either cohesion or purpose leaves a leadership vacuum into which military officers march."[39] Samuel Huntington supports this interventionist argument, noting that the principal cause of military intervention in politics is "not the social and organizational characteristics of the military establishment but the political and institutional structure of the society."[40]

In Southeast Asia, it was not so much the failure of postindependence democratic political and institutional structures that ensured the intervention of the military as the lack of a political or an institutional history prohibiting such involvement—as compared with the Western polities, in which separation of military and civilian political power and subordination of military authority to civilian governmental authority are more institutionalized. Moreover, in Southeast Asia's societal context, given the bankruptcy of traditional religious bases of legitimacy, claims of participation in the revolution eventually became potent forms of legitimacy primarily for military leaders. At the same time, Western concepts such as representation and civilian predominance in politics failed to gain credibility or substance in the realities of Southeast Asian politics. In fact, in countries such as Indonesia, Vietnam, and Burma, military exploits of their revolutions harked back to the romanticized military campaigns described in the traditional chronicles, which gave the contemporary governments a legitimacy that could be understood in traditional terms.

Traditionalism and the State

In the postindependence years, the urban orientation of the elite grew more acute until, for example, many political parties became essentially urban cliques, with little beyond their revolutionary heritage to offer to rural peasants. Political elites have had only a minimal understanding of the peasant agricultural base upon which their systems rest and have often initiated government policies that insulate the rural population from the outside world to the extent possible. The single exception to this trend has been the leadership of communist parties in Vietnam and elsewhere, as Marxism came to stand essentially for land reform and its proponents spoke out against the corruption and materialism of Westernized urban elites. In Vietnam, the Viet-Minh worked to ensure support among the rural population because they were "convinced of the value of their own cause" and they had found a "population which, after decades of disorientation, was predisposed to change."[41] In a similar way, the communist party in Indonesia, before its destruction in 1965–1966, claimed a membership in excess of 3 million people and a "web of mass organizations including 15 million members."[42] Scholars have warned that the lack of effective representation of the interests these parties succeeded in mobilizing—particularly those of the peasantry—could become a source of serious instability.[43] But peasant populations have endured because their expectations of responsiveness from government, drawn from the still traditional political culture, remain low or nonexistent. Even more, their expectations of government intervention are so negative that a lack of policy and nonaction are regarded as good.

In these postindependence centrist systems, the extension of power from national to international contexts quickly became blurred. Because the geographic boundaries of each state were established by colonial fiat with little or no consideration of national identity, the extension of the states' authority rarely coincided with the territories shown on maps. Boundaries as a fixed demarcation line were unknown as a traditional political structure and were anathema to the patterns of loyalty among ethnic groups on the periphery. The ability of the contemporary centrist states, as their traditional procedures, to extend their authority outward from the capital depended on their military capabilities, the remoteness of the areas in question, the infrastructural capacity, the loyalties of the local populations, and the capacities of competing sources of authority. One or more of these limiting factors has been evident in some border region of every Southeast Asian state.

Another aspect of the urban orientation that harked back to traditional Southeast Asia was the direction of power—which has extended from the center toward the state's borders. Largely because of the deep ethnic divisions within each newly independent state and also, coincidentally, because many of these ethnic splinter groups inhabited border regions, every state in the region has had difficulties in maintaining its borders and extending its authority throughout its territory. In Burma, for example, Shan and Karen areas constitute nearly separate states in which taxes are collected, law and order are maintained, and authority is exercised outside the realm of the government in Rangoon. In Thailand, Laos, and Cambodia, Lao peoples on both sides of the Mekong continue to view the river as an artery of communication rather than a border. Muslim separatists remain a problem for the Philippines, and the Malay states of Sabah and Sarawak have variously sought independence—sometimes in association with the Sulu separatists from the Philippines. Indonesia, although relatively stabile in recent decades, experienced separatist resistance in Sumatra as well as in the eastern islands and continues to struggle with the island of Timor. For years, Sihanouk preserved peace and independence for Cambodia through de facto concession of large parts of Cambodia to Vietnamese control.

Because the state was not secure in its own territory, and because most of the territorial claims were subject to challenges on ethnic, ideologic, economic, or other grounds, concepts of state sovereignty (coupled with territorial security) remained weak. All of the contemporary states have accepted standard Western concepts of fixed and clearly demarcated borders, although they have not always accepted the borders as drawn. However, traditional concepts of fluid frontiers and borders remain extant in many areas because centrist states lack the capacity to extend authority fully to officially recognized borders. Moreover, ethnic minority groups, accustomed to maintaining their separate identities even under vassal status in the traditional period, have been impossible to assimilate and have also been very slow to accept any form of national identity that gives dominance to a different ethnic group. When the lack of capacity exists simultaneously in contiguous neighboring states, the frontier may become a buffer zone that overlaps the border on both sides. This has commonly been the case when rivers—traditionally central arteries for communication—have become political dividing lines for ethnic or cultural groups who live astride the river. When such groups have sufficient capacity, they may organize their own "polity," with local guerrilla or traditional clan practices filling regulatory needs, as has been the case in Shan areas of Burma. In other cases, when one state has more power than its neighbor, the more powerful state may extend its authority beyond the official border, as was the case for many years when the Vietnamese effectively controlled parts of Laos and Cambodia.

Lack of ethnic cohesion and related limits to territorial integrity have a direct impact on the state's ability to conduct foreign policy. Cynthia Enloe has pointed out that among such fragmented states, clear patterns indicate that these problems (1) induce greater dependence on foreign powers, especially for military and economic assistance; (2) provide opportunities for other powers to interfere in the domestic political arena, especially in the border areas occupied by ethnic splinter groups; and (3) forestall intraregional cooperation because the national leadership is not sufficiently secure within its own political and territorial base.[44]

The Contemporary State

The states of Southeast Asia (see Map 7.1) have survived the pains of independence and outlived the disillusionment of unmet expectations. Preindependence hopes did not come to fruition, but these states did not collapse. Burma has shown that a Southeast Asian state can survive by itself; Vietnam has demonstrated that a Southeast Asian state can outlast, if not defeat, a superpower; and Malaysia and Singapore have demonstrated that states can survive without revolutionary fervor. Singapore and recently Malaysia and Thailand, with Indonesia not far behind, have shown that economic development is possible—perhaps without parallel political development. These states are demonstrating forms of political development, based in part on traditional or at least non-Western political values, that will take them in different directions from those predicted by Western social science theories and models.

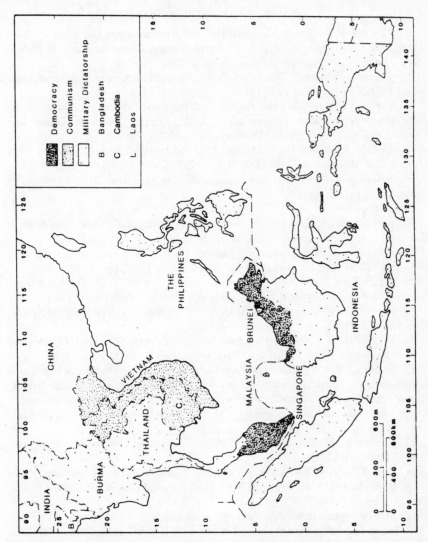

MAP 7.1 From Ashok K. Dutt, *Southeast Asia: Realm of Contrasts*, 3d rev. ed. (Boulder, CO: Westview Press, 1985), p. 2. Used by permission.

NOTES

1. Dorothy Hess Guyot, "Communal Conflict in the Burma Delta," in *Southeast Asian Transitions: Approaches Through Social History*, edited by Ruth T. McVey (New Haven: Yale University Press, 1978), p. 195.

2. Robert L. Solomon, "Boundary Concepts and Practices in Southeast Asia," *World Politics* 23 (October 1970), p. 7.

3. Guy J. Pauker, "National Politics and Regional Powers," in *Diversity and Development in Southeast Asia*, edited by Guy J. Pauker, Frank H. Golay, and Cynthia E. Enloe (New York: McGraw—Hill, 1977), p. 20.

4. Donald K. Emmerson, *Indonesia's Elite: Political Culture and Cultural Politics* (Ithaca: Cornell University Press, 1976), pp. 223–224.

5. Peter Lyon, *War and Peace in South-East Asia* (London: Oxford University Press, 1969), pp. 45, 49.

6. *Ibid.*, p. 68.

7. James C. Scott, *The Moral Economy of the Peasant: Rebellion and Subsistence in Southeast Asia* (New Haven: Yale University Press, 1976), pp. 35–55.

8. Samuel L. Popkin, *The Rational Peasant: The Political Economy of Rural Society in Vietnam* (Berkeley: University of California Press, 1979), pp. 30–31.

9. D.J.M. Tate, *The Making of Modern South-East Asia* vol. 2, *The Western Impact: Economic and Social Change* (London: Oxford University Press, 1979), p. 317.

10. John F. Cady, *Southeast Asia: Its Historical Development* (New York: McGraw-Hill, 1964), p. 364.

11. J. S. Furnivall, *Colonial Policy and Practice: A Comparative Study of Burma and Netherlands Indies* (New York: New York University Press, 1956), p. 318.

12. Charles F. Keyes, "State Schools in Rural Communities: Reflections on Rural Education and Cultural Change in Southeast Asia," in *Reshaping Local Worlds: Formal Education and Cultural Change in Rural Southeast Asia*, edited by Charles F. Keyes (New Haven: Yale University, Center for International and Area Studies, Monograph no. 36, 1991), p. 7.

13. Gordon P. Means, *Malaysian Politics; The Second Generation* (Singapore: Oxford University Press, 1991), p. 3.

14. Ruth T. McVey, "Introduction," in McVey, *Southeast Asian Transitions*, p. 27.

15. R. William Liddle, *Ethnicity, Party, and National Integration* (New Haven: Yale University Press, 1970), p. 206.

16. McVey, "Introduction," in McVey, *Southeast Asian Transitions*, p. 27.

17. James C. Scott, *Political Ideology in Malaysia: Reality and the Beliefs of an Elite* (New Haven: Yale University Press, 1968), p. 251.

18. Karl D. Jackson, "The Political Implications of Structure and Culture in Indonesia," in *Political Power and Communications in Indonesia*, edited by Karl D. Jackson and Lucian W. Pye (Berkeley: University of California Press, 1978), p. 42.

19. Koentjaraningrat, "Villages in Indonesia Today," in *Villages in Indonesia*, edited by Koentjaraningrat (Ithaca: Cornell University Press, 1967), p. 389; see also Gerald C. Hickey, *Village in Vietnam* (New Haven: Yale University Press, 1964), p. 285.

20. Liddle, *Ethnicity, Party, and National Integration*, p. 207.

21. Clark D. Neher, "Political Values and Attitudes," in *Thailand: Its People, Its Society, Its Culture,* edited by Frank J. Moore (New Haven: HRAF Press, 1974), p. 375.

22. Lucian W. Pye, *Politics, Personality, and Nation Building* (New Haven: Yale University Press, 1962), p. 83.

23. John L.S. Girling, *The Bureaucratic Polity in Modernizing Societies: Similarities, Differences, and Prospects in the ASEAN Region* (Singapore: Institute of Southeast Asian Studies, Occasional Paper no. 64, 1981), p. 12.

24. D. E. Brown, *Principles of Social Structure in Southeast Asia* (Boulder: Westview Press, 1976), pp. 214–215.

25. Lucian W. Pye, *Asian Power and Politics, The Cultural Dimensions of Authority* (Cambridge: Belknap Press of Harvard University Press, 1985), p. 336.

26. Joseph La Palombara, "An Overview of Bureaucracy and Political Development," in *Bureaucracy and Political Development,* edited by Joseph La Palombara (Princeton, N.J.: Princeton University Press, 1967), pp. 8–9.

27. Max Weber, *The Theory of Social and Economic Organization,* translated by A. M. Henderson and Talcott Parsons (New York: Free Press, 1964), pp. 333–334.

28. Karl D. Jackson, "Bureaucratic Polity: A Theoretical Framework for the Analysis of Power and Communications in Indonesia," in Jackson and Pye, *Political Power and Communications,* p. 4.

29. Fred W. Riggs, *Thailand: Modernization of a Bureaucratic Polity* (Honolulu: East-West Center Press, 1966), p. 328.

30. Douglas A. Pike, *War, Peace and the Viet Cong* (Cambridge: MIT Press, 1969), p. 61.

31. Anthony Reid, "Trade and the Problem of Royal Power in Aceh," in *Pre-Colonial State Systems in Southeast Asia,* edited by Anthony Reid and Lance Castles (Kuala Lumpur: Malaysian Branch of the Royal Asiatic Society, Monograph no. 6, 1975), p. 51.

32. Mavis Puthucheary, *The Politics of Administration, The Malaysian Experience* (Kuala Lumpur: Oxford University Press, 1978), p. 82.

33. Ann Ruth Willner, "The Neotraditional Accommodation to Political Independence: The Case of Indonesia," in *Cases in Comparative Politics—Asia,* edited by Lucian Pye (Boston: Little, Brown, 1970), pp. 244–245.

34. Pike, *War, Peace and the Viet Cong,* pp. 63–64.

35. Pye, *Asian Power and Politics,* p. 49.

36. Russell H. Fifield, *The Diplomacy of Southeast Asia* (New York: Praeger Publishers, 1958), p. 59.

37. J. Stephen Hoadley, *Soldiers and Politics in Southeast Asia: Civil-Military Relations in Comparative Perspective* (Cambridge: Schenkman Publishing Company, 1975), p. 163.

38. Roger Scott (ed.), *The Politics of New States: A General Analysis with Case Studies from Eastern Asia* (London and Sydney: George Allen & Unwin and Australasian Publishing Co., 1970), pp. 39–40.

39. Hoadley, *Soldiers and Politics in Southeast Asia,* p. 162. See also Edward Shils, "The Military in the Development of the New States," in *The Role of the Military in Underdeveloped Countries,* edited by John J. Johnson (Princeton, N.J.: Princeton University Press, 1962), p. 40.

40. Samuel P. Huntington, *Political Order in Changing Societies* (New Haven: Yale University Press, 1968), p. 194.

41. Milton Osborne, *Region in Revolt: Focus on Southeast Asia* (Victoria: Penguin Books Australia, 1971), p. 120.

42. Donald Hindley, "Political Power and the October 1965 Coup in Indonesia," *Journal of Asian Studies* 26 (February 1967), p. 237.

43. Daniel S. Lev, "Indonesia 1965: The Year of the Coup," *Asian Survey* 6 (February 1966), p. 110.

44. Cynthia H. Enloe, "Foreign Policy and Ethnicity in 'Soft States': Prospects for Southeast Asia," in *Ethnicity and Nation-Building: Comparative, International, and Historical Perspectives*, edited by Wendell Bell and Walter E. Freeman (Beverly Hills: Sage Publications, 1974), p. 226.

8

The Global System in the Post–World War II Era

The international system that the newly independent states of Southeast Asia joined in the years following World War II was fundamentally different from the earlier traditional or colonial international systems. World War II had left Europe and much of Asia, the vanquished as well as the victorious, in shambles, and "only two nations—the United States and the Soviet Union—had the military strength, the ideological conviction, and the political will to fill these vacuums."[1] The collapse of the Soviet Union in 1989 raised questions, certainly in hindsight, about that nation's strength even as far back as the end of World War II. In any case, the world soon engaged in a new type of competition following the war.

Ideological competition and military confrontation quickly dominated the global system following the war as the United States and the Soviet Union engaged in a struggle that became known as the cold war. The system spawned by this war lasted from approximately 1947 until 1989, although it underwent several important changes during this period. With the destruction of the Berlin Wall in 1989 signaling the crumbling of the Soviet empire, the global system entered an era of fundamental changes that have not yet resulted in the establishment of another, clearly structured system.

The international environment, particularly in the years immediately following World War II, was very volatile and hostile. Ideological conflict, rapidly expanding communications technology, and even more rapidly expanding technical complexities and power of weaponry made commonplace aggressive forms of interstate behavior that had not previously been possible. Although intrigue and subversion had been common in the earlier international systems, growing superpower competition, bolstered by modern communications techniques and other technology, made these characteristics the hallmark of the postwar international system. Much of this competition took place in Southeast Asia.

There were three basic differences between the contemporary system and previous systems in which Southeast Asian states had functioned as independent actors. First, the traditional interstate trading system was a series of loosely connected and largely autonomous regional trading systems that shared and exchanged some common values and patterns of behavior but between which communication was so relatively slow that regionally isolated and independent political action was the norm. Colonial conquest destroyed this traditional system, replacing it with nearly global monopolistic economic systems for certain commodities, but global interaction and instant communication were not possible until the post–World War II international system emerged. Unique regional systems of isolated communities nurturing particularized patterns of behavior were gone, and the multistate system that had originated in Europe expanded to the entire globe.

A second new feature of the post–World War II international system was the ability of some states (actors) to extend their political power or influence throughout the globe, whereas others, as in the traditional system, could extend power and influence regionally but no further. The limits of power applied primarily to offensive or initiating political influence as contrasted with the negative or rejecting influence a weaker (regional) actor might exert locally on a stronger (global) actor. In the traditional system, with its primarily commercial focus, commodity pricing in one region or subsystem influenced the cost of goods throughout the several interdependent regional trading systems, but few states could exert political influence beyond their immediate region. Although colonial powers did extend political power considerably beyond their national borders and could extend that power, at least on occasion, to almost any point on the globe, it was not until after World War II that states were able to extend political power continuously and to sustain it at will throughout the globe.

By contrast, in the contemporary global system the United States and, after some time, the Soviet Union had the ability to initiate and sustain foreign policy actions anywhere in the globe, whereas states such as Singapore and Thailand had the ability to act throughout Southeast Asia and, at times, to rebuff external intrusions within those states or elsewhere by mobilizing public criticism of the initiatives. However, even in the contemporary world, the capacity of global powers such as the

United States to initiate *and control* foreign policy actions is neither globally uniform nor constant over time. The Vietnam War demonstrated the limit of U.S. military power. The inability of the United States—even with the sanction of the United Nations—to maintain limited humanitarian efforts in Somalia (late 1993) further illustrates these limits, as does the impotence of all major states and the United Nations in securing a peaceful settlement in Bosnia. This general dichotomy of regional and global power is, in actuality, a continuum involving the relative power of each state actor and the issues involved.

A third unique feature of the post–World War II international system has been the tremendous increase in the number of states participating in the system. The system of equal actors based on the sovereignty of the state had its genesis in the much smaller and more homogeneous European arena. Previous systems that developed elsewhere were based on the superior-vassal relations between states in which the theoretical single state as the center of the world was to dominate. As most former colonies have gained independence, the number of states—theoretically all sovereign and equal and all holding membership in the United Nations—has grown from approximately 60 in 1950 to more than 150 in 1990. Not only has this growth strained the ability of the system to maintain communication links between and among these states, the very wide differences in economic, military, and other state capacities, as well as the social and political instability of some of these states, have called into question the very concept of a sovereign state.

The policy problem for any state, then, is to establish a proper mix of global and regional perspectives. Newly independent states especially, such as those in Southeast Asia, found their abilities to influence foreign events and decisions at any level severely circumscribed. In the immediate postwar years, events were often dictated by the United States, the only global power to survive the war largely unscathed. As the Soviet Union gained stature and power, the global agenda was increasingly defined by the conflict between it and the United States. The growing intensity of this conflict increased the dominance of global issues at all policy levels and lessened the abilities of the superpowers to acknowledge the variations and exceptions that were essential at the regional and national levels while limiting the freedom of regional powers to define foreign policy issues outside the context of global ideological confrontation.

During the cold war, most regions and regional states were at some time victims of the global or regional policies of the superpowers. Southeast Asia was no exception. Although various nationalist, revolutionary, and military ventures successfully defeated all of the former colonial powers, they were less successful in limiting later regional interventions by global actors—particularly the superpowers, which sought political or other advantages in the region. Moreover, regional policy initiatives taken on the basis of global objectives often had serious and unforeseen consequences at the regional and global levels. As World War II ended and the cold war unfolded, it was largely the United States that first focused on Southeast Asia as an arena for global conflict.

The hallmark of the bipolar system was the competition between the United States and the Soviet Union, often characterized as the free world versus the communist world. Three variants of the system gave shape to most international activities after World War II. Although these variants were not mutually exclusive with respect to time, the first period essentially evolved into the second, which altered the environment sufficiently to enable the third to emerge: (1) the *tight bipolar system,* during which only the Soviet Union and the United States were truly global actors; (2) *détente,* during which the Soviet Union and the United States made serious efforts to ease the tensions inherent in bipolar competition; and (3) the *loose bipolar system* or *multipolar system,* in which other states began to play major global roles. Transitions from one system variation to another were generally evolutionary and overlapping; it is therefore difficult to specify precise sequential time frames for these periods. Moreover, episodes of intense bipolar competition were not infrequent even throughout the détente period, and the superpowers remained immune to many dictates of the emerging multipolar world.

The Bipolar World and the Cold War

Even before the end of World War II, competition between the United States and the Soviet Union intensified, becoming more hostile and ideologically based. Much of international politics became polarized to one of the two sides. Although the U.S.-Soviet competition was initially focused in Europe, the Chinese communists' 1949 success in defeating the U.S.-sponsored nationalist Chinese and establishing the People's Republic of China (PRC), and the 1950 North Korean attack on South Korea, brought the cold war to Asia quickly and dramatically. The European dimension of the cold war diminished further following the Berlin Crisis of 1962; even more of the competition shifted to the Third World, which often seemed somewhat removed from vital interest areas and, therefore, a "safer" place to compete. A number of newly independent states, seeking to avoid this polarization, formed the Non-Aligned Movement but to little avail.

The United States

Two perspectives governed much of U.S. foreign policy after World War II. First, even though the United States was the only major military force in Asia at the end of World War II, its policies were influenced by a strong Atlantic-European bias, which was strengthened by the Soviet consolidation of power and control throughout Eastern Europe. Second, the vision of communism as a global threat obscured regional, national, and local differences in the political evolution of many developing states. This global perspective in U.S. foreign policy became galvanized when the Asian heartland—China—fell under communist control and North Korea sought to penetrate the Asian rimland, launching its attack on South Korea. The U.S. response was to "seal" the communist monolith of the Soviet Union and China—which taken together now controlled the entire Eurasian landmass, by building an alliance system throughout the rimlands of Europe, the Middle East, and Asia.

Heartland versus rimland theories of international politics had been thoroughly expounded by scholars throughout the first half of the twentieth century, but in the post–World War II era this view led to the U.S. policy of *containment of communism*. The containment strategy was simple: (1) concede the Soviet Union, China, and Eastern Europe to the communist sphere but isolate them from the rest of the world by creating an alliance system that would reach around the globe, and (2) provide support and assistance to all countries of the free world to ensure that no additional states fell to communism. Because in actual implementation the containment policies gave greater emphasis to the first objective, these policies greatly reduced U.S. flexibility in decisions predicated upon purely regional issues. Communism was a global ideology and containment was a global strategy, requiring, in U.S. eyes, the active participation of all global actors.

The primacy of the containment mentality affected other aspects of U.S. foreign policy. For example, long before World War II, the United States was clearly on record as supporting independence for colonial areas. Although specific dates had not been proposed, it was generally expected that transition procedures not unlike those created for the Philippines would be appropriate in most cases. The United States had made its commitment to the Philippines soon after the defeat of the Spanish in 1898 and had only halfheartedly encouraged similar policies among other colonial powers by the 1930s, despite Woodrow Wilson's enunciation of an official program of Filipino independence in 1912. Nevertheless, establishing independence for colonies had clearly been a U.S. foreign policy commitment for nearly fifty years.

The apparent ambivalence toward independence for colonies was heightened after World War II, when the United States was caught between its desire to support nationalist movements in Southeast Asia and the need to support the rebuilding of Europe as the bulwark of the containment policy against further Soviet expansion—even at the cost of a return to the colonial past. The United States tried to support both its European allies and the Southeast Asian nationalists, and its policies shifted from one side to the other over time. The dilemmas of trying to rationalize a regional foreign policy position (supporting the independence of former colonies) and a global policy position (containing communism) became particularly acute following the 1949 communist takeover in China. For example, the United States had pressured the Dutch to reach an accord with Indonesia's nationalists in the period from 1945 to 1949 and continued to do so until West Irian was turned over to Indonesia. In Vietnam, however, once it became clear that the Communist Lao Dong Party would control an independent Vietnam, the French were encouraged to remain there; they were eventually financed by the United States and were finally replaced by the U.S. military. In the end, and perhaps in necessary deference to its global perspective, the United States was unable to resolve either the contradictions in its policies of support for new independent states versus the European colonial powers or those between global and regional perspectives in its foreign policy.

The military containment policy took form in a series of regional alliances of which the North Atlantic Treaty Organization (NATO) was the anchor. The alliance network extended from Europe through Southeast Asia, surrounding the Eurasian heartland which was controlled by the Soviet Union and the PRC. Added to these regional alliances were the bilateral treaties with Japan, South Korea, and Taiwan, as well as the Pacific Security Treaty also known as the ANZUS pact with Australia and New Zealand. Each of three regional alliances—NATO in Europe, the Central Treaty Organization (CENTO) in the Middle East and South Asia, and the Southeast Asian Treaty Organization (SEATO)—was linked to the others through a swing member: Turkey was a member of both NATO and CENTO, whereas Pakistan was a member of both CENTO and SEATO.

From the global perspective and in terms of conventional military action, the U.S. alliance system appeared impregnable. An attack at any point in the system would bring a chain reaction in order to deter "open armed aggression . . . by making it abundantly clear that an attack on the Treaty area would occasion a reaction so united, so strong, and so well placed that the aggressor would lose more than it could hope to gain."[2] This treaty system, parts of which are still functioning, provided the foundation of U.S. cold war policies. During the 1950s and 1960s, the

United States expected and demanded that other states actively support the side of freedom in the global confrontation of communism, thereby creating a zero-sum environment in which any commitment to the communist "side" was viewed as a policy or strategic loss for the free world. Moreover, neutrality—the policy choice of many states trying to avoid the conflict and the domination inherent in the cold war alignments—came to be viewed by the United States as support for communism.

In Asia, the U.S. containment policy struck directly at China's own self-interested Southeast Asian strategy to limit the power of other global actors in the region; the policy also probably mitigated China's growing conflict with the Soviet Union for some years, whereas Chinese support for insurgent movements in Southeast Asia probably prolonged the U.S. presence in the region. The PRC was unable to curtail U.S. influence directly, but, feeling the Soviet Union had already lost its revolutionary zeal by the time of the Geneva meetings in 1954, China used the Bandung forum in 1955 to challenge the superpowers with conciliatory messages for newly independent states (whether reactionary bourgeois or revolutionary in nature), which had enormous propaganda value among the states attending the conference.

After Dwight Eisenhower had been elected president and took office in 1953, U.S. policies toward the Soviet Union became somewhat more flexible. Eisenhower's style was less confrontational than Truman's had been, and as the most highly decorated U.S. soldier, Eisenhower was not politically vulnerable to criticism of being "soft" on communism, which especially the State Department under Truman had been. Also, the 1954 Geneva Conference had relieved some cold war tension, and Soviet Premier Khrushchev's 1959 visit to the United States reduced competition in the global system. Nevertheless, the cold war continued, and Third World countries especially continued to have great difficulties in maneuvering between the United States and the Soviets and in protecting themselves from unwanted intervention and subversion.

The global and pervasive nature of the communist specter was well suited to the moralist U.S. policy perspective of leading the free world. Unsophisticated with respect to the nuances of international politics after decades of isolation, the American people accepted the black-and-white nature of the cold war issues. Americans did not know nor were they highly motivated to learn about far away regions like Southeast Asia. Structured policies that supported economic development, which might have broadened the national political bases of support for Southeast Asian regimes, seemed slow and haphazard in achieving results, and they lost favor against military assistance programs that were bolstered by the moralist rhetoric of fighting communism. It is probable that during the 1950s and 1960s the American public, which was conservative in its worldview and lacked any real knowledge of Southeast Asia, would not have understood or supported massive economic development policies. Moreover, it was often difficult to determine whether a regional or local conflict was, in reality, communist inspired or the result of narrowly defined local issues. U.S. policymakers have long understood the connection between security and economic development in the Third World, but sustaining a consistent policy rationale for foreign assistance—particularly the open-ended costs of foreign aid—proved impossible even in the face of the overt and pervasive challenge of communism.

Most damaging for U.S. foreign policy was the propensity of U.S. policymakers to define any anticommunist regime as "freedom loving" and, therefore, as deserving of U.S. support. It seemed to matter little that such military assistance could become a tool for repressive antidemocratic regimes. There may have been value in numbers in this global confrontation of communism, but the U.S. willingness to accept and support boldly repressive regimes throughout the cold war era cost precious time during which reform-minded governments in these countries might have been able to move socioeconomic development to the point at which communist or other insurgencies would have withered for lack of constituencies.

Although interpretations of motives, causes, and realities in U.S. foreign policy vary greatly, the period from the mid-1950s through the 1960s has been considered the *Pax Americana*.[3] It was not an entirely peaceful period, but it was a time in which the United States, despite occasional symbolic setbacks, held sway throughout the globe. Soviet influence and power grew during the period, but that country's continued domestic economic problems, the cost of its military development programs, and its own ambivalence toward much of the world limited its global capacities. U.S. policies were defeated in some regional contests, but overall, the United States was the only state that possessed clearly global capacities. Ironically, this cold war turned into a kind of cold peace, as the superpowers averred the confrontation that might have brought about World War III:

> We can now see that the cold war, the most dangerous, bitter, and protracted rivalry between Great Powers in modern history, did in time become the most protracted period of freedom from Great Power war in modern history. Whether or not one approves of the *means* by which this happened, whether or not one even agrees on the *way* in which it happened, the simple fact is that the cold war did evolve into a Long Peace.[4]

An evaluation of U.S. policy in Southeast Asia, however, reveals greater deficiencies when the global context is set aside. U.S. policies, beginning shortly after World War II, showed a lack of knowledge and understanding of Southeast Asia. U.S. interests in Asia historically focused on Japan and China, and as the economies of the Southeast Asian colonies became more tightly linked to Europe during the nineteenth and twentieth centuries, U.S. concern for the region narrowly focused on the Philippines. By World War II, U.S. policies supporting independence for other regional colonies had receded considerably, as the isolationist policies of the interwar years had done little to encourage active policies toward Southeast Asia. The United States defined the global agenda as constituting confrontation and defeat of the Soviet Union, and although it was unable to accomplish this task, it did succeed in making this the primary objective of world politics in the postwar years.

The Soviet Union

Soviet policymakers had traditionally directed their focus—which was inherited from the czarist period and was reinforced by the experiences of two world wars—toward Europe, although for centuries a historical sense of eastward expansion had also drawn Russian and Soviet adventurers and state leaders toward Asia. Moreover, the ideological homestead of Marxism was the industrial West, not Asian agrarian peasant cultures. Whereas Marxist concepts had easily transferred to Asia, many of the young intellectuals of Southeast Asia, who had been trained in Europe during the colonial period, were quick to identify with broadly conceived Marxist notions as a rationale for opposing both colonialists and the traditional aristocratic elite, who still had some vestiges of respect and authority. Nevertheless, "whatever role the Soviet Union plays in Asia and whatever aims and interests she may have are those of a European and a global power in Asia, not those of an Asian power."[5]

The first impetus for Soviet policy in Southeast Asia, well before confrontation with the United States became an issue, was support for the region's nascent communist parties in their opposition to colonial regimes. Soviet policies were ambiguous and confusing on such issues as whether communist elements in places such as Southeast Asia should cooperate with bourgeois nationalists against colonial authority. However, among Southeast Asian communists only Ho Chi Minh remained active in the Comintern during the 1930s, by which time the issue had been resolved in favor of confrontation with the nationalist leadership.[6]

Although the late 1940s may have held possibilities for cooperative strategies between the superpowers as envisioned in the concept of the United Nations, the confrontation between them was beyond reversal by the time the United States announced the Marshall Plan for European reconstruction (officially the European Recovery Plan, announced in 1948)—which, pointedly, did not include the Soviet Union. After World War II, the Soviet Union countered U.S. influence and success in Western Europe by establishing itself as the champion of the newly emerging countries in Asia and Africa. Turning away from Europe, the Soviet Union stimulated a number of communist rebellions in Southeast Asia, such as the uprising along the Sittang River in Burma, which followed strong communist agitation at the Southeast Asian youth conference held in Calcutta in 1948.[7] In addition, soon after the Indonesian communist leader, Musso, returned from Moscow, a coup was attempted in Sumatra.[8]

Yet in the years immediately following World War II, Soviet policy in remote regions such as Southeast Asia could be little more than reactive with respect to U.S. initiatives. Seeking to position the Soviet Union more favorably vis-à-vis many Third World countries, Khrushchev offered a more accommodating view of neutralism than did the United States. Using the phrase "positive neutrals," Khrushchev at times praised Indonesia, Burma, and Cambodia, among others, for their adherence to nonparticipation in military blocs.[9] Soviet foreign assistance projects were largely symbolic. In Indonesia, for example, Soviet support of the Collagen Steel Project and the Senayan sports complex was largely political in nature, designed to enhance Sukarno's stature as a leader of the nonaligned states and to strengthen Soviet influence there. Despite such support, Soviet policy never achieved the level of influence it sought: "The more Moscow gave Sukarno materially and verbally, the more he seemed to feel he could disregard Soviet policy recommendations and do as he pleased, including pursuing many policies, such as closer relations with China, inimical to the interests of the U.S.S.R."[10]

The policy benefits of supporting the national communist parties in Southeast Asia were dubious. Over time, these parties usually proved too headstrong and nationalistic to consistently follow Comintern or Soviet direction, making the Soviets mainly a passive rider on the roller-coaster movements of the parties in the region. The number of ill-fated communist military rebellions throughout the region is indicative of the problem: Years of training leaders, building cells, developing auxiliary mass organizations, and nurturing political respectability were wasted again and again because of badly timed and poorly planned military action against incumbent regimes. Moreover, although the Soviet Union was viewed as safe by some regional communist groups because of its distance from the region (as compared with the Chinese communists), this same distance undercut the relevance of Soviet ideological thinking for the region's communists, who found Maoist theories of peoples' wars of liberation more meaningful than Soviet Marxism-Leninism. The Maoist emphasis on communal interests, with precedence over those of the individual, found ready-made cultural support, and the concept of class struggle, when adapted (as in China) to landlords and other forms of agrarian class discrimination, found receptivity throughout Asia. And as the first generation of communist Asian leaders—educated in Europe and intellectual and elitist in outlook—gave way to younger leaders, revolutionary Maoist ideas gained further support.

After Stalin's death in 1953, the Soviet's antagonistic views of the United States softened somewhat, and such concepts as *peaceful coexistence* crept into the superpowers' vocabulary. At the same time under Khrushchev the Soviet Union continued to attack U.S. containment policies with proposals such as creating several zones of peace—including Southeast Asia—in attempts to gain further friendships among communists but also, importantly, to give noncommunist states an alternative to the U.S. security umbrella and to bring about the dismantling of the U.S. global security system.[11] Approaches to noncommunist states required diluting Soviet ideological fervor and, in some cases, even sacrificing local communist parties to achieve better relations with bourgeois governments—a strategy that was successful in the global system vis-à-vis the United States but costly in the communist system vis-à-vis China.[12] These policies enabled the Soviet Union to counter the vastly superior U.S. forces around the globe because although the Soviet Union was considered a global power from the time of the end of World War II, it was not until after the Cuban missile crisis that Soviet forces developed the capacity to project force virtually anywhere in the globe.

Détente and the Weakening of Bipolarity

Détente, or the easing of competition between the superpowers, had its beginnings in the mid-1950s when Soviet Premier Khrushchev began to talk about the possibilities of peaceful coexistence. Détente gained further credibility when the United States established diplomatic relations with China, and it received another important boost with the end of the U.S. involvement in Vietnam. Support for détente by either superpower was hardly zealous, but it was continuous because the intense competition within the bipolar system could not be sustained. Neither the United States nor the Soviet Union could effectively implement and maintain the tight alignment of all or even most of the states in the international system. The costs associated with bipolar competition in terms of military expenditures, weapons systems research in an increasingly technological-ly complex environment, and payments and material assistance to client and potential client states grew too heavy—particularly in the context of growing domestic social and economic demands in both countries.

The bipolar system also continued to weaken, or loosen, because the superpowers, having agreed to the possibility of peaceful coexistence, could no longer command the rigid and absolute loyalties of their client states. Although peaceful coexistence was not so much a statement of a positive policy outcome for either superpower as it was an acknowledgment that little or nothing could be done to change the situation, it defined limits, however tentatively—beyond which neither superpower would take action. Without doubt, each would have preferred to eliminate the other, but both countries recognized that the costs and potential risks associated with direct confrontation and defeat were too high.

Neither the United States nor the Soviet Union was ever entirely comfortable with détente. The Soviets maintained something of an "embattled fortress" mentality in response to U.S. containment. Yet there was intense debate among Soviet policymakers as to whether they should seek influence beyond the communist sphere or protect only their own vital interests, which were defined as constituting the communist world. In the United States, there was a continual political debate about the merits of trying to negotiate with the atheistic communists. In reality, neither side was willing to completely reject the idea of ultimate victory, and yet each realized that the costs of victory would be too high. This ambivalence regarding ultimate policy goals, especially in the face of the rampantly mounting costs of confrontation, eventually stimulated change.

The superpowers also perceived the idea of détente differently. For the Soviets, détente signaled parity and equality with the United States in global status and meant the end of U.S. efforts to dominate them in regional political competition. For the United States, however, détente was perceived primarily as a restraint on Soviet adventurism throughout the world, especially in the Third World. Consequently, whereas the Soviet Union expected to play an expanded role in regional politics, the United States expected the Soviets' role to diminish.[13]

The United States

The U.S. containment policies began to unravel in the late 1960s, although they were never formally abandoned; indeed, elements of the idea of stopping, or containing, communist expansion in the Eurasian heartland were still evident through the Bush presidency. Considerable evidence suggests that the resurgence of competition and confrontation instigated by the United States during the Reagan presidency and continued through the Bush presidency was responsible for bankrupting the Soviet Union.

Ironically, policies developed earlier during the Nixon presidency, including moving toward détente with the Soviet Union and establishing relations with the People's Republic of China, seriously undermined the policy rationale for containment. The American public's confusion over the evident contradiction between détente on the one hand and the war in Vietnam on the other was important in sustaining domestic opposition to U.S. policy in Vietnam. The majority of Americans could not distinguish between global and regional issues because U.S. policymakers did not develop that distinction. The contradictions between the policy that brought the United States into the war in Vietnam—cold war containment—and the policy that undermined U.S. credibility there—détente—were never satisfactorily resolved.

As early as 1969, Richard Nixon sought to establish a new basis for U.S. foreign policy. What has become known as the Nixon Doctrine (or, for Southeast Asia, the Guam Doctrine) recognized the changing U.S. status. Its principal policy points included: (1) maintenance of U.S. treaty commitments, (2) extension of the nuclear shield to any nation whose survival was vital to U.S. security if that nation was threatened by a nuclear power, and (3) provision of such military or economic support as was required by treaty or requested by a government to meet aggression but with the expectation that each nation will assume primary responsibility for its own defense. This doctrine represented a major U.S. policy change away from containment and its subsidiary domino concept vis-à-vis Southeast Asia. Some regional leaders saw the doctrine as a "device to cover an American abandonment of responsibility in the region."[14] The domestic travails that later engulfed the Nixon administration, as well as the insecure leadership that followed, confirmed this view for many regional leaders. The subsequent Carter administration's emphasis on human rights as a primary consideration for full American support heightened the belief that U.S. leaders neither understood the problems of Southeast Asia nor maintained a sufficient commitment to the region to act as a positive force.

The U.S. military collapse and withdrawal from Vietnam may have had a positive side in that the United States realized it could no longer police Southeast Asia and shore up fading domestic elites in an effort to preserve its faltering global containment policy. From a domestic perspective, détente had proceeded to an extent that the logic of containment was no longer sufficient to ensure public support for military ventures in far-off lands. From a regional perspective, the converse of abandonment was a recognition, implicit in the third point of the Nixon Doctrine, that regional states must take responsibility for determining their own futures. To the extent that this recognition has been linked to a better understanding of regional problems as the basis for U.S. decisionmaking (rather than its standard practice of applying global policy rationales to regional issues), the United States has improved the likelihood of successful policy implementation in the region.

At the same time, core U.S. interests in the region were redefined around Southeast Asia's geopolitical position on the sea lanes between the Pacific and Indian Oceans—that is, between East Asia and the Middle East. This fact had important military and strategic importance for the United States, and it also recognized the Japanese dependence on these sea lanes for obtaining oil from the Middle East. Southeast Asia's economic potential was increasingly acknowledged as an important U.S. interest. The market potential of the region had been recognized since colonial times, but with real economic growth in the region exceeding 6 percent during the ten-year period 1985–1995, that market potential has become even greater. The rapid economic growth of Singapore, Malaysia, and Thailand, with Indonesia not far behind, has signaled a new era of economic relations between the United States and Southeast Asia.

The Soviet Union

The Soviet response to U.S. containment policies was mixed and was hotly debated in Soviet policy circles. At issue was the strategy of response: whether to confront U.S. containment globally and actively or, more conservatively, protect vital interests only within the communist sphere, leaving most of the rest of the world to the bourgeois nationalists or, at best, supporting communist political parties in those states.

From the mid–1950s onward Khrushchev, perhaps reacting to Stalin's previous siege mentality, advocated the more activist policy of breaking out of the capitalist encirclement. Some policy initiatives, such as Soviet assistance to allow Egypt to complete the Aswan Dam on the Upper Nile after the United States canceled its funding in an attempt to punish Nassar, drew great public attention, highlighting the intense competition between the United States and the Soviet Union. The most spectacular success of the "breaking out of the capitalist encirclement" policies was the Cuban Revolution of 1959, which, although not attributable to Soviet initiatives, brought the communist world almost to U.S. shores. Ironically, it was also Cuba that pulled the superpowers the greatest distance from détente in 1962 during the Cuban missile crisis. Yet that crisis served to define the limits of confrontation and thereby strengthened the likelihood that détente would remain the primary policy focus for both the Soviet

Union and the United States. Except for Vietnam, the Soviet Union had few other major successes in breaking out of U.S. encirclement.

In a military sense, however, Soviet capacity never equaled the U.S. ability to project military power throughout the globe. The more conservative Russian view prevailed in the argument that conventional forces were primarily responsible for defending local borders and, at most, immediately contiguous areas.[15] Although Khrushchev and later Brezhnev did seek to expand Soviet military influence by providing military equipment, training, and advisers to many Third World countries, the Soviet Union never undertook a policy of placing significant ground forces in Asian or other Third World locations.

At the same time, the Soviet Union under Khrushchev sought aggressively to strengthen relationships with neutral Southeast Asian states in order to encourage policy stances independent of the West. Khrushchev made trips to Southeast Asia in 1955 and again in 1960. Soviet relations with Burma under U Nu and with Indonesia under Sukarno were key to the Soviet strategy, but they also portended differences with China, which saw Southeast Asia as being essentially within its sphere of influence. Further, it was necessary for the Soviet Union, particularly in Indonesia, to balance its policies between support for a bourgeois nationalist government and a vigorous Indonesian Communist Party, the PKI.

The approaching division within the communist world was foreshadowed by the failure of the Soviet Union to gain an invitation to the 1955 Bandung Conference of Asian and African States, at which China made great strides in building relations with other Third World states by portraying itself as the leader (a label that could have been construed to apply to the Soviet Union) of the anti-imperialist and neocolonial forces.[16] China also drew the distinction between its agrarian version of communism, which appealed to most of Asia, and the Soviet industrial, more European form of communism.

The Soviet Union had significantly increased its global capabilities by the late 1960s and was in a stronger position to define limitations of the U.S. containment policy. In 1969, Soviet Premier Leonid Brezhnev proposed a "collective security" system for Asia. Its objective was to go directly to regional powers, "draw[ing] on the interests of the non-aligned states in strengthening collective security arrangements, to steer their support behind Soviet proposals for regional and global security regimes."[17] The system was designed in part to by-pass further agreements with the West on regulating superpower activities in the Third World, but "Southeast Asian countries suspected the Soviet plan was intended to draw the Asian countries into a defence system with the U.S.S.R. directed primarily at China."[18] Although Brezhnev's proposal received scant support in Asia, it became the cornerstone of Soviet Southeast Asian policy and was a sign of the USSR's increasing regional interests.

After 1975, with the fall of South Vietnam and the U.S. withdrawal from Southeast Asia, the Soviet's regional policy context changed abruptly. Not only did its major adversary retire from a major regional conflict, but the USSR soon gained an ally in Vietnam, with which it signed a treaty of friendship in 1978. This alliance benefited the Soviets as the Vietnamese agreed to let them use port facilities and airfields, thereby giving the Soviets a new strategic flank position in the competition with the PRC and creating the Soviet version of a containment policy for China. The Vietnamese were reluctant to allow the Soviets full use of vacated U.S. military facilities at Cam Ranh Bay and elsewhere, but their dependence on Soviet support (given the draining of Vietnamese energies in Cambodia and the surprisingly universal isolation of Vietnam) made continued denial of Soviet demands difficult.

Access to former U.S. military facilities in Vietnam gave a tremendous boost to Soviet strategic policy at both the regional and global levels and became key to Moscow's "two foremost global objectives—containing China and competing with the United States for worldwide influence and power."[19] Although they had not been utilized to the level of previous U.S. operations, the naval facilities in Vietnam significantly increased the Soviet ability to counter U.S. operations in Southeast Asia, South Asia, and the Middle East. When the second strategic gain—that of flanking China—was considered as well, the full value of Soviet support of Vietnam became evident. Soviet redeployment of military force to Asia began as early as 1963 and included increased military support to North Vietnam; moreover, although the Soviets were willing to discuss some Cambodian issues, there was no reason to expect that they would readily relinquish this strategic position. The Soviet Union, however, was not interested in expending (or able to expend) substantial resources in Southeast Asia; instead, it encouraged Vietnamese restraint in order to minimize the possibility of a Vietnamese conflict with Thailand, a major U.S. client.

Under Gorbachev, Vietnam remained the Soviet Union's most important client in Southeast Asia, although relations between the two were often strained because the Soviets began to pressure Vietnam to withdraw from Cambodia. The Soviet Union also actively sought better relations with noncommunist states. Thai-Soviet relations grew warmer as the Soviets pressured the Vietnamese to leave Cambodia. The Soviet Union also gave consistent verbal support to Malaysia's regional peace plan which called for Southeast Asia to be recognized as a "zone of peace and neutrality." Gorbachev even worked to improve relations with the

Philippines, seeking to encourage those pressing for closure of the U.S. bases there.[20]

China

The foreign policy of the People's Republic in Southeast Asia has continued to be influenced by traditional Chinese views of the world: "One could not be Chinese without having a dedicated conviction of the innate worth and superiority of Chinese culture. . . . In short, Peking's intractable mood comes out of China's history, not just from Lenin's book."[21] China has promoted Southeast Asia as a traditional sphere of influence that should be "militarily quiescent" and "politically accessible."[22] The PRC has at different times followed traditional Chinese strategies—leading by example or by force. However, China's foreign policy, particularly in the early years following World War II, was often limited to rhetoric because its very scarce resources were devoted to domestic needs.

China followed the Soviet lead in developing the global strategy of peaceful coexistence in the early 1950s, compromising in Korea and participating in the 1954 Geneva talks on Vietnam. However, following the Geneva talks, China began to separate itself from the Soviet Union's peaceful coexistence policy and capitalized instead on its image as the revolutionary model for the Third World—particularly in Asia, where the similarities in traditional agricultural bases were obvious.[23] Because traditionally Southeast Asia fit within the closer circles of the Chinese world, China expected to maintain a special relationship there and sought the "development of a safe belt, if not a sphere of influence, through the establishment and strengthening of friendly or neutralist regimes in such peripheral areas as Southeast Asia,"[24] thereby limiting the pressure of the superpowers.

China played a prominent role at the Bandung Conference of newly independent states in 1955 and presented an image of support for nationalist and anti-imperialist forces. Moreover, Zhou Enlai replaced Nehru of India as the central figure in the Afro-Asian group of states. More important, the conference positioned China as a leader of progressive forces in the Third World, clearly upstaging the Soviet Union.

Revolutionary China had major difficulties in dealing with the conservative nationalist Southeast Asian governments. Relationships were complicated by PRC support for communist parties there, some of which were outlawed or maintained a state of rebellion, but even in Vietnam relations were instabile. China balanced diplomatic relations with revolutionary policy by lessening its support for insurgents when government-to-government relations were good and increasing its support of the revolutionaries when formal relations soured. The PRC's relations within the region were also influenced by the pressure in Southeast Asia of large numbers of ethnic Chinese, who still control significant portions of the economy wherever they reside but who have usually spurned assimilation into the culture of their adopted countries and have sometimes been involved in communist insurrections.

For years the decline in fraternal communist relations between China and the Soviet Union was hidden under the veil of the united front against U.S. involvement in Vietnam. What began in the 1950s as China's attempt to revolutionize its own agrarian society led to a rejection of the Soviet model of urban industrial development. The PRC hardened its revolutionary line to contradict the Soviet policy of peaceful coexistence. Because of the remnants of China's traditional worldview, such a split might have been inevitable in any case, with the Chinese finding it impossible to accept second place in the global communist hierarchy. As early as 1964, China reportedly offered the Vietnamese an assistance package in excess of US $1,000 million per year if the Vietnamese would refuse further Soviet aid.[25] The doctrine of "wars of national liberation" announced in September 1965 was an indirect criticism of Vietnam's increasing reliance on the Soviet's more sophisticated military program.[26] When the Soviet Union replaced the United States in Vietnam, the division between the PRC and the USSR deepened.

The Rise of Regional Powers and Multipolarity

Détente between the United States and the Soviet Union introduced sufficient flexibility to the global system to enable other states to prosper. In reality, there had always been some flexibility in the system, which various states had sought to exploit. A bloc of states, seeking to avoid bipolar entanglements, forged the Non-Aligned Movement in 1961. Although it provided an important forum for many Third World states, it did not develop sufficient political capacity to influence the global agenda or otherwise compete with the superpowers. Ironically, the greatest challenges to the bipolar nature of the global political system came not from politics or political movements but from the economic sector, as global economic growth, international trade, and international investment began to supplant the politics of ideology as the primary moving forces in global interaction. Japan's rise as a global economic power without comparable military strength remained unique, but a resurgent Germany led the rest of Europe into a major economic rebirth. The Middle Eastern and other oil-producing states created a commodity cartel, the Organization of Petroleum Exporting Countries (OPEC), that gave them considerable global influence.

The Non-Aligned Movement

The Non-Aligned Movement did not take shape until the 1961 Belgrade Conference. Prior to that time a number of states had individually articulated foreign policies of nonalignment or neutrality vis-à-vis the bipolar blocs. Many of these states were former colonies and had much in common. Most had met for the first time at the 1955 Bandung Conference, but this conference, which included all of the newly independent states of Asia and Africa—some of which were strongly aligned with a superpower bloc—did not signal the birth of the non-aligned movement. Egypt, Yugoslavia, and India under Nassar, Tito, and Nehru, respectively, played leading roles in the formation of the Non-Aligned Movement.

Nonalignment is often confused with neutrality, but the two are not synonymous. Traditional neutrality is recognized as a *legal* status and not simply a policy position.

> Neutrality was a passive, isolationist policy of non-involvement and generally was practiced by stable, established states. . . . Neutrality involved abstention from all conflicts, whereas non-alignment only involves abstention from the cold war. Non-alignment has not implied neutrality in the anti-colonial struggle nor in conflicts between the developing and the developed nations. . . . Non-alignment is a policy of new states that are still involved in a search for their identity. It rejects the claim that the cold war is everybody's business and rejects the attempt to impose alien ideas. It is mainly due to ideological pressure coming from the bloc leaders and the need to develop a coherent and distinct reply that non-alignment could not remain a policy but itself had to develop into an ideology.[27]

Nonaligned states were primary targets of superpower influence and manipulations. The United States fairly aggressively pursued a policy demanding that all states make a commitment to the cold war blocs, whereas the Soviet Union was more inclined to interpret nonalignment more favorably and gave verbal and material support more freely to nonaligned states in an effort to improve state-to-state relations and to ensure that these states would remain outside the Western orbit.[28] For its part the Non-Aligned Movement—although successful in influencing some issues at the United Nations, in providing verbal and policy positions to enable participating states to remain removed from the cold war, and in keeping the anticolonial political agenda alive even in the face of the cold war—was unable to take command of the global political agenda or even to influence its direction. The greatest weakness of the movement was that because most of its members were newly independent, internally instabile, and economically underdeveloped, it could not translate its goals into effective policies in order to affect the global political agenda. Yet it did provide a measure of security in numbers to better withstand the pressures brought by bloc leaders to adhere to one of the poles throughout the duration of the cold war.

From the beginning the Non-Aligned Movement was weakened by the disparate interests of its member states, many of which found common ground only in their desire to maintain independence of action between the superpower alignments. With the collapse of the Soviet Union, the Non-Aligned Movement faced the loss of its raison d'être. However, in recent years it has shifted its focus to other concerns, and under Indonesia's leadership has been "brought back from the brink of irrelevance to make significant contributions to the debate on global economic issues."[29]

Japan

Japanese foreign policy since that country's defeat in World War II has been dominated by its relationship with the United States. The U.S. constitutional prescription for Japan—that it not redevelop a military capacity—meant Japan played no role in power politics. Yet under U.S. protection and despite the presence of hostile neighbors in China and the former Soviet Union, Japan remains the only state in modern history to develop as a global actor on the basis of its economic capacities without a similar military capacity. Japan's future as a military power remains a regional foreign policy issue of considerable importance, but Japan has survived for the fifty years since World War II without such capacity. More important, it experienced tremendous economic growth in the essentially hostile bipolar global political environment.

Japan entered the twentieth century as the single Asian model for modernization. Its rising industrial capacities and its defeat of the Imperial Russian naval fleet in 1905 demonstrated that European powers were not invincible. Yet their language, cultural introversion, and lack of access to the core of Southeast Asian intellectuals prevented the Japanese from achieving leadership in the growing anticolonial and national independence movements. As militarism increased in the 1930s, the Japanese challenged non-Asian privileges in China; when they entered Southeast Asia after the outbreak of World War II, they were received as liberators by many. Disillusionment followed, with the harsh realities of war and Japanese exploitation, but the Japanese also took steps to strengthen independence movements, to provide basic military training for much of the local population, and (as defeat neared) to establish independent governments to ward off the return of European colonial powers. But overall, the legacy of these experiences did not leave Japan in a strong position in Southeast Asia.

After the war and throughout the 1950s, when Japan as well as the new states of Southeast Asia were rebuilding their domestic economies, Japan took little cohesive action in the region. War reparations were paid to some states, and Japan began to "build [its] position in Southeast Asia on the basis of economic diplomacy,"[30] but aggressive corporate economic investment did not begin until early in the 1960s.

Japan's primary foreign policy goals were and remain intimately linked to its commercial policies, especially the search for trade in raw materials and hard currency. In effect, Japan has hidden behind the U.S. alliance while "enlarging overseas contacts for the purpose of maximizing economic well-being."[31] This trade orientation gave Japanese policy a dual focus: The industrial states of the West were the market zone, whereas Asia and particularly Southeast Asia became raw materials zones and, more recently, manufacturing zones. For example, after the Thais approved policies to induce local investment of foreign capital in 1963, Japan's share of Thailand's auto market rose from approximately 10 percent to more than 80 percent in less than ten years.[32] This pattern was repeated with numerous products throughout the region. By the late 1960s, nearly two-thirds of Japan's private investments in Asia and three-quarters of its foreign aid for Asia were directed to Southeast Asia.[33] Although Southeast Asia remained less important to Japan than Western countries, oil-producing countries, or China, Taiwan, and Korea, Japanese investments there have been heavy. Geographically—located on China's southern flank and astride the sea lanes that carry Middle Eastern oil—the region is very important to Japan.

Growing economic imbalances between Japan and Southeast Asia had important political consequences for both the region and for the future of Japan's relations and investments there. Japanese investment policies and practices also did little to create a positive image. Although shrewd economic and business practices were the hallmark of Japanese corporations, the Japanese lacked skill at interpersonal-intercultural relations, demonstrated a limited appreciation of the still growing nationalist feelings, and exhibited an overall unwillingness to accept local responsibility for personal or corporate development. These traits and behaviors alienated Southeast Asians. For example, Japanese businesspeople sought the best local business expertise, but such expertise was invariably found in the Chinese community, a group already resented by the local population. Japanese corporate policies for introducing local management remained limited; they retained rigid fiscal control so that spillover to the local economy was minimal; and their rigid demeanor and strict business practices alienated the more ebullient Southeast Asians, thereby leaving an impression—rightly or wrongly—of exploitation.

The frustration of this real and imagined exploitation continues to stimulate anti-Japanese feelings and occasional demonstrations. Widespread demonstrations took place in 1974 when Japanese Prime Minister Kakuei Tanaka toured Southeast Asia. He was greeted by student riots, first in Thailand and then in Indonesia. These outbreaks of violence, although they had local as well as anti-Japanese overtones, stirred debate in Japan about its role in Southeast Asia and its seeming inability to relate to other Asians.

This debate resulted in a series of policies aimed at countering the negative image. In 1977, Japanese Prime Minister Takeo Fukuda attended the second Association of Southeast Asian Nations (ASEAN) summit meeting in Kuala Lumpur, where he stressed the need for Japan to develop closer personal and cultural understandings and to support ASEAN's economic security plans.[34] This was followed by a policy statement that became known as the Fukuda Doctrine for Southeast Asia and that aimed to (1) establish relationships of mutual trust and confidence, (2) guarantee Japan's policy of nonmilitarism, and (3) offer Japan's "good offices" in stabilizing Indochina and ASEAN relationships. The doctrine also included nearly US $3 billion in assistance and loans for ASEAN industrial and development projects.

The Fukuda Doctrine represented a high point in Japan's Southeast Asian policy, but overall it brought little change in Japanese–Southeast Asian relations. Although the fault did not lie primarily with the Japanese, few of the ASEAN development projects were successful. The ASEAN states also remained suspicious of Japan's overtures toward Vietnam, fearing increased activities there would draw Japanese resources away from them and strengthen Vietnamese military capacities.[35]

Japan has become more engulfed in global issues and has sought to define a global leadership role for itself. Its policy definitions remain obscure and its actions are limited, but three issues have been central to Japan's nascent global position: (1) to ensure global peace and security, (2) to respect freedom and democracy, and (3) to guarantee world prosperity through open-market economics. A second policy debate for Japan has focused on the value of its bilateral relationship with the United States versus its growing range of relationships with other Asian states.[36] It is unclear how these policy goals are to be achieved and, particularly, how Japan is going to lead any global system to these goals. Moreover, as Japan has faced domestic political and economic problems of its own, concerns with global leadership have lagged.

As a policy, broader Pacific Basin cooperation has also drawn Japan's attention away from the narrower focus of Southeast Asia. Japan's image in Asia has improved in recent decades as its industrial structure has continued to adapt to the wider region, in effect integrating the region's economies. Japan's stronger position in the broader Asian economy "reflects the attraction of power, an increasingly sensitive Japanese diplomacy, Japan's promise as a source of needed capital and technology, and growing annoyance with U.S. foreign economic policies."[37] Malaysia and Thailand have welcomed this more prominent Japanese role; on the other hand, U.S. pressures for Japan to increase its military capabilities were not well received in Southeast Asia.

Japanese economic domination in Southeast Asia will continue, regardless of whether it is made more or less palatable with development assistance or with changes in Japanese personal or official behavior. Japan has also taken steps to open a dialogue with ASEAN states on security issues. The states of Southeast Asia have been better able to deal with Japan collectively, as ASEAN has demonstrated, but they must recognize that they remain vulnerable to economic penetration.

With the end of the cold war, new questions have arisen about the relationships between Japan and both the United States and Japan's other primary economic partners, including Southeast Asia. Talk of Japanese leadership is common, and questions about a rising Asian regional market led by Japan resound. However, Japanese concepts of leadership do not encourage quick change; rather, leadership emerges slowly. Moreover, Japanese leadership has been slowed by its uncertainty concerning the global environment: "The relative stability of the cold war has been supplanted by a diffuse security environment that is in many ways more dangerous . . . [enhancing the] Japanese sense of uncertainty and foreboding."[38] Thus far, although Japan's international participation has grown rapidly, it is mostly commercial and routine in nature. Moreover, Japan remains highly ambivalent about many issues surrounding global leadership; these include the unsettled view of Japan's accountability for militarist activities in Asia during World War II; the breakdown of the domestic political consensus and continuing resignations and humiliations of leading politicians because of corruption charges; and the issue of global leadership, including a permanent seat on the United Nations Security Council. These issues, particularly the intensity of domestic opinion concerning them, suggest that Japan has not yet found a comfortable image of itself as global political (as opposed to economic) leader and, consequently, is not ready to step forward with confidence to play a specific global role.

Europe and the Economic Community

Among the former colonial powers, the Dutch and the French were particularly determined to reestablish their colonial authority, despite revolutionary opposition from indigenous nationalist forces. The British were less vigorously challenged in Malaya and Singapore, although Burmese relations were more difficult. But once the issue of independence for the colonies had been settled, these European states devoted most of their energies to rebuilding their own economies and strengthening the U.S.-led and European-focused NATO alliance system.

From the beginning these European states played important roles in the global international system, despite its bipolar construction. Western Europe, much weakened by the war, clearly understood the implications of a communist victory for their mostly socialist systems. Contrary to the common view that the United States dominated and manipulated the global system, including Europe, some Europeans saw the United States quite differently:

> Far from seeing President Truman . . . as an anti-Soviet zealot hustling a reluctant Europe into a gratuitous cold war, the [British] Foreign Office saw him for a considerable period as an irresolute waffler distracted by the delusion that the United States could play mediator between Britain and the Soviet Union. Ernest Bevin, Britain's Socialist foreign secretary, thought Truman's policy was to "withdraw from Europe and in effect leave the British to get on with the Russians as best they could."[39]

Yet on balance, policy initiatives the United States took for Europe—the Truman Doctrine, the Marshall Plan, and the North Atlantic Treaty Organization—were essential for the future of Europe because they "restored self-confidence among the Europeans . . . [and] preserved the idea of freedom in Europe by a narrow and precarious margin at a time when Europeans themselves, reeling from the effects of two world wars, had almost given up on it."[40] Europeans clearly understood the Soviet plan for Eastern Europe and invited the United States to create and support a balancing force: "Compared to the alternative, American hegemony—for there is no denying that such a thing did develop—definitely seemed the lesser of two evils."[41]

Europe set about its own rebuilding process, aided in its economic rebuilding through the U.S. Marshall Plan and shielded from the Soviet Union by the United States through the NATO alliance. Nationalism played an important role in this redevelopment, and some states were able to reestablish relations with former colonies. The French were not driven from Vietnam until 1954 and had little input there after that until the collapse of Vietnam's communist benefactor, the Soviet Union, forced Vietnam to seek accommodation with other states. The British were successful in maintaining close relations with Malaysia and Singapore, to the economic benefit of both, but the Burmese remain less receptive to any outside contacts. Dutch relations with Indonesia improved considerably during the 1970s but have faltered again over human rights issues, especially concerning the Indonesian takeover of East Timor.

Along with Japan, the economic strength of Europe led by Germany grew to rival that of the United States; thus by the early 1970s the dominant position of the U.S. dollar as the single global reserve currency had ended, which forced the United States to drop its fixed-price policy for gold. The European Economic Community (EEC) combined the economic strength of its leading members—Germany, France, Britain, and Italy. Although the EEC was organized in 1957, nationalism and other barriers slowed its development for several decades. The EEC's goal remains to create a single market of sufficient size to compete globally, whereas individually its members would be disadvantaged. Despite delays in its development, the EEC represents a global market second in capacity only to the United States.

The collapse of the Soviet empire also changed the situation for the EEC. The unification of Germany raised that country's economic potential in a positive sense for EEC goals but also created concerns within the organization about German domination. In addition, other Eastern European states are eager to become members of the EEC, which could change the dynamics of the community entirely. At the end of the twentieth century, Europe is better positioned for global leadership than at any time since the early decades of the century.

The Organization of Petroleum Exporting Countries

In 1973, OPEC crashed onto the international scene and into the global system by announcing an embargo on the export of crude oil and raising prices to previously unheard-of levels. The result was severe economic disruption throughout the industrialized world, which had been constructed on the basis of very low-cost fuel and oil. For the fourteen members of OPEC—among Southeast Asian states only Indonesia is a member—every day seemed like Christmas as oil revenues filled state treasuries beyond imagine. OPEC demonstrated that a commodity cartel, under very specific conditions and with an essential commodity, could manipulate the system in its own interests. Superpower nuclear weapons were of very little value in meeting the OPEC challenge.

Indonesia, like many other OPEC members, became somewhat myopic about oil revenues and began to spend more than the cartel could generate even at the higher prices. By the late 1970s, demand for crude oil had shrunk because of the global recession and the introduction of new non-OPEC sources, particularly from Alaska and the North Sea, which had become feasible as sources because of the higher prices. Indonesia has subsequently broadened its economic base beyond crude oil, but there can be no question that the OPEC strategy—which was put together by a group of states typically outside the main power arenas of the global system—successfully used economic power to challenge the global political system in order to generate significantly higher revenues for petroleum-exporting states.

The OPEC strategy presented a major systemic economic and psychological challenge to the United States and the industrialized world. Although the United States and other industrial economies made the transition from low-cost energy to high-cost energy more smoothly and more rapidly than anticipated, at the time the effect on the U.S. global image in both the political and the economic spheres was unmistakable. OPEC forcefully demonstrated the rising power of economic factors over political or military factors in the increasingly interdependent global system.

China

From the late 1960s onward, the PRC and the Soviet Union found themselves increasingly in competition, particularly as the Chinese pressed their revolutionary ideological differences throughout Southeast Asia. During the war against the United States, Vietnam was careful to balance its relations with the Soviets and the Chinese while trying to maximize its own independent positions. Sihanouk in Cambodia was also able to manipulate Soviet interests to balance the Chinese, and Sukarno used the Soviet connection until it became too conservative after 1963, then vaulted to a closer relationship with China. The Burmese, although in many respects structurally and ideologically close to the Soviets, allowed them to play only a limited economic role and even less of an ideological role.[42] This transition in Sino-Soviet competition took place when the Chinese moved away from supporting insurgency movements and toward developing state relations, even with noncommunist states.

For centuries China has perceived Vietnam as a buffer state within its sphere of influence, protecting the southern flank. The Chinese view of Vietnam, part of China's age-old worldview, "contains the conviction that China has an *inherent right* to monitor the destinies of the peoples on its perimeter, those around the Middle Kingdom, and that these peoples have an *obligation* to defer to China."[43] The 1979 Chinese military incursion into Vietnam, a challenge to the Vietnamese invasion of Cambodia, was a gesture of support for China's Cambodian allies but was also an expression of Chinese frustration with the Soviet influence in Indochina, as historically the Chinese had taken military action to bring ungrateful vassals into line. In this case, the Vietnamese not only rejected China's ideological leadership but also had refused to acknowledge Chinese revolutionary support dating back to the 1940s. In addition, the 1979 border skirmishes were aimed at reestablishing China's premise that extraregional powers do not belong in Southeast Asia, but in reality, little changed: The Soviet Union was not dislodged from Vietnam, nor were the Vietnamese dislodged from Cambodia. Worse, China's military move into Vietnam demonstrated the weakness of its military threat, although it did place pressure on Vietnam's northern border. At the same time, the Soviet Union offered little protection to its ally, Vietnam, and the perceived value of Soviet protection declined in the aftermath of China's incursions. Vietnamese domination of Cambodia was unacceptable to China, and until the Vietnamese withdrew, China—at very little cost—was able to manipulate the situation in such a way as to add significantly to Hanoi's problems.[44]

Finally, as a counter to Soviet influence following its alliance with Vietnam, China came full circle and begai to focus on state-to-state relations, even with noncommunist governments and with states that maintained a U.S. presence. It reversed the radical revolutionary line it had initially developed in opposition to the Soviet Union in order to seek a new regional balance of power. China improved its links to the noncommunist ASEAN states, particularly Thailand—which, although for decades a prime target of China's revolutionary insurgency policy because of its conservative government and linkages to the United States—had become the frontline state against Vietnamese expansion through Cambodia. The fact that this support for the Thai monarchical regime came at the expense of the Communist Party of Thailand showed clearly that traditional balance-of-power politics carried more weight in Chinese policy formulation than did ideology. Burma received a great deal of attention as Beijing tried to counter Soviet influence on its southern flank.[45] Prime Minister Tun Abdul Razak in explaining Malaysia's lessening fear of Chinese-supported insurgents, observed that China wants "Southeast Asian goodwill and would prefer 'bourgeois' governments that were not hostile to it rather than radicals who could come under the influence of its arch-enemy, the Soviet Union."[46]

China has faced decades of frustration in Southeast Asia. The region provided opportunities for its global adversaries to maintain positions on

China's southern flank and to construct a strategic containment of China itself. On the regional level, China realized few successes among other communist groups and experienced several spectacular failures, most notably the destruction of Indonesia's PKI in 1965 and the ouster of the Khmer Rouge from Cambodia in January 1979. China has sometimes added to this frustration by supporting insurgency movements and taking ambivalent or inconsistent approaches to the ethnic Chinese living in Southeast Asia, but its policy of developing state-to-state contacts stabilized its relations with most states, lessened the fears and propensities of those states to rely on extraregional support, and isolated Vietnam in the region.

Collapse of the Soviet Union and the End of the Cold War

Transitions in the international system—from a tight bipolar system to the détente-supported loose bipolar system to the economically oriented multipolar system—represented changes in degree within essentially the same bipolar global structure. Throughout, the United States and the Soviet Union were the two strongest military powers in the world, and other states' abilities to successfully challenge either nation were determined more by the superpowers' lack of will than by these challengers' potential power. Even this bipolar system did not allow the superpowers to act uninhibitedly, and the American defeat in Vietnam and the Soviet defeat in Afghanistan demonstrated the limits of the superpowers' capacities to control events even when they used military force. It seemed at times that the superpowers were as much captives of their various client states as they were leaders of vast hegemonic alignments of states.

The collapse of the Soviet Union and the disintegration of the Warsaw Pact, which ended the cold war, also signaled the end of the bipolar system. Simply stated, no single state remained that had sufficient military power to challenge the United States, and although communism was sustained in some states—most notably the People's Republic of China—its global threat ended. Yet one factor often overlooked in considering the breakdown of the bipolar system is that much of the development of power during the cold war was economic rather than military, political, or ideological and that other states such as Japan and Germany survived the cold war perhaps stronger economically than the lone remaining superpower. It is ironic that even the United States, whose "military prowess [in the Gulf War] could not disguise the fact that Washington had to cajole and beg its allies to pay for the war effort," was left with an "image of a military giant with economic feet of clay."[47]

New Economic Powers

Long before the end of the cold war, it had become apparent that economic power, as much as or more than military power, was becoming a major determining factor in the global system. As military power became more lethal, the political will to use that lethal force diminished and global consensus emerged on the unacceptability of the use of extreme force. Ironically, this constraint severely limited the superpowers' abilities to police global conflicts; at the same time, it enabled conflicts to spread using conventional force which became more accurate and lethal with advanced technology but was not subject to global opposition as are nuclear weapons.

The United States may be the only remaining superpower in full command of a nuclear arsenal, but military forces in places such as Cambodia, Bosnia, and Rwanda have little fear of that arsenal's potential. At the same time, other states such as Japan, which has eschewed any military role; Germany, as the divided West Germany and now the unified Germany; Britain and France, as middle-ranking European economic powers; and a gaggle of rising Asian states including Taiwan, South Korea, Singapore, Malaysia, and Thailand (referred to collectively as newly industrializing countries, or NICs) have used their more demonstrative roles in international trade and commercial activities to give them a voice in global political issues as well. The cold war may be over, but many feel Germany and Japan won.[48]

The Islamic States

The global Islamic reawakening is focused primarily on domestic politics in many of these states. At the same time, however, Islam has a great deal to say about international relations, particularly relations among states in the community of faith. The Islamic resurgence may initially have been more a rejection of Western practices and values than a positive statement of an alternative model. Islamic revivalism has drawn great strength not only from the Iranian revolution in 1979 but also from the collapse of the Soviet Union in 1989, which freed the Muslims of Central Asia to again seek participation in the Islamic world. Turkey, Saudi Arabia, and Iran have made serious efforts to gain influence and leadership there. Revolutionary Islam has sought to use violence as a tool for achieving its antiestablishment or anti-Western goals, and some states have been willing to provide support for these activities.

Perhaps seeking to facilely create another monolithic adversary, many in the West see Islam as a highly unified global movement, but there are great divisions between fundamentalist groups who see Islam as an "unchanging medieval, patriarchal, rule-frozen structure" and the more liberal, modernizing, and secular groups.[49] But as more adherents of the revitalized Islam move into positions of power in more states, we should expect that they will seek a unity among states with similar outlooks and will also seek to assert their views and practices in the international system.

> On the global scene, Moslems must develop the confidence to become actors rather than passive spectators. . . . To begin, we should accept the reality of a pluralistic world. Within the Moslem world, pluralism is far from an alien concept. . . . Intellectual reconstruction, which can only be based on free expression, [is urgent]. . . . Only under the free flowering of the Moslem intellect can we jettison the rigid polemics and intolerance of thought and develop credibility with the rest of the world community. . . . We must develop the potential to construct and maintain an economic infrastructure which is self-reliant as well as globally competitive. Only on that basis can we begin to improve the living conditions of our people and provide them with the basic amenities of life. . . . Then we can realistically aspire to fulfill the moral imperative of Islam—the promotion of universal education, prudent management of resources, respect for basic human rights and fair distribution of wealth.[50]

Thus stated, Islam has undertaken a major revision of the world order. Islam's internal debate—between the fundamentalist or conservative view and the liberal view—will continue. In whatever form, Islamic revitalization has been accompanied by a new assertiveness and vigor in espousing Islam's values and beliefs and has focused on three principal issues: (1) the development of Islam as a total way of life, as contrasted with the narrower definition of a religion; (2) the recognition of the Islamic community as a global community despite political, ethnic, or cultural differences among its adherents; and (3) the creation of a variety of organizations to give expression to this revitalized belief system.[51] Whatever the outcome, its imperatives will be dramatic for the Islamic world and, potentially, for the entire world.

Substate Nationalist, Ethnic Nationalist, and Irredentist Movements

Ethnic and cultural cleavages have always been present in state construction and tend to become more visible in instabile times. Some international systems are more effective in managing these cleavages than others. For example, Southeast Asia's traditional vassal system allowed for continued maintenance of minority ethnic-cultural identities, whereas the current nation-state system requires that everyone within the state's boundaries pledge alliance and attach his or her primary identity to the state. Ironically, movements that in some times and places are considered heroic struggles for self-determination are seen at other times as ethnic cleansing or intertribal slaughter.

With the disintegration of the Soviet Union and its Eastern European empire, various forms of nationalism and ethnic cleavages reemerged, often in irredentist forms. Apparently, without the ideological overlay or authoritarian control provided by Soviet hegemony, these age-old hatreds gained new life: "Eastern Europe too has provided a rich literature of the experience of the 'small nations,' for whom singular 'Progress,' the march of 'History' and 'Reason' as defined from the point of view of Berlin or Moscow has meant subordination."[52] But former Soviet territories are not the only places in which nationalist and ethnic cleavages offer potential fractures and conflict in the international system.

A great deal of such ethnic, racial, and intercultural strife finds its roots in the European imperial period when colonies were created by fiat, sometimes binding ancient enemies under a single jurisdiction without concern for local interests or linguistic, economic, political, or cultural patterns. Wherever they occur, cultural, linguistic, and ethnic differences cause peoples to separate from each other and to label others as "outsiders" who are to be regarded with fear, suspicion, and hatred. And ethnic nationalism seems to become more militant when it is suppressed or threatened and often results "when irrational treaties cause significant numbers of one's people to live on the wrong side of the border."[53]

Ethnic nationalist movements will continue to express themselves violently, in part because the present international system does not provide effective mechanisms for relieving tensions or meeting separatist demands. The logic of the nation-state requires that it be sovereign within its boundaries, and no other nation-state can violate that logic with-out—at least by implication—calling into question its own structural logic. Internal state structures, such as federal systems, can offer some relief within the context of the state, but the primary approach remains violent revolutionary action that seeks independence and the creation of a new state in conformity with ethnic divisions and boundaries.

Russia

The new Russian state that emerged from the collapse of the Soviet Union can sustain little influence in Asia, particularly in Southeast Asia. Soviet influence had been largely military since its takeover of the former U.S. base at Cam Ranh Bay, its ideological influence having essentially been lost to various forms of Maoism. Russia has "abandoned former Soviet pretensions toward significant air and naval power capabilities" in

Asia, the former Soviet security agreement with Vietnam has no force, and "most of the Pacific Fleet is rusting in port, [with] only a token force remain[ing] in Vietnam's Cam Ranh Bay to show the flag."[54] The agreement on the use of Cam Ranh Bay remains intact, but the Russian navy has little hope of projecting significant force from there.

Russia's Asian interests—even more than those of the former Soviet Union—are limited by its traditional focus toward Europe, its geographic isolation from Southeast Asian economic growth areas, and a crumbling infrastructure that makes it nearly impossible to extend or sustain power and influence over such great distances. Whatever its capabilities, Russia does have serious interests in the future of Asia. Perhaps the most important and potentially most volatile of those interests is in China's continued economic growth and military development, particularly the possibility of an expanded Chinese Pacific naval capacity. Similarly, the potential for Japanese military development is a serious concern for Russia, given its continued interests in the Kurile Islands. Ironically, except in the case of China these military-strategic interests are not reflected in similar economic interests, which have been characterized as "stagnant" for Japan and "minuscule" for Southeast Asia.[55] Russian interests in Asia are now more parallel to those of the United States, but Russia has so little capacity to extend influence into the region that it will not be a significant factor in shaping the future of the region or in determining U.S. policies there.

U.S. Global Leadership Without a Foil?

The cold war was not supposed to end as it did. The Soviet Union was not supposed to collapse. From the early days of peaceful coexistence, both superpowers had inched toward an acceptance of the division of the world into respective spheres of influence. Much of the expected scenario included an increasing number of ever broader agreements on arms control and other thorny issues in order to diminish the potential for conflict, particularly conflict resulting from errors in communication or misunderstanding. But the U.S. adversary—the communist bloc (regardless of whether it was as monolithic as once thought)—remained in place, giving the United States an ideal and much needed amoral and atheistic whipping post through which to maintain consensus and assist in policy formation.

There are few remaining compelling security challenges facing the United States and, perhaps unfortunately, none as simple and simplistically compelling as a monolithic, communist authoritarian monster positioned to take over the world. Americans as a people are not well schooled in global politics and tend to remain comfortable in their own surroundings, in effect preferring the Holiday Inn and McDonald's even if they are in Paris or Hong Kong. At the same time, the U.S. vastness provides an insulation that gives global issues a surreal quality except to the extent that blood or suffering is seen on the evening news. Despite eloquent rhetoric to the contrary, the world remains a very far-off place for most Americans. They make few serious efforts to learn about or understand that world, although the average American is certain that (1) little money should be spent on things foreign, and (2) few or no U.S. soldiers should be put at risk to protect foreign interests, except on those occasions when Washington—in cooperation with the television news media—can successfully engender a "Rambo mentality" on Main Street.

Americans view themselves as a chosen people. From the earliest days of the republic, people in the United States have seen themselves as the *new* people, buttressed by a government founded on the highest political principles and sanctioned by the moral righteousness of reformed Christianity. Americans have often chosen to avoid the immoral and dirty world of global politics; on those occasions when U.S. involvement was required, it was always on the side of right, justice, and goodness in combatting the forces of evil, however construed.

With the global evil now not only vanquished but disintegrated, where does the United States anticipate identifying the next generation of evil forces? Can the United States articulate a coherent set of political goals, develop a supporting set of policies, and implement them without such a foil? The answers to these questions are not clear, but indications are not entirely positive. The engine that drove the United States through the cold war—the military and foreign policy bureaucracies as well as the military-industrial groups—still commands much of the U.S. policy-making apparatus. Moreover, during those periods in U.S. history when no compelling global target for moral certitude has been available, national or domestic partisan politics has taken over the definition of U.S. international political goals linking foreign policy closely to the ideological divisions between the Republican and Democratic political parties.

The United States is in no position to abandon its perspective on or commitment to global politics, although policies supporting its global position are less than clear. The world may continue to be hostile and disorderly, but few of the conflicts will involve issues of vital U.S. security interest; further, the United States has not yet come to consider economic issues as being as vital as security issues. During the Bush administration, global stability was central to foreign policy, "serv[ing] as the primary rationale for preserving Washington's network of increasingly obsolete and irrelevant cold war–era military alliances."[56] The second principle of the Bush administration's foreign policy was derived from the perspective of the United States as the sole remaining superpower to which the rest of the world should dutifully look for guidance and leadership. Even if this view were accurate for security issues (which it is not), it is certainly not true for economic issues. Unfortunately, U.S. policy remains mired in post–cold war security issues while the rest of the world is focusing increasingly on economic issues. Under the Clinton administration, foreign policy has had such secondary importance that policy has often been shaped in response to public pressure stimulated by the nightly newscasts of violence and human tragedy around the globe.

The alliance system developed to implement the Soviet-China containment policies cannot be sustained as a pretext for U.S. involvement in regional politics. It is critical for the United States to formulate its policies based on a full and clear understanding of the regional variables influencing any situation, even when global variables may ultimately determine the policy. However, before global policy goals are transferred directly to the regional level, their relationship to "basic cultural and philosophical values and experience and contemporary trends and developments"[57] must be understood and accounted for in policy prescriptions.

The United States can continue to play a leading role in international politics, but such leadership will not be automatic and cannot be assured. The diversity that is present in the post–cold war global system will require more sophisticated policies and a flexibility of response that belies many past foreign U.S. policy practices. Leadership will not emerge solely because the United States "won" the cold war nor because the world recognizes the inherent virtues of the American society and U.S. political system. In the new international environment, the United States must develop a new set of defense policies that do not waste economic resources or unnecessarily risk U.S. military forces, which will require a careful redefinition of America's vital interests as compared with important and lesser interests. In the context of these redefined interests, the United States should carefully review all of its international commitments and alliances with the goal of reducing them in order to increase decisionmaking flexibility and autonomy. Finally, the United States must carefully determine the limits for corporate—particularly military—action, recognizing its changed vital interests and the limits inherent in the will of the American people to sustain high-cost global projects.

The End of Hegemony

The cold war has ended, leaving one superpower in collapse and the other facing a crisis of economy and will that limits its capacities to act as the world's sole remaining superpower. As the cold war began to thaw, some states chose to focus resources on economic development rather than nuclear weapons development, leaving them in relatively strong positions at present but without sufficient power or influence to undertake any amplified hegemonic role.[58] Yet another group of states, having eschewed Western modernism, is revising the social contract between its peoples and governments using religious (Islamic) principles as its guide.

The global system at the close of the twentieth century will remain diverse. Greater expressions of interests will emerge—whether Islamic, ethnic nationalist, or Asian capitalist—to challenge the system's power managers. This greater diversity will enable the states of Southeast Asia to play a more independent and important role in the global system than would have been possible during the cold war. At the same time, this diversity will create a broader range of possible negative factors that are capable of attacking the state and the system at any time.

NOTES

1. Arthur Schlesinger Jr., "Some Lessons from the Cold War," in *The End of the Cold War, Its Meaning and Implications*, edited by Michael J. Hogan (Cambridge: Cambridge University Press, 1992), p. 54.

2. John Foster Dulles, "Manila Conference Address," U.S. Department of State, *Bulletin* 31 (1954), p. 432.

3. This phrase was popularized in a study that was highly critical of U.S. post–World War II foreign policy. See Ronald Steel, *Pax Americana* (New York: Viking Press, 1967); see also Amaury de Riencourt, *The American Empire* (New York: Dell Publishing Co., 1968).

4. John Lewis Gaddis, "The Cold War, the Long Peace, and the Future," in Hogan, *The End of the Cold War*, p. 21.

5. Malcolm Mackintosh, "Soviet Interests and Policies in the Asia-Pacific Region," *Orbis* 19 (Fall 1975), p. 764.

6. Evelyn Colbert, *Southeast Asia in International Politics, 1941–1956* (Ithaca: Cornell University Press, 1977), pp. 116–117.

7. John F. Cady, *The United States and Burma* (Cambridge: Harvard University Press, 1976), pp. 196–197.

8. Colbert, *Southeast Asia in International Politics*, p. 83.

9. Roy Allison, *The Soviet Union and the Strategy of Non-Alignment in the Third World* (Cambridge: Cambridge University Press, 1988), pp. 21–22.

10. Robert C. Horn, "Soviet Influence in Southeast Asia: Opportunities and Obstacles," *Asian Survey* 15 (August 1975), p. 660.

11. Allison, *The Soviet Union and the Strategy of Non-Alignment*, p. 84.

12. Vernon V. Aspaturian, "The Foreign Policy of China," in *World Politics*, edited by James N. Rosenau, Kenneth W. Thompson, and Gavin Boyd (New York: Free Press, 1976), p. 85.

13. W. Raymond Duncan and Carolyn McGiffert Ekedahl, *Moscow and the Third World Under Gorbachev* (Boulder: Westview Press, 1990), p. 45.

14. Donald E. Weatherbee, "The United States in Southeast Asia: Continuity and Discontinuity," paper presented at the International Studies Association meeting, Cincinnati, Ohio, March 1982, p. 4.

15. Melvin A. Goodman, "Introduction," in *The End of Superpower Conflict in the Third World* edited by Melvin A. Goodman (Boulder: Westview Press, 1992), p. 7.

16. R. A. Longmire, *Soviet Relations with South-East Asia* (London: Kegan Paul International, 1989), pp. 49–50.

17. Allison, *The Soviet Union and the Strategy of Non-Alignment*, p. 84.

18. *Ibid.*, p. 133.

19. Donald S. Zagoria and Sheldon W. Simon, "Soviet Policy in Southeast Asia," in *Soviet Policy in East Asia*, edited by Donald S. Zagoria (New Haven: Yale University Press, 1982), p. 153.

20. Duncan and Ekedahl, *Moscow and the Third World Under Gorbachev*, pp. 154–159.

21. See John K. Fairbank, *The People's Middle Kingdom and the U.S.A.* (Cambridge: Belknap Press of Harvard University Press, 1967), p. 46. See also Udo Weiss, "Imperial China's Tributary Trade and the Foreign Trade Policy of the People's Republic of China: A Comparison of Attitudes," *Asian Quarterly* 1 (Bruxelles, 1976), n.p.

22. Melvin Gurtov, *China and Southeast Asia—The Politics of Survival* (Lexington: Heath Lexington Books, 1971), p. 167.

23. Robert C. North, *The Foreign Relations of China* (Belmont, Calif.: Dickenson Publishing Co., 1969), p. 122.

24. Shao-chuan Leng, "Chinese Strategy Toward the Asian Pacific," *Orbis* 19 (Fall 1975), p. 776.

25. Roland-Pierre Paringaux, "The Indochinese Power Seesaw," *The Guardian* (October 29, 1978), n.p., cited in Chan Heng Chee, "The Interests and Role of ASEAN in the Indochina Conflict," in *Indochina and the Problems of Security and Stability in Southeast Asia*, edited by Khien Theeravit and MacAlister Brown (Bangkok: Chulalongkorn University Press, 1981), p. 188.

26. D. R. Sardesai, "Vietnam's Quest for Security," in *Changing Patterns of Security and Stability in Asia*, edited by Sudarshan Chawla and D. R. Sardesai (New York: Praeger Publishers, 1980), p. 225.

27. Peter Willetts, *The Non-Aligned Movement: The Origins of a Third World Alliance* (London: Frances Pinter, 1978), p. 20.

28. Allison, *The Soviet Union and the Strategy of Non-Alignment*, pp. 33–35.

29. Andrew MacIntyre, "Indonesia in 1993, Increasing Political Movement?" *Asian Survey* 34 (February 1994), p. 118.

30. Russell H. Fifield, *The Diplomacy of Southeast Asia* (New York: Praeger Publisher, 1958), p. 83.

31. Donald C. Hellmann, *Japan and East Asia: The New International Order* (New York: Praeger Publishers, 1972), p. 61.

32. Reijiro Toba, "Japan's Southeast Asia Policy in the Last Decade," *Asia Pacific Community* 19 (Winter 1982), pp. 30–43.

33. Sheldon Simon, "East Asia," in Rosenau, Thompson, and Boyd, *World Politics*, pp. 534–535.

34. William W. Haddad, "Japan, the Fukuda Doctrine, and ASEAN," *Contemporary Southeast Asia* 2 (June 1980), pp. 10–29.

35. Guy Sacerdoti, "A Doctrine of Suspicion," *Far Eastern Economic Review* (September 11, 1981), p. 36.

36. Eugene Brown, "Japanese Security Policy in the Post–Cold War Era," *Asian Survey* 34 (May 1994), p. 431.

37. Danny Unger, "Japan's Capital Exports: Molding East Asia," in *Japan's Emerging Global Role*, edited by Danny Unger and Paul Blackburn (Boulder: Lynne Rienner Publishers, 1993), pp. 164–165.

38. Brown, "Japanese Security Policy in the Post–Cold War Era," p. 432.

39. Schlesinger, "Some Lessons from the Cold War," citing Alan Bullock, *Ernest Bevin: Foreign Secretary, 1945–1951* (London, 1983), p. 216, in Hogan, *The End of the Cold War*, p. 60.

40. Gaddis, "The Cold War, the Long Peace, and the Future," in Hogan, *The End of the Cold War*, p. 27.

41. *Ibid.*

42. Horn, "Soviet Influence in Southeast Asia," pp. 662–663, 667.

43. Douglas A. Pike, *War, Peace, and the Viet Cong* (Cambridge: MIT Press, 1969), p. 36. Emphasis added.

44. John F. Copper, "China and Southeast Asia," in *Southeast Asia Divided: The ASEAN-Indochina Crisis*, edited by Donald E. Weatherbee (Boulder: Westview Press, 1985), p. 61.

45. Edwin W. Martin, "Burma in 1975: New Dimensions to Non-Alignment," *Asian Survey* 16 (February 1976), p. 173.

46. "Malaysia: Foreign Relations," *Asia 1974 Yearbook* (Hong Kong: Far Eastern Economic Review, 1975), p. 211.

47. Ted Galen Carpenter, "Strategic Independence," *New Perspectives Quarterly* 9 (Summer 1992), pp. 20–21.

48. Robert Gilpin, "The Debate About the New Economic Order," in Unger and Blackburn, *Japan's Emerging Global Role*, p. 24.

49. Michael M.J. Fischer, "Is Islam the Odd-Civilization Out?" *New Perspectives Quarterly* 9 (Spring 1992), p. 54.

50. Anwar Ibrahim, "Moslems Must Stop Blaming Their Problems on the West," *New Perspectives Quarterly* 8 (Summer 1991), p. 65.

51. Hussin Mutalib, "Islamic Revivalism in ASEAN States," *Asian Survey* 30 (September 1990), pp. 878–879.

52. Fischer, "Is Islam the Odd-Civilization Out?" p. 55.

53. Andrew Oldenquist, "The Case for Ethnic Nationalism," paper presented at the Mershon Center, The Ohio State University, Columbus, Ohio, January 1994, p. 6.

54. Charles E. Ziegler, "Russia in the Asia-Pacific, A Major Power or Minor Participant?" *Asian Survey* 34 (June 1994), pp. 532, 534.

55. *Ibid.*, pp. 537, 539.

56. Carpenter, "Strategic Independence," p. 20.

57. Norman D. Palmer, "The United States and the Security of Asia," in Chawla and Sardesai, *Changing Patterns of Security and Stability in Asia*, p. 139.

58. Deborah L. Haber, "The Death of Hegemony: Why 'Pax Nipponica' Is Impossible," *Asian Survey* 30 (September 1990), pp. 892–905.

9

Foreign Policy in the Bipolar World

At independence, the states of Southeast Asia, with the exception of Thailand, were led by elites that had little international experience or training in diplomacy and few defined national interests to guide them. The tenets of the European interstate system, first introduced to Southeast Asia through colonial conquest, provided the framework for a tightly structured global system governed by protocol, ideology, and power. The loosely connected regional systems that had formed the precolonial international commercial system were gone, and the Chinese imperial system that anchored the Asian end of the interlinked regional commercial subsystems had collapsed early in the twentieth century under pressure from Europeans and Americans. In the new global multistate system, each state was viewed as sovereign within its territory and as equal among others internationally, concepts that were significantly different from those of traditional systems. Southeast Asian leaders adapted to the confusing, protocol-controlled diplomatic system with little difficulty, drawing policies from their experience in shaping statehood but finding it necessary to mold foreign policy responses to demands and pressures from the increasingly hostile, polarized, and aggressive global system actors.

Foreign Policies in the New Era of Independence, 1945–1957

Among states in which independence was strongly contested by former colonial powers, competing nationalist elites, or ethnic groups seeking separate statehood, initial foreign policies became extensions of their domestic revolutions. Seeking international recognition and diplomatic and material support, leaders adopted often simplistic and moralist international postures that emphasized freedom, independence, and democracy. Yet support from the global system for the independence of former colonies was scant; most major world powers were hostile or ambivalent, a fact that stimulated moral indignation among the Southeast Asian elites.

Early postindependence foreign policies were often conditioned by the actions of returning colonial powers. Most obviously in Burma, Indonesia, and Vietnam, conflicts with former European metropoles prompted policies that rejected political alignments with former colonial powers. Burma—although not forced to fight a war of independence—rejected relations with the British, demurring on membership in the British Commonwealth and developing a foreign policy of active neutrality. Indonesia, because of its revolutionary struggle against the Dutch, vigorously repudiated policies of alignment with the Netherlands and the Western bloc. Vietnam, the most extreme case, rejected the West entirely and allied itself ideologically with the communist world. Recent experiences with colonial practices had made these states rightfully wary of further major-power domination.

The Philippines, Malaysia, and Singapore acquired independence under friendlier terms and were quicker to cooperate and to ally themselves with former colonial powers. The Philippines welcomed returning U.S. forces and remained firmly aligned with the United States, providing sites for two major military bases and joining SEATO in 1954. The Federation of Malaya (Malaysia after 1963) linked its foreign policy closely with that of Britain, as did Singapore in 1965; both states maintained defense agreements with the British. Thailand's foreign policy was continuous because it had avoided colonization but had moved closer to the United States as the conflict in Indochina expanded. Thailand became the second regional member of SEATO in 1954. Cambodia and Laos maintained foreign policies of neutrality, which was established by the Geneva agreements of 1954 and the Zürich agreements of 1961, respectively.

Few Southeast Asian states pursued policies of cooperation or even frequent communication with regional neighbors. Their varying colonial experiences had linked them to disparate European metropoles, providing the elites with widely divergent educational experiences and outlooks on global politics. Also, traditional foreign policy behavior provided few examples of regional cooperation. Although developing good relations with immediate neighbors was one of Indonesia's first publicly outlined foreign policy goals,[1] there was little precedent on which to build such relations.

The traditional centrist view of the state governed the perceptions with which leaders dealt with other states. Domestic power in traditional, as well as the contemporary, centrist systems extended from the center—literally, the capital—and reached only as far as military force could be sustained, which significantly influenced elite perceptions and foreign policy implementation. Most of these states were still economic and, at times, ideological competitors, and their competitive stances strengthened links to states and movements outside the region.

Economic competition among Southeast Asian states traditionally involved exports of kapok, pepper and spices, quinine, copra, palm oil, tin, and rubber. Rice, as the dietary staple of the region, was in sufficient demand in some states to take up most of the surplus produced in others. Contemporary states have also searched competitively for foreign capital, and petroleum became a surplus commodity for some and a deficit for others.

At independence, Vietnam (first North Vietnam) was the only regional state to establish a communist government. Indonesia, by contrast, moved through three different ideological periods but has always entertained concepts of its own leadership role in the archipelago, if not the entire region. Burma and Cambodia, as well as Indonesia, played prominent roles in the Non-Aligned Movement during the 1960s, but their mutual interests in nonalignment had little impact regionally. U Nu of Burma, Sihanouk of Cambodia, and Sukarno of Indonesia were preoccupied instead with the global stage.

Early foreign policies were largely the prerogative of the governmental elites and were dominated by strong charismatic leaders such as Sukarno and Sihanouk, who kept competing elite groups off balance in order to broaden their own latitude in foreign policymaking,[2] which remained the personal domain of premiers, presidents, dictators, and other leaders, who often shaped foreign policy to fit the needs of their continuing domestic revolutions as they saw them. By contrast, Thailand's foreign ministry had a longer tradition and greater expertise, which gave a bureaucratic perspective to foreign policy. Public opinion among all of these newly independent states played a very limited role in foreign policy, except when mass demonstrations orchestrated by or against the government were occasionally successful in influencing foreign policy.

Responses to the Cold War and Global Bipolarity, 1950–1970

Southeast Asian states looked out on an increasingly hostile world as they developed foreign policy positions, so that "from 1945 to the early 1960s, most decisions and actions of the major Asian statesmen were responses to the cold war conflict between Washington and Moscow."[3] As the world became increasingly polarized, policy options narrowed. An alignment with either the communist or the Western bloc meant the end of meaningful relations with the other. The United States manipulated foreign assistance incentives in order to attract support, whereas the Soviet Union stimulated rebellions to replace conservative governments with communist regimes. States that braved nonaligned policies found some latitude between the two blocs as well as some issue-by-issue flexibility, and each superpower contributed some foreign assistance in hopes of winning the allegiance of these states.

The Philippines: Joining the Bipolar System

The Philippines found it easy to align with the United States. Former colonial status and disagreements on both economic relations and postwar compensatory payments did impart a negative cast to bilateral relations between the two countries, but Philippine support for U.S. leadership was strong at the global and regional levels. Manila's frustration was focused primarily on the U.S. Congress, in which war compensation claims were delayed for years and various trade quotas and other economic restrictions were initiated.

Despite the U.S. failure to protect the Philippines against the Japanese, the Filipinos quickly moved back under the U.S. wing—joining SEATO as a founding member, providing military facilities for U.S. naval and air forces, contributing troops to the U.S. effort in Vietnam, and for years supporting the United States on the issue of UN membership for Taiwan and opposing PRC membership. Philippine foreign policy was governed by staunch anticommunist views, as was seen when the Philippines advocated SEATO action in Laos in 1961.[4] Filipino anticommunism was also strengthened by elements of "Sino-phobia."[5] Throughout most of the 1950s and 1960s, Philippine foreign policy was "a mirror image of American policy," best interpreted as "American policy with a lag-time of five to ten years."[6]

The closeness of the Philippine-U.S. relationship also set the tone for Philippine foreign policy with respect to Southeast Asia. As late as April 1949, the Philippines had established formal relations in Asia only with the Republic of China (Taiwan). To shed its image as the client of a non-Asian state, from the early 1950s the Philippines attempted to cultivate closer ties with Asians, and by 1963, "for the first time since independence, the Philippines' relations with Asia . . . became more important than [its] relations with the West."[7] Filipino policies began to contradict U.S. positions, as when Manila—which had always been outspoken against colonialism—gave strong support to Indonesia's struggle to claim Irian Jaya.

The Philippines also sought closer relations with Indonesia as a way of confirming its Asianness. The regional organization MAPHILINDO (a confederation composed of *Ma*laysia, the *Phil*ippines, and *Indo*nesia) was an attempt to link the Philippines directly to Indonesia and Malaysia, key states in the Malay world. The Filipino strategy for MAPHILINDO was also designed to contain Malaysia's diplomatic and political pressure against Philippine designs on Sabah, part of Malaysia's North Borneo territory. Manila claimed part of Sabah as successor to the old Sulu sultanate and demanded that the claim be resolved by the World Court. The Philippine claims to Sulu originated with claims of the heirs of the last Sulu sultan, which had long interested Diosdado Macapagal. As president of the Philippines, he saw some domestic political value in the Sulu claims, particularly in raising Filipinos' awareness that they were part of the Malay world.[8] As a foreign policy issue, the Sulu claim offered an opportunity for the Philippines to separate itself from the United States, although it challenged another tenet of Filipino foreign policy—development of closer ties to Southeast Asia. The claim was put forward with varying intensity from 1961 until 1968, when it became apparent that it had severely inhibited the Filipino transition to an Asian foreign policy.

Filipino concern for its Asian identity was strong and stemmed from the successive, intensive Spanish and U.S. colonial experiences that obliterated much of their indigenous cultural identity. Filipino writers and historians have made considerable effort to find links to archipelago Southeast Asia's precolonial past—for example, identifying links to Indonesia during the Śrīvijayan period. Others have described great Muslim kingdoms located in the southern Philippines. The Sulu claims served to reinforce these perspectives.

Throughout the 1950s and especially in the 1960s, there was a dualism in Philippine foreign policy based on the felt need to establish stronger economic ties within Southeast Asia while recognizing that the United States remained the principal source of the country's economic and security support. This extraregional link was often disdained by other Asian states; moreover, on several occasions it brought with it certain policies, such as Philippine support for Indonesia's confrontation with Malaysia, that did little to serve long-range Philippine interests.

Malaysia: Maintaining the British Connection

Malaysia found it easy to sustain links to the British and chose to participate in the British Commonwealth. Its principal security concern, which stemmed from a twelve-year communist insurgency, was addressed through a mutual defense and assistance treaty signed with the British in 1957. Economic links to Britain remained strong, but Malaysia became anxious about possible British entry into the EEC and the potential negative effects on Malaysian exports of palm oil, rubber, and tin.

Malaysia also tried to maintain some measure of an independent foreign policy by limiting the ability of the British to use military forces stationed in Malaysia to support such organizations as SEATO, even though its strong anticommunist views had placed Malaysia among the first countries to provide technical support to South Vietnam after the fall of the French.[9] Under Tunku Abdul Rahman's leadership, Malaysia took other independent stances: It strongly criticized South Africa's policies of apartheid, supported China's claim for UN membership, and opposed such military interventions as the Soviet move into Hungary and the Chinese takeover of Tibet. Despite this mix of policies, Malaysia's firm links to the British and its strong anticommunist policies made it difficult for the country to sustain its position in the Non-Aligned Movement, as in 1965 when it feared it would not be seated at the Algiers conference of nonaligned powers.[10]

Malaysia's territorial integrity became a major foreign policy issue when Indonesia challenged the addition of North Borneo and Sarawak in the formation of the Federation of Malaysia, describing the new state as a British neocolonial creation. At the same time, the Philippines pushed its claim to North Borneo. In seeming contradiction, these three states cooperated to form the short-lived, Malay-oriented regional organization MAPHILINDO until Malaysia severed diplomatic relations with both Jakarta and Manila in 1963. Within two years of Malaysia's formation, a new foreign policy issue arose when Singapore separated from Malaysia. Except for the dispute with the Philippines over North Borneo, these conflicts had been resolved by 1967 when Malaysia and its neighbors formed ASEAN.

After the confrontation with Indonesia had ended and ASEAN had been formed in the late 1960s, Malaysia began to move away from its relationship with the British. Relations with the Soviet Union expanded after 1967, when several trade missions were exchanged, and diplomatic relations were established in 1968. By 1970, having brought its domestic insurgency under control and having settled its differences with its neighbors, Malaysia was prepared to step into the global arena with less concern about the protective blanket of the British military.

Singapore: British Support for Economic Growth

Singapore's foreign policy has been linked closely to that of Malaysia. It obtained self-government in 1959, but foreign affairs and defense remained under British control, and Singapore was the primary base for support of the British-Malaya defense agreement. After two years as part of the Federation of Malaysia (1963–1965), Singapore found itself independent and isolated—a reincarnation of the traditional Malaccan entrepôt center but without the coercive power to control the economic and political future of the region. Moreover, its largely Chinese population located in the midst of the ethnic Malay archipelago left it isolated and regarded with considerable suspicion by its neighbors.[11]

Singapore broke this isolation in 1966–1967 with a foreign policy that gave strong support to nonalignment and Third World states in general in addition to strongly criticizing Western and particularly U.S. imperialism. However, domestic economic realities intervened, and Singapore soon turned back to the West in search of trade, aid, and investment. It maintained its global, investment-oriented policies until the late 1960s.

Although Singapore maintained a strong anticommunist position and supported the U.S. action in Vietnam, it also avoided any temptation to replace its old British commitment with a similar commitment to the United States, feeling that the latter was not dependable in the longer term.[12] China has also posed problems for Singapore, which did not immediately establish official relations with the PRC—even though their common heritage drew them together and their private economic links have always been strong. For some time, Singapore felt vulnerable to China's policies of infiltration and subversion because of the close cultural bond between that country and the Singapore Chinese. As the leading center of capitalist development in Southeast Asia, Singapore approached the PRC cautiously.

Thailand: Seeking Security in the Bipolar System

Thailand, the only Southeast Asian state to avoid colonization, capably bent to necessity, maintaining a reputation for skilled and knowledgeable diplomacy. It has been noted of Thai foreign policy that the "glory of the tradition has perhaps been overstated and the role of luck understated," while at the same time "Thai statecraft has been much more principled, much less like the bamboo" than has been recognized.[13]

Throughout most of the twentieth century, especially in the 1950s and 1960s, Thai policy followed a propensity to lean away from China and to cultivate relations with any states that opposed China.[14] In 1949, following the communist victory in China, Thailand developed stronger anticommunist positions that led to closer technical, military, and economic relations with the United States, and by 1954 it was sufficiently committed to U.S. foreign policy to enter the SEATO alliance system. However, Thailand also attended the Bandung Conference, where cordial conversations with Zhou Enlai left the Thais wondering whether, through SEATO, they had overcommitted themselves to the cold war.[15] They overcame these misgivings, but when the United States approved neutrality for Laos in 1962, the Thais first felt the "weakening of American determination to hold the line on the Southeast Asian mainland."[16] Nevertheless, Thai-U.S. relations remained strong, with increasing economic and military support through the 1960s until the U.S. announcement of the Guam Doctrine in 1969.

Thailand supported regional cooperation as a means of ensuring independence for its foreign policy. Bangkok became the headquarters for SEATO; however, when the Laos crisis of the period 1960–1962 showed that SEATO could not provide effective security, Thailand began to search for regional alternatives and was a leader in the founding of both ASA and, later, ASEAN.[17]

Despite its emphasis on regional cooperation, Thailand's relations with its immediate neighbors—Burma to the west and Laos and Cambodia to the north and east—have not been good. These borders constitute some of the least stabile areas in Southeast Asia. The Thai-Burmese border has never been secure, and the Burmese have frequently accused the Thais of encouraging instability there. Border problems also had a serious impact on Thai-Cambodian relations, particularly because each state interpreted older Thai-French border treaties to its own advantage.[18] Thailand found Cambodian Prince Sihanouk's neutralist policies and continued assertions of the inevitable communist triumph in Southeast Asia particularly grating. After Sihanouk accepted North Vietnam's use of Cambodian territory, relations with Thailand deteriorated further.

Vietnam: Balancing Communist Giants and Fighting for Independence

Foreign policies in Vietnam were dominated by the long war fought there, which began in 1946 when the French returned. In 1950, the French resurrected the former emperor, Bao Dai, to provide a governmental alternative to Ho Chi Minh and set the stage for the 1954 Geneva agreements that divided Vietnam. The partition of Vietnam caused severe economic and social disruptions in both the north and the south and greatly expanded the influence of the major benefactors of each side—the United States in the south and the Soviet Union and China in the north. The south never overcame its image as a client, even though the Diem government sometimes ignored U.S. advice and refused directives. Its immediate neighbors, Laos and Cambodia, maintained official neutrality toward both Vietnams but held little optimism that the south would survive. Most nonaligned states, including Burma and Indonesia, deferred direct relations with South Vietnam; Sukarno actively supported the north. Other Asian states such as Malaysia and Singapore, as well as Japan, gave verbal support to noncommunist South Vietnam but were careful not to be drawn into an alignment with that country or the United States. Only a few Asian allies—such as South Korea, Taiwan, the Philippines, and Thailand—provided varying amounts of troops, material, and other support to South Vietnam.

Meanwhile, the Sino-Soviet rift brought difficulties to North Vietnam as it tried to balance its two increasingly provocative mentors. Moreover, Hanoi was determined to "go its own way" in matters of ideology and felt the Sino-Soviet dispute prevented the two communist powers from working together to maximize support.[19] Practical considerations of continuing material support, ideology, and traditional power and cultural biases all figured in North Vietnam's calculations, as did domestic power coalitions and competing ideological groups within the Lao Dong Party politburo. Although Sino-Vietnamese differences were evident as early as the 1954 Geneva talks, North Vietnam did not have sufficient strength to consider a pro-Soviet policy in the face of Chinese opposition. Yet from 1957 to about 1960, the Vietnamese were drawn closer to Moscow, whereas after 1963, as the war intensified, they came again to rely on the Chinese.[20] The Soviet Union downplayed the Vietnamese revolution, hoping to contain the conflict as a regional struggle and minimize U.S. involvement there.

North Vietnam also actively stimulated subversion in Laos and Cambodia, although Hanoi accepted Sihanouk's neutrality and his opposition to Thailand and South Vietnam. In Laos especially, the North Vietnamese practiced the time-honored regional policy of extending their own power into territory in which a power vacuum existed. They utilized much of southeastern Laos for supply routes to the south. Elsewhere, North Vietnam sought support among the nonaligned states, especially Burma and Indonesia; in the early 1960s, as Jakarta under Sukarno moved to the left, the North Vietnamese found their first solid regional support.

Beyond the region, all of North Vietnam's primary relations were within the communist world. A few nonaligned states maintained relations, but among the countries of Western Europe only Sweden maintained full diplomatic relations with Hanoi in the early 1960s.[21]

Cambodia and Laos: The Failure of Guaranteed Neutrality

Cambodia and Laos entered the contemporary era in the most precarious positions of all Southeast Asian states. French colonial rule had saved Cambodia from the relentless pressure of the Thais from the west and the Vietnamese from the east, as Cambodia's decline from the heights of the Khmer kingdom at Angkor in the thirteenth century had been nearly continuous, interrupted only by French protectorate status in the 1860s. Laos, by contrast, had only the barest historical framework in the state of Lan Chang, which appeared in the 1350s; in its present form, "only by cartographic and diplomatic convention [could] Laos seriously be considered as a single state."[22] Both Cambodia and Laos were confronted with foreign policy contexts not appreciably different from what might have been expected in the fourteenth or fifteenth century traditional system; however, the mid-twentieth century, multistate system left them more vulnerable to collapse or external annihilation.

Cambodian and Lao foreign policies were governed by their proximity to the Vietnam conflict. For Laos, where neutrality had been guaranteed by the Zürich agreement signed in 1961 by all major powers and all relevant regional actors, foreign policy was largely a struggle to implement that neutrality in the face of overwhelming pressure from North Vietnam. As with South Vietnam, the Laotian government of Prince Souvanna Phouma received support from the United States, whereas the opposing Pathet Lao were supported by North Vietnam, China, and the Soviet Union. From the beginning, the Lao Communist Party was led by individuals who were very sympathetic to North Vietnam.[23] The U.S. presence on the one hand and the North Vietnamese on the other effectively divided Laos territorially, rendering neutrality ineffective and providing a continuous threat to its future as an independent state.

Similarly, Cambodia's foreign policy sought guarantees for its existence—in the global system against communist confrontation and in the regional system against the irredentist claims of its neighbors, especially Thailand.[24] During the period before the fall of Prince Norodom Sihanouk (1970), Cambodia maintained an aggressive and independent foreign policy. As with that of Laos, Cambodian neutrality was guaranteed by international treaty. Cambodia was surrounded by hostile or potentially hostile countries—Vietnam, Thailand, and China—that it could not risk antagonizing. Sihanouk also recognized, however, that a vulnerable Cambodia needed external assistance, and he acknowledged this legally in 1957 when the Cambodian National Assembly passed a neutrality act that included a clause allowing for foreign assistance against military invasion. Sihanouk accepted both U.S. and Soviet technical and economic aid as well as U.S. military assistance, and he strongly encouraged the United States to provide support to Laos in the early 1960s.

Cambodia's relations with Thailand and South Vietnam were poor at best because Cambodian neutrality was seen in Bangkok and Saigon as constituting tacit support for communist North Vietnam. This situation became even more critical after 1965, when Cambodia agreed to North Vietnam's use of Cambodian territory for logistical and supply purposes. Relations with the United States deteriorated and were broken in 1965; they were not restored until 1969.

As pressures from Thailand, South Vietnam, and North Vietnam increased in the late 1960s, Cambodia sought to strengthen its neutrality; however, by this time both the right and the left had insurgent armies—the Khmer Serai backed by Thailand and the Khmer Rouge backed by China.

Burma: Positive Neutrality Leads to Positive Decline

Of the neutral Southeast Asian states, Burma was the most constant in its pursuit of neutralist policies. The Burmese chose "positive" neutrality, which translated into an issue-by-issue choice of involvement or noninvolvement, alignment or nonalignment, or an independent position. Perhaps because Burma had been governed for such a long period as a subunit of British India, there was little domestic support for post-independence linkages within the British Commonwealth. This became generalized as a foreign policy strategy of avoiding most special relationships. Burma's foreign policy was governed by two principles: (1) Small, weak, and underdeveloped states should stay out of global blocs; and (2) geographic proximity to China and the obvious inequality of the two countries meant Burma had to be circumspect in all of its foreign policy decisions so as not to provoke China.

From the early 1950s, Burma also established a course of friendly relations with Thailand. Historical antagonisms and contemporary border and ethnic problems between the two nations made this difficult, and Thai alignment with the United States through SEATO further separated them. Burma, contrary to the strategies of many other regional states, did not seek to expand its borders; because of the extremely tenuous relations with the various ethnic minorities residing near its borders, however, it sought formal border agreements with all of its neighbors.

Border issues occupied the major part of Burma's foreign policy toward its immediate neighbors. As was the case among traditional states, Burma experienced severe problems with ethnic minority groups that occupied the border regions and effectively rejected state authority. Its first concern was the border with China, and an agreement was reached in 1960 that demarcated the border and transferred disputed territory. Thailand and Burma signed a common-border agreement in 1963, but continued movement of Karen and Shan dissidents across the border, as well as smuggling of consumer goods into Burma, continued to cause difficulties. Additional border agreements were reached between Burma and Thailand in 1963 and again in 1968, but the Thai-Burmese border remained a virtual sieve as people and goods move back-and-forth to take advantage of or escape the economic distortions in Burma. China's reductions in support of Burmese communist insurgents forced the communists into alliances with noncommunist ethnic minorities and drug-smuggling groups along the Thai-Burmese border. In 1967, Burma reached separate border agreements with both India and Pakistan and settled disputes over the islands in the Naaf River.

Burma accepted foreign assistance from a number of sources including the United States, Russia, Japan, China, Britain, and Israel. However, the country remained sensitive to "strings" attached to foreign assistance, and some assistance programs were terminated because of suspected anti-Burmese activities on the part of the donor. The United States felt the brunt of Burmese sensitivities, having been asked to end its foreign assistance programs in 1953 and again in 1966. Chinese support to Rangoon, however, increased steadily throughout most of the 1960s.[25] Israeli assistance was appreciated because Israel was not a leading member of either of the power blocs and Burma had no significant Muslim community that might be critical of Israeli assistance.

Beginning in 1968, Burma began to change its foreign policy focus following six years of a nearly reclusive policy. In 1969, travel restrictions were relaxed somewhat to encourage tourism, and Burma chartered a plane from a U.S. airline to shuttle tourists between Hong Kong and Rangoon.[26] Burma accepted assistance for offshore oil exploration from Gulf Oil Corporation in 1972, the first time it had taken aid from a private, nongovernmental organization.[27]

Within the region, Burma maintained good relations with all states, and it was active in the Non-Aligned Movement and the United Nations. However, it rejected invitations to participate in regional organizations such as ASEAN, although it occasionally sent observers to regional meetings. Patterns of isolation in Burmese foreign policy again became evident as the Burmese espoused self-sufficiency even when it brought economic or other deprivation.

Indonesia: Left or Right but Always Independent and Active

Indonesia, the largest and most populous state in the region, has had great fluctuations in its foreign policy that, not surprisingly, have been closely linked to shifts in domestic politics. However, although veering at times more to the left or to the right, Indonesia has retained a consistent concept of an independent and active foreign policy in which some distance or aloofness has been maintained at all times, even toward its apparent major global benefactors of the moment. The underlying caution in this policy strategy may stem from the bitter experience of the revolution and the development of an underlying elite perception of the world as a hostile place—a perspective that also developed through the revolutionary experience. Indonesia at first developed a pro-Western neutralism—a commitment to nonalignment that envisioned the establishment of exclusive relations with Western countries.[28] Indonesia hosted the Asian-African conference at Bandung in 1955, and—along with Burma and Cambodia—it increasingly voiced its concern and resentment over the impositions of both the Western and Eastern power blocs. By the mid-1950s, Indonesia had developed its independent foreign policy to protect itself from the "duplicitous" Dutch and their Western allies.

Throughout the 1950s, Indonesia essentially balanced its criticisms of both East and West. However, as President Sukarno became increasingly convinced of his global mission, Indonesian foreign policy became decidedly more critical of the "old established forces" of the West and more tolerant of the "new emerging forces" of the East and the Third World. Sukarno regionalized these concepts in Indonesia's confrontation with Malaysia, a state he labeled a neocolonial creation. Regardless of whether Sukarno seriously intended to crush Malaysia or whether the anti-Malaysia policy was actually designed for Indonesian domestic purposes, it was an economic disaster for Indonesia because most Western capital disappeared.

As Sukarno's claims of encirclement by the old established forces became more frequent throughout the early 1960s, Indonesia's relations with the United States slowly deteriorated. There were increasingly frequent instances of conflict in these relations, as, for example, when U.S. covert aid to the rebellion in the Eastern Islands was publicized or when Indonesia's claim to West Irian was defeated at the United Nations. These conflicts further shifted Indonesia's foreign policy to the left, but they did not preclude the development of another U.S.-sponsored assistance package following Indonesia's takeover in West Irian.

By 1964, Indonesia's relations with the West had greatly declined, and a "Jakarta-Hanoi-Peking axis" appeared on the horizon.[29] Also at this time, Indonesia's confrontation with the established world order peaked in its withdrawal from the United Nations. Indonesia's conservative military leaders were sufficiently concerned that they sent peace feelers to Malaysia, apparently without Sukarno's knowledge,[30] but Indonesia's leftward foreign policy movement continued until Sukarno was removed from power following the October 1965 coup attempt by the communist party.

The Suharto government that emerged in 1966 and 1967 dramatically reversed Indonesian foreign policy. Within two years the Malaysian confrontation was ended, and both states became members of a new regional association. Relations with China were frozen in 1967, and the activities of the Soviet Union were sharply curtailed. Negotiations with the Soviet Union for the rescheduling of debt payments were very slow, and Indonesia did not respond positively to the Soviet proposal for a Southeast Asian collective security pact.[31]

Indonesia again embarked on a pro-Western foreign policy, although it continued to search for opportunities to exercise its own independent and active policy. Suharto's New Order government gave most of its attention to domestic economic stabilization. Major Western donors formed the Inter-Governmental Group on Indonesia (IGGI) both to guarantee steady financial support and to provide a framework for making difficult economic decisions, but Indonesia's relations with IGGI also inhibited Jakarta's flexibility in foreign policy. Under the New Order government, regional relations gained a higher priority. Although it was careful to avoid being criticized for trying to dominate the region, Indonesia began to develop its leadership potential within the ASEAN framework.

Foreign Policy Responses, 1950–1970

The foreign policies of all of the states of Southeast Asia were limited by their lack of resources, organization, and experience in international diplomacy. Early foreign policy initiatives tended to be short-term responses to contemporary issues and were formulated within the context of the immediate past experiences: Revolutionary states tended to reject former colonial authority, whereas those states that experienced a nonrevolutionary transition to independence tended to stay close to the former metropole. Regional relations were slow to develop because most states remained dependent upon former colonial metropoles or became dependent on one of the leaders of the global power blocs. However, as these states gained experience, new foreign policy orientations and strategies—combining a core of historical and cultural experience with the newly defined goals of the independent states—began to emerge.

NOTES

1. Mohammed Hatta, "Indonesia's Foreign Policy," *Foreign Affairs* 31 (April 1953), p. 352.

2. Arnfinn Jorgensen-Dahl, *Regional Organization and Order in South-East Asia* (London: Macmillan Publishers, 1982), p. 159.

3. H. Wriggins, "The Asian State System in the 1970s," in *Asia and the International System*, edited by Wayne Wilcox, Leo E. Rose, and Gavin Boyd (Cambridge, Mass.: Winthrop Publishers, 1972), p. 346.

4. David Wurfel, "The Philippines," in *Governments and Politics of Southeast Asia*, edited by George McT. Kahin (Ithaca: Cornell University Press, 1964), p. 758.

5. Peter Lyon, *War and Peace in South-East Asia* (London: Oxford University Press, 1969), p. 44.

6. Robert O. Tilman, "The Foreign Policies of the Smaller Asian States: Malaysia, Singapore and the Philippines," in Wilcox, Rose, and Boyd, *Asia and the International System*, p. 218.

7. David Wurfel, "A Changing Philippines," *Asian Survey* 4 (February 1964), p. 706.

8. Jorgensen-Dahl, *Regional Organization and Order in South-East Asia*, pp. 191–194.

9. *Asia 1976 Yearbook* (Hong Kong: Far Eastern Economic Review, 1977), p. 216.

10. J. Norman Parmer, "Malaysia 1965: Challenging the Terms of 1957," *Asian Survey* 6 (February 1966), p. 117.

11. Nancy McHenry Fletcher, *The Separation of Singapore from Malaysia* (Ithaca: Southeast Asia Program, Data Paper no. 73, 1969), pp. 1–89.

12. Tilman, "Foreign Policies of the Smaller Asian States," in Wilcox, Rose, and Boyd, *Asia and the International System*, pp. 215–216, especially n. 27.

13. James E. McCarthy, "National Image and Diplomacy: The Case of Thailand," *Southeast Asia, An International Quarterly* 2 (Fall 1972), p. 428.

14. David A. Wilson, "Thailand," in Kahin, *Governments and Politics*, p. 66.

15. Donald E. Nuechterlein, *Thailand and the Struggle for Southeast Asia* (Ithaca: Cornell University Press, 1965), pp. 122–131.

16. David A. Wilson, "Thailand: Old Leaders and New Directions," *Asian Survey* 8 (February 1968), pp. 120–121.

17. *Ibid.*, p. 88.

18. Ganganath Jha, *The Foreign Policy of Thailand* (New Delhi: Radiant Publishers, 1979), pp. 113–121.

19. William J. Duiker, *The Communist Road to Power in Vietnam* (Boulder: Westview Press, 1981), p. 256.

20. Donald S. Zagoria, *Vietnam Triangle: Moscow, Peking, Hanoi* (New York: Pegasus Books, 1967), pp. 102–109.

21. Robert A. Scalapino, "The Foreign Policies of the Smaller Asian States: Vietnam," in Wilcox, Rose, and Boyd, *Asia and the International System*, p. 178.

22. Lyon, *War and Peace in South-East Asia*, pp. 85–86.

23. Paul F. Langer and Joseph J. Zasloff, *North Vietnam and the Pathet Lao, Partners in the Struggle for Laos* (Cambridge: Harvard University Press, 1970), p. 171.

24. Bernard K. Gordon, "Cambodia: Where Foreign Policy Counts," *Asian Survey* 5 (September 1965), pp. 433–448.

25. Frank N. Trager, "Burma: 1967—A Better Ending than Beginning," *Asian Survey* 8 (February 1968), pp. 112–113.

26. Josef Silverstein, "Political Dialogue in Burma: A New Turn on the Road to Socialism," *Asian Survey* 10 (February 1970), p. 139.

27. Jon A. Wiant, "Burma: Loosening Up on the Tiger's Tail," *Asian Survey* 13 (February 1973), p. 186.

28. Franklin B. Weinstein, "The Foreign Policies of the Larger Asian States: Indonesia," in Wilcox, Rose, and Boyd, *Asia and the International System*, p. 128.

29. Justus M. van der Kroef, "The Sino-Indonesian Partnership," *Orbis* 8 (Summer 1964), pp. 332–356.

30. Weinstein, "Indonesia," in Wilcox, Rose, and Boyd, *Asia and the International System*, p. 139.

31. John M. Allison, "Indonesia: The End of the Beginning?" *Asian Survey* 10 (February 1970), pp. 144–145.

10

Foreign Policy in a Multipolar World

As the bipolar system weakened, Southeast Asian states faced greater ambiguity in the global system but also gained considerable policy flexibility. Ambiguity was greatest with respect to ideology and willingness to utilize the vast military power that had been accumulated by some states. The Guam Declaration (1969) signaled the decline of the U.S. containment strategy, and the fall of South Vietnam demonstrated its end, at least for Southeast Asia. Both the Sino-Soviet rift—which had begun in 1959 and peaked in the Ussuri River conflict in 1970—and the Sino-American rapprochement in 1971 had long-term policy implications. But now Southeast Asian states had gained confidence and experience in international affairs and were better prepared to apply their own interpretations to interstate policies.

Following World War II, the Southeast Asian states (except for North Vietnam) came to recognize that the Soviet Union's commitment to countering U.S. involvement in the region would entail very limited Soviet economic or military assistance. Yet by the early 1970s, Soviet naval capabilities extended into Southeast Asia, raising for the first time the possibility of superpower confrontation in a "spectator" region.[1] The Soviet's policy bid for regional prominence came through its proposed collective security system. However, regional leaders, including those in North Vietnam, also recognized that China's assertion of greater independence from its Soviet partner made Southeast Asia even more vulnerable to external competition and manipulation.

British withdrawal from Malaysia and Singapore left both countries weakened defensively, despite the new British defense agreements and the continued presence of Australian and New Zealand troops. The vivid demonstrations of the American public's unwillingness to sustain its anticommunist containment policy and the failed military operation in Vietnam meant external military force was no longer available to prop up incumbent elites. Japan, neither a strategic threat nor a support, became feared because of its growing economic domination. Regardless of whether external military support had been welcomed (which it usually had not, at least publicly), when U.S. military forces were no longer available and elites in Southeast Asia found themselves rethinking many foreign policy positions, the result was the gradual assertion of an Asian international system that became "more autonomous, generating its own dynamic pattern of relationships independent of the Moscow-Washington conflict."[2]

Foreign Policy After 1970

These changes in the global system had important impacts on all of the states of Southeast Asia and on the region as a whole. At the same time, the regional states, by this time having gained several decades of experiences in foreign policy, were better prepared to pursue foreign policy goals based on their own national interests—which after decades of independence were also more clearly defined and understood. Foreign policies of the regional states reflected more sophisticated responses to an increasingly complex world.

The Philippines: Seeking Asian Friends

The earlier dualism in Philippine foreign policy intensified as relations with the United States weakened and the presence of the military bases became a more sensitive issue. In addition, domestic "disappointments and the expectations for a better life" forced Manila to look for new, more pragmatic policy options.[3] In 1968, state visits by President Marcos to Indonesia, Malaysia, and Thailand signaled changing policies, and Japanese economic activity in the Philippines continued to grow, especially in joint ventures for natural-resource exploitation.[4] But Philippine relations within Southeast Asia—despite its increasingly active ASEAN membership—remained uncertain, in part because of the still festering Sabah conflict between Malaysia and the Philippines.

A second foreign policy change involved dropping opposition to trade and diplomatic relations with communist states. President Marcos announced a reorientation in Filipino foreign policy in early 1971, stressing his desire to broaden contacts around the globe. This new policy became more evident and important throughout 1971—for example, when the Philippines shifted its support and voted in favor of UN membership for the People's Republic of China. Unofficial trade contacts were also opened between the two countries.

The Philippines soon broadened this new strategy to include unofficial contacts with the Soviet Union and other Eastern European countries. Official relations were established with seven Eastern European countries in 1972; in 1975, relations were established between Manila and Beijing and in 1976 with Moscow and Hanoi. Regionally, the competing claims to the Spratley Islands by China, Vietnam, and the Philippines, as well as Taiwan, were better managed because of stabile diplomatic relations among those states. The Filipino strategy of improving relations with communist states added pressure on the United States to mitigate the perceived weakening of security guarantees for Manila.

Key to loosening the almost total dependence on the United States was the development of better relations with neighboring states. The former quixotic search for Asianness through cultural ties with Indonesia, as well as claims to Sabah, was gradually replaced with realistic policies focused on regional cooperation, especially through ASEAN. The Philippines was the earliest advocate of an ASEAN summit, and as early as 1971 the Marcos administration raised the issue of an ASEAN free-trade zone. The Philippines remained frustrated by the lack of movement toward freer intra-ASEAN trade and viewed Indonesia's proposals for limited trade adjustments as unsatisfactory.[5] Manila gave minimal support to ASEAN's regional neutralization proposal, "accepting the intellectual arguments of neutralization" but labeling it long-range.[6] Nevertheless, Filipino relations within ASEAN forged "closer and stronger" bilateral ties in a "true multilateral alliance that would benefit all member nations through economic cooperation rather than through military entanglements."[7]

A third strand of the diversified Philippine foreign policy involved contact with the nonaligned states. Beginning in the 1970s, Manila curtailed its use of force against Muslim insurgents to "avert worsening relations with Arab states."[8] In an attempt to reach nonaligned Muslim states, the Philippines sponsored a national Muslim conference and attended the Islamic Foreign Ministers' Conference in Malaysia.[9] In February 1976, the Philippines hosted the Group of 77, at which a Manila Declaration was formulated; the declaration called for the indexing of raw materials prices, debt rescheduling, increased foreign aid on more concessionary terms, tariff preferences for imports to developed countries, and unrestricted technology transfers.[10] Manila also sought observer status in the nonaligned meetings in August 1976, but the delegation was limited to guest status. The United Nations Commission on Trade and

Development (UNCTAD) meetings were successfully hosted in Manila in May 1979.

Despite this broader base for Filipino foreign policy, the United States remained strong, if not dominant, in Manila's international perspective. In the mid-1970s the Philippines threatened to close the U.S. bases, but it did not do so. The military bases continued to be a volatile political issue, used sometimes by the government as leverage against the United States and sometimes by the opposition as a challenge to Marcos. Manila did negotiate increased compensation and reduced U.S. extraterritorial rights. Some inequities in economic relations were resolved through bilateral agreements. But although the U.S. security agreements offered Manila protection from external threat, the U.S. military bases also ensured that the Philippines would be an automatic target in a general war.[11]

In response to the declining intensity of the cold war and the breakdown of global bipolarity, Manila took advantage of the wider range of available policy options and oriented itself "toward independence, pragmatism, and development."[12] Issues such as the Sabah dispute with Malaysia receded, and concern over U.S. withdrawal from the region lessened. Expanding Filipino relations with neighbors in Asia "led to more realistic policies" in both the regional and the global systems.[13] Although it was disrupted by domestic political problems, over a period of two decades the Philippines built a foreign policy framework that, although continuing its U.S. links, sustained a greater balance in the regional and global systems, reduced the country's dependence on extraregional powers, and provided broader expression of Filipino interests in foreign policy.

Malaysia: Looking East and Looking to Islam

By the late 1960s, the British had declared their intent to withdraw from Southeast Asia, but Malaysia remained under the defense umbrella of the new Five Power Defense Pact, which included Britain, Australia, New Zealand, Malaysia, and Singapore. Malaysia opposed British withdrawal and also saw Britain's decision to join the European Economic Community as a sign of its declining interest in Asia. Nevertheless, Britain remained Malaysia's key contact in Europe, and Malaysia relied on British advice and service until British protectionism and decisions such as increasing university fees for foreign students studying in the United Kingdom forced the Malaysians to broaden their international contacts.

In 1970, Malaysia formally declared a nonaligned foreign policy, although its antecedents stemmed from the late 1960s when the country opened closer relations with nonaligned Muslim states. As early as 1968, a political entrepreneurship element in Malaysian foreign policy was introduced that included links with communist countries—especially the Soviet Union and China—despite Malaysia's experience with communist insurgents and its strong anticommunist stance.[14]

Trade with the Soviet Union grew as the Soviets increased their purchases of Malaysian rubber. Trade missions and cultural exchanges with China began in 1970, as China sought improved relations with Southeast Asian states in an attempt to counter growing Soviet influence. Trade with China subsequently increased. By 1970 Malaysia's new nonaligned stance included advocating U.S. withdrawal from Vietnam, proposing to replace U.S. troops with a neutralization guarantee for Southeast Asia. Malaysia had established diplomatic relations with East Germany and with most other Eastern European communist states by 1973. After more than a year of negotiations, Malaysia led the ASEAN states in opening diplomatic relations with China in 1974.

Dramatically increased participation in various Islamic organizations caused Malaysia to oppose U.S. support for Israel. In addition, pan-Islamic issues became entangled in bilateral relations with the Philippines, where repression of Moro Muslims had driven refugees to Malaysia. Malaysia hosted the Fifth Islamic Conference in Kuala Lumpur in 1976, but trade with and investment from Islamic countries grew slowly.

Finally, Malaysia's new foreign policies included a regional perspective. ASEAN's growth gave Malaysia a stronger self-identity and a willingness to articulate regional policy positions, such as the Southeast Asian neutrality proposals. Despite the nagging dispute with the Philippines over Sabah, relationships within ASEAN prospered. Although the observation that Malaysia practiced "self-induced subordination to Indonesia on foreign policy matters" is an overstatement, relations with Indonesia became close during the 1970s.[15]

A high point of Malaysia's foreign policy was ASEAN's adoption of its proposal for neutralizing Southeast Asia by creating a regional Zone of Peace, Freedom, and Neutrality, "free from any form or manner of interference from outside powers."[16] Recognizing that Western—particularly British and U.S.—protection was no longer dependable against China, Malaysia formulated its neutrality proposal, stating that "apart from its own internal and subregional problems, the biggest single 'external' problem of Southeast Asia is the uncertainty surrounding China's future intentions."[17] The neutrality proposal brought a global character to Malaysian foreign policy and gave it greater legitimacy among nonaligned states.

Singapore: The Politics of Economic Growth

Singapore, which was not independent until 1965, took an initially strong stance toward nonalignment and assumed a somewhat confrontational position within the region.[18] This "go-it-alone" strategy peaked in the crisis with Indonesia over Singapore's decision in October 1968 to hang two Indonesian marines still held captive from the old Indonesian confrontation, despite appeals from Indonesia's President Suharto and Malaysia's Prime Minister Tunku Abdul Rahman. Also in 1968, Singapore and the Soviet Union established diplomatic relations and exchanged ambassadors.

Singapore subsequently developed a foreign policy based on positive neutrality and the recognition of its own position, size, and long-term economic needs. For example, it stressed regional economic cooperation while maintaining a publicly self-effacing posture with respect to Malaysia and Indonesia in an attempt to lessen its conspicuously Chinese character. At the same time, as a latter-day incarnation of the traditional Southeast Asian entrepôt city-state, Singapore accepted and encouraged a balanced presence of global powers in the region—a position strikingly different from Malaysia's advocacy of regional neutrality. Singapore's foreign minister, S. Rajaratnam, said "Singapore was 'puzzled and alarmed' that China had never developed an Asia policy . . . [and that Singapore] welcomed the increased interest shown by Japan and the Soviet Union in Southeast Asia but at the same time stressed the need for a continuing U.S. presence in the post-Vietnam era."[19] Although it did not invite the Americans to occupy the facilities of the departing British, Singapore consistently argued for a continued U.S. "economic and strategic presence" in the region.[20]

Despite Britain's disengagement policies, Singapore hosted the Commonwealth Heads of State Conference in 1971 and continued to rely on British security support. Singapore also expanded economic ties with the EEC. Although it expected continued British economic support, Singapore realized that capital and investment would also be needed from Japan, Western Europe, the United States, and the Eastern bloc countries. With the largest oil-refining capacity in the region, Singapore prudently strengthened relations with Middle Eastern states.

Relations with Japan were built slowly during the 1970s. Investment in Singapore as well as political relations were strengthened by Japanese Prime Minister Kakuei Tanaka's visit in 1974. Singapore, which favored an active regional role for all global powers, was supportive of Japan's increasing military capabilities.

Singapore developed a unique foreign policy position toward China. Recognizing both Indonesian and Malaysian suspicions of China,

Singapore repeatedly stated that it would not open formal relations with China until all ASEAN states had done so; yet Singapore's informal relations with China remained very active and correct. Brisk trade continued between the two, directed mostly from China to Singapore, although Singapore also had extensive unofficial contacts with Taiwan and sent military officers there for training.

Regional relations, especially in the archipelago, remain critical to Singapore. Following the 1974 visit of Indonesian President Suharto, when several basic economic agreements were signed, a triangular relationship developed among Singapore, Malaysia, and Indonesia. Disagreements, such as water problems between Malaysia and Singapore and competing freight rates between Indonesia and Singapore, remained but did not prove insurmountable, although the imbalance in economic strength among the three continued to cause friction. Singapore led ASEAN initiatives against protectionist policies in Japan, the United States, the EEC, and Australia and was also sympathetic toward Thailand as a result of joint fears of communist expansion and of Thailand's vulnerable strategic position on the mainland.

Singapore's nonalignment has always had a certain capitalist tilt given the nature of its economy, but it refused to join the Asia and South Pacific Area Council (ASPAC) because of the council's anticommunist profile. Singapore retained relations with Eastern Europe as well as with the West, and it maintained relations with both North and South Vietnam. Singapore's official position on nonalignment in the early 1970s was summarized by President D. B. Sheares: "Singapore is neutral and non-aligned insofar as we are asked to take sides between competing power blocs. . . . But where our survival is concerned, we cannot afford to be neutral. We will not stand non-aligned if we are threatened by superior force."[21]

Within Southeast Asia, Singapore was originally pessimistic about prospects for regional cooperation but found a positive foreign policy forum in ASEAN. Continuing its self-effacing posture, Singapore used ASEAN to rationalize its position among the regional states, following the theme "to be complementary within ASEAN, to be competitive world-wide."[22] The ASEAN theme of greater economic cooperation stimulated slow but steady changes in regional economic policies that were advantageous to Singapore. Maritime relations between Indonesia and Singapore stabilized, and joint military exercises were held. After the early 1970s, Singapore became the regional entrepôt and transshipment center, despite the efforts of other regional states to improve their own port facilities.

Developments in Indochina during the 1980s prompted closer ASEAN coordination and cooperation. Singapore was the advocate of the

Cambodian opposition coalition and led the ASEAN campaign to seat the coalition in Cambodia's vacant spot at the New Delhi nonaligned meetings; it was also instrumental in pressuring Japan to withhold economic aid to Vietnam. At the same time, however, Singapore's strong verbal criticism of Vietnam was mitigated by trade in excess of US$200 million by 1983.[23] Meanwhile, the Soviet Union's growing role in Indochina prompted Singapore's leaders to urge the United States to continue or expand its regional security role.

Singapore's foreign policy reflected tenets of the traditional Southeast Asian entrepôt states. As a modern regional commercial center, however, Singapore has emphasized tourism and regional finance as well as commodity trade. First, it sought to stabilize relations throughout the region, ignoring the traditional propensity to employ military, especially naval force to maintain its position and instead using regional cooperation—through ASEAN—as the cornerstone of its foreign policy. Second, it actively sought the involvement of extraregional powers both to enhance its economic position and to increase its security. At the global level, Singapore recognized its dependence on the world economy; at the regional level, it patiently relied on ASEAN economic growth to provide widening local markets for its financial and technical services.

Thailand: Regional Security Replaces Bipolar Security

Its proximity to military conflicts and long-standing ethnic and historical animosities made Thailand watchful of Vietnam's revolution and its spreading power. Because of its strongly anticommunist policies, Thailand found itself linked to South Vietnam and U.S. global containment policies. This linkage became intense when Thailand was under military control and its foreign ministry was kept in the background of Thai foreign policy.[24] The U.S. failure in Vietnam was difficult for successive Thai governments as they extricated their troops from direct combat, reduced the U.S. presence on Thai soil, and tried to expand relations with numerous states with which they had had virtually no previous contact.

In early 1969, Thailand began to signal a changing policy publicly when Foreign Minister Thanat Khoman informed the Thai parliament that "there should be less reliance on non-Asian countries to enable countries in the region to fill the vacuum of a U.S. withdrawal from the area."[25] At the same time, talks aimed at a planned withdrawal from Vietnam began, although President Nixon visited Thailand in July 1969 and reiterated U.S. support for SEATO. Thailand was also criticized in the United States by antiwar groups, the media, and congressional opponents of the war.

The pace of the Thai-U.S. separation quickened in the early 1970s as the Thai government, which was under civilian control from late 1973 through 1976, underwent intense policy introspection that focused on domestic institutions as well as foreign relations. The government sought control of U.S. activities in Thailand by regulating contracts more strictly, limiting the numbers of U.S. personnel at certain sensitive bases, and restricting or terminating some intelligence posts focused on areas other than Indochina.

Thailand supported Lon Nol's anticommunist government in Cambodia, although it declined to send troops there to assist against the Vietnamese and Cambodian communists. With the fall of Saigon and, later, of Lon Nol's Cambodian government, Thailand's separation from the United States moved to its conclusion. A subsidiary problem arose when U.S. forces from Thai bases were used to rescue the freighter *Mayaguez*. The Thais notified the United States that all U.S. military personnel remaining on Thai soil would be subject to new and more restrictive regulations; when the United States rejected these limitations, the remaining troops left.

The emerging Thai foreign policy sought to balance more evenly the country's relations with extraregional powers. As Thailand reduced its U.S. links, it improved relations with old enemies, particularly China but also the Soviet Union and the Eastern European countries. The Thais had had formal relations with the Soviet Union, but in 1968 and 1969 they encouraged trade mission activities and other exchanges. There were reports of secret Thai missions to China in early 1970.[26]

Thailand dropped its opposition to UN seating for the PRC in 1971, although it supported Taiwan's continuing membership. Communications, sports delegations, and unofficial visits to China followed for several years until formal relations were established in 1975. Relations and contacts with other communist states, including a trade delegation to North Korea in 1974, were also expanded, but the most important of these were with the Vietnamese. Thailand had made intermittent unsuccessful overtures to Hanoi beginning in 1972, so when North Vietnam sought the release of South Vietnamese aircraft and other equipment left on Thai soil, Thailand pressed for better relations. The Thais eventually turned over most of the equipment, and diplomatic relations were established. Communications between the two countries remained limited because of their different ideologies and their competing interests in Indochina.

The long border between Thailand and Laos and Cambodia, as well as the historical ethnic problems and territorial irregularities among these states, has meant that relations have been difficult at best. Thailand's strong anticommunist position included supplying military forces to fight against the Pathet Lao. However, the Thais also sought to maintain Lao and Cambodian independence from Vietnam. Thailand, for example, was the first noncommunist country to recognize the Khmer Rouge regime, and it maintained relations with Laos even after the last neutral coalition had become a communist government. By the mid-1980s, Thai-Laotian relations were strained because of border disputes, a conflict that was prompted by Vietnam.[27] The strong influence of the Vietnamese in Indochina also helped to rejuvenate Thai-U.S. relations.

Consolidation of Vietnam's control over both Laos and Cambodia placed a great strain on Thailand because these areas had served as buffers between the Vietnamese and Thai kingdoms even before the arrival of the French. Vietnam's control of the buffer zone was a direct threat to Thailand: From the Thai foreign policy perspective, Cambodia was no longer independent; the Vietnamese army had moved to (and over) the Thai border; there were thousands of refugees in Thailand; and Thailand had to substantially increase its military expenditures.[28] Despite Thailand's efforts to stabilize relations after the unification of Vietnam, the two states remain opponents in almost every respect.

Meanwhile, Thailand tried to strengthen relations within ASEAN. Continuing problems on the Thai-Malaysian border did not inhibit the development of good relations between the two countries. The Thai foreign ministry established an ASEAN bureau in 1975 and looked to the organization for diplomatic support as the Indochina situation worsened.

Thailand's security and foreign policy perspectives underwent a basic revision after Vietnam took control of the traditional buffer states between them. Essentially, Thailand became a frontline state against the Vietnamese-controlled and communist Indochina. The Thais moved much closer—perhaps too close—to China, seeking support for the common short-term goal of dislodging the Vietnamese from Cambodia.[29] Although closer relations with China strained Thai relations within ASEAN, they also served to again bring Thailand and the United States into closer alignment. As long as Indochina remained instabile, Thai foreign policy vacillated as it dealt with imminent internal as well as external threats. Much like traditional kingdoms, Thailand experienced countervailing pressures at its borders, and with the Cambodian buffer removed, competing Thai and Vietnamese power could have clashed in search of a new equilibrium.

Vietnam: Victory and Neoimperialism

U.S. military support for South Vietnam wavered in the late 1960s. By 1968, negotiations between Washington and Hanoi had become a reality Saigon could no longer ignore. Faced with possible abandonment through an agreement that did not include them, a South Vietnamese delegation went to Paris. South Vietnam tried to sustain relations with its military allies—Australia, New Zealand, South Korea, Taiwan, Thailand, and the Philippines—but these states reevaluated their cold war policies and rejected continued support for South Vietnam. In 1969, both the Philippines and Thailand announced plans to withdraw from South Vietnam. Eventually, all of South Vietnam's allies indicated that their support would end with the U.S. withdrawal.

Diplomatically, South Vietnam became increasingly isolated as previously neutral or nonaligned states, many having already formally recognized North Vietnam, accepted also the Provisional Revolutionary Government (PRG) in the south. The PRG was recognized at the 1973 nonaligned conference in Algiers, by which time more than a dozen states had sent representatives to PRG-controlled zones. South Vietnam countered by encouraging states to recognize both the Democratic Republic of Vietnam in Hanoi and the Republic of Vietnam in Saigon but not the provisional government in the south.

For North Vietnam, the closing years of U.S. involvement in Indochina were also complicated: Policies to counter South Vietnam's initiatives had to be developed, and pressure had to be maintained on the war-weary United States without appearing intransigent to the latter's friends and allies. At the same time, North Vietnam had to operate within the growing rift between the Soviets and the Chinese, knowing that the policies of both countries were changing unpredictably because of the global politics of détente. Moreover, the continued resurgence of parochial interests among communist states meant North Vietnam was no longer a priority.[30] Finally it was necessary for North Vietnam to continue to absorb the high cost of sustaining the war effort in the south.

The Soviet Union and China advocated different positions regarding Hanoi in negotiations with the United States. China held a relatively harder line than Moscow and urged the Vietnamese to persevere in the war, even after the United States offered to negotiate in 1968. China also stressed military tactics that did not require advanced military equipment (presumably available only from the Soviet Union). For its part, North Vietnam, balancing the appearances of friendship with China and the USSR in order to avoid the political gulf between them and in the hope of receiving as much aid as each might be willing to give, expanded its relationship with the Soviet Union to counter China's more local and traditionally dominant position.

As the likelihood of a North Vietnamese victory became more apparent, more states recognized Hanoi and its southern revolutionary arm. Sweden, which had opened diplomatic relations with North Vietnam in early 1969, was the first Western state to do so, but during the next several years many other states followed. North Vietnam rejected several ASEAN invitations but opened more active relations with India, a state whose independent foreign policy was more compatible with North Vietnam's views.

The collapse of Saigon not only unified Vietnam but also signaled the end of global bipolar conflict there. The parallel fall of Cambodia's U.S.-supported Lon Nol government removed the last vestige of Western colonial and imperial power, although extraregional power soon returned as the Chinese began to provide support to the Khmer Rouge.

Meanwhile, Hanoi embarked with exhilaration on a new foreign policy designed to enhance the global solidarity of the communist states and peoples and to gain greater global recognition of the special relationship among the fraternal peoples of Vietnam, Laos, and Cambodia in the regional system. Vietnam defined five fundamental foreign policy goals: (1) to protect political independence from all non-Vietnamese challenges, (2) to stabilize independence that was free from external economic, military, or material aid, (3) to guarantee ethnic and territorial unity and integrity, (4) to ensure Vietnamese defense against any military threat, and (5) to establish Vietnam as the dominant influence in Indochina and as a major influence throughout Southeast Asia.[31]

With diminished concern over the Sino-Soviet rift, Hanoi moved quickly to improve its ties with the Soviet Union. In Beijing in 1975, Le Duan, general secretary of the Vietnamese Communist Party, refused to renounce Soviet "hegemonism" in Asia, thus formally rejecting China's view.[32] New technical aid agreements were signed in early 1975, and Moscow financed the building of a Ho Chi Minh mausoleum in Hanoi. Relations with China cooled dramatically.

Vietnam began a global diplomatic initiative that increased the number of states according Vietnam diplomatic recognition to ninety-seven and brought Vietnam membership in twenty-two international organizations.[33] It also worked to stabilize relations with the ASEAN states, replacing its frequently used criticism of the ASEAN states as "stooges and henchmen for the United States" for diplomatic recognition and the beginnings of quiet, nonpolemical, and constructive dialogue. Relations with Thailand remained strained but were somewhat improved. Vietnam sought to establish a credible nonaligned foreign policy position. However, having tipped the Sino-Soviet scale in favor of Moscow, Vietnam needed another counterweight—the United States—if it were to sustain a nonaligned posture. Vietnam expected aid from the United States as indicated in the Paris agreements. Hanoi tried to open the door to the United States by returning the remains of some U.S. troops and publicly stating its desire to normalize relations. Through 1978, Vietnam continued a broader diplomatic program in Southeast Asia in an attempt to ease U.S. and ASEAN fears, enunciating a four-point policy of (1) noninterference in the domestic affairs of others, (2) exclusion of foreign bases from the region, (3) regional economic cooperation and peaceful settlement of disputes, and (4) support for a modified version of ASEAN's proposed ZOPFAN.[34] The opportunity for conciliation was not taken by the United States, which rejected requests for aid and blocked Vietnam's admission to the United Nations.

Hanoi and Moscow signed a treaty of friendship in 1978; then, after this commitment had been made, Hanoi turned to confrontation, insisting that Moscow support the elimination of China's ally, the Khmer Rouge, in Cambodia. Vietnam's Indochina policies were strengthened by the treaty with the Soviet Union, allaying Vietnamese fears of Chinese rivalry and domination in Southeast Asia because of the counterpoise of Soviet protection. Relations between Vietnam and China deteriorated rapidly after the end of the Vietnam War, although Vietnam had recognized "no later than 1972 that China was not favoring the unification of Vietnam."[35] These relations were complicated after 1975 by the growing friendship between the new Cambodian Khmer Rouge regime and China.

Vietnam's perspectives were derived from the long history of Indochinese conflict dating back to the seventeenth-century Vietnamese expansion into Kampuchea Krom (Cochin China). The roots of the conflict predated the organization of any communist party in Indochina, but the immediate causes were related to Khmer Rouge paranoia toward the Vietnamese and the concomitant breakdown in communications between Phnom Penh and Hanoi, as well as to Phnom Penh's growing relations with China. As violence in Cambodia increased, the numbers of refugees moving into Vietnam grew also, providing the nucleus for a Cambodian resistance group. Continued Khmer Rouge military activities in Vietnamese border areas threatened stability in several new economic zones, and from a strategic standpoint Vietnam may have feared that a prolonged border war with Cambodia would become a two-front war with China.[36] Vietnam's invasion of Cambodia took place with Soviet approval, but the Chinese retaliated by sending their own troops across the border into Vietnam.

The Vietnamese should have welcomed the victory of the Khmer Rouge in Cambodia, which brought another communist government to power and eliminated a right-wing military government with close ties to the United States. The initial conflict with the Khmer Rouge focused on border areas that had been under Vietnamese control for nearly a decade. However, the roots of the conflict lay deep in Vietnamese-Cambodian relations and in differing interpretations of such concepts as the "Indochina Federation" or Vietnam's desire for a "special relationship" in Indochina, which the Khmer Rouge interpreted as meaning Vietnamese domination.[37] Moreover, there were differences in the two countries' respective interpretations of socialism and the global situation of communism that were based on the different socioeconomic and political conditions in each country. The conflict, which had been precipitated by a border dispute, escalated into a Vietnamese campaign to destroy the Khmer Rouge. Vietnam believed neutralism in Laos and Cambodia could not work—that probabilities of external intervention from states such as the United States and China made neutralism impossible. Vietnam took action to ensure that governments in Laos and Cambodia were reliable and supportive.

The regional power balance shifted in three ways as the result of the Vietnamese conquest of Cambodia. First, Indochina was consolidated under the leadership of communist Vietnam. Second, and linked to the first, Vietnam reestablished the traditional interstate pattern of conquering neighboring states but of maintaining them in suzerainty rather than destroying or annexing them. Third, the Soviet Union gained strategic military access to former U.S. facilities in Vietnam.

At first, Hanoi seemed confident that the Cambodian issue would be settled quickly, but as resistance groups made stabilization impossible, Vietnam's global isolation increased in the early 1980s. China, the United States, and the ASEAN states were successful but not united in sustaining global opposition to Vietnam's occupation of Cambodia. China, unable to force any decisions, appeared satisfied to maintain pressure on Vietnam through Cambodia and along the China-Vietnam border. The United States perhaps still psychologically vulnerable as a result of the Vietnam conflict, seemed only too willing to follow China's lead without seriously examining its own regional interests. Meanwhile, the ASEAN states could not agree on whether China or Vietnam was the greater enemy of regional stability.

Vietnam's strategy nearly succeeded, as trade with noncommunist countries began to increase, Australia moved to improve relations after the change to a Labor government, and there were some signs that linkages between Jakarta and Hanoi were warming—although UN opposition to seating Vietnam's client-Cambodia grew stronger each year.[38] Vietnam tried to localize the conflict—to move it out of the United Nations, persuade other Southeast Asian states to accept the status quo, and undermine the Chinese ability to influence any negotiations.[39]

Cambodia: Under Vietnam's Imperial Thumb

Cambodia, caught in the middle of the cold war confrontation, also found itself hopelessly intertwined in ethnic competition and regional changes that made the preservation of independence nearly impossible.

Cambodia sought neutrality as the only potential refuge from these larger conflicts, but other nations' policies intruded in the sense that their global and regional strategies were often played out within Cambodia's borders. As the war in Vietnam escalated, U.S. pressure on Cambodia intensified in response to the continuing Vietnamese presence along the border regions.

Cambodia had some success in sustaining neutralist policies until 1965, when North Vietnam began using its territory and it became increasingly enmeshed in the regional aspects of the war. With Sihanouk's tacit acceptance of Vietnamese troops on Cambodian soil, the political right began to coalesce; in 1969, when Lon Nol became prime minister, Cambodia moved away from neutralism, although the transition was not immediate. During 1969 and 1970, relations with communist states remained positive. Sihanouk was the only head of state to attend Ho Chi Minh's funeral, and Prime Minister Lon Nol visited Beijing. At the same time, relations with the United States resumed in 1969 after a four-year break. Also in 1969, Cambodia joined the International Monetary Fund and the Asian Development Bank, both of which were supported by the West.

Sihanouk had been able to sustain neutralist positions in cultivating relations with China and the Soviet Union while also receiving such conservative leaders as Indonesian President Suharto and Emperor Haile Selassie of Ethiopia. Conversely, as late as 1968, Sihanouk reiterated Cambodia's rejection of membership in and protection from SEATO.

Recognizing Cambodia's vulnerability, Sihanouk made great efforts to secure its borders, despite the North Vietnamese army. Cambodia sought and received formal bilateral confirmations of its borders from states as diverse as Britain, Japan, Pakistan, Guinea, and Ceylon. Sihanouk also continually sought border guarantees from the North Vietnamese and the National Liberation Front, as well as from the South Vietnamese and the Thais. Border problems were acute on the Mekong, and as relations with Thailand deteriorated, the Thai-sponsored Khmer Serai took advantage of sanctuaries in Thailand. Territorial encroachment was a traditional pattern of regional interstate behavior; from independence Cambodian territory had been threatened by the Thais on the west and the Vietnamese on the east.

These conflicts were contemporary versions of the traditional inter-ethnic conflicts that had been interrupted by the French. From its zenith in the twelfth and thirteenth centuries during the Angkor period, Cambodia was continually pressured by Champa, Annam, and Vietnamese dynasties on the east and Ayudhya on the west. Vietnamese expansion signaled the rise of a new ethnic, or cultural, group at the territorial and political expense of the declining Cambodian politico-cultural entity. Thai expansion was more conservative, focusing less on territory than on the neutralization of any competing political entities in the Mekong Basin. Colonial domination also exacerbated the conflicts by establishing artificial boundaries between states. Shifts and changes that began in the mid-1960s and continued into the 1980s reflected both the region's readjustment to its own internal power dynamics and the rise or decline of particular ethnic groups at the expense of others.

Cambodia's neutrality ended in 1970, and U.S. military forces entered the country from South Vietnam for the first time. Cambodia was briefly dependent upon the United States and its two nearest allies, Thailand and South Vietnam. Sihanouk, meanwhile, went into exile in Beijing as China's policy of seeking a Cambodian counterbalance to an increasingly aggressive and independent Vietnam took shape. However, under Lon Nol Cambodia was unable to deal militarily with either the North Vietnamese army or the local communist insurgents. In the end, Cambodia's pro-Western regime was a local victim of the breakdown of the global system when the United States withdrew its military support for the containment policy.

Even before the end of the U.S. involvement in Indochina, Cambodia had begun to slide into another global conflict. China, seeking to flank Vietnam, gave its support to the Royal Government of Cambodia, which was in exile in Beijing, and later to opposition forces inside Cambodia; the Soviet Union, meanwhile, maintained relations with the rightist Lon Nol government until forced to close its embassy when it was embarrassed by public criticism of its lack of support for Third World countries.[40]

Following the collapse of the U.S.-supported regimes in Indochina, the new Khmer Rouge government in Phnom Penh entered a secretive period during which it focused largely on reformulating domestic society. Most of its foreign policy initiatives were announcements of its intention to follow a Maoist line, but in actuality that policy was ultranationalist and often xenophobic. Its links to the radical left in China were very close, dating back to earlier than the Cultural Revolution, and political maneuvering among the Khmer Rouge factions followed the fortunes of political groups in the PRC: When "Teng's rightists staged their comeback against Chiang's radicals, Pol Pot intensified his purges," and the Stalinist faction tightened its control and increased the level of internal and external violence in Cambodia.[41]

Continual conflict took place along the Vietnamese border, but Cambodia managed to reach border agreements with Thailand and established diplomatic relations with Bangkok. Cambodia also took a more conciliatory posture toward ASEAN than did Vietnam or Laos, ignoring the organization for the most part but also avoiding such labels as "imperialist tool."

As Cambodia's drift toward Beijing became clearer in the 1970s, Cambodian-Vietnamese relations deteriorated. Border clashes became more frequent and rhetoric more heated. Concomitantly, as relations between Vietnam and China worsened, Cambodia again became vulnerable in a conflict over which it exercised little or no control. The resolution of this conflict began in December 1978 with the Vietnamese invasion of Cambodia and the subsequent installation of a pro-Vietnamese government under Heng Samrin.

This new stage of Vietnamese control in Cambodia completed a process that had started in the 1700s and that was only temporarily inhibited by French colonial intervention. The French had unwittingly enhanced the Vietnamese position in Indochina, especially in Cambodia, by relying heavily on Vietnamese bureaucrats in colonial administration throughout the area. China's brief intrusion across the northern border of Vietnam was intended to pressure Vietnam into withdrawing from Cambodia, but it also demonstrated that China, like other global powers, did not want to enter a sustained armed Indochina conflict. There was no countervailing force in the region to challenge Vietnam's control and no global power with the will to intervene, but Vietnam reached a crisis of will because of pressure from all sides to reverse its position in Cambodia.

Laos: My Neighbor, My Guardian

Laos was even less successful than Cambodia in sustaining neutrality. Neutralist coalition governments were established there in 1957, 1962, and 1975, but none withstood the external pressures for long. By 1970, the estimated total of U.S. assistance to Laos had reached US$500 million,[42] with many clandestine military operations and groups receiving military support. Direct military action by the North Vietnamese army in Laos increased at the same time, as did North Vietnamese support of the Laotian Patriotic Front (Pathet Lao) forces.[43]

Laos tried to maintain its neutralist complexion through diplomatic relations with the Soviet Union, China, and both North and South Vietnam, but when South Vietnamese troops moved into Laos in early 1971—provoking only mild Laotian protests—and relations with the Thai military continued to expand, its neutral image was lost. In late 1971, the United States announced that it would no longer comply with the 1962 Geneva agreements guaranteeing Laotian neutrality.

However, in 1972 a new Lao coalition government was formed. Prince Souvanna Phouma engineered a compromise with rightists, who may have already realized that U.S. support was waning. The last neutralist government did not have time to stabilize: With the fall of Phnom Penh and Saigon in 1975, the remaining rightist leadership fled Laos. The coalition government was abolished, the king abdicated, and the Lao People's Revolutionary Party replaced the Patriotic Front. Laos had again passed from neutrality to alignment, this time with the communist bloc.

Abandoning neutrality for the third time in 1975, Laos was caught in the struggle between the Soviet Union and China, as well as in the regional struggle between Thailand and Vietnam. At the global level, through the late 1970s Laos sought to balance the USSR and the PRC, but at the regional level it turned totally toward Vietnam and minimized relations with Thailand. This imbalanced regional position reduced Laotian foreign policy flexibility. Following Vietnam's intervention in Cambodia, the Vietnamese position in Indochina became preponderant, and Laos had even less foreign policy flexibility.[44]

In the early 1980s, Laos sought more latitude in relations with noncommunist states. The prospect of new initiatives from the United States that would provide aid in exchange for information on American soldiers missing in action (MIAs) was rumored, but little of substance followed. Relations with Thailand also improved. With an estimated five Vietnamese army divisions in Laos,[45] nothing extraordinary was expected. Then in the mid-1980s, Laotian-Thai border disagreements were manipulated by Vietnam in an attempt to ease pressure on the Thai-Cambodian border by increasing pressure along the Thai-Lao border and to generally ensure that Thai-Laotian relations did not become too cordial.[46]

The three states of Indochina appeared destined for a long-term "special relationship" under Vietnamese leadership.[47] Since Cambodian opposition to the relationship was badly fragmented and Laotian opposition was nearly nonexistent, these two states had few options but to fill roles as traditional vassal states in Vietnam's extended Indochina system.

Burma: Perfecting Isolation and Decay

Nonalignment, neutrality, and isolation are policies Burma has consistently maintained. In foreign and domestic politics, Burma has evolved a peculiarly Burmese way toward socialism at home and a Burmese way toward independence in its foreign policy. For instance, it has steadfastly tried to maintain stabile relations with its neighbors, especially India, China, and Thailand. Recognizing China's dominant regional position, the Burmese have made foreign policy decisions within the context of their perceptions of China's likely reactions, according China de facto veto power over Burma's foreign policy. China, in turn, has used its financial, material, and moral resources to expand or withdraw support from the Burmese communist insurgents as a reward mechanism for the Burmese government's policy decisions. One outcome of this Chinese influence was a very carefully managed and limited relationship between Burma and the Soviet Union. Yet relations with China were not always harmonious; they soured in 1967 and improved after 1970, although concerns remained about the treatment of Chinese living in Burma. The treatment of Indian minorities in Burma has also been a source of difficulty, and border problems with Thailand have never been satisfactory. Thai-Burmese relations were also threatened when Thailand granted political asylum to former Burmese Prime Minister U Nu.

Other aspects of Burma's foreign policy have sustained its nonaligned posture. For example, Burma was among the few states to maintain relations with both North and South Vietnam and North and South Korea, although its relations with North Korea were severely strained when assassins from there attempted to murder South Korea's President Chun Doo Hwan during his state visit to Burma in 1983. Burma also maintained good relations with the Soviet Union and the United States, although it carefully restricted aid from and involvement with both. Burma received technical assistance from Japan and the United Nations through the United Nations Development Program (UNDP). Its relations with the British remained correct but not warm; and its relations with West Germany and Finland were friendly, as Burma found in the latter sympathy for both its neutralist position and its proximity to a global power.

Within Southeast Asia, Burma maintained policies of friendly but limited and always bilateral cooperation. It welcomed the changes in Indochina that ended U.S. involvement but withheld recognition of Cambodia's Heng Samrin regime, arguing that the Khmer Rouge—however inhumane its domestic policies—was the only legitimate government there.[48] Burma showed some interest in ASEAN, attending meetings occasionally as an observer but declining membership. It continued to respect Chinese wariness of ASEAN and its capitalist-oriented members, and indicated that it would join a regional organization only if all Southeast Asian states were members.

Through the early 1970s, Japanese investment and assistance expanded, focusing on petroleum exploration. Ne Win made several trips within Southeast Asia and by 1973 had visited all of the ASEAN countries. He also visited India, Pakistan, and China. By the mid-1970s, Burma was again accepting assistance from the World Bank and the Asian Development Bank, both of which it had previously rejected. In the early 1980s, it received a new US$30 million agricultural assistance grant. However,

Burma maintained its aloof perspective on both global and regional politics despite persistent speculation that ASEAN membership was planned.

Burmese neutrality and links to both ASEAN and Vietnam led to suggestions that Rangoon might play a role in negotiating a Cambodian settlement.[49] Moreover, within the context of the Sino-Soviet split, Burma's policy options between the two communist giants were very carefully managed. Characteristically, the Burmese restructured relations with Western states such as the United States, which became a more legitimate partner for the Burmese after U.S. military involvement in Vietnam had ended. U.S.-Burmese cooperation remained modest, but joint efforts in narcotics control, for example, were undertaken.[50]

In addition to the effect of its proximity to China, Burmese foreign policy has been governed by a not always healthy suspicion of foreigners and of Western modernization. As early as the mid-1960s, the closure of World Bank operations in Rangoon was prompted by "an antipathy to having foreigners observe closely the Burmese economy."[51] Its development policies remain based on an obscure perception that Burma must follow its own development model. For example, tractor power for agricultural production was rejected in favor of the water buffalo because of continued shortages of parts and gasoline in the domestic market.[52] Thus, despite its desire for Western goods and technology, Burma has held fast to its generally aloof and nonaligned policies.

Burma is the only Southeast Asian state to sustain a more or less constant foreign policy course, despite the pressures and changes in global and regional systems. Its geographic position has perhaps aided the situation. The country was beyond the fringes of the cold war confrontation in Indochina and lies between two volatile, underdeveloped giants—India and China. Its attraction to neutralism has not meant an inactive foreign policy but rather a policy of selectively deciding each issue on its own merit. In addition, Burma has been very active in what has been called "conference diplomacy."[53] Finally, its willingness to impose strict developmental goals on itself—rejecting assistance moneys if terms were not suitable—has given the state a measure of insulation against overcommitment to any one donor state.

Indonesia: Politics of Regional Leadership

Although it was not subject to direct military confrontation in Indochina, Indonesia was the target of considerable competition among global powers—a fact that had an impact on its foreign policy. Size, resources, and a strategic regional position combined to make Indonesia attractive to both East and West.

In 1965, Indonesia turned toward the West. The government that evolved following the October coup designed a foreign policy to stabilize Indonesia's domestic inflation problems and to establish a development program keyed to financial assistance from major Western donors. Gone was Sukarno's flamboyant rhetoric of "newly emerging forces" in global confrontation with the established world order; "reality," said one writer, "was gaining control over romance."[54]

Foreign policy suddenly became one of the least interesting topics in Jakarta. The Suharto government met with international creditors to reschedule debt payments and review austere development plans. Indonesia also redressed its regional foreign policy by ending its confrontation with Malaysia and expanding relations with Singapore, Thailand, the Philippines, and Burma.

Indonesia's traditional "independent and active" foreign policy was retained, but that description came to stand for a pragmatic mixture of policies that acknowledged the position of its Western creditors while allowing some breadth of action within non-Western circles in order to defend a nonaligned label for its foreign policy.[55] Recognition of its creditors included strong commercial and assistance-oriented relations with the United States and Japan, although distrust and fear of economic domination at times inhibited relations, particularly with Japan. Also included in this policy was a reconstituted role for the Dutch. Links to the Inter-Governmental Group on Indonesia became a target of domestic criticism because of perceived Indonesian dependence on donors who, it was claimed, were concerned with protecting their investments at the expense of Indonesia's development.[56] Such criticism also addressed issues of domestic corruption and arbitrary governmental decision-making, but it largely reflected the deep-seated concern, which had been present since independence, that Indonesia would become too close to either the East or the West. Worries about economic dependence continued; these concerns focused increasingly on Japan and culminated in the January 1974 riots, which broke out when Japanese Prime Minister Kakuei Tanaka arrived in Jakarta.

Limits on Indonesia's Western "tilt" remained; nevertheless, the country's international stance became more pro-Western under the New Order government than at any time since independence. It has been argued that this shift away from nonalignment was possible because no effective domestic opposition remained to restrain the government: "The New Order's freedom to carry out a foreign policy of development . . . reflects the latitude afforded the absence of serious political competition."[57] When the New Order came to power, however, Indonesia was near bankruptcy, and "Indonesia's long-standing allegiance to nonalignment in foreign policy has been overshadowed by its critical need for enormous economic assistance . . . [which] can only come from the developed countries of the West and Japan."[58]

Indonesia retained or expanded its activities in several non-Western organizations. By 1969, it was ready to support a summit meeting of nonaligned states, and Indonesian foreign minister Adam Malik attended the summit in Algiers in 1973. Indonesia also participated in Islamic organizations, although it did not take strong positions in the Middle East conflicts. An oil-exporting nation, Indonesia also became a member of OPEC.

In bilateral relations, Indonesia sought to retain its image of independence. In 1968, it implemented a policy of dual recognition for divided states, establishing contacts with South Korea and informal relations with South Vietnam while retaining relations with North Korea and North Vietnam. In 1972, Indonesia established relations with East Germany. Relations with the Soviet Union were maintained, although arduous negotiations were required before the Soviet Union accepted debt rescheduling as called for by Indonesia's Western creditors. Indonesia remained very cool toward Moscow because it refused to supply military spare parts after the coup in 1965; nevertheless, the Soviet Union maintained one of its largest embassies in Jakarta.[59]

China remained a major foreign policy enigma for Indonesia. Because of suspected complicity in the 1965 coup, Indonesia froze its relations with China. The exact terms of the freeze were never clear: Although the entire diplomatic staffs of each country departed under duress, relations were not considered formally broken. Informal contacts were maintained, and some trade continued through Singapore and Hong Kong. Rumors of improved relations were frequent, and although various Indonesian government officials declared at times that relations would be restored "soon," it was not until 1985 that Indonesia's first trade mission visited Beijing and trade relations were formalized through an exchange of memoranda.

China was perceived as a double threat. Because of that country's alleged collusion with the Indonesian Communist Party, the Indonesian military feared Chinese support of internal subversion. These fears were exacerbated by ethnic Chinese living in Indonesia, who for generations had rejected assimilation and were often seen as agents for subversion. Formalization of Indonesia's relations with the new Malaysia was made easier by the fact that the Chinese population of Singapore had already been separated from Malaysia,[60] although Indonesia's relations with the independent Singapore were extensive.

Having long feared problems in an independent Timor, in 1976 the Indonesian government took decisive action in Portuguese Timor despite an expected furor of world opinion. Jakarta obviously feared the possibility of a communist client state in the archipelago and, holding little hope that Timor could ever sustain independent economic or political status, acted to annex the territory to Indonesia. It has since become clear that this annexation is permanent, although the Indonesians "are realistic about the speed with which measures of integration will effect change" in Timor.[61] Global opinion led by the Netherlands and Australia remained highly critical of Indonesia's policies in Timor and increasingly focused on reported violations of human rights and continued repression in Timor. While Indonesia took some steps to improve its handling of Timor, the issue did not find a solution acceptable to all sides.

In regional politics, Indonesian foreign policy matured throughout the 1970s. By the early 1970s, relations with Malaysia had grown very strong, enhanced by such changes as the new unified spelling system and an agreement on reciprocal recognition of university degrees. With the fall of Indochina in 1975, Indonesia assumed an even more active role in regional politics. It played a significant leadership role in ASEAN, and it was selected to host the permanent secretariat in Jakarta for which Indonesia pressed very hard against an alternative bid from Manila. At ASEAN's Bali summit, President Suharto demonstrated his quiet consensus-building approach to regional politics and the importance he attributed to the regional organization. The Indonesian concept of "national resilience" was transformed into one of "regional resilience" to connote the greater level of regional unity and confidence. Indonesia also expanded its regional role by strengthening its relations with non-ASEAN states, particularly Burma. Specific policies have changed from time to time, but Indonesia has consistently sought regional leadership "based on an exclusive pattern of relations among the resident states," although it did not have the power to shape that pattern.[62]

Brunei: Oil Everywhere

The sultanate of Brunei gained independence on January 1, 1984, and developed a foreign policy plan that would bring it directly and positively into regional politics. As early as 1981, Brunei began to seek an association with ASEAN.[63] Malaysia had its differences both with Brunei and with the British handling of the independence process, and there were suspicions of Indonesian plans for annexation, but these problems did not hinder Brunei's ASEAN membership, which was strongly supported by Indonesia.

Brunei's major concern as Southeast Asia's second ministate was the maintenance of its oil production, which approached 200,000 barrels per day.[64] Even as the terms of independence were being developed, security was a major concern. Brunei wanted to retain a battalion of British Army Gurkhas under the sultan's command. However, the British balked at this prospect, feeling that any national security threat would likely "originate from sources within the country . . . yet the philosophy behind the deployment of the Gurkhas stems from the perception of an external threat."[65]

Brunei also developed close relations with nonregional Islamic and oil-producing states. Following independence, Brunei increasingly "look[ed] to international bodies to amplify its voice." It became an active participant in ASEAN, the British Commonwealth, the Islamic Conference Organization, and the United Nations.[66] Brunei also developed close bilateral relations with Japan as its major trading partner for oil, natural gas, and beef.

Foreign Policy Responses, 1970–1985

During this period the states of Southeast Asia gained considerable strength and experience in responding to the challenges of international politics. In the course of managing domestic politics in the years since independence, they also shed many of the foreign trappings of government and politics that were inherited from the colonial period or adopted erroneously in the immediate postindependence period. Although they all remained weak in terms of foreign policy capabilities, as a region the states defined a common ground for regional diplomacy where none existed previously and at the same time placed some limits on the ability of extraregional powers to act in the region. Regional interaction and cooperation grew significantly, and the client-state status of many of these countries diminished. Although many of the more dramatic goals of revolution and independence remained unfulfilled, the regional states adopted more low-key approaches to domestic growth and development, as well as toward international relations. In both domestic politics and foreign policy, patterns of regional interaction, diplomacy, and leadership took on more autochthonous meanings.

NOTES

1. Donald C. Daniel, "The Soviet Navy in the Pacific," *Asia Pacific Community* 4 (Spring–Early Summer 1979), pp. 66–84.

2. H. Wriggins, "The Asian State System in the 1970s," in *Asia and the International System*, edited by Wayne Wilcox, Leo E. Rose, and Gavin Boyd (Cambridge, Mass.: Winthrop Publishers, 1972), p. 349.

3. Estrella D. Solidum, "Philippine Perceptions of Crucial Issues Affecting Southeast Asia," *Asian Survey* 22 (June 1982), p. 536.

4. John H. Adkins, "Philippines 1972: We'll Wait and See," *Asian Survey* 13 (February 1973), p. 146.

5. Guy J. Pauker, "Hegemonical Aspirants in Southeast Asia," in *Diversity and Development in Southeast Asia: The Coming Decade*, edited by Guy J. Pauker, Frank H. Golay, and Cynthia H. Enloe (New York: McGraw-Hill, 1977), p. 55.

6. Dick Wilson, *The Neutralization of Southeast Asia* (New York: Praeger Publishers, 1975), pp. 69–70.

7. "The Philippines: Economy," *Asia 1975 Yearbook* (Hong Kong: Far Eastern Economic Review, 1976), p. 263.

8. Rolando V. del Carmen, "Philippines 1974: A Holding Pattern—Power Consolidation or Prelude to Decline?" *Asian Survey* 15 (February 1975), p. 136.

9. Bernard Wideman, "An Approach to the Muslim Rebels," *Far Eastern Economic Review* (November 22, 1974), p. 12.

10. Guy J. Pauker, "The North-South Conflict," in Pauker, Golay, and Enloe, *Diversity and Development in Southeast Asia*, p. 83.

11. Carlos F. Nivera, "National Threat Perceptions in the Philippines," in *Threats to Security in East Asia–Pacific*, edited by Charles E. Morrison (Lexington, Mass.: D. C. Heath and Co., 1983), pp. 129–130.

12. Solidum, "Philippine Perceptions of Crucial Issues Affecting Southeast Asia," p. 546.

13. Lela Garner Noble, "The National Interest and the National Image: Philippine Policy in Asia," *Asia Survey* 13 (June 1973), p. 575.

14. Stephen Chee, "Malaysia's Changing Foreign Policy," in *Trends in Malaysia II* (Singapore: Institute of Southeast Asian Studies, 1974), p. 47, cited in Wilson, *The Neutralization of Southeast Asia*, p. 65.

15. Stephen Chee, "Malaysia and Singapore: Separate Identities, Different Priorities," *Asian Survey* 13 (February 1973), p. 157.

16. Gordon P. Means, *Malaysian Politics: The Second Generation* (Singapore: Oxford University Press, 1991), p. 47.

17. Wilson, *The Neutralization of Southeast Asia*, p. 67.

18. R. S. Milne, "Singapore's Exit from Malaysia: The Consequences of Ambiguity," *Asian Survey* 6 (March 1966), pp. 175–184.

19. "Singapore: Foreign Relations," *Asia 1970 Yearbook* (Hong Kong: Far Eastern Economic Review, 1971), p. 250.

20. Chee, "Malaysia and Singapore," p. 161.

21. "Singapore: Foreign Relations," *Asia 1974 Yearbook* (Hong Kong: Far Eastern Economic Review, 1975), p. 272.

22. Prime Minister Lee Kin Yew, "National Day Speech" (August 17, 1980), cited in Lim Joo-Jock, "Singapore in 1980—Management of Foreign Relations and Industrial Progress," in *Southeast Asian Affairs, 1981*, edited by Leo Suradinata (Singapore: Institute of Southeast Asian Studies, 1981), p. 276.

23. *Far Eastern Economic Review* (April 5, 1984).

24. James E. McCarthy, "National Image and Diplomacy," *Southeast Asia: An International Quarterly* 2 (Fall 1972), p. 448.

25. *Asia 1970 Yearbook* (Hong Kong: Far Eastern Economic Review, 1971), p. 290.

26. David Morell, "Thailand: Military Checkmate," *Asian Survey* 12 (February 1972), p. 165.

27. Juree Vichit-Vadakan, "Thailand in 1984: Year of Administering Rumors," *Asian Survey* 25 (February 1985), p. 234.

28. Khien Theeravit, "Thai-Kampuchean Relations: Problems and Prospects," *Asian Survey* 22 (June 1982), pp. 569–571.

29. Leszek Buszynski, "Thailand: Erosion of a Balanced Foreign Policy," *Asian Survey* 22 (November 1982), p. 1052.

30. Allan Goodman, "Is It Too Late to End the Vietnam War?" *Southeast Asia: An International Quarterly* 1 (Fall 1971), p. 367.

31. Lee E. Dutter and Raymond S. Kania, "Explaining Recent Vietnamese Behavior," *Asian Survey* 20 (September 1980), pp. 931–942; and Carlyle A. Thayer, "Vietnamese Perspectives on International Security: Three Revolutionary Currents," in *Asian Perspectives on International Security*, edited by Donald Hugh McMillen (London: Macmillan Publishers, 1984), pp. 57–76.

32. D. R. Sardesai, "Vietnam's Quest for Security," in *Changing Patterns of Security and Stability in Asia*, edited by Sudarshan Chawla and D. R. Sardesai (New York: Praeger Publishers, 1980), p. 239.

33. "Vietnam: Foreign Relations," *Asia 1977 Yearbook* (Hong Kong: Far Eastern Economic Review, 1978), p. 329.

34. Sheldon Simon, "Vietnam: Regional Dominance Arising from the Failure of Great-Power Balances," in *The Great-Power Triangle and Asian Security*, edited by Raju G.C. Thomas (Lexington, Mass.: D. C. Heath, 1983), p. 85.

35. Philippe Devillers, "An Analysis of the Vietnamese Objectives in Indochina," in *Indochina and Problems of Security and Stability in Southeast Asia*, edited by Khien Theeravit and MacAlister Brown (Bangkok: Chulalongkorn University Press, 1981), p. 92.

36. Craig Etcheson, *The Rise and Demise of Democratic Kampuchea* (Boulder and London: Westview Press and Frances Pinter, 1984), pp. 192–194.

37. Stephen P. Heder, "The Kampuchean-Vietnamese Conflict," in *The Third Indochina Conflict*, edited by David W.P. Elliot (Boulder: Westview Press, 1981), p. 35.

38. Michael Eiland, "Kampuchea in 1984: Yet Further from Peace," *Asian Survey* 25 (January 1985), p. 110.

39. Pao-min Chang, "Beijing Versus Hanoi—The Diplomacy over Kampuchea," *Asian Survey* 23 (May 1983), p. 607.

40. "Cambodia: Foreign Relations," *Asia 1974 Yearbook*, p. 113.

41. Etcheson, *The Rise and Demise of Democratic Kampuchea*, p. 176.

42. "Laos: Foreign Relations," *Asia 1971 Yearbook* (Hong Kong: Far Eastern Economic Review, 1972), p. 215.

43. Paul F. Langer and Joseph J. Zasloff, *North Vietnam and the Pathet Lao: Partners in the Struggle for Laos* (Cambridge: Harvard University Press, 1970), pp. 151–163.

44. Geoffrey C. Gunn, "Foreign Relations of the Lao People's Democratic Republic: The Ideological Imperative," *Asian Survey* 20 (October 1980), pp. 990–1007.

45. "Laos: Foreign Relations," *Asia 1984 Yearbook* (Hong Kong: Far Eastern Economic Review, 1985), p. 206.

46. Arthur J. Dommen, "Laos in 1984—The Year of the Thai Border," *Asian Survey* 25 (January 1985), pp. 119–120.

47. Dennis Duncanson, "Ideology, Tradition and Strategy in Indochina's Foreign Policy," *Journal of the Royal Society for Asian Affairs* 15 (February 1984), p. 44.

48. Aung Kin, "Burma in 1980—Pouring Balm on the Sore Spots," in Suradinata, *Southeast Asian Affairs, 1981*, p. 121.

49. Kin, "Burma in 1980," in Suradinata, *Southeast Asian Affairs, 1981*, p. 122.

50. Edwin W. Martin, "Burma in 1975: New Dimensions to Non-Alignment," *Asian Survey* 16 (February 1976), pp. 175–176.

51. David J. Steinberg, *Burma: A Socialist Nation of Southeast Asia* (Boulder: Westview Press, 1982), p. 123.

52. "Feeding On the Past; New is Not Always Better on Burma's Farms," *Far Eastern Economic Review* (August 15, 1985), pp. 64–66.

53. Josef Silverstein, *Burma: Military Rule and the Politics of Stagnation* (Ithaca: Cornell University Press, 1977), pp. 167–196.

54. Werner Levi, *The Challenge of World Politics in South and Southeast Asia* (Englewood Cliffs, N.J.: Prentice-Hall, 1968), p. 22.

55. Lalta P. Singh, "Indonesian Foreign Policy: The Linkage Between Domestic Power Balance and Foreign Policy Behavior," *Southeast Asia: An International Quarterly* 1 (Fall 1971), pp. 379–394.

56. Allan A. Samson, "Indonesia 1973: A Climate of Concern," *Asian Survey* 14 (February 1974), p. 163.

57. Franklin B. Weinstein, "Indonesia," in Wilcox, Rose, and Boyd, *Asia and the International System*, p. 142. For an excellent detailed development of this thesis, see Weinstein, *Indonesian Foreign Policy and the Dilemma of Dependence* (Ithaca: Cornell University Press, 1976).

58. Robert C. Horn, "Soviet Influence in Southeast Asia: Opportunities and Obstacles," *Asian Survey* 15 (August 1975), p. 661.

59. "Indonesia: Foreign Relations," *Asia 1975 Yearbook*, p. 191.

60. Michael Leifer, *Indonesia's Foreign Policy* (London: Allen & Unwin, for the Royal Institute of International Affairs, 1983), p. 175.

61. Donald E. Weatherbee, "The Indonesianization of East Timor," *Contemporary Southeast Asia* 3 (June 1981), p. 17.

62. Leifer, *Indonesia's Foreign Policy*, pp. 180–181.

63. Donald E. Weatherbee, "Brunei: The ASEAN Connection," *Asian Survey* 23 (June 1983), p. 723.

64. *Ibid.*, p. 725.

65. Hamzah Ahmad, "Oil and Security in Brunei," *Contemporary Southeast Asia* 2 (September 1980), p. 188.

66. K. Mulliner, "Brunei in 1984: Business as Usual After the Gala," *Asian Survey* 25 (February 1985), p. 219.

11

Coming of Age in
Foreign Policy Responses

The bipolar system ended with the disintegration of the Soviet Union in 1989, followed by the collapse of the communist regimes in Eastern Europe and the U.S. diffidence toward a continued role as global leader, which was characterized by growing domestic problems and a lack of foreign policy knowledge or interest on the part of U.S. administration under President Bill Clinton. Concomitantly, other states, although less powerful than the United States in a military sense, stepped into the vacuum created by the superpower decline and asserted their own independent policy positions—many basing that independence on economic rather than military capacity. The pressure to align with either the free world or the communist world had repressed divergent policy perspectives for decades, and the ideological straitjacket of the cold war had produced a uniformity of perspective that clouded deep differences in political views.

Foreign Policy Responses to the Collapse
of the Bipolar World

Confidence was the hallmark of the foreign policies of the states of Southeast Asia as they entered the era of international relations without the overarching presence of superpower control and manipulation of the global system. That confidence had grown through the years of experience implementing foreign policy in the generally hostile environment of the bipolar world. Particularly satisfying and important to the confidence that these states felt was their success in expanding policies of regional cooperation. However, the foundation of their confidence was found not in their foreign policy experiences at all but in growing domestic economic productivity and successful redefinition of domestic political structures that were more compatible with their own unique political cultures. This confidence was buttressed by their sustained domestic economic growth, which was taken as "proof" of the validity of their domestic political practices. In the international arena, Southeast Asian states implemented policies that more clearly reflected their precise objectives for serving their own locally defined interests. No longer could the global policy agenda be so readily dominated by the great powers or even by the Western powers acting in concert, and no longer could the foreign policies of individual states be dominated by the global agenda.

The Philippines: Trying to Build a New Model

During the early years of Corazon Aquino's presidency which began in 1986, the idealist and romantic notions of political and social renewal slowly vanished. Yet Aquino's assumption of power solved at least one dilemma because the ASEAN summit could be held in Manila as scheduled once Marcos had left office. Equally important, the willingness of ASEAN leaders to come to Manila was a solid show of support for Aquino.

The ASEAN summit resulted in what has become known as the ASEAN Manila Declaration, a rather general statement on economic cooperation among regional members. Perhaps of greater importance, the summit added a protocol to the 1976 Treaty of Amity and Cooperation that allowed other regional states to initial the document, which was later significant in providing Laos, Cambodia, and Vietnam with a mechanism for establishing formal links to the ASEAN group.

The Aquino government also strengthened the Philippines' image as an Asian state, as opposed to a Western client state, when she made state visits to Indonesia and Singapore before making the traditional trek to the United States. Manila also made efforts to ease its dispute with Malaysia over the Sulu archipelago.

Yet despite these policy leanings toward Southeast Asia, the Philippines also came under increasing pressure to resolve the future of the U.S. military bases located there since the agreements were scheduled to expire in 1991. The issue of the bases provided an essential focal point for Filipino foreign policy because the bases were a continuing reminder of Manila's unequal position in its relations with the United States.

Differences concerning territorial sovereignty, the presence of nuclear weapons, and U.S. manipulation of economic and military aid packages in the bargaining process were extremely unpopular with the general public in the Philippines, making the bases not only Manila's dominant foreign policy issue but an increasingly sensitive domestic issue as well. The strain in relations was intensified as many inside the U.S. government became critical of Aquino's management of the government. At the same time, changes in the global political structure slowly diminished the strategic importance of the bases, and Singapore's agreement to open naval repair and storage facilities, as well as to permit regular visits by U.S. fighter planes, further eroded the value of the bases in the Philippines. By the time the United States withdrew from the bases, Filipino domestic opposition to a continued U.S. presence was so strong that a rational foreign policy or strategic decision from Manila was nearly impossible.

Following the closure of the U.S. military bases, Filipino foreign policy became focused on its economic base in Southeast Asia. Economic diplomacy took the form of trade missions and other official visits to ASEAN partners. The ASEAN Free Trade Agreement (AFTA), signed in Singapore in 1991, further strengthened Manila's economic relations in the region.

At the same time, domestic political problems continued to hamper the Philippines' ability to undertake positive political or economic foreign policy initiatives:

> As presently (and historically) constituted, the Philippine state is ill-equipped to serve as a neutral arbiter of economic and political affairs. State autonomy and capacity are constrained by elite penetration of the state, the exclusionary nature of Philippine democracy, and the institutional structure of power. . . . Economic competition and state neutrality in economic affairs are constrained . . . by the predatory behavior of the socioeconomic elite, the concentration of wealth, and the oligopolistic and monopolistic nature of the private sector.[1]

These imbalances in the political and economic systems have resulted in "paralysing infighting . . . plaguing organizations as diverse as the Communist Party—split asunder by disputes over policy and dogma—and the feuding Manila and Makati stock exchanges."[2] In the increasingly pragmatic Southeast Asian environment, such economic and social paralysis has left the Philippines in a marginal competitive position.

Malaysia: From the British Shell to Regional Leadership

Malaysia's foreign policy was jolted into recognizing the new regional reality when Vietnam invaded Cambodia. Fearing that Vietnam—particularly a Vietnam buttressed by its treaty with the Soviet Union and with Soviet military forces at hand at Cam Ranh Bay—would use military force, or at least the threat of the use of force, to intimidate other regional states, Malaysia sought assurances against this eventuality. Malaysia and China, both of which had failed to reach understandings directly with Vietnam, exchanged official visits in late 1978 and early 1979 during which they came to mutual understandings with respect to "checking Vietnamese expansionism and the growing Soviet military capabilities from the bases in Vietnam."[3] Whereas Malaysia had previously launched independent foreign policies, such as its ZOPFAN proposal for Southeast Asia and its diplomatic initiatives toward Moscow and Eastern European countries in the late 1960s, these had been undertaken with the knowledge that British security support was available and viable. In addressing the Vietnam situation after the U.S. withdrawal, there was a sense of urgency and perhaps maturity in Malaysia's policy based on the recognition that Western security guarantees were suspect and that the state's long-term survival probably depended singularly on its own actions and capacities.

Malaysia also strengthened its links to the ASEAN group, which developed a unified strategy opposing Vietnamese occupation of Cambodia. In early 1980, Malaysia and Indonesia jointly issued the Kuantan Principle, appealing to the Soviet Union and China to stay out of Southeast Asian politics and seeking a negotiated end to the Cambodian conflict. The ASEAN states also sought to assure Thailand that Vietnamese aggression would be countered, and Malaysia announced that it would provide assistance to Thailand in the event of a Vietnamese attack.

When Mahathir bin Mohamad became prime minister, he introduced a new image to Malaysia's foreign policy. The West was held in increasing suspicion with regard to domestic as well as international issues. Trade issues, commercial air transport landing rights, as well as criticism of Malaysia's racial policies intensified the state's displeasure with the British and with Commonwealth activities in general. Malaysia responded with the "Look East" policy announced in early 1982. Prime Minister Mahathir argued that the West would use a variety of policy issues—human rights, trade unionism, exchange rates, media treatment, environmental protection, and democratic values—to keep developing states off balance and under economic control. To counter this perceived Western domination, Mahathir proposed the creation of a new East Asia

Economic Caucus (EAEC), a forum in which Asian interests could be discussed and planned without Western interference. The Look East policy sought to stimulate economic development by emulating Japan and South Korea, but in implementation it led to some confusion, criticism, and divisiveness at home. Nevertheless, Korean and Japanese investments in Malaysia increased rapidly through the 1980s.

For the previously demure Malaysia, Prime Minister Mahathir's foreign policy stances have been fairly strident. Not only has he been a strong voice for Asian togetherness through the Look East policy, but as early as 1988 he proposed a bilateral payment scheme to pool resources in an effort to enable developing countries to bypass financial institutions controlled by the West. He also proposed the creation of the South Investment, Trade, and Technology Data Exchange Center to provide opportunities for linkages among technology leaders and entrepreneurs in the southern countries. Malaysia's increasingly confrontational policies vis-à-vis the West seem to presume that the West is maintaining a sophisticated conspiracy to sustain its supremacy in global political and economic spheres and to be "accus[ing] the larger industrial powers of attempting to monopolize world trade and determine the trade policies of smaller states."[4]

Critics of the Look East policy saw it as Mahathir's rather visceral expression of an anti-British and anti-Western bias. On the other hand, the Look East policy also signaled a new primacy of Asianness in Malaysia's foreign policy and the end of its preoccupation with things Western, particularly British. It also reflected a clear transition in Malaysia's foreign policy from an insecure and inexperienced state to an effective and pragmatic actor. Malaysia ranked its foreign policy priorities as ASEAN, the Muslim countries, the nonaligned movement, and the Commonwealth countries, in that order. In another sense, it reconstructed the essential foreign policy focal points of traditional states on the Malay Peninsula: The Strait of Malacca in relations with Indonesia; competing entrepôt centers in relations with Singapore; and concern for extraregional powers in relations with China.

Malaysia has aggressively broadened its global contacts and relationships. Jettisoning its outmoded British links, the state built solid relationships with its nearest neighbors, expanded its global support through Islamic and nonaligned states, and came to terms with its greatest external threat—China. Within Southeast Asia, Malaysia began exporting autos to Indonesia. It has used its Islamic connections to gain an economic foothold in the Middle East. Concerned that China's expanded blue-water naval capacities resulting from the purchase of an aircraft carrier would greatly strengthen Beijing's presence in Southeast Asia and its claim in the Spratleys and the Paracels, in mid-1993 Malaysia bought Russian MiG-29 jet fighters[5] in addition to the usual military hardware it purchased from the West.

Singapore: Economic Foreign Policy

Singapore maintains dual strategies—regional and global—in its foreign policy. In the global perspective, trade and investment are the key issues, and Japan, Europe, and the United States are the primary targets. Technology transfer is also an important part of Singapore's strategy vis-à-vis the industrialized states. On the regional front, trade and investment are also primary objectives, but a host of secondary variables—ranging from security issues to intercultural sensitivities—gives a different complexion to the state's policies.

Singapore's relations among ASEAN states have generally been good. Singapore is cognizant of and low-key about its economic prowess as well as its Chineseness. Relations with Malaysia have occasionally been disturbed by minor irritants, but few significant issues have appeared. Singapore has provided important technical and policy-planning assistance to Brunei since the latter's independence, perhaps finding strength of friendship in the two countries' mutual ministate problems. Indonesia and Singapore have also developed closer relations as the former has gained more economic confidence.

At the global level, many of Singapore's foreign policy issues are also economic. For example, in 1989 Singapore and the United States underwent a period of highly strained relations when Singapore "graduated" from the Generalized System of Preferences (GSP), which allowed certain commodities from developing countries to enter the United States without duty. Although GSP status is always understood as temporary, the way in which it was terminated by the United States left Singapore highly disturbed, although its economy adapted very quickly.

The GSP dispute did not impede the United States and Singapore from signing a military facilities use agreement in 1990, providing for repair and storage facilities for the U.S. Navy and some landing and other rights for U.S. military aircraft. From Singapore's perspective, this agreement signaled the continuing U.S. commitment to maintain a presence in Southeast Asia, although Malaysia in particular disagreed, seeing the agreement as a violation of the ZOPFAN proposal.

Despite this disagreement over the U.S. military presence in Singapore, Malaysia and Singapore continued to maintain close relations. Particularly important was the water rights agreement through which Singapore was to receive water from Johore. Also, Singapore, Malaysia, and Indonesia developed the "Triangle of Growth," opening the industrial and economic growth areas of Johore in Malaysia and Bantam in Indonesia to joint ventures and other investment by entrepreneurs from any of the three countries.[6] However, perhaps feeling the vulnerability of a small state, Singapore was much more outspoken in its criticism of Iraq's invasion of Kuwait than were Malaysia or Indonesia, where stronger Islamic anti-Western sentiments among at least some segments of the population made muted reaction the better policy choice. Singapore maintained flexible policies in the face of the rapidly changing situation in the Soviet Union and Eastern Europe, attempting not only to maintain a balance in terms of the old bipolar global division but also to position itself to take advantage of changing economic opportunities in Eastern Europe.

Thailand: Finding Security in Economic Growth

In the 1980s, Thai foreign policy was dominated by its concerns about Vietnamese expansionism and about finding solutions to the Cambodian situation. As it became apparent that Vietnam could not sustain its domination of Cambodia, divisions appeared among Thai policymakers regarding the best mechanisms for dealing with Vietnam—whether to continue the hard-line approach or develop a more flexible policy in the hope of easing Vietnam's reluctance to withdraw from Cambodia. In this context, Indonesia played a key role as Thailand nervously supported Indonesia's diplomatic approaches to Vietnam and its efforts to define solutions for Cambodia. The Thai military, taking the more conservative approach, gave continued support to the Khmer Rouge in Cambodia and continued to strengthen Thailand's security arrangements with China. It is a credit to the growing political and diplomatic skills of the Thai and Indonesian foreign policy establishments that regional solidarity through ASEAN was preserved while innovative strategies for breaking the Cambodian stalemate without totally isolating Vietnam were explored.

With other neighbors, Thailand has had success in expanding relations, and it sought to "serve as a gateway to Indochina for trade and invest-ment."[7] Relations with Laos have improved dramatically after years of ideological as well as more mundane border conflicts. Changing policies in Laos have made improved relations productive, as opportunities for Thai investment became significant. Thai relations with Burma have remained positive but were hampered by public opposition to the Burmese military crackdown on prodemocracy opposition groups in Rangoon. By 1990, however, Thai relations with Burma had improved to the extent that Thailand advocated reducing Burma's global isolation, which had been imposed by the United States and others critical of Burmese domestic policies.

The changing global environment has continued to challenge Thai foreign policy strategies. Relations with the United States came increasingly to focus on economic issues and away from security issues, which had previously dominated Thai-U.S. relations, although Thai domestic issues related to the military's control of politics continued to bring problems to its relations with the United States. As Thailand's economy showed increasing strength, the Thais continued to encourage and seek U.S. investment as a balance to the Japanese. Although Thai-Japanese relations were strained when the Thai royal prince—who was in Japan to celebrate the centennial (1987) marking the establishment of diplomatic relations between the two states—was insulted by a number of lapses in protocol,[8] Thailand proposed that the Japanese Navy join it in joint exercises.[9]

Thai foreign policy has adjusted continually in response to the collapse of the Soviet Union and the Eastern bloc countries and to the implications of this changing environment for Southeast Asia, particularly Indochina. Thailand's increasing economic strength has required that it develop foreign economic policy in a global rather than national or even regional contexts. Thai-U.S. relations have continued to focus on economic issues in contrast to the past, when the relationship was almost entirely security-based.

Vietnam: The Trauma of Peace and the Realities of Rebuilding

After the defeat of the U.S. forces, Vietnam was unable to turn immediately to the challenges of economic development.

> That veteran generation was brilliantly successful in realizing the . . . objective of unifying the entire country under communist rule . . . [but] its record of achieving the post-war goal of bringing peace and prosperity to the Vietnamese people has been considerably less impressive. The national economy, plagued by a lack of capital and technology after a decade of mismanagement, was in shambles. The chronic failure of Party leaders to manage problems of the post-war era led to factional infighting and widespread discontent.[10]

Not until 1986, when the "renovation," or *doi moi*, policy was instituted, did the situation begin to change. Importantly, the enunciation of this policy change had been preceded by key changes in political leadership at the Politburo and in upper leadership levels of the government and the party. The *doi moi* was aimed primarily at domestic—agriculture and industrial—policies; however, foreign policy could not be far removed because of the gaping needs for capital and technology from abroad.

Reform, although slow, has been sufficient to allow entrepreneurship and private initiative to be rewarded, but the state's socialist cooperative structure remains in place.

Vietnam's resources continued to be drained by its occupation of Cambodia and Laos. Although domination of Indochina was a historically logical progression for the Vietnamese, they were unable to sustain military supply and logistics needs, let alone finance the managerial and developmental needs of Laos and Cambodia—particularly in the face of continual and growing external opposition. For example, the occupation of Cambodia brought strong opposition from China to the north and all of the ASEAN states to the south. During the occupation, which began in late 1978 and continued until the late 1980s, the occupation army reached a total of approximately 140,000 troops in 1987 before the withdrawal process began.[11]

The Vietnamese position regarding Cambodia—basically, its opposition to the Khmer Rouge and particularly Pol Pot—abated over a period of years as Vietnam found itself increasingly isolated. Although it had sought to establish a "special relationship" with its client government in Cambodia—the culmination of the centuries-long drive to the south and west—it became obvious that Vietnam could not sustain the situation alone. As Soviet support dissipated and finally disintegrated, it became necessary for Vietnam to reshape its position. By 1988, Vietnam was ready to negotiate, and it set the process in motion through a series of contacts to and through Indonesia.

The negotiation process was a long one, with the Cambodian agreement not completed until 1991 in Paris, but Vietnam succeeded in extricating its military forces more quickly and in reducing its expenditures there. Settlement also awaited improvements in Vietnam's relations with China, which, following high-level talks in China during July 1991, "served to reinforce Sino-Vietnamese support for a comprehensive political settlement."[12]

Vietnam's policies toward China remained tense through much of the 1980s. China vigorously opposed Vietnam's expanded role in Indochina; even more important, it opposed the growing influence of the Soviet Union in Vietnam, particularly Soviet use of the former U.S. military bases. To counter the Soviets, the Chinese had reportedly tried to induce the Vietnamese to distance themselves from the Soviets, offering to replace "the entire Soviet aid program . . . [and to] supply all the major commodities previously provided by the USSR—oil, cement, steel and cotton—in return for which Vietnam would agree to 'coordinate' its foreign policy and develop closer political ties with China."[13]

Recognizing that "China is the one power with the capacity and motivation to fill the vacuum" left by the collapse of the Soviet Union and the declining U.S. foreign policy interest, Vietnam became much more concerned about mutual relations.[14] Relations with China were normalized in 1991 based on an agreement by both sides not to seek hegemony or the imposition of ideology or values, but no alliance or other security guarantees were included. Territorial and maritime disputes remained unsettled, and in 1992 conflict arose again over Chinese agreements for offshore oil exploration and military occupation of Da Ba Dau Island in the Spratley group.

Also, with the collapse of the Soviet Union Vietnam's policies came to reflect the fact that the socialist "camp" no longer existed and that, consequently, it could pursue policies broadly defined as being in its national interest. For the first time in its modern history, Vietnam was "no longer dependent on any single country and was now free to construct its own foreign policy, although geopolitical constraints mean that China is still a factor."[15] It opened diplomatic relations with South Korea specifically to encourage the growth of economic activities. By late 1992, Vietnam had also completed negotiations with Japan to resume aid, which had been suspended in 1979. Vietnam also initialed the ASEAN Treaty of Amity and Cooperation and was granted observer status in ASEAN.

As part of an attempt to improve regional relations, Prime Minister Vo Van Kiet visited Malaysia, Brunei, the Philippines, and Singapore in October 1991. Impressed with Singapore's development, he invited its former Prime Minister Lee Kuan Yew to serve as a development adviser to the government of Vietnam.

Less positively, Vietnam's policies toward the United States could be characterized as "seeking to no avail." Vietnam had entertained hopes of receiving U.S. economic assistance soon after the end of the war, but the United States did not respond. Such issues as Americans missing in action and Vietnam's less than helpful attitude toward returning the remains of U.S. service personnel served to strengthen American bitterness toward Vietnam. Following the settlement of the Cambodia conflict, expectations were high that the United States and Vietnam could restore some measure of normal relations. Third countries—especially France, Japan, and the ASEAN states—encouraged Vietnam to be more forthcoming regarding MIAs and the United States to soften its hostile position toward Vietnam, but not until 1992 did the United States partially lift its economic embargo and "provide educational and humanitarian aid, and through a variety of envoys and unofficial contacts . . . encourage the Vietnamese to think that by early 1993 much greater progress toward normalization would have been made."[16] Although Vietnam demonstrated that it could undertake significant development programs without American aid or investment, it eagerly welcomed the

U.S. decision in early 1994 to end the nearly twenty-year-old economic embargo. The Vietnamese, like many others in Southeast Asia, fear potential Chinese economic and even military domination and hope a U.S. regional presence will provide a counterbalance to China's widening aspirations.

Cambodia: Trying Again with International Guarantees

Always seemingly vulnerable to external manipulation and control, Cambodia came under Vietnam's domination through direct military aggression in 1978. That control began to weaken and finally collapsed as the result of continuing internal pressure by guerrilla groups and increasing external pressure for free elections and for removal of the Vietnamese-controlled regime. Consequently, much of Cambodia's policy—whether foreign or domestic—has of necessity focused on the cessation of violence, the creation of a functional government, and the restoration of basic support services for the population.

The changing policies of the Soviet Union even before its collapse had an enormous impact on the situation in Cambodia because the Soviet Union "recognized that its détente with China and ability to find new friends in the Pacific [were] limited by its support for Vietnam's occupation of Kampuchea."[17] Ultimately, the Soviet Union and, subsequently, Russia worked with the United States and the West to pressure Vietnam to withdraw from Cambodia. Without Soviet financial and materiel support, Vietnam could not sustain its presence in Cambodia.

Chinese support for a Cambodian settlement was equally important, as China had financed and armed the extremely violent Khmer Rouge in an effort to counter Vietnam's expanded Indochina role. Unable to affect Vietnam's policies through direct military action, China had found supporting the Khmer Rouge to be an easy, low-cost alternative, but global events—particularly in Eastern Europe and the Soviet Union—made the settlement of Chinese-Vietnamese differences more urgent: "Events in the Persian Gulf, combined with the Soviet Union's rapid deterioration, pointed to the United States as the world's unchallenged superpower . . . [a] new geopolitical reality [that] moved the two key players—Vietnam and China—to do what was necessary to gain the acquiescence of the [Vietnamese-sponsored government] and the Khmer Rouge in a compromise settlement."[18]

Finally, Vietnamese support diminished gradually as Soviet support for Vietnam declined and as the Chinese reduced their support for the Khmer Rouge. Ultimately, Vietnam failed to effectively operationalize its concept of a "special relationship" among the states of Indochina as a means of establishing its traditionally structured suzerainty over

Cambodia because Vietnam and its Cambodian client regime were unable to "build a strong and reliable armed force . . . that would permit their promised withdrawal by 1990 without some arrangement preventing a return of the Khmer Rouge."[19] As had been the case for centuries, Vietnam could not sustain its armed forces fully extended to the borders of its intended empire.

The changes began when, after more than ten years of war, domestic violence, and diplomacy by great and small states, a compromise was reached in the Agreement on a Comprehensive Political Settlement of the Cambodia Conflict, signed in Paris on October 23, 1991. The agreement was "the most ambitious peacekeeping effort ever attempted by the United Nations . . . brokered by outside powers and accepted only with deep reservations by the Cambodian parties themselves."[20] It established a UN transitional authority (UNTAC) and combined the four antagonist groups in Cambodia—three groups under the Coalition Government of Democratic Kampuchea (CGDK) including the Khmer Rouge communists, the National United Front for an Independent, Neutral, Peaceful and Co-operative Cambodia (FUNCINPEC) led by Prince Norodom Sihanouk and his son Norodom Ranariddh, and the Kampuchean People's National Liberation Front (KPNLF) led by Son Sann, the former prime minister; plus the then current Vietnamese-created and sponsored People's Republic of Kampuchea (PRK)—into a coalition government. In early 1992, the United States lifted its economic embargo of Cambodia, which provided an important stimulus for foreign investment.

From the signing of the agreement through the UN-supervised elections in May 1993, Cambodia sought to implement the terms of the agreement and stave off disintegration. Yet frustration remained acute because political leaders were unable to achieve peace and stability following elections. Fearing that the country would again collapse into factional fighting, Prince Sihanouk—who was elected king and head of state by the parliament—proposed to return to a more active role in the government, including, importantly, appointing Khmer Rouge leaders to government posts in an effort to end their guerrilla attacks on the government.

Laos: The Freedom to Pursue New Foreign Policy

Laos, too, felt the shocks of readjustment in the global and regional systems as its major benefactors—the Soviet Union and Vietnam— reduced support. Laos did not figure as prominently as Cambodia in global and regional politics because of its relatively more stabile domestic political environment, but general inefficiency in the system has meant that Laos has "experienced low productivity, weak industrial growth and a lack of export diversification . . . accentuated by a fall in the level of economic growth."[21] In early 1986, Laos began a more aggressive search for American MIAs as a means to encourage the United States to upgrade relations. In 1988, the government undertook further policy changes and reforms designed to stimulate economic productivity and attract foreign investment. These efforts were enhanced by diplomatic efforts to reduce international isolation and dependence on Vietnam.

Relations with the Soviet Union remained friendly during the late 1980s, although Gorbachev made it clear that improved efficiency in Lao economic management was essential. Relations with China also improved during that same period, and diplomatic relations were established following "Vietnamese troop withdrawals from the northern Lao-China border and assurances from Beijing to Vientiane that support for anti-government guerrillas was being terminated."[22] Although Vietnam did not block Laotian overtures to China, it remained the principal Lao benefactor based on their Treaty of Friendship and Cooperation signed in 1977, which defined their mutual "special relationship," including the stationing of Vietnamese troops in Laos. By 1989, however, most of those troops had been withdrawn.

Laotian economic reforms of 1986 and 1988 meant that by the latter date all preferential policies for such socialist structures as cooperatives had been eliminated. Implementation of economic reforms stimulated immediate new trade and investment interest from Thailand, which led to greatly improved Lao-Thai relations. Thai Prime Minister General Chatichai Choonhavan led a trade delegation to Laos in late 1988. Previous border conflicts, which had focused on illegal teak logging, were brought under control, and trade between the two countries expanded quickly. Economic reform also brought renewed interest from Japan, which pledged new aid for agricultural and port development, but the United States remained aloof.

Laos remains one of the poorest countries in Asia, and its inefficient management and limited infrastructure make economic growth problematic at best. Nevertheless, the economy has improved. Relations with Thailand continued to expand into the early 1990s, particularly in joint-venture and other economic activities. Also in 1990, Thai Princess Chakri Sirindhorn visited Laos, and political-military relations were improved. China, particularly Yunnan province, has become the largest provider of foreign investment in Laos.[23]

U.S. relations with Laos have improved as progress continues to be made on issues concerning American MIAs, local political detainees, and drug trafficking. U.S. bilateral assistance programs, which had been suspended in 1975, were restored in 1990. Also in 1990 a joint memorandum on narcotics control was signed. U.S. private investment has also returned for petroleum exploration.

Despite the growing diversity of Laotian relations with the outside world, it has not totally divorced itself from its special relationship with Vietnam. Politically, the two states remain very close and pursue similar policies with respect to domestic development as well as international relations. Laos remained supportive of Vietnam's policies in Cambodia. At the same time, "The [Vietnamese] effort to turn Laos's economy away from Thailand and toward Vietnam has foundered on bad roads, antiquated ports, and rapacious Vietnamese officials. [Consequently,] Vietnam, consumed with its own economic difficulties and almost equally poor, can do very little for Laos."[24]

Continuing its moves toward a more independent Laotian foreign policy, Foreign Minister Phoun Sipaseut initialed ASEAN's Treaty of Amity and Cooperation and gained observer status in ASEAN in 1992. Relations with the United States were raised to the ambassadorial level after a seventeen-year break. Although Lao leaders still acknowledge their special relationship with Vietnam, the latter's influence has decreased as other competitors seek trade and investment opportunities. Increasingly, Thailand plays a primary economic role for Laos, and China fulfills the role of socialist leader and "validates the path the Lao party is following."[25] One observer has noted that for the first time since 1789, Laos has no dominating patron or partner, and although relations with Vietnam still hold "some concern over the delineation of their border and illegal Vietnamese immigration," Laos has no "fear of absorption by Vietnam."[26] As private trade and enterprises have reemerged under reformed Laotian policies, Laos's economy has generally outperformed those of both of its Indochinese neighbors.

Burma: Deeper into the Abyss

Although Burma has continued to view its relationship with China as the delimiter of its foreign policy, it has also attempted to maintain correct and open contacts with other countries. In 1987, Ne Win visited such nations as the United States and West Germany in an effort to stabilize relations with the West. Nevertheless, China still provides most of the technical and material support needed to sustain Burma. And although signs of Burma's plan to develop more open policies continue, little has changed. Speculation concerning fissures within the Burmese elite has fueled debate about likely scenarios for the post–Ne Win era, but as yet no one can answer two essential questions: (1) whether the dominant elite can maintain its unified position, and (2) whether this elite, even assuming complete unity, can maintain the will to ruthlessly repress dissent in the face of internal and external pressures.

Not surprisingly, much of Burma's foreign policy has been dominated by its domestic problems. Riots in Rangoon and other cities in 1988, which were brutally repressed, drew strongly negative reactions from most of the outside world—diplomatic missions were reduced in size, formal protests were filed with the government, and aid programs were canceled. In response to these negative sanctions, Burma's military government announced plans for and carried out general elections in 1990; however, the elections produced an overwhelming victory for the opposition, which caused the military to negate the election results in order to maintain its power. The net impact of the elections has been to further isolate Burma from the international community.

Burma has made some efforts to break out of this isolation and to repair its international image. It has maintained generally good relations with China and Thailand. Relations with the industrialized world have remained weak, but Burma succeeded in persuading Japan to resume its foreign aid program, although Japan appears to have been influenced as much by its worried business community as by the moral dilemma of giving aid to a repressive regime.[27] In 1992, after a fourteen-year break, Burma rejoined the Non-Aligned Movement, which it had quit because of the movement's close links to the Soviet Union. Also, the ASEAN states have been slow to criticize Burma, refusing to join the United States and other industrialized states in criticizing human rights abuses and instead sending the Filipino foreign minister to Rangoon to discuss the issue. Even Malaysia and Indonesia criticized Burma, however, when large numbers of Arakanese Muslims fled to Bangladesh to avoid conscription for corvée labor.[28]

Burma's primary foreign policy objective is to end its political isolation and increase foreign aid and investment without increasing the inflow of foreign ideas and people. It has had some success in achieving this objective, as China and the ASEAN states have been slow to take actions that would isolate Burma, and Japan has recently moved to expand its relations with Rangoon. Singapore, Portugal, Poland, and Czechoslovakia have increased arms shipments to Burma.[29] Singapore, Korea, and Japan have also provided funds for hotel construction and have supported other improvements to develop Burma's tourism industry, an increasingly lucrative source of much needed hard currencies for Rangoon. Thus, the United States has become the leader of a relatively small and, to Burma, less important group of antiregime critics.

Indonesia: The Quiet Approach to Regional Leadership

Indonesia's foreign policy has become more dynamic compared with the early years of the New Order, although there has been no return to the flamboyant policies and practices of the Sukarno days. In fact, contrasting styles have been evident, as leaders such as Singapore's Lee Kuan Yew and Malaysia's Prime Minister Mahathir have become more assertive and vocal on foreign policy issues, whereas Indonesia's Suharto appears to prefer the quiet, behind-the-scenes approach. Regardless of style and with increased confidence, the New Order government reestablished Indonesia's "rightful" position as regional leader, especially with respect to ASEAN. This newly invigorated foreign policy stance was first given recognition in a seminar sponsored jointly by the Foreign Ministry and Gadjah Mada University in 1988 and attended by the current and two former foreign ministers. The seminar, which called for Indonesia to play a greater role in international affairs, was compared to former Vice President Hatta's speech of forty years earlier, which had provided the vision for Indonesian foreign policy for decades.[30]

Tangible evidence of its new and more active foreign policy was found in Indonesia's opening of bilateral contact with the Vietnamese in an effort to find a solution to the Cambodian conflict. Indonesia played an active role in the Indochina settlements under the International Commission of Control and Supervision following the U.S. withdrawal from Vietnam. Further evidence of the new policy was seen in Indonesia's initiatives and dialogue with the Soviet Union. Clearly, Indonesia has sought a significant regional leadership role, at least in the archipelago, comparable to that of the great historical kingdoms of Śrīvijaya, Majapahit, and Mataram. Whether Indonesia can sustain this leadership role, which is implicit in its size (in terms of both population and geography), and successfully meet the regional challenges remains to be seen. Indonesia still has significant domestic problems that hinder its international leadership potential, but its capacities are enormous, and some of its diplomatic successes have been impressive.

Geopolitics has had a significant impact on Indonesia's foreign policy thinking as evidenced in its diplomatic initiatives toward Vietnam with respect to the Cambodian crisis. For many years, Indonesia sought to engage Vietnam in a regional dialogue in an attempt to seek a settlement despite strong opposition from Indonesia's ASEAN partners, particularly Thailand and Singapore. Although Indonesia carefully managed ASEAN sensitivities, it also appeared keenly interested in keeping regional communication with Vietnam open—often in the face of strong rejection from Vietnam—a policy that reflected Indonesia's long-term concern for regional solidarity against China.[31]

Indonesia's leadership roles in both the regional and the global arenas have continued to expand. Its role in resolving the Cambodian crisis was crucial. Importantly, in this effort Indonesia put into practice a key precept of its foreign policy, stressing the "responsibility of the countries of a given region—including Southeast Asia—to work together in limiting the role of external powers and promoting a sense of indigenous regional unity and cooperation, even if this requires the transcending of ideological barriers in the region."[32] Indonesia has consistently expressed a preference for finding regional solutions to problems as a way of limiting opportunities for external powers to influence and manipulate the situation.

Beyond Southeast Asia, in the late 1980s Indonesia sought a more active role in such groups as the Non-Aligned Movement, although problems with East Timor have somewhat weakened Indonesia's leadership claims. Other factors limiting Indonesia's leadership potential include its domestic difficulties with human rights and the press, which have occasionally affected its relations with Australia and other Western countries. Also, its limited contacts with China diminished its leadership claims.

After years of rumors and speculation, Indonesia normalized relations with China. By 1990, the world had changed sufficiently and communism had lost most or all of its international vitality, so officially sanctioned Chinese communists in Jakarta appeared much less fearsome. Important for Indonesia, stabile relations with China helped to dispel criticism of its Western leanings and added to its credibility as a state capable of dealing with all of the world's powers. Over the longer term, stabile relations with China should also provide new economic opportunities for Indonesia. With the Soviet Union no longer in existence and the United States a problematic player in Southeast Asian politics, China's relative regional influence will increase over time, and Indonesia will hope to hold together its ASEAN and other regional partners to deal with China from a position of strength.

Indonesia succeeded to the chair of the Non–Aligned Movement in 1992 for a three-year term and demonstrated its leadership by turning the organization's focus to economic issues and to the debate between the industrialized states and the underdeveloped states. Using this forum to promote its nonconfrontational approach to challenging the West as contrasted with other Southeast Asian leaders such as Malaysian Prime Minister Mahathir, Indonesia sought to establish a "dialogue between the industrialized countries of the North and the developing countries of the South . . . to be constructed on the basis of a spirit of interdependence rather than the confrontational style adopted in the 1970s and early 1980s."[33] But despite this new emphasis on economic cooperation,

Indonesia has insisted that the Non-Aligned Movement maintain its goals of opposing colonialism and racism and ensuring that such world forums as the United Nations are not dominated by any one country or small group of countries.

Yet Indonesia's coveted position as senior leader of the Southeast Asian states remains tempered by criticisms of its human rights record, particularly with respect to East Timor, and growing problems with its labor policies, particularly its unwillingness to allow the establishment of independent labor organizations. Timor became critical to all of ASEAN when Portugal, as chair of the European Community–ASEAN negotiations, blocked further discussions because of Indonesia's record there.[34] The United States reduced its military assistance to Indonesia, and both the United States and Japan reviewed their Indonesian foreign aid programs because of problems in Timor. Even relations with Malaysia were strained over the treatment of Acehenese separatists who sought political asylum in Malaysia.[35] As a foreign policy issue, Indonesia has vigorously opposed linking human rights issues to other issues such as economic development.

As the Asian region has been continually defined and redefined as an economic unit, Indonesia has also played a leading role in these new regional forums. Preempting further Dutch criticism of human rights, Indonesia announced in 1992 that it would no longer accept aid from the Dutch and dissolved its foreign assistance planning and coordination group, the Inter-Governmental Group on Indonesia—which included the Dutch—and reconstituted the Consultative Group on Indonesia (CGI), excluding the Netherlands. Indonesia was among the first states to support the Asia-Pacific Economic Community (APEC) and hosted its plenary meeting in 1994, which furthered Indonesia's leadership position within the broader Asian context.

Brunei: ASEAN, Islam, and Oil

Three focal points dominate Brunei's foreign policy—relations with its Southeast Asian neighbors, which are reflected largely in activities within ASEAN; relations with the Islamic world; and relations with other oil-exporting countries. A fourth, increasingly visible focus is Brunei's interest in a nonaligned foreign policy; Brunei joined the Non-Aligned Movement in August 1992.

In regional relations, Brunei has continued to act through ASEAN and to strengthen bilateral relations with Singapore and Malaysia. Relations with Thailand and the Philippines are cordial but less intense, although President Aquino visited Brunei during her tenure in office. Regional economic cooperation through ASEAN has been fundamental to Brunei's foreign policy. Brunei also hosted Vietnamese Prime Minister Vo Van Kiet and established diplomatic relations with Vietnam at the ambassadorial level in late 1992. In other regional affairs, Brunei pledged US $1 million toward the rehabilitation of Cambodia and offered a small military contingent for the UN peacekeeping force there.

Oil revenues have provided Brunei with a foreign policy tool few other states enjoy. For example, when Brunei was accepted into membership in the United Nations, the sultan presented the United Nations Children's Fund with a US$1 million grant to mark the occasion.[36] More recently, Brunei continued to cement its relationship with the Islamic world with a pledge of US$1 million for relief work in Bosnia.

Britain continues to play a major role in Brunei's defense posture through the Anglo-Brunei Defence Arrangement, although there have been signs that Brunei is interested in increasing its defense contacts with the United States.[37] In 1988, Britain demonstrated its defense capabilities through military exercises known as Setia Kawan, landing more than 3,000 troops in Brunei.[38] Singapore, among others, has encouraged Brunei to join the British-sponsored Five Power Defense Agreement, but Brunei has taken no action. On the other hand, the sultan wants the British-officered Gurkha garrison to remain in Brunei beyond its scheduled 1998 departure.

Foreign Policy Responses After 1985

Underlying the fundamental changes in the foreign policies of Southeast Asian states is the fact that they no longer automatically accept policy directives from superpowers or other external sources. Moreover, there is a willingness to evaluate and judge the fundamental perceptions on which policy prescriptions are based. Throughout Asia, but with significant input from Southeast Asian leaders, Asian alternatives to Western thought in terms of language, philosophy, and ideology are being defined for topics ranging from democracy and human rights to trade and defense.[39] Malaysia and Singapore have taken positions that are outspokenly critical of the West, whereas Indonesia has been more muted in its criticism. Even communist states such as Vietnam and Laos have redefined their policies to open their economies while trying to retain political control.

The experience of the post–World War II era undoubtedly left its mark on Southeast Asian interpretations of international relations. First, these states now recognize that they are on their own. Despite the most virulent rhetoric of cold war alliances, Southeast Asian leaders understand that the United States, the former Soviet Union, the British, the

French, and other European powers are unreliable regional partners because they have consistently acted in their own narrow self-interests as defined at any current point in time. This was certainly the message perceived by Thailand after years of dependence on the United States. Similarly, Malaysia and, to a lesser extent, Singapore hold a greatly diminished confidence in British steadfastness. Southeast Asian states do not presume the great powers will withdraw from the region but recognize that these powers will pursue their own interests regardless, and to the potential detriment, of the interests and demands of the regional states themselves. This understanding—perhaps somewhat of a reality check for Southeast Asian states—has left them with a more pragmatic understanding of their positions vis-à-vis the global system. Now that ideology has largely been removed from the formula, more realistic understandings of interstate relations have evolved.

Pragmatism has also been transferred from the political sector to the economic sector as the states of Southeast Asia have seen the inadequacy of military capacity in the face of unmet popular expectations concerning well-being and economic growth. Economic development is no longer a polemical or an ideological political issue, as was the case in the early years of independence. The ASEAN group of states especially have learned that economic growth requires balancing appropriate government policies, stimulating essential capital formation, and developing a committed and capable workforce. More recently, Laos and Vietnam have implemented policies that reflect a similar pragmatism, whereas Cambodia has undertaken some changes but has been hampered by vestiges of political and ideological conflict. Ideology continues to give way to pragmatism as issues are now focused on how to sustain these balances in continually changing national and international contexts.

These learning experiences have led to the development of a concept of Asian exclusiveness—more broadly defined than Southeast Asian but a concept to which Southeast Asians have contributed greatly. In direct opposition to such concepts as a developing *world culture*, Asians are focusing on refining individual and societal attributes that seem to be unique to Asia or that are at least found in unique patterns there. Whether the label is "communal democracy" or "soft authoritarianism," the fundamental message is that Asian approaches to society—especially to government and authority—will differ from those of the West.

NOTES

1. Jeffrey Riedinger, "The Philippines in 1993, Halting Steps Toward Liberalization," *Asian Survey* 34 (February 1994), pp. 139, 143.

2. Rigoberto Tiglao, "Philippines, Paralysed by Politics," *Far Eastern Economic Review* (May 12, 1994), p. 22.

3. Gordon P. Means, *Malaysian Politics: The Second Generation* (Singapore: Oxford University Press, 1991), p. 77.

4. Fred von der Mehden, "Malaysia in 1991, Economic Growth and Political Consolidation," *Asian Survey* 32 (February 1992), p. 118.

5. Jyotirmoy Banerjee, "Implications for Asia-Pacific Security, The Russian Enigma," *Asian Survey* 34 (June 1994), p. 552.

6. Shee Poon Kim, "Singapore in 1990, Continuity and Stability," *Asian Survey* 31 (February 1991), p. 176.

7. Suchit Bunbongkarn, "Thailand in 1991, Coping with Military Guardianship," *Asian Survey* 32 (February 1992), p. 138.

8. Clark D. Neher, "Thailand in 1987, Semi-Successful Semi-Democracy," *Asian Survey* 28 (February 1988), p. 199.

9. Scott R. Christensen, "Thailand in 1990, Political Tangles," *Asian Survey* 31 (February 1991), p. 201.

10. William Duiker, "Vietnam, A Revolution in Transition," in *Southeast Asian Affairs, 1989,* edited by Ng Chee Yuen (Singapore: Institute of Southeast Asian Affairs, 1989), p. 353.

11. Ronald J. Cima, "Vietnam in 1988, the Brink of Renewal," *Asian Survey* 29 (January 1989), p. 68.

12. Carlyle A. Thayer, "Sino-Vietnamese Relations, The Interplay of Ideology and National Interest," *Asian Survey* 34 (June 1994), p. 521.

13. *Ibid.,* p. 517, citing *Canberra Times,* December 17, 1990, n.p.

14. John W. Williams, "The United States and Vietnam: What Is Next?" *Midwest Newsletter, International Studies Association* 1 (September 1994), p. 5.

15. Thayer, "Sino-Vietnamese Relations," p. 514.

16. Allen E. Goodman, "Vietnam's Post–Cold War Diplomacy and the U.S. Response," *Asian Survey* 33 (August 1993), p. 833.

17. Gerald Segal, "The USSR in Asia in 1987: Signs of a Major Effort," *Asian Survey* 28 (January 1988), p. 3.

18. Frederick Z. Brown, "Cambodia in 1991, An Uncertain Peace," *Asian Survey* 32 (January 1992), p. 90.

19. Nayan Chanda, "Cambodia in 1987, Sihanouk on Center Stage," *Asian Survey* 28 (January 1988), p. 107.

20. Brown, "Cambodia in 1991," p. 95.

21. William Worner, "Economic Reform and Structural Change in Laos," in Ng Chee Yuen, *Southeast Asian Affairs, 1989,* p. 187.

22. *Ibid.,* p. 205.

23. Geoffrey C. Gunn, "Laos in 1990, Winds of Change," *Asian Survey* 31 (January 1991), pp. 91–92, citing "China Is Largest Foreign Investor in Laos, Says Agency," *Straits Times* (Agence France Presse), November 26, 1990, n.p.

24. Stephen T. Johnson, "Laos in 1991, Year of the Constitution," *Asian Survey* 32 (January 1992), p. 86.

25. *Ibid.,* p. 81.

26. *Ibid.*

27. Donald M. Seekins, "Japan's Aid Relations with Military Regimes in Burma, 1962–1991," *Asian Survey* 32 (March 1992), p. 260.

28. David I. Steinberg, "Myanmar in 1992, Plus Ça Change . . . ?" *Asian Survey* 33 (February 1993), p. 182.

29. Susumu Awanohara and Irene We, "Hard Line, Soft Target: Washington Will Get Tough with Burmese Junta," *Far Eastern Economic Review* (March 31, 1994), p. 31.

30. Jon Halldorsson, "A Higher Profile for Indonesia," in Ng Chee Yuen, *Southeast Asian Affairs, 1989*, p. 147.

31. Andrew J. MacIntyre, "Interpreting Indonesian Foreign Policy, the Case of Kampuchea, 1979–1986," *Asian Survey* 27 (May 1987), p. 527.

32. Gordon R. Hein, "Indonesia in 1988, Another Five Years for Soeharto," *Asian Survey* 29 (February 1989), p. 126.

33. Andrew J. MacIntyre, "Indonesia in 1992, Coming to Terms with the Outside World," *Asian Survey* 33 (February 1993), p. 207.

34. *Ibid.*, p. 205.

35. David McKendrick, "Indonesia in 1991, Growth, Privileges and Rules," *Asian Survey* 32 (February 1992), p. 251.

36. K. U. Menon, "Brunei Darussalam in 1987, Modernizing Autocracy," *Asian Survey* 28 (February 1988), p. 256.

37. Abu Bakar Hamzah, "Brunei Darussalam, Continuity and Tradition," in Ng Chee Yuen, *Southeast Asian Affairs, 1989*, p. 102.

38. K. U. Menon, "Brunei Darussalam in 1988, Aging in the Wood," *Asian Survey* 29 (February 1989), p. 144.

39. See Denny Roy, "Singapore, China, and the 'Soft Authoritarian' Challenge," *Asian Survey* 34 (March 1994), pp. 231–242.

12

The Emergence of
Neotraditional Values

Now approaching their fifth decade of independence, the Southeast Asian states are exhibiting increased confidence. Although their methods and organization may not find understanding or approval in the West, their neotraditional approaches to government constitute a statement that Southeast Asians have rediscovered and reasserted an indigenous identity. The tenacity of traditional behavior patterns within the domestic context is visible in the structures and functioning of government as well as in policy prescriptions. This is not to argue against change, however, for change is occurring everywhere in Southeast Asia. I am also not arguing that neotraditional behavior is a euphemism for emerging "backwardness." Change takes place as new patterns of behavior and institutions are adopted by Southeast Asians, and this happens largely as *adaptation* within the framework of historical and cultural understandings. Southeast Asians may readily adopt new forms or practices, but the adoption process requires familiarization with and adaptation to forms that are comfortable and understandable within the context of local experience. With the passage of time, responses to change have been defined more consistently in indigenous terms, even when Western forms, labels, or concepts may continue to be employed.

The emergence of the indigenous identity may offer greater assurance of success in the development and functioning of political institutions and social structures. It is clear that political values and structures cannot or will not be adopted wholesale from external models. In effect, the depth and vitality of indigenous values are too great to be overridden by new and different structures. Singapore, for example, is "characterized by both industrialization and modernization . . . [in which] new innovations, technology, and values are adopted from the advanced countries. Nevertheless, the "new elements resulting from them are added to supplement and not to substitute the indigenous cultures."[1] New structures and each political change must be constructed in terms that are amenable to local values (which also change, although at a slow pace) so that their adoption finds substantive referents in local political culture. Yet it must be emphasized that this process will not inhibit political change in Southeast Asia; just the opposite is true, and change is pervasive in the political systems there. This proposition only indicates that change must come within terms acceptable to and understood by the participants in the political system.

Problems remain, and further disjunction and sociopolitical collapse are possible. There is uncertainty about how or whether the governments of Southeast Asia can solve the problems confronting them by drawing upon ancient cultural values. Moreover, it is not certain *which* traditional values will be useful or exactly what they will mean when brought to bear on contemporary problems by individuals who are also products of the late twentieth century. For example, as the influence of Islam has extended in various part of East Java, tensions have arisen between orthodoxy and popular-magical forms of religion,[2] which have yet to be resolved. Nevertheless, faced with continuing challenges because of population growth and the continued destruction of precapitalist social formations, established elites have become more firmly entrenched— despite some expansion of the middle class—and incipient mass protests have generally been met with political repression. The state, although ostensibly lacking many of the finer points of Western political organization, has been redefined in more characteristically indigenous terms and continues to develop a formula for growth and development that uses this traditional context, no doubt somewhat homogenized by contemporary interpretations of traditional values: "As [postindependence] ruling elites failed to 'deliver' the developmental goods in the overwhelming majority of Third World states, their own legitimacy was called into question by religious and/or ethnic leaders, who often framed their criticisms in religious doctrinal or sub-national terms."[3]

Southeast Asian traditions tend to accept or acquiesce to the existing governors in the seats of power; historically, popular legitimacy has been weak. In the traditional system, "There was no political participation by the individual villager in the decisions made by the council. Neither was the individual involved in the court-mandarin structure. . . . Individuals got virtually no experience with government, certainly none of the educative experiences of a citizen in a democracy."[4] Currently as well, most states derive much of their legitimacy through acquiescence, but it is uncertain whether this can be sustained indefinitely. In fact, it is likely that education—both formal and informal, through the global spread of ideas—will continue to erode local village and clan identification and turn the attention of the individual more directly to the state. As ever larger numbers of Southeast Asians are exposed to formal education and external values, the challenges for the elites will be to adaptively integrate the new forces these people and their ideas represent while maintaining a cultural and political unity. In the short run, education remains largely a luxury of the elite, and the training that is reaching broader segments of the population is largely technical in nature, which reflects the governments' preoccupations with human-resource needs for economic development and their disinterest in a broadly educated citizenry. The Philippines, with a longer history of mass education than most Southeast Asian countries, may be an exception, but the extent to which political participation there has moved beyond patron-client relationships is not clear. As education in the more liberal sense penetrates these societies, elites will find it necessary to broaden participation in these systems. This does not mean it is only a matter of time until Western political ideas are accepted through education. The challenge will be to define indigenous techniques and forms through which participation can be broadened.

The process of redefining national identity and, by extension, the social and political institutions that make up contemporary society has not been easy or uniform. Some values such as religion have been obvious areas for revitalization. Others, such as political practices and structures, have evolved more haphazardly and have sometimes been driven as much by the propensity of incumbent elites to protect their interests as by a disinterested and thoughtful process of development of appropriate political institutions. Yet in one sense, even this ad hoc approach to political reorganization and development has shaped modes of operation that more closely approximate indigenous processes and structures for government. A substantial element in this definitional process remains the elucidation of the way these societies will differ from the West, which until recently had maintained a monopoly on the definition of such terms as *developed* and *modern*, essentially shaping them in its own image.

Interestingly, this definitional process, although in part generational within Southeast Asia, also has an economic base. As Southeast Asian states have gained in economic stature—as they have "developed" in the Western economic definition of the term—they have become increasingly independent and vocal in their criticisms of Western political and social practices, pointing vigorously to ways in which particular Western practices fail to apply to them or to fit their cultural context. Criticisms of the West also focus on the breakdown of social institutions such as the family and the apparent decline in the work ethic coupled with excessive demands for social support services from the government. It is true that some first-generation Southeast Asian leaders were critical of the West—Sukarno and others regularly castigated the United States and the Soviet Union for failings and shortcomings in world politics. The Bandung Conference of 1955 drew broadly different pictures of the world as envisioned by the superpowers and by the Third World states, respectively. Sukarno also criticized Western democratic processes, but it has been later generations that have turned the discussion to the full range of domestic political and economic practices and, importantly, focused on traditional values for the ideas that will shape these institutional changes.

Generational Change and Neotraditional Values

The first generation of revolutionary and independence leaders adopted many of the roles of their Western counterparts. Since they sought to replace Western colonial leadership, it was imperative for them to demonstrate their capacities to do so—not by prescribing some outmoded models of state organization (the institutions that had enabled the colonial powers to gain control in the first place) but by acting out their bona fides through emulating the colonial style in everyday life and in governmental management. Speaking of Indonesia, it has been noted that:

> Insofar as they [nationalist elites] acquired the trappings of modernity, it legitimized their claims to replace the Dutch as the rulers of Indonesia, for it was by their expertise in dealing with the modern world that the Netherlanders had argued their tutelary right. It also legitimized the new nationalist leaders' precedence over traditional ruling elites in Java and the Outer Islands, for the old chiefly families could be portrayed as *feodal* and outmoded, incapable of meeting the challenge of the West.[5]

In the years following independence, this first-generational elite group continued to define its mission as consisting of: (1) the imperative of bringing modernity to the nation and the state, and (2) the definition of the role of the state in the *modern* global political system.

Importantly for later political meanings and contexts, modernity was defined largely in Western terms. Modernity came to be equated with an urban lifestyle and an official governmental appointment, and Western education was the key criterion for admission to this modern elite group. The measure of success for this group was, to a large extent, the degree to which it was able to emulate its colonial predecessors. To the extent that modernity was defined in these urban terms, the mass of the rural population was, by definition, backward; thus, to the (mostly limited) extent that policies were focused on the rural populace, the emphasis was on bringing modernity to them rather than solving immediate social and economic problems. The intricacies of agriculture policies such as land tenure, commodity production, marketing systems, and infrastructural support received much less attention than did food prices in major urban markets.

In the international political arena, which generally appeared more interesting and important than rural sectors and was certainly more familiar, the great number of new states appearing on the scene created a momentum that seemed to consume much of the policy focus of these newly independent governments. In the attempt to define their independence in the midst of the growing cold war, many states sought to be free of the bonds or strings attached to alignment with either superpower camp; the Non-Aligned Movement was born in this mentality and was committed to a new world order. The rejection of foreign assistance—which was often aimed at rural development, improved agricultural production, or education—because of demands made by donors that pertained to global political alignments highlights the dilemma faced by these early postindependence leaders. The result frequently left Southeast Asia's political elites more isolated from their rural constituencies.

The sociopolitical model formed by the composite of policies, actions, and values of the first generation of postindependence leaders has been rejected with increasing stridency by second- and third-generation leaders because "however useful modernity was as a mystique, it created the problem of establishing a sense of cultural self that was something more than a hybrid of European and local traits. Hence the great concern—psychological as well as political—for establishing . . . [a] national identity, and the intense ambivalence towards things deemed as 'Western' or 'foreign.'"[6] Education and training during the period since independence have had an important impact on some of these problems. As second and third generations since independence have come to maturity, the intellectual complexion of the elite groups has begun to change:

> Gradually, however, a new generation of elites began coming to the political scene with more of a vernacular education and with greater concern for some of the core values of their ethnic cultural heritage and often with a heightened awareness of the potential to mobilize mass support for themselves by appealing to the "primordial sentiments" of their ethnic community, frequently in the form of religious revivalism.[7]

Popular notions of nationalism and independence, which have received great emphasis in the local public-education systems, coupled with an overall decline in the quality of mass educational instruction have shaped the basic value structure of growing segments of the population and have given traditional values ever stronger popular support. Such values as the premium placed on foreign language skills among first-generation leaders (no doubt motivated by the added status derived from conversational links to the colonial elite) were lost in the socialization processes that gave greater emphasis to national language as part of the new national identity. In the end, there may have been too much to accomplish within a single generation, so that securing independence became the major achievement of the first generation of political leaders while defining the polity and refining political practices would, of necessity, wait for later generations.

The success of these new Southeast Asian leaders, measured at least in economic terms, has been undeniable. As economic stability has increased, political, social, and environmental issues have been given greater focus. Whether traditional values have stimulated or structured this success is another issue, but some of the key elements of this dramatic growth are definable: "holding special-interest politics at bay (which is sometimes an excuse for keeping opposition politicians at bay); . . . swift and sometimes brutal punishment of crimes with no hand-wringing at all over their 'causes'; and leaving enterprising individuals and families with lots of both resources and responsibilities by keeping taxes and welfare low."[8]

There are expectations to this contrasting of first- versus second-generation leaders—Singapore's Lee Kuan Yew being the most obvious example of a first-generation leader who has become a spokesperson for traditional values. However, even Lee is a recent convert to these views and earlier espoused a wide range of Western methods and ideas. Lee makes a doubly interesting example because as prime minister in Singapore he put into practice many policies based on traditional Asian practices, especially their propensity for government control, strong top-down political structures, restriction on opposition practices, and other policies based on the sense of preference for the community as contrasted to the individual's rights and freedoms.

Neotraditional Values and Ideologies Underpinning the State

During the 1960s, many domestic issues were overshadowed by external issues and global politics. This became less true in the 1970s and 1980s as superpower politics waned, providing a respite from the pressures of global conformity and greatly reducing the likelihood of external penetration and subversion. In this more relaxed environment, elements of traditional state practices have reemerged in the contemporary period:

> Any discussion of sociopolitical development . . . must take into consideration two factors: (1) the distinctive character of . . . cultural values, which contribute their own meaning to . . . development, while at the same time setting limits of interpretation on such commonly used terms as democracy, basic human rights, political rights, constitutional state, rule of law, and so on; and (2) the history of . . . [the] struggle for self-determination, which continues to influence the present-day course of political development.[9]

Although there are exceptions and variations, in many respects the states of Southeast Asia have become traditional in both domestic and international outlooks. But the basic issue for Southeast Asians is how to organize a modern, growing industrial society without encouraging or experiencing the negatives exemplified in Western society as they see them. Where are the balances between community and individual, order and freedom, exploitation and equitable growth, and government control and service? Moreover, what can traditional values tell Southeast Asians about maintaining the balances in these relationships?

Semantic difficulties aside and recognizing that there is little uniformity throughout the region, there are three fundamental elements around which Southeast Asians diverge from the West in their sociopolitical views: (1) the rejection of Western commercialism and consumer culture; (2) the rejection of Western concepts of the primacy of the individual versus the community; and (3) although less widely discussed, the rejection of Western concepts of the welfare state or, stated more bluntly, rejection of the concept of public service in favor of control as the primary responsibility of government. Of course, one does not have to look very far to see conspicuous consumption in Southeast Asia, but—particularly for the substantial Muslim populations—the revitalization of Islam has provided a strong, value-based orientation and framework for redirecting their lives. In articulating the view of this group, a Thai parliamentarian noted that "those who are overtly Western in their thinking are finished. What the region needs now are people who can blend ideas and technologies acquired from outside the region with the values and traditions of Asia's indigenous societies, [such as] consensus-building which is derived from traditional Asian virtues of rationality, tolerance and modernization."[10] The rejection of individualism is both more subtle and pervasive, but it finds expression in current challenges to human rights issues, in disenchantment with certain

Western democratic political concepts and processes, and in discomfort with Western concepts of freedom of speech, information, and the press.

The new Southeast Asian assertiveness has stimulated overt actions in an effort to demonstrate to the West that the Asian environment is changing and is no longer automatically subservient to Western influence or approval. Malaysia, for example, imposed trade sanctions on British businesses (an act that would have been unthinkable a decade ago) when the London *Sunday Times* published allegations that Malaysian Prime Minister Datuk Seri Mahathir Mohamad had accepted bribes from a British contractor. Singapore took very indignant exception to criticisms by U.S. President Bill Clinton of its inhumane punishment—caning—of an American youth convicted of vandalism there. In the current Southeast Asian environment of assertive independence, the publicity attracted by the president's statement solidified Singapore's resolve to pursue its own course.

Ideology and Religion

In both Burma and Vietnam, ideology has replaced metaphysics as the basic legitimizing mechanism for the state, although Buddhism remains an important political force in both. Indonesia has relied increasingly on vague pronouncements of *Pancasila*, or its "five principles"—a weak form of ideological support—to counter Islamic and other demands for greater influence in government, and Malaysia has given greater voice to Islam as a state ideology. Catholicism dominates the social and political fabric of the Philippines. Most states have also relied upon variations of an economic development theme as important elements of legitimization. However, whether communist ideology or economic development has provided the state's philosophical base, the urban orientation and extractive nature of the state have changed very little. Moreover, every state with a substantial Muslim population has had to defer to some extent to Islamic political demands.

Although Islam has played an important role in shaping Indonesia's nationalist movement since the early twentieth century, its dynamism was latent in Malaysia until events outside the region stimulated its rise. Islam gained some strength in identity as a result of the Arab-Israeli War of 1967 and experienced a substantial increase in vitality following the revolution in Iran (1978–1980), but it stimulated a stance of greater militancy during and following the 1990–1991 Gulf War against Iraq. Malaysia has experienced the strongest growth of Islam, and the government there—which has long represented itself as the protector of Islam—is in danger of losing control of the Islamic agenda to radical groups. Much of the new activism can be seen in Islamic groups called *dakwah*, meaning "call" or "call to worship," which have organized and become more militant and politically active. The government faces an enormous dilemma because whereas it relies on the support of these groups, their increasing mobilization of the Muslim community poses both a threat and a challenge as the government seeks to maintain its responsibility for interpreting and enforcing Islamic law and to ensure continued support of them and individuals while not allowing the groups to take over the interpretation of Islamic law (thereby forcing the government, as the protector of Islamic law, to comply with the dictates of these small but strident groups). More radical Islamic groups, such as the *Darul Arqam*, have raised governmental concern because of their growing influence within Malaysia's middle class, where UMNO has predominated for decades.[11] Conversely, the Islamic Party of Malaysia's (PAS) basic policy stresses the need for the preeminence of ethnic Malays in all matters of politics, the economy, and culture as the only reliable means of protecting Islam.[12] Control of Islam has continued to be a problem for the government of Malaysia as it banned the controversial Al-Arqam sect in late August 1994.[13]

In the Philippines, in Mindanao—although conflicts still abound within Islam and between Muslims and Christians—Islamic religious activity has increased dramatically since the mid-1970s. Muslim minorities in Thailand and the Philippines face uncertain futures unless both they and the non-Muslim majorities develop flexible responses to the numerous arbitrarily hardened politico-religious issues that separate and isolate the minority groups while feeding suspicions and myths on both sides. Examples of the synthesis of Islamic and Western law exist, and Singapore has passed the Administration of Muslim Law Act (1966), which provides for a council to advise on religious matters relating to Islam there.

From the time of the traditional period, there has been no separation of religion and politics in Southeast Asia, and most traditional states supported their legitimacy with a variety of religious themes and claims. In many respects, religion has been in competition with secular nationalism in the definition of political ideology among postindependence states. Whereas in the earliest times religion, particularly Hindu conceptions of state, offered a weak but workable structure for interstate relations, it became politicized when Islam arrived in the region and became even more highly politicized as Christian colonialists sought to confront Islam wherever possible.

This politicization of religion has extended to the contemporary era. Secular modernization has failed to produce the equitable and open societies promised in its manifesto; thus, people in Southeast Asia have sought indigenous and neotraditional alternatives. Moreover, the Gulf

War and other problems in the Middle East gave credence to the Muslim view that the Christian West still plans to impoverish if not destroy Islam. The fact that the disgruntled and disenfranchised in Southeast Asia have looked to religion for political solutions should come as no surprise; rather, the West has been too quick to envision its own models of secularism as the inevitable end result of modernity. In the 1960s, Islamic dress was adopted by many people among the lower classes because it was inexpensive; however, by the 1980s, "Islamic dress took a different, more sophisticated form . . . [as] middle and wealthy classes adopted an expensive and fashionable sort of Islamic attire."[14]

Although conservatism in Christianity may or may not lead to a parallel political conservatism, Islam does more consistently stimulate conservative political pressures because of the lack of separation between religious and political concepts in Islamic thinking. Even within Islam, however, there may be significant differences in its political significance for ordinary people in rural towns and villages compared with that for urban political and religious leaders and activists. Yet Islam also presents enormous contradictions for political practices in Southeast Asia because its propensity to readily and sharply delineate between good and evil conflicts with the more obscure and uncertain perceptions of power and interpersonal relationships that are common in the region's cultures.

The Community and the Individual

From very early history in Southeast Asia, the community has taken precedent over the individual in social thought. Many have argued that this philosophy developed from the communal nature of the agricultural village, particularly in irrigated agricultural systems, and from the interdependence and reciprocity of relationships that evolved in this closed community. Greater credence was given to conformity and harmony than to freedom of individual expression and thought:

> The interests of the society as a whole are emphasized over those of the individual member. Thus, basic rights including political rights are accompanied by social responsibilities, which are weighted equally. It is expected that each individual will exercise self-restraint and will be willing to make sacrifices for the sake of serving the interests of society in the course of safeguarding his personal rights.[15]

This may have appeared to be a small price for the individual who in return received protection and sponsorship guaranteed by the community. The origin of this philosophical view matters less than does the recognition that this concept of the primacy of the community over the individual permeates every aspect of life in Southeast Asia and creates for the average citizen there a completely different pattern of thoughts and expectations than that of the average citizen in the West. Moreover, the Western concept of development, which places great emphasis on the ever increasing autonomy of the individual, has not found acceptance in Southeast Asia, particularly as it applies to politics.

Human rights is one of the issues derived from these community versus individual differences that has come to the fore in recent years as a measure of the distinction between Western and Asian societies. Some argue that this is only the most recent Western stratagem to redefine its superior status, which stems from the colonial era when moral, religious, and technological rationales provided the underpinnings of that superiority. Nevertheless, as a general principle, Southeast Asians place greater value on community rights than on individual rights. As characterized by the Malaysian prime minister, "To us, democracy means welfare of the majority. While the individual must have his rights, these must not extend to the point where they deprive the majority of their rights."[16] Importantly for the future of political institutions in Southeast Asia, most individuals there know, understand, accept, expect, and act in accordance with this differentiation in relationships.

Thus framed, for Southeast Asians the human rights debate has become focused on the issue of universality versus culturally specific versions of these rights. There are also salient questions about whether human rights grow out of some inalienable human condition or whether they are— taken largely from Western political development—a set of constitutional rights as defined in the social contract between the governed and the governor: "Although the general idea of the right of man and certain corresponding themes are shared by humanity's major value systems, no system provides a systematic and comprehensive list of rights comparable to those in [certain] Western constitutions."[17] But the most comprehensive statements on human rights have been developed by the United Nations and are summarized in various UN documents and declarations, to which most of the states of the world have agreed.

Despite such general agreements, differences have emerged, practices continue to vary greatly, and no consensus seems to be on the horizon as the crux of the debate remains the issue of universality versus the cultural or time-specific context of human rights. The Vienna Declaration (June 1993) developed at the World Conference on Human Rights conveniently skirted the issue by acknowledging "the principle of universality and indivisibility" of human rights while simultaneously adopting the principle that "the significance of historical, cultural and religious backgrounds must be borne in mind in the protection and promotion of human rights."[18] Those who argue from the universality point of view—mostly Westerners—criticize Asian leaders for excessive control of political systems and for lopsided economic policies that favor industrial and corporate interests over the interests of individual workers. These arguments are seen in many Asian quarters as Western efforts to impose currently defined Western values on the rest of the world and are sometimes labeled "neo-" or "cultural" imperialism. Moreover, some argue that Western interest in human rights has grown only as its economic dominance has waned.

The role of economics in this issue is important. Third World countries have insisted that the right to development and the interdependence of development, democracy, and overall individual rights be considered universal and inalienable—a position often not supported by developed states. Extensive evidence shows that as part of the development process, individuals have been willing to defer many sociopolitical advantages, including some forms of individual human rights, in favor of opportunities for improved economic position. This may give or may have given some of Southeast Asia's political leaders an opportunity to defer political development processes temporarily while focusing on economic development, at least as long as the economic pie is growing larger and spreading through ever wider segments of society. At some point, however—perhaps as economic growth levels off or as a critical mass of the population achieves a relatively comfortable economic status—new political issues seem to arise and to become more important. Alternatively, Vietnam has deferred economic development in favor of political goals, and Burma has stagnated in both its economic and political development. The ways these variant approaches will change in the future is not clear.

Human rights has become an issue of concern for the international political system, whereas once it was under internal sociopolitical control. Most developed countries seek stronger enforcement mechanisms for human rights, most likely through the United Nations. Many developed nations have also made strong commitments to linking foreign aid funding to progress on human rights issues within specific developing countries. Whether Western or developed countries will allow for variation in human rights practices and whether developing countries will reject such intrusions, as Indonesia has done with respect to assistance from the Netherlands, will be determined individually. Nevertheless, it is clear that the states of Southeast Asia are not prepared to accept automatically Western definitions of human rights the way they once accepted Western definitions of democracy.

Democratic and Political Values

For Southeast Asians, democratic values also fall under the community versus the individual debate. Few in Southeast Asia reject democracy outright; however, the Western model—often labeled "50 percent + 1 democracy," referring to voting patterns in which a single vote (an individual) can determine the success of an election or a decision for the entire community—finds little support there:

> The ideal of democracy is a weakly held sentiment among almost all people in Vietnam. This has always been the case, and it remains so today. Few Vietnamese strongly favor Western style democracy, and if anything the number grows steadily smaller with each passing year. . . . Both knowledge and appreciation of democracy are largely absent.[19]

Southeast Asians appear to prefer the idea of *communal democracy* which relies on discussion and consensus building and in which the vote—often unanimous—is not taken until after a consensus has been established. To Westerners this looks a great deal like a system designed to apply pressure on individuals to conform, and in many senses it is. Whereas Western social scientists have romanticized this notion for years within the concept of Asian village democracy, the practice is rejected out of hand when applied to the state. However, the pressure to conform is precisely what Southeast Asians see as the expression of the *community will*, bringing errant individuals into line for the greater community good. In this context it is perfectly normal to protect or maintain the (greater) community good from disruption or destruction by the (lesser) individual good. Southeast Asians are quick to point to many instances when, in their views, the West has suffered because of its total commitment to individual rights at the expense of the community.

Concepts of democracy that emphasize community rights as much as or more than individual rights are being transferred to the political systems in Southeast Asia. The disintegration of most of the parliamentary systems organized after independence in the 1950s and 1960s reflected in part the failure of these structures to accommodate the propensity toward community and consensus as opposed to individual independence of action. Independent action by parliamentarians, bureaucrats, and other members of the elite came to be seen as largely self-serving. As a result, "serious political activity in Vietnam is not found in legislative debate, election speeches, or even in political party activities, but in the work of these major social, political, and religious organizations. . . . The mutual-protection association is the basic unit of politics in Vietnam and will remain so in the foreseeable future."[20] Many of the political structures that have been constructed since that time have been attempts to create systems that allow for the expression of the community will. Whether these institutions have the breadth and the capacity to arbitrate such a consensus may remain open to question, and many would argue that consensus is only derived from an authoritarian elite. Nevertheless, the ultimate success of these institutions will be determined on the basis of their utility for the community, rather than for the individual.

The objective of this reconstruction is to redefine political processes using fundamental Southeast Asian (which may also be more widely Asian) political concepts. The underlying principle has been the primacy of the community in relation to the individual, in which politics is essentially the building of consensus. The pandemonium of individual demands fully articulated and perhaps endlessly debated in public is anathema to the collective, consensual processes that are the norm in Southeast Asia. In the eyes of Westerners collective decisionmaking may readily appear to be authoritarian, but it is the norm—tempered perhaps by paternalism and the pressure on leadership to represent the highest standard for the polity in its interface with the cosmos. At the same time, paternalistic consensus-building *requires* participation: "In Asian politics patrons and clients seek each other out for different but equally compelling reasons, and the spirit of mutual dependency is quite different from the Western expectation that the bonds which tie superiors and inferiors are likely only to allow the former to manipulate the latter for their own interests."[21] The issue confronting most Southeast Asian states at this point in their development is how to transform political institutions in a way that will raise the efficiency and expand the participation inherent in these community-based processes.

Structures of the State and Neotraditionalism

It is one thing to reject as unsuitable for Southeast Asian political needs the institutions of democracy the West has evolved over centuries of its own development; it is quite another to define a new set of institutions and supporting processes that will meet these political needs. Early postindependence Southeast Asian political leaders thought Western-style political parties and parliaments, perhaps with a little adjustment, would meet these needs, but experience has demonstrated otherwise. Now, political institutions in most Southeast Asian states barely resemble those of their Western counterparts even though Southeast Asian states continue to use Western labels for most political institutions. And although the processes that support these institutions may not meet with the approval of Western theorists, it appears increasingly obvious that these structures and processes can and will function with greater and lesser degrees of efficiency in Southeast Asia.

Political Parties

Political parties in Southeast Asia have rarely been similar to those in the West. They have sometimes played strong and important but not independent roles in the region's political systems. In keeping with the centrist nature of these states, political parties have tended to fill roles in mass orientation and mobilization and have served as outreach tools of the government. Although political parties in the West also fulfill these educational and mobilization roles, they are mechanisms for the *upward* movement of ideas and political aspirants. Parties in Southeast Asia rarely perform this latter function and in many situations are in reality little more than cliques, loose groupings of like-minded individuals, or patron-client groups. Even at those points in time when mass participation becomes important—such as during elections—participation tends to be controlled by the elite rather than spontaneous. Two factors seem critical in limiting both the independence and the overall effectiveness of Southeast Asian political parties: (1) Political structures in the region remain centrist in focus, and there is little grassroots participation in national political organizations; and (2) such organizations as do exist outside the capital usually reflect the fragmentation—ethnic, cultural, and economic—of the society at large.

Perhaps the most common format for political parties is the single party or dominant party structure. In most of these cases, the single or dominant party has some type of official sanction from the government. Burma—now under martial law—is currently without a viable party system; Vietnam is a single-party state, and Singapore and Malaysia are effectively so because opposition parties have been unable to define an alternative agenda or, lacking access to the apparatus of government, to build grassroots support. Indonesia has forced its once myriad political parties into two semi-independent parties representing all former Muslim parties (the Development Unity Party, PPP) and all non-Muslim parties (the Indonesian Democratic Party, PDI), plus GOLKAR, the government-controlled functional group. GOLKAR dominates this system, and even in their consolidated forms, Indonesia's historically fractious political parties have been unable to build broad national support. (The Indonesian Communist Party, the PKI, remains a curious anomaly as until its destruction in the mid-1960s, it appeared to be structuring itself around massive grassroots support.) In Malaysia the coalition, first as the alliance and then as the National Front, or Barisan Nasional (BN), composed of three ethnic parties—the United Malays National Organization (UMNO), the Malayan Chinese Association (MCA), and the Malayan Indian Congress (MIC)—has long supported the government; smaller independent parties have existed but have been unable to affect the political system significantly. The BN, which has made room for smaller parties—particularly from Sabah and Sarawak—has been more successful in recent years in developing an image as a consociational winning national team rather than that of a simple coalition of convenience, as the earlier alliance sometimes appeared.[22] Despite this seeming success at the level of the political parties, Malaysia's Chinese are faced with two issues that make full political participation difficult: (1) The Malaysian Chinese are themselves divided in terms of language, place of family origin, and class; and (2) within the Chinese Confucian political culture there are no "guidelines for minority leadership in a community dominated by non-Confucian culture . . . that a Chinese leader should be subordinate to a 'foreigner' is culturally unthinkable."[23]

When the government has not sought to use a dominant political party as a mechanism for political mobilization, parties have tended to be even more highly fragmented and reflective of larger divisions in society. Thailand's system of political parties has been as multifarious as its constitutions, general elections, coups, and cabinets. Parties have been formed, split, unified, and redivided, but in no case have they successfully built a constituency base for political action. For the most part, political parties have been loose groupings of like-minded individuals or patron-client groups. Parties have sometimes been created by law, but seldom have they been organized to give voice to issues of concern to the electorate. Even during those periods of civilian government, factionalism and infighting among political parties have made governing almost impossible, furthering views—widely held within the bureaucracy—that political parties cause political instability and disunity.

Political parties in the Philippines have similarly gone through a number of periods of greater or lesser division. Although political parties were introduced under American tutelage, much as in the rest of Southeast Asia parties here evolved as personalized organizations based on traditional patron-client relationships rather than as organizations defining a particular political philosophy, set of principles, or even policy goals. Until 1972 a two-party system—based on the Nacionalista and Liberal Parties, with a number of small parties or independent candidates occasionally challenging for seats in the House—predominated, but both of these leading parties were typical of the centrist parties found elsewhere in the region: "They sought not mass membership, only mass support and were run by a small group of government officials and ex-officials, the professional politicians."[24] National leaders maintained patron-client relations with shifting coalitions of provincial and local leaders who also depended on patron-client relations in very instabile arrangements. But Filipino parties before 1972 had tended to be national in scope (compared with those elsewhere, which were divided along ethnic or religious lines) but drew heavily from the same upper socioeconomic strata.

Major election reforms were implemented in the Philippines during 1972, but they were soon superseded by Marcos's declaration of martial law. Under martial law, patron-client relations became even more important for continued political access, strengthening the network of provincial political families that have dominated the economic and political systems. Marcos created the Kilusan Bagong Lipunan (KBL), or New Society Movement, but it failed to reach the scope of such similar government-sponsored parties as GOLKAR in Indonesia. The rise of Corazon Aquino, who won the presidential elections (although she had to lead a minor revolution forcing Marcos into exile in order to claim her inauguration) as the leader of a broad coalition of political parties, worker's groups, religious organizations, and both leftist and rightist leaders, brought the Philippines into a multiparty system as chaotic as any in the region. Ultimately, Aquino was unable to convert her overwhelming personal popularity into a strong political base from which to counter regional and provincial political forces that remained in place from the Marcos era.

Parliament

It may be reasonable to ask how, if political parties could not aggregate the larger political issues extant in the society, one could expect a parliament—as the forum within which these parties were to work—to function effectively? The fact that parliamentarians, even as representatives of political parties, frequently pursued parochial or self-serving interests ensured the ultimate failure of both the parties and the parliament. As early as the mid-1950s, Sukarno in Indonesia was already vocally critical of standard Western practices of democracy as being unworkable. Although the reasons for the failure of Western-style parliamentary structures are complex, in most Southeast Asian democracies the parliament has been the most conspicuous failure among imported Western institutions. Reflective of the centrist nature of these states, and given the essential role of the parliament in the democratic system, its failings were both devastating and very public.

Yet all of the governments of Southeast Asia have sought to establish and maintain some type of deliberative body through which to aggregate political ideas, minimize and resolve political conflicts, and legitimize the government and its political decisions. It has also been important for this institution to play major ritual roles in support of both the center (government) and the society at large. Sukarno's ideas for a guided democracy, developed years earlier but implemented under the New Order, called for decisions in parliament to be made not by majority vote but by *musyawarah* (consensus building). Operationally, this has meant that discussions and informal "deals and horse trading" often take place in the halls, in committee, or entirely outside the confines of the parliamentary structure, and the outcome is determined and fully known by all participants before the parliament is called to order.

Importantly for Indonesian political stability, for example, this process has saved the government-sponsored GOLKAR from publicly humiliating the weak political parties by defeating them on every issue with public votes. The independent parties, which are too weak to veto government issues, do have some hope of influencing the consensus during the informal discussions. It does not appear that GOLKAR (the government) can dictate every decision, so it must seek to build a consensus that includes dissenters: "The government has withdrawn bills because no *mufakat* [consensus] was emerging. It is said that over 650 bills have been shelved in parliamentary committees . . . before they even reached the plenum simply because the opposition refused to give its assent."[25] Reflecting the village heritage of maintaining consensus and harmony (supported heavily by the primacy of the community over the individual), this style of deliberative operation—whether it is called parliamentary or something else—seems to have found long-term viability among Southeast Asian states as long as minority groups have sufficient opportunity to contribute to and occasionally deny consensus.

The work of the parliament in Singapore is, perhaps more than anywhere else in Southeast Asia, the work of a single political party—the People's Action Party (PAP), which has dominated the political scene there since coming to power in April 1959. The government faces some disaffection because of its paternalism and heavy-handedness with a population that is increasingly younger, better educated, and highly sophisticated. Because of the PAP's dominance of the general elections, some parliamentary functions—particularly the role of a local opposition—have never materialized. At the same time, as with political parties in much of the rest of Southeast Asia, the PAP is not a grassroots mass organization. Yet one of the more important functions of the MPs (parliamentarian) is the "weekly 'Meet the People' sessions where the MP receives feedback from his constituents."[26] The uniformity within the government among the elite, the bureaucracy, and elected officials—made possible by decades of PAP domination—has made Singapore an administrative state in which the political arena is increasingly less competitive and the bureaucracy and political institutions such as the parliament find their functions merging.

Malaysia's record of parliamentary democracy appears at first to be as strong as any in the region. Despite the suspension of parliament following communal riots in 1969, parliamentary rule was reestablished, and Malaysia has sustained a "remarkable and enviable record of political stability and general social peace [in which] there have been three consecutive changes of heads of government, seven general elections, and continuing institutionalization of the processes of government in which, *inter alia*, the supremacy of civilian authority has been unquestioned."[27] Yet even with this success, Malaysia's democratic practices are more a matter of form than of substance. Reflecting frustrations with the tenets of Western democracy similar to those expressed elsewhere, the government has used its legislative success to pass increasingly restrictive—by Western definitions—laws, many, such as the 1975 Amendment to the Universities and Colleges Act and the Societies Act (1981), designed to curb political expressions that criticize the government. Perhaps because of the fear of interethnic conflict (as confirmed by the experience of 1969), Malaysia has developed electoral and bureaucratic systems that work side by side, that are almost indistinguishable from one another, and that have been led on both sides by UMNO under the Alliance and BN banners.

The Thai parliament, or National Assembly, was first formed in 1932; however, since half of the assembly was appointed—mostly military or civilian government officers—"the legislative process became an extended arm of, and provided an additional function for, the bureaucracy."[28] The result was the rapid politicalization of the Thai bureaucracy. The elected members of parliament devoted most of their efforts to internal legislative activities rather than building a national political power base, which was left to certain national civilian leaders and the military. From the beginning of parliamentary government, the Thai Ministry of the Interior has played an important role in mobilizing rural voters. Successive governments—usually ushered in by the military—have shaped and reshaped the parliament, written and rewritten constitutions, and abolished and resurrected political parties, but Thailand has largely remained a "semidemocratic government in which the bureaucratic elite has made certain concessions to the non-bureaucratic forces to allow participation in the political process."[29] This system reflects the unique composition of the Thai political system which is based on respect for the king, acknowledgment of the legitimizing value of the constitution (or a constitution), and the weakness of political parties or any form of extrabureaucratic power and authority.

The weaknesses in parliamentary structures and processes perhaps bring into focus the essential question for the development of political institutions in communal democracy. Because political parties have not become effective as channels of communication between the general population and the government as represented in parliament, the question of how political issues and other concerns are communicated *upward* through the political system remains unanswered. (We have already seen that, in fact, political parties have been used successfully for *downward* communication.) Without the link to the broad base of citizens, parliaments in most Southeast Asian countries have tended to become one more element of bureaucracy in essentially bureaucratic states. Such strategies as Singapore's "meet the people" can be viable mechanisms for grassroots communication between the government and its citizens; whether such strategies can be used to adequately articulate the broad-based interests of Singaporeans remains unclear.

The Bureaucracy

Some aspects of bureaucratic structure closely match traditional Southeast Asian values, and these seem to be magnified in contemporary performance. Although most Southeast Asians "have an instinctive understanding of the finest gradations of hierarchy and so are never confused as to who outranks whom, they are less certain about how power should be used."[30] Numerous bureaucratic attributes, however, are quite alien to traditional Southeast Asian culture, and these seem to be readily ignored. For example, traditional deferential attitudes toward authority have been easily assimilated into bureaucratic practice, but in operation this has meant that subordinate officers rarely make decisions. On the other hand, the abstract rules and regulations that are common to bureaucratic practice conflict with typical Southeast Asian paternalistic and other personalized forms of interaction: "The imperative that people should above all recognize their personal obligations and their ties of acquaintanceship meant that any attempt by powerful officials to advance impersonal public policies [was] usually seen as a way of avoiding personal obligations and duties."[31] Consequently, formal rules and regulations may be written, but they are frequently ignored or are only used when an officer does not want to make a decision. Ironically, this conflict between the abstract bureaucratic form and actual operation has produced highly politicized and very insecure bureaucracies because pressure to void rules is constant from both political and personal sources, but the abstract rules exist in the background and thus can threaten the security of an individual officer at any time.

The duality of this conflict, along with other traditional proclivities toward indecision and inaction, reinforce bureaucratic tendencies to do nothing. High degrees of personal insecurity lead to a general lack of innovation and creative thinking and to an absolute aversion toward decisionmaking. Moreover, the lack of bureaucratic responsiveness to popular demands and needs is sustained, as in Vietnam but also elsewhere, because "neither the survival of the civil service nor the tenure of its officials is affected by such demands."[32] Although the bureaucratic idea of public service is acknowledged, the focus of the service is the government itself and not the general population. The bureaucracy is "system-oriented, not program-oriented," and individual bureaucrats see government service as "an avenue to success, a means of getting rewards from society."[33] The emphasis on service to the government as an end in itself has roots that are deep in Asian culture: "Asia's peasants . . . have long identified government with the tax collector and the oppressor, friend and protector of money-lender and landlord."[34] Bureaucratic structures and methods established before and during the colonial period and refined since, whether military or civilian, have reinforced the traditional extractive nature of the state in Southeast Asia.

Singapore has developed some policies for a basic welfare state, with programs in subsidized housing and other health and social services. But even Singapore has been characterized as an "administrative state" in which the "fusion of professional party leaders with leading elements of the bureaucracy and its 'neo-Confucianist' ethos [is] entirely compatible with bureaucratic values."[35] Vietnam carried out major social reorganizations in the north, but years of war have drained resources, made welfare programs impossible, and preserved the extractive orientation prevalent elsewhere. Burma also embarked on an ideological road that stressed social reorganization, but it provided little in the way of a welfare return for the general population. Moreover, none of the Southeast Asian states has exhibited a political form that has enabled the mass of the population to determine the political agenda or control the political elite.

Most Southeast Asian states are rapidly becoming bureaucratic polities: "The failure to recognize the importance of external controls has resulted in the growth of a civil service which to a large extent is accountable only to itself."[36] Lack of accountability has been particularly critical in Malaysia, where the bureaucracy has the additional responsibility of protecting the Malay community, and Malays have been promoted to ensure that the highest policymaking positions will be filled by ethnic natives. In Vietnam, where the Confucian ethic should influence bureaucratic behavior, in the traditional period "there was no Puritan-in-politics tradition, no sense of obligation. No one went into government to become a civil 'servant.' Much of this attitude carries over today and strongly influences the present system."[37] The Malaysian combination of "ethnic mission" and lack of external accountability led the prime minister to take several actions against bureaucratic inefficiency: (1) Time clocks were installed so workers could record their arrival and departure, (2) name tags were issued to all officers so citizens could identify them in making complaints, (3) top planning and administrative agencies were strengthened, (4) the Malaysian Administration and Planning Unit was instructed to make surprise inspections in an attempt to raise productivity and weed out deadwood, (5) the National Bureau of Investigations was given a new mandate to pursue corruption, (6) the Public Complaints Bureau was reactivated, (7) civil servants were required to declare assets, and (8) the Anti-Corruption Agency was reactivated.[38] There is an irony in these actions in that most of the reforms—those relating to the planning and administrative agencies, the Malaysian Administration and Planning Unit, the National Bureau of Investigations, the Public Complaints Bureau, and the Anti-Corruption Agency—represent further expansion of the bureaucracy, exactly what they were meant to correct. There is no evidence to indicate that these reforms have brought any long-lasting change.

Bureaucratic domination of these political systems appears to be one of the most uniform aspects of all Southeast Asian states. Moreover, the bureaucracy is so completely interlinked with other parts of the political system, ranging from political parties to the military, that few external checks to its authority are possible. Further, given the traditional Southeast Asian expectations concerning government performance and responsiveness, there should be little expectation that the bureaucracy will lead the state through any serious reform efforts.

The Military

In Southeast Asia, there appears to be little difference in outlook between civilian and military elites, as the military elites are closely linked "with the members of the elite's cosmopolitan mainstream."[39] The traditional authority of a king, a sultan, or a chief in Southeast Asia was directly linked to his personal ability to field a military force; although in reality the king's power was inhibited by the weakness of the system, there were no institutionalized taboos against the expansion of the use of power if and when better forms of power—such as improved military organization, techniques, and equipment—or better forms of control—such as bureaucratic organization and regulation—became available. In this context, the colonial regimes provided the "better mousetrap," introducing new concepts of command structures and organization, as well as the concept of the professional military. They did not (or could not) impart the concept of the subordination of the military to civilian authority. The concept of direct military involvement in politics gained additional legitimacy through the various revolutionary experiences against the British, French, and Dutch—in Burma, Vietnam, and Indonesia especially, the army was the revolution. In Thailand the military, the civilian bureaucracy, and the private commercial sectors have been intertwined for decades. Singapore and Malaysia are exceptions to this generalized regional situation; civilian oversight of the military is well established in both countries, although civilian control of the military in the Philippines under Marcos led to the greatest amount of military corruption that has been experienced anywhere in the region.

The military's involvement in politics has not been an aberration; rather, it is tied to the reemergence of political structures that are basically compatible, or at least not incompatible, with the history and tradition of the region. Vietnam may be an exception, but its unique situation of nearly three decades of continuing warfare makes it difficult to establish with certainty the primacy of civilian and party rule. The military preoccupation with war in Vietnam and Indochina—fighting the French, Americans, Khmer Rouge, and Cambodian rebels in succession—may have distracted the Vietnamese military from any possible involvement in domestic politics.

The distinction between the Western philosophy of appropriate military behavior and the philosophy extant in Southeast Asia brings into focus the depth of the cultural differences involved. The perspective of Southeast Asian military officers has been summarized by Ulf Sundhaussen, whose views reflect those of Abdul Haris Nasution, one of the region's leading military thinkers: "The army should not be seen as trying to dominate the country, but as a social-political group entitled to play a role as one of the forces determining and executing national policies."[40] Alexander Woodside has noted, in referring to Vietnam, that "it was in the crucible of the 'people's war' that East Asian tradition and Western political theories finally did complete their joint production of a new kind of populist egalitarianism."[41]

It is by no means clear, however, that populism—even in Vietnam—will determine the nature of military politics in Southeast Asia. The evidence suggests instead that military politics will feature forms of bureaucratic traditionalism that will continue to divide society into two groups—a small, governmental elite and the uninvolved mass of the population. The direct association of the military with the political system has gained its clearest statement from the Indonesian experience in which, following the revolution, the army defined "dual functions" for itself: (1) military force, as in the traditional role of protecting the state from external (and, later, also internal) attack; and (2) social and political force arising from the need to protect the ideological, political, social, economic, cultural, and religious underpinnings of the revolution.[42]

The growth of military-bureaucratic polities further limits access to decisionmaking in the bureaucratic polity because of the distinctions and restrictions placed on civilian bureaucrats. In Indonesia, the group known as technocrats exists largely at the behest of its military patrons, although the latter recognize that these technocrats are necessary in order to satisfy major assistance and donor agencies. In Thailand, by contrast, there is a greater and more recognizable division of labor between military and civilian bureaucracies. Burma's military bureaucrats fill supervisory and oversight roles throughout the bureaucracy; in addition, the military-bureaucratic polity has a propensity to extend its control into commercial and business activities through partnerships and joint ventures with local and international commercial interests. In Burma, this control has taken the form of the nationalization of most commercial establishments and the elimination of Chinese and Indian business interests in the name of developing the government's socialist programs.

In other states, private business interests have been co-opted in those instances in which the typical partner from the bureaucracy provides contacts and access to the bureaucracy itself and the partner from the private sector provides the capital and business management expertise. In this way, political power has become a tool for claiming economic power, and economic power becomes a tool for sustaining political power. The penetration of the bureaucracy into nongovernmental sectors reduces the possibility for the autonomous development of major economic-political groups outside the control of the bureaucracy. The bureaucracy, having thus co-opted the economic sector, establishes as its primary goal—and that of its business cohorts—the maintenance of its power and interests.

Authoritarian Governments and Communal Democracy

The capital city is still the locus of political activity, and the new states are primarily resource extractive and nonwelfare in orientation. Typical extractive patterns of state organization are evident in Indonesia, Thailand, Malaysia, the Philippines, Burma, Vietnam, and Laos, where political systems have been dominated by ethnic, educational, family, or other elites. Singapore has exhibited some social programs that seem to set it apart, and Brunei is unique with respect to its vast per capita wealth. Economic systems remain controlled by resident Chinese, often with close links to the political elite. Concomitantly, there has been little participation by the general populations in the political system, but recent economic growth is impacting wider population segments.

Elections are held, but the ability of the masses to influence the political system through voting or other means (except for occasional violence) remains limited. Singapore's governing party, the PAP, has tried to be responsive to fluctuations in voter support at the polls. Characterized as "soft-authoritarian" societies, most Southeast Asian states are "ordered according to inegalitarian group hierarchies that emphasize conformity to group interests over individual rights."[43] Agricultural production—the primary economic activity of all of the states except Singapore—remains in the hands of peasants, but their limited access to land, capital, and markets guarantees continued domination of the economic system by outsiders. Thailand has invested heavily in infrastructure and human-resource development and has offered significant tax incentives to encourage industrial development outside the greater Bangkok area, but the pull of the center is so strong that these incentives have had little impact. External capital in the form of foreign investment or development assistance has been available, but investments seem to reinforce the positions of the economic and political elites; development assistance has achieved success only in isolated contexts, with little overall impact on the quality of life among the rural poor.

The traditional centrist structure of the state has been evident in the actions and policies of the governments. The capital city remains the center of control. Provincial military and government assignments are often used as political punishments, whereas ambassadorships to small, distant, unimportant states remain a convenient way to "exile" political competitors. Burma has not allowed dependents to accompany diplomats and other travelers abroad—a policy reminiscent of the traditional system of retaining hostages in the capital to ensure the loyalty of retainers and officials. Singapore has established public social controls to the point of excess, at least in Western eyes. And Malaysia has become more expansive in implementing Islamic rules and restrictions.

Control of the political agenda remains important in most of these states, and there is a propensity to use government institutions and procedures to protect that control. In Malaysia, for example, the Societies Act Bill, as amended in 1981, gave the Registrar of Societies powers to deregister any group that challenged the government, Islam or other religions, the national language, the special position of Bumiputras, or legitimate interests of other communities.[44] In 1994, the government used the Societies Act to ban the radical Islamic group Al-Arqam. Singapore's Newspaper and Printing Act has been used to control various media, including such prestigious journals as the *Far Eastern Economic Review* and *Time*, which published views that "serve only to strengthen

a weak opposition and . . . eventually bring down the government."⁴⁵
Indonesia has demonstrated its penchant for control, particularly over the
press, as in 1986, when the government closed the respected newspaper
Sinar Harapan and, more recently, in 1994, when it closed the most
respected magazine in Indonesia, the weekly *Tempo*. In the Philippines,
the Marcos regime especially "took strong measures to ensure that
messages critical of his regime would not reach the public, [and] muzzled
the press and used arrest, detention and even torture to try to immobilize
his opposition" while creating a new Department of Public Information
to enforce control and censorship.⁴⁶ The broad and arbitrary nature of
these controls quickly raises Western concerns about abuse, but within
the Southeast Asian context of the primacy of the community, such
concerns are much less demonstrable.

A Prospective Overview

The nature of the state in Southeast Asia has evolved since independence and now more closely reflects indigenous forms that have been
amalgamated from resurgent neotraditional values tempered and shaped
by pressures and demands of the late twentieth century. It is not
democratic in form, at least not in the Western definition of the term, but
neither is the form purely a dictatorship (except perhaps in Vietnam).
Most states seem to reflect the greater Asian respect for authority (or lack
of concern or fear of too much authority) that gives stronger voice to
community values than to individual values and emphasizes outward
appearances of harmony over conflict. The states have developed "market
economies with a kind of paternalistic authoritarianism that persuades
rather than coerces."⁴⁷ Institutional mechanisms for the absorption of
dissenting and minority views do not yet appear to be well established,
but evidence suggests that such views can be accommodated through
political parties and parliaments, at least within the community-harmony
context. Competition in the contemporary global system will require
additional changes in decisionmaking processes within Southeast Asian
states, perhaps streamlining those processes and introducing some greater
measure of depersonalization of policy prescriptions.

There are two areas of political practice in which change appears
necessary, if not imperative. First, the balancing of public demands,
needs, and opposition views against the political penchant for consensus
and—more negatively—control through repression continues to inject

instability in the Southeast Asian state; and processes that adequately allow for dissent and for competing views to be heard (whether publicly or in less public forums) without being construed as threats to the system must be established before practices of communal democracy can be sustained and become institutionalized. Such actions as Indonesia's imprisonment of leading figures in the 1984 Tanjung Priok riots— including Dharsono, a decorated and popular general and former commander of the West Javanese Siliwangi army division—demonstrated that the Indonesian government, as with most Southeast Asian governments, "can break anybody at any time for any reason and no one in this society has either the power or . . . the will to do anything about it."[48] Second, bureaucratic practices will have to be revised to limit or reduce personalized patron-client relationships so that the system can function routinely. Douglas Pike noted more than twenty-five years ago that the "system is inadequate to engage in planning, forecasting, team leadership, decision making, and follow-through, because it lacks a sufficient number of individuals with necessary managerial skills and experience."[49] Pike was partly correct in his observation when he added that "we are concerned . . . [not with] the abilities of Vietnamese as individuals—[but with] a system."[50] He was wrong in his prescription for correcting the problem: The system clearly perpetuates and reinforces many neotraditional practices, and numbers of trained individuals cannot mitigate against this. That is, in most Southeast Asian countries sufficient numbers of well-trained individuals now exist, but the system still dictates their behavior in neotraditional terms, relying on patron-client and other personalized relationships to maintain their positions and encouraging continued lack of action and decisionmaking even among bureaucrats trained through graduate levels in Western institutions. The system remains pervasive, smothering individual initiative; yet the system must be revised because it cannot be replaced: "Of course, the final mix will be authentically Vietnamese, or it will not endure. Vietnam will define and work out the details. Heritage will continue to limit her."[51]

State power in Southeast Asia is still derived in large measure from the acquiescence of the people, and rising levels of education may reduce this propensity. It is clear, however, that the end of acquiescence will not result in Western democratic political structures but instead should stimulate the further refinement of neotraditional values and the concomitant political practices in the development of communal democracy to give greater play to individual participation but within the communal context.

NOTES

1. Peter S.J. Chen, "The Cultural Implications of Industrialization and Modernization in South-East Asia," in *The Sociology of South-East Asia: Readings on Social Change and Development*, edited by Hans-Dieter Evers (Kuala Lumpur: Oxford University Press, 1980), p. 239.

2. Robert W. Hefner, "Islamizing Java? Religion and Politics in Rural East Java," *Journal of Asian Studies* 46 (1987), pp. 553–554.

3. Jeff Haynes, *Religion in Third World Politics* (Boulder: Lynne Rienner Publishers, 1994), p. 9.

4. Douglas A. Pike, *War, Peace and the Viet Cong* (Cambridge: MIT Press, 1969), p. 69.

5. Ruth McVey, "The *Wayang* Controversy in Indonesian Communism," in *Content, Meaning and Power in Southeast Asia*, edited by Mark Hobart and Robert H. Taylor (Ithaca: Cornell University, Southeast Asia Program, 1986), p. 27.

6. *Ibid.*

7. Gordon P. Means, *Malaysian Politics: The Second Generation* (Singapore: Oxford University Press, 1991), p. 3.

8. "Asian Values," *The Economist* (May 28, 1994), p. 14.

9. Jusuf Wanandi, "Sociopolitical Development and Institution Building in Indonesia," in *Asian Political Institutionalization*, edited by Robert A. Scalapino, Seizaburo Sato, and Jusuf Wanandi (Berkeley: University of California, Institute of East Asian Studies, 1986), p. 184.

10. Michael Vatikiotis, "Value Judgment: Younger Leaders Search for New 'Asian' Directions," *Far Eastern Economic Review* (February 10, 1994), p. 28.

11. Michael Vatikiotis, "Radical Chic, Islamic Fringe Groups Gain Influence Among the Elite," *Far Eastern Economic Review* (May 26, 1994), p. 33.

12. Chandra Muzaffar, "Malayism, Bumiputraism, and Islam," in *Readings on Islam in Southeast Asia*, compiled by Ahmad Ibrahim, Sharon Siddique, and Yasmin Hussain (Singapore: Institute of Southeast Asian Studies, 1985), pp. 356–357.

13. Doug Tsuruoka, "Malaysia: In the Name of Security," *Far Eastern Economic Review* (August 11, 1994), pp. 25–26; and "Al-Arqam Outlawed," *Far Eastern Economic Review* (September 8, 1994), p. 13.

14. Mona Abaza, *Changing Images of Three Generations of Azharites in Indonesia* (Singapore: Institute of Southeast Asian Studies, Occasional Paper no. 88, 1993), p. 21.

15. Wanandi, "Sociopolitical Development and Institution Building in Indonesia," in Scalapino, Sato, and Wanandi, *Asian Political Institutionalization*, pp. 185–186.

16. L. Gordon Crovitz, "Nobody Elects the Press: Mahathir Speaks Out on the Media, Culture and Trade," *Far Eastern Economic Review* (April 7, 1994), p. 20.

17. Ta Van Tai, *The Vietnamese Tradition of Human Rights* (Berkeley: University of California, Institute of East Asian Studies, 1988), p. 2.

18. Vincent Lingga, "Universality of Rights Reaffirmed," *Jakarta Post* (June 26, 1993), p. 1.

19. Pike, *War, Peace and the Viet Cong*, p. 67.

20. *Ibid.*, p. 82.

21. Lucian W. Pye, *Asian Power and Politics: The Cultural Dimensions of Authority* (Cambridge: Belknap Press of Harvard University Press, 1985), p. 51.

22. Stephen Chee, "Consociational Political Leadership and Conflict Regulation in Malaysia," in *Leadership and Security in Southeast Asia, Institutional Aspects*, edited by Stephen Chee (Singapore: Institute of Southeast Asian Studies, 1991), p. 54.

23. Pye, *Asian Power and Politics*, p. 251.

24. David Wurfel, *Filipino Politics* (Ithaca: Cornell University Press, 1988), p. 95.

25. Ulf Sundhaussen, "Indonesia: Past and Present Encounters with Democracy," in *Democracy in Developing Countries: Volume 3, Asia*, edited by Larry Diamond, Juan J. Linz, and Seymour Martin Lipset (Boulder: Lynne Rienner Publishers, 1989), p. 440.

26. Lee Boon Hiok, "Political Institutionalization in Singapore," Scalapino, Sato, and Wanandi, *Asian Political Institutionalization*, p. 208.

27. Zakaria Haji Ahmad, "Malaysia: Quasi Democracy in a Divided Society," in Diamond, Lind, and Lipset, *Democracy in Developing Countries: Volume 3, Asia*, pp. 348–349.

28. Chai-Anan Samudavanija, "Thailand: A Stable Semi-Democracy," in Diamond, Linz, and Lipset, *Democracy in Developing Countries: Volume 3, Asia*, p. 308.

29. *Ibid.*, p. 319.

30. Pye, *Asian Power and Politics*, pp. 255–256.

31. *Ibid.*, p. 48.

32. Allen E. Goodman, *Politics in War: The Bases of Political Community in South Vietnam* (Cambridge: Harvard University Press, 1973), p. 223.

33. Pike, *War, Peace and the Viet Cong*, p. 62.

34. Michael Brecher, "The Search for Political Stability," in *International Politics of Asia*, edited by George P. Jan (Belmont, Calif.: Wadsworth Publishing Co., 1969), p. 45.

35. John L. S. Girling, *The Bureaucratic Polity in Modernizing Societies: Similarities, Differences, and Prospects in the ASEAN Region* (Singapore: Institute of Southeast Asian Studies, 1981), p. 12. The concept of the administrative state is taken from Chan Heng Chee, "Politics in an Administrative State: Where Has the Politics Gone?" in *Trends in Singapore*, edited by Chee Meow (Singapore: Singapore University Press for the Institute of Southeast Asian Studies, 1975).

36. Mavis Puthucheary, *The Politics of Administration: The Malaysian Experience* (Kuala Lumpur: Oxford University Press, 1978), p. 120.

37. Pike, *War, Peace and the Viet Cong*, p. 62.

38. Means, *Malaysian Politics*, pp. 84–85.

39. Girling, *The Bureaucratic Polity in Modernizing Societies*, p. 11.

40. Ulf Sundhaussen, "The Military: Structures, Procedures, and Effects on Indonesian Society," in *Political Power and Communications in Indonesia*, edited by Karl D. Jackson and Lucian W. Pye (Berkeley: University of California Press, 1978), p. 47.

41. Alexander B. Woodside, *Community and Revolution in Modern Vietnam* (Boston: Houghton Mifflin, 1976), p. 239.

42. Harold Crouch, *The Army and Politics in Indonesia* (Ithaca: Cornell University Press, 1978), pp. 24–45.

43. Francis Fukuyama, "Asia's Soft-Authoritarian Alternative," *New Perspectives Quarterly* 9 (Spring 1992), p. 60.

44. Means, *Malaysian Politics*, p. 85.

45. Thomas A. Bellows, "Singapore in 1988, the Transition Moves Forward," *Asian Survey* 29 (February 1989), p. 152.

46. Wurfel, *Filipino Politics*, p. 122.

47. Fukuyama, "Asia's Soft-Authoritarian Alternative," p. 60.

48. Lincoln Kaye, "Guilty as Charged: Dharsono is Sentenced to 10 Years' Imprisonment for Subversion," *Far Eastern Economic Review* (January 23, 1986), p. 10.

49. Pike, *War, Peace and the Viet Cong*, pp. 61–62.

50. *Ibid.*, p. 62.

51. *Ibid.*, pp. 83–84.

13

Regional Politics: Fragmentation and Cooperation

At independence, the states of Southeast Asia found little to bind them together. Although many regional leaders spoke prominently of regional politics and the importance of cooperation among neighboring states, their links to Europe, which were based on the residual economic and social linkages of the colonial era, and the allure of global politics, which were based on the ideologically charged cold war, were stronger than their links to each other. Despite the strain in relations between London and Rangoon at Burma's independence and in spite of the fact that Burma did not join the British Commonwealth, Burmese Foreign Minister U. E. Maung suggested that his country might consider a defense pact with India or Pakistan—both Commonwealth members. The British also continued to supply arms to the Burmese for use against Karen and other rebels. The Non-Aligned Movement, a defensive response to the magnetism of global bipolar pressures exerted by the Soviet and U.S. superpowers, did little to draw its regional proponents together. Premier U Nu of Burma, President Sukarno of Indonesia, and Prince Sihanouk of Cambodia followed Indian Prime Minister Nehru's lead but chose to compete for leadership and stature within the Non-Aligned Movement rather than develop a common regional approach. The United Nations (as opposed to a regional bloc of states) became the primary organized supranational forum through which smaller states such as those in Southeast Asia might exert leverage and seek redress against global powers.

Further, the traditional regional political system offered few models for interstate cooperation. A key element for such cooperation—acceptance of the concept of sovereign and equal states—had no political basis in the concepts of the traditional system. Superior-vassal relations and subjugation by force had been the primary means for dealing with neighbors and were the standards for conducting interstate relationships. Although the concept of national sovereignty was readily accepted by all of these states at the end of the colonial period (with a few polemical objections such as Indonesia's reaction to the creation of Malaysia and Singapore), their traditional and colonial experiences left Southeast Asian states with a legacy of isolation and limited knowledge of regional politics and approaches to problem solving.

Regional Bilateral Relations

Since independence, the states of Southeast Asia have maintained bilateral relations, although there have been breaks between states and the two Vietnams were not universally recognized. Bilateral relations have frequently been governed by domestic political climates, which in turn were governed by the rhetoric of the cold war. Reactions to the foreign policy initiatives among regional states were often similarly polemical or ideological. For example, the common revolutionary experiences of Vietnam and Indonesia drew them very close together at the height of Sukarno's power and later sustained an ambiguous but substantive military élan between them, despite Indonesia's dramatic shift to the political right. Indonesia had criticized Malaysia because the latter's road to independence was "too easy" and lacked revolutionary struggle, but their relations later shifted from hostile confrontation to intimate friendship. Thailand and the Philippines were held at arm's length by other regional states because of their alliance relationship with the United States, yet opposition to the presence of U.S. military bases in those countries did not inhibit their cooperation in the establishment of ASEAN.

Actual breaks in relations between two regional states have occurred only rarely. In 1962, the Philippines claimed the territory of North Borneo (Sabah) in opposition to the British plan to make it part of Malaysia. Ambassadors were withdrawn for a time after late 1963, but consular relations were reestablished in early 1964. The new Federation of Malaysia and Indonesia did not establish relations immediately at Malaysia's formation, although informal communications were maintained. In the period when Vietnam was divided into two states, not all regional states recognized both or either. In the early years of independence—despite the general continuity of bilateral relations within the region—cooperative interactions were few, and external relations remained strong: "All the Southeast Asian countries more or less regularly consult with other nations—mostly those outside Southeast Asia."[1]

Regional Association and Cooperation

The historical experience of the Southeast Asian states may explain much of the initial lack, and subsequent slow evolution, of regional cooperation. On the other hand, the propensity for conflict in the traditional system, the intraregional isolationism maintained by the colonial powers, and the magnetism of the postindependence bipolar global system make it somewhat surprising that cooperation evolved as rapidly as it apparently did. Nevertheless, progress in regional cooperation was often found lacking, particularly by Western analysts who argued, for example, that "the phrase 'regional cooperation' has already inspired so much high-sounding prose and so little action that it is naive to hope for some solid progress."[2] In the decade of the 1950s, regional cooperation was limited, and "fragmentation and dependence on external influences [were] the result of absence of regional solidarity and lack of common culture and communications, and also a consequence of the dependence of the structures of resources on external assistance."[3] Only when they gained sufficient confidence and experience were the states of Southeast Asia able to define an agenda that was more appropriate for local and regional needs.

In the four to five decades since independence, these states have developed a creditable record in the area of regional cooperation. Cooperative patterns in intraregional relations developed both because and in spite of the traditional interstate system. Although little emphasis was placed on interstate cooperation in the traditional system, that system provides the politico-cultural base that defines the contemporary region. Despite Southeast Asia's great diversity, a sense of regional identity has grown among Southeast Asians that sets them apart from the rest of both Asia and the world now more than at any time in history. This sense of identity was notably weaker among the traditional states at the time of the first arrival of the European colonial powers. But at the end of the twentieth century, political leaders throughout Southeast Asia have become confident and outspoken in defining the social, political, and cultural features of the region in both national and regional contexts.

The Framework for Regional Cooperation

Many explanations exist for the development of regional cooperation. The fact that the elites (if not all of the peoples) of Southeast Asia have accepted the concept of the nation-state from the Western international system provided the essential building blocks for regional cooperation. Then, too, the experience of coping with cold war politics reinforced a sense of being exploited and manipulated from the outside, thereby stimulating the need to find an alternative sense of commonality and identity. This sense of commonality, perhaps based initially on geographic and cultural proximity, has given added meaning to the regional commitment. Negative experiences in relations with the seemingly fickle global powers encouraged the early recognition of the value of a common approach to regional and global political issues. Such global networks as the Non-Aligned Movement were too diverse to effectively counter the major global powers. Over time, regional relations have eclipsed those with other states such as the states of Africa, which remain "sparse and seemingly haphazard."[4] Some Southeast Asian states have found common linkages in Islamic organizations, although differences between Middle Eastern and Southeast Asian Islam seem to lessen the potential for Islam to provide an effective organizational framework for regional or all but the broadest global political action.

The similarities of views and experiences among the leadership elites have also been important in the development of regional cooperation. With a few notable exceptions such as Indonesia's Sukarno, most first-generation political leaders accepted Western political concepts, adopting the framework and vocabulary of the cold war in international politics as well as Western definitions of economic and political development. These leaders were therefore left with a predetermined set of goals and expectations that diminished or placed a lower priority on regional cooperation unless it fit within the Western, global context of bipolar competition and the cold war. Although political leaders in Southeast Asia were sometimes thought to inhibit regionalism because "insecure national elites cannot risk compromising national goals,"[5] others believed regionalism could be enhanced because elites did not have to "negotiate and bargain with an array of well-entrenched, politically organized popular interest groups prior to making decisions on regional affairs."[6]

It has become increasingly clear that second and later generations of government elites have found common interests not only in their backgrounds but also in the problems they face. Through slow and evolutionary processes, these elites have shed the baggage of simply emulating Western social, political, and economic thinking in favor of adapting and adjusting Western ideas into concepts that are more in tune with indigenous experiences and traditional values, thus creating a neotraditional perspective on development. This process was first undertaken in the domestic arena, largely because imported Western concepts and practices failed to produce the expected viable institutions or to bring about the anticipated growth and progress in economic development.

In the international arena, regional contacts and cooperation gained strength as the contrast between cold war rhetoric and reality became evident, particularly in the realization that global powers consistently made and altered policies based on narrowly defined global interests over which the Southeast Asian states had little or no control. Initially perhaps, regional cooperation gained its impetus simply through the realization that there was no other arena in which these states, whatever their differences, could find dependable relationships. Over time, as these relationships developed, historical as well as contemporary commonalities added considerable resilience to regional cooperation. In meeting their most urgent needs, these states have not sought to compromise national independence in favor of regional integration but, quite the opposite, have sought to use regional cooperation to further national development and strength.

Regional cooperation has taken many organized forms in attempts to meet a wide range of economic, security, and general political objectives. Some organizations, such as SEATO, were controlled substantially by outside forces, whereas others have been largely regional creations. Yet even those created by regional states have not always been successful: The MAPHILINDO experience demonstrated that regional organizations cannot survive if the member states do not have a common purpose for the organization. Some organizations have been more successful, and ASEAN, which has been functioning for nearly thirty years, appears to have demonstrated that a regional organization supported by a group of states that have common objectives can not only survive but can prosper.

Security organizations have been held in suspicion by some of the states of Southeast Asia because they required alignment—particularly in the years during the cold war—with one of the superpowers. The policies of "active neutrality" pursued by these states have meant that security agreements and organizations are often unwelcome. Most of the regional states came to feel their principal security threat was internal instability and subversion. Organizations such as the U.S.-sponsored SEATO, aimed at countering expansionist goals of the Soviet Union and China, carried too many strings and offered too few advantages. Moreover, SEATO accentuated the very deep differences in security thinking between the United States, which viewed massive military action by the Soviet Union and its allies as the primary threat, and the states of Southeast Asia, which saw the principal threat as domestic economic or political subversion.

Nevertheless, extraregional organizations and alliances offered some states in Southeast Asia the support and security they had not found in regional groupings, particularly in the early postindependence years. The United Nations has been one such organization. Various Islamic organizations have been of interest to Indonesia and Malaysia. Thailand and the Philippines participated in the U.S.-dominated SEATO alliance and still maintain bilateral agreements with the United States, although Thailand's frustration with seemingly capricious U.S. policy shifts after the fall of Saigon and Manila's experience with the closure of U.S. military bases there left both states highly suspicious of U.S. commitments and dependability. Vietnam signed a friendship treaty with the Soviet Union, but it, too, found Soviet—and later Russian—support variable and dependent upon external Soviet or Russian interests beyond its control. Malaysia and Singapore have maintained security treaty ties to Britain, Australia, and New Zealand but rejected membership in ASPAC because of its ostensible anticommunist bias.

These extraregional linkages provided a valuable sense of continuity and strength where none had previously existed within the region. The external security organizations and agreements strengthened some regional states at certain periods of time and in specific political situations, but most were detrimental to the development of intraregional cooperation. The SEATO alliance, although focused primarily on China, also provided a real threat to North Vietnam. The British defense agreements with Singapore and Malaysia were at one time perceived as threats by Indonesia. The Soviet-Vietnamese treaty of friendship and cooperation, although again primarily focused on China, also increased the potential Vietnamese threat to other states in the region—particularly Thailand—and contributed to the polarization of the region. At the same time, virtually all of these externally supported alliances broke down when the external patron no longer found it convenient, practical, or financially feasible to sustain the relationship. Regional security issues were given little consideration, and the inevitable conclusion regional states have drawn from these experiences is that external powers are unreliable partners for achieving effective regional growth or stability.

The Politics of Regional Organization

There have been numerous attempts at creating organizations to serve the interests of regional states that were not led by extraregional powers. Created to serve a variety of ends, these early attempts at regional organization were probably doomed from the beginning by early Southeast Asian leaders' lack of experience, confidence, and common knowledge. These organizations were not, for the most part, specifically focused on either security or economic integration; nevertheless, they provided learning mechanisms for cooperation that neither the traditional nor the colonial system offered. And with the passage of time, as second and later generations of leaders took power they were better prepared to build viable linkages among themselves and to understand their importance, given the capricious nature of relations with many extra-regional global powers.

The first attempt at regional cooperation through a formal, locally created, and locally managed organization was the Association of Southeast Asia which included Malaya, the Philippines, and Thailand. Established in 1961 in response to increasing sentiment from key regional leaders for some type of regional organization, ASA was the precursor of ASEAN. Although ASA was originally advocated by Malaya and the Philippines, Thailand's foreign minister, Thanat Khoman, became the principal force behind its founding. ASA was successful in developing an infrastructure for regional cooperation that consisted of annual foreign ministers' meetings, several high-level working parties, and a series of functional committees. But it suffered from a membership only three states, and it sorely missed the participation of Indonesia and Burma. Nevertheless, ASA cut across the major ethnic and religious divisions in Southeast Asia, bringing together Buddhist (Thailand), Muslim (Malaya), and Christian (Philippines) cultural streams while lacking only sinicized Vietnam among the region's major cultural groups. ASA was nearly immobile during the conflict between Malaya and the Philippines over North Borneo, and by the time it was revived for the foreign ministers' meeting in July 1966, the region (especially Indonesia) was in the midst of a major reorientation that ultimately transformed ASA into a new organization with wider participation and a stronger mandate.

Another early attempt at regional cooperation in 1962 and 1963 was the creation of "politics of the moment." As proposed by Philippine President Macapagal, the confederation of ethnic Malay states known as MAPHILINDO was created to serve the immediate political goals of its members. Malaysia sought to assuage its confrontations with the Philippines and Indonesia. The Philippines hoped to prevent the incorporation of North Borneo into the new Malaysia, whereas Indonesia believed its support of MAPHILINDO would strengthen Manila's support for Indonesia's confrontation with Malaysia.

MAPHILINDO had a very brief history. The conflicting goals of its members ensured that little could be achieved. When Indonesia and Malaysia ended their confrontation, negotiations took place within a bilateral framework sponsored by third parties such as Thailand, the United States, and Japan; MAPHILINDO served no role in ending this confrontation. Yet the potential for ethnic unity and the expanse of archipelagic territory under one organization captured the imagination of many in Asia and demonstrated the potential of any regional organization that included Indonesia. Moreover, although MAPHILINDO left serious doubts within Malaysia's political elite regarding cooperation with Indonesia, Sukarno's previous commitment to the confederation made Suharto's subsequent decision to join the Association of Southeast Asian Nations much easier. In their commitment to MAPHILINDO, both Malaysia and the Philippines formally and publicly acknowledged that Western military bases were "temporary in nature"[7]—an important concept for the future growth of regional cooperation. It was always doubtful, however, whether the idea of a united Malay people, espoused particularly by some people in Indonesia,[8] had the potential for political expression because the clan and ethnic suspicions that inhibit national integration make regional integration even less probable.

MAPHILINDO also had strong anti-Chinese overtones. For Indonesia in particular, regional cooperation offered possible protection against subversion by the local Chinese. MAPHILINDO also accentuated the fact that fear of the Chinese, whether local or mainland, had "the regional states sufficiently worried to talk frankly about collective security."[9] The formation of Malaysia was particularly threatening because of the expanded hinterland it would provide for the economically potent—and ethnically Chinese—Singapore. This view was clearly articulated by one of Indonesia's elder statesmen who opposed the formation of Malaysia because "the new state . . . would inevitably become a second China. The Singapore Chinese would then be able to extend their power through the entire area."[10]

Strengthening the Foundations for Regional Cooperation

With the end of Indonesia's confrontation policies against Malaysia, as well as the Philippines' recognition that its North Borneo claims were unlikely to succeed, the archipelagic area of Southeast Asia entered a new period of stability, and a greater degree of cooperation than had been envisioned under either ASA or MAPHILINDO became possible. Although by 1967 Indonesia was under Suharto's leadership and the New Order government was dismantling most of the old Sukarno policies, the declaration of the Association of Southeast Asian Nations restated ideas borrowed not only from ASA but also from the politically inspired MAPHILINDO—particularly the need for regional responsibility for regional security and stability and criticism of the presence of foreign bases in Southeast Asia.

Views at the time differed as to whether a new organization should be formed or whether ASA should be expanded, but policy positions on this issue were determined by domestic political factors. Philippine President Marcos favored ASA and reportedly wanted a new organization only if it could somehow be shown to bear his imprint. He reportedly wanted to establish his own position in Filipino posterity among previous Filipino Presidents Carlos P. Garcia and Diosdado Macapagal, who had been instrumental in forming ASA and MAPHILINDO, respectively. Malaysia's Prime Minister Tunku Abdul Rahman also opposed a new organization at first, insisting that the ASA framework was sound and could be expanded if Indonesia wanted to join. Although he remained suspicious of Indonesia's intentions, he also found it difficult to work with the Philippines in giving continued support to ASA. Furthermore, it was important in domestic terms that the Malaysian government not appear subservient to Indonesia. Indonesia, for its part, had perceived itself as the leading state in the archipelago, if not the entire region, and the idea of humbling itself by applying for membership in an organization in which Malaysia and the Philippines held a veto on approval did not seem domestically feasible for the fledgling Suharto government. Singapore, skeptical of regional cooperation, was not involved in early discussions about the formation of ASEAN but quickly recognized the potential of regional cooperation for strengthening its Southeast Asian, as opposed to Chinese, identity. But it was the strong commitment of Thailand's foreign minister, Thanat Khoman, to regional development, as well as the rapport between Khoman and Malaysian Prime Minister Tunku Abdul Rahman, that made ASEAN possible. Also important was the work of Indonesia's new foreign minister, Adam Malik, who placed great value on the need for broader regional cooperation and sincere assurances of new directions for Indonesia.

Consolidation and Confidence-Building in Regional Cooperation

The formation of ASEAN heralded a new era in regional cooperation for Southeast Asia since it included most of the noncommunist states of the region, especially Indonesia. More important, this step toward regional cooperation was adapted to Southeast Asian needs. In a manner historically similar to the borrowing of political concepts from outside the region and molding them to meet indigenous needs, Western concepts of regionalism—which focused on the integrative processes seemingly inherent in regionalism—were rejected in favor of building a regional organization that would strengthen rather than diminish national identity and autonomy: "ASEAN is not a confederation, not to mention a federation, but simply an organization of sovereign states preserving their 'national identities,' all equal partners with no leaders [in theory], freely associating with one another."[11] This was the Indonesian view at ASEAN's formation. A close adviser to President Suharto said regional cooperation "is a diplomacy based on national interest, based fully on the condition and objective demands of the country concerned."[12] Put in its simplest terms, regional cooperation in Southeast Asia should be understood as the "collectivisation of interests aimed at national survival and the improvement of the international status quo."[13] Particularly at the time of its founding, the individual member states were far too fragile to risk making compromises for regional goals. Yet Western scholars, overlooking Southeast Asia's realities, still insisted that "meaningful economic integration . . . has yet to progress beyond a preliminary stage of economic regionalism."[14] Few considered the facts of historical experience, which provided no precedent or models that might have shaped the patterns of regional cooperation. In some fundamental ways the states of Southeast Asia—at both the elite and popular levels—did not know one another.

The first decade of ASEAN cooperation witnessed much discussion as member states explored the problems and possibilities of cooperation through a formal institution. Their progress was limited because of the continuation of several bilateral conflicts among them. The continuing Sabah conflict between Malaysia and the Philippines during 1968 and 1969 made full cooperation impossible. Relations between Singapore and Indonesia were strained nearly to the breaking point when, despite a personal appeal from President Suharto, Singapore executed two Indonesian marines captured during Sukarno's confrontation with the new Malaysia. Domestic instability and ethnic fragmentation further limited the ability of ASEAN member states to act cohesively. The primary constraints to more sophisticated regional cooperation were the continued domestic vulnerability of the member states—which deflected their attention and inhibited their abilities to compromise or to alter firmly entrenched national policies—and the time required to define common understandings to shared problems and to create a vocabulary based on common approaches to these problems.

Analysts repeatedly expressed a mixture of hope and concern for ASEAN's potential, but outside observers, ignoring the lack of historical precedent for cooperation, created hopes and established goals that were premature and unattainable. The learning process involved in cooperation and the time needed to define problems in common terms have never been adequately recognized by critics of ASEAN's achievements. For example, before joining ASEAN, Singapore Prime Minister Lee Kuan Yew had not visited any ASEAN state and had made only one brief stopover in Bangkok in 1966.[15] The region's overwhelming propensity toward fragmentation, based on the traditional regional system—which emphasized conflict, not cooperation, as the dominant mode of interaction—and the colonial system, which further fractured the region while artificially integrating the fractured pieces into the global system, required great efforts to overcome.

There were substantive accomplishments in policies and programs during ASEAN's early years. For instance, in recognition of the organization's vulnerability to political change, a system of meetings among foreign ministers or heads of state was put in place. Funding for ASEAN came through a joint account established in 1969 with contributions of US$1 million from each member state. These funds were used in projects subsequently approved by the foreign ministers in conference. Numerous agreements covered mostly uncontroversial issues such as tourism and educational exchange and coordinated such activities as assistance for planes and ships in distress. In its external relations, ASEAN was initially unsuccessful in attracting other regional states, particularly Burma, as members. South Vietnam's membership application was rebuffed, although South Vietnamese participants attended early meetings as observers. ASEAN played an important role in restoring bilateral diplomatic relations between Malaysia and the Philippines in 1969.

In November 1971, the ASEAN foreign ministers approved the Kuala Lumpur Declaration, ASEAN's first significant regional policy declaration. It stated that the ASEAN states would increase their solidarity and cooperation in order to create in Southeast Asia a universally recognized Zone of Peace, Freedom, and Neutrality, that was free from external manipulation, interference, and intervention. First articulated by Malaysia less than one year after ASEAN's founding and given varying degrees of support by other ASEAN members, ZOPFAN represented an important new level of strategic thinking within ASEAN. Although implementation strategies remained obscure, the doctrine gave coherence to several important concepts by acknowledging that extraregional powers could not be removed from the region by weaker regional powers, even acting collectively, and that neutralizing global struggles through regional cooperation was the only likely way for smaller states to avoid becoming pawns in superpower struggles.

ASEAN's framework was obviously political inasmuch as economics cannot be separated from politics, particularly for developing countries, although only limited possibilities for early intraregional economic cooperation appeared within the ASEAN framework. But politics in the sense of formal regional security or strategic policies was very limited from the beginning. The only military terminology included in the ASEAN declaration is the reference to foreign bases. Ignoring the varying forms of member governments (and with no reference to democracy), the declaration stresses regional linkages of history and culture, mutual interests, and common problems. Much of ASEAN's first decade was spent defining these ties.

ASEAN and the Coming of Age in Regional Cooperation

The Bali summit in 1976 was held in a "new" Southeast Asia, devoid of the U.S. military presence in Vietnam. Although the meeting included "much more public attention to political and security matters than usual," the five state leaders reconfirmed the belief that "economic rather than military cooperation was the key to stability in the region."[16] At Bali, the ASEAN heads of state also agreed to establish a permanent ASEAN secretariat, which gave the organization much greater institutional strength, and signed a Treaty of Amity and Cooperation for the settlement of disputes through processes established in the treaty, which gave the earlier Bangkok Declaration the force of treaty. The Treaty of Amity and Cooperation later became important as a mechanism through which other regional states could gain observer status in ASEAN.

ASEAN's tenth year (1977) proved to be its most substantive up to that time. Early in the year, a preferential trade agreement was signed. Several other agreements included a declaration of mutual assistance in natural disasters, as well as commodity-sharing agreements for oil products and rice. The nineteenth ASEAN ministerial conference was held in 1977 in Manila and was also attended by the prime ministers of Japan, New Zealand, and Australia, who participated in discussions concerning development assistance for ASEAN and its members. Despite residual fears of Manila's domestic instability, the ASEAN group accepted a certain urgency to take more positive initiatives to offset the previously slow pace of substantive interaction. Japanese Prime Minister Fukuda added substance to Japan's efforts to rebuild its image in the region by pledging US$1 billion in credits for five regional industrial projects. Also in 1977, the first talks between ASEAN and the United States took place in Manila. The world had apparently begun to recognize the progress and prospect for regional cooperation: "ASEAN is a positive reality . . . an organic international organization, in the critical sense that like nations modify their interest in the regional collective cause."[17]

ASEAN and Global Politics

If ASEAN's first decade focused introspectively on defining areas of commonality, the second decade took a different direction. Economic cooperation and integration through such agreements as an ASEAN free-trade zone did not develop; nor did the five highly publicized Japanese-funded, regional industrial projects succeed. Low-level economic adjustments were made, but Indonesia—which held the weakest economic position among the ASEAN states—blocked significant progress because of its sense of vulnerability, especially to Singapore. Nevertheless, ASEAN began to develop a role for itself as a regional agent in the global system.

Based on the recognition that "regional associations will afford bargaining power with foreign powers that individual governments lack,"[18] the ASEAN states found the organization to be a useful mechanism for unified dealings with larger, extraregional economic powers. In 1972, ASEAN ministers created the Special Coordinating Committee of ASEAN Nations (SCCAN) and later formed its subsidiary, the ASEAN Brussels Committee (ABC), both of which have coordinated activities and negotiated agreements among the members of the EEC. In the following years, relations between ASEAN and the EEC grew and joint ministerial meetings were held, although the level of activity between them remained comparatively small because ASEAN and Southeast Asia were "relatively low in the European scale of global priorities."[19] With the consolidation of Vietnam's control in Indochina, however, the EEC took a greater security interest in ASEAN. ASEAN also engaged in active dialogue with such organizations as the Economic and Social Commission for Asia and the Pacific (ESCAP) and the United Nations Development Program.

At other levels of external relations, ASEAN dealt directly with such states as Japan, Australia, New Zealand, Canada, and the United States to negotiate more favorable trade and investment positions. In some cases, these negotiations focused on a specific commodity, as in the Japan-ASEAN Forum on Synthetic Rubber through which ASEAN tried to protect the production levels of natural rubber, which had come under pressure from the increased production of synthetic rubber. However, despite the Fukuda Doctrine, Japan continued to be slow in dealing directly with ASEAN, preferring separate bilateral agreements. Negotiations with other bilateral partners—especially the United States and Australia—were initially difficult, but from the ASEAN perspective they demonstrated that collective bargaining and action could substantially strengthen the negotiating positions of these individually relatively weak states. In an effort to better deal with external organizations, ASEAN formed a coordinated system of assignments in which each member state undertook responsibility for relations with a particular state or organization.

ASEAN also played a key role in the development of the Pacific Community concept. In 1984, the ASEAN foreign ministers "strongly endorsed the so-called Pacific concept which called for increased cooperation among littoral states of the Pacific Ocean."[20] On the other hand, early considerations of the Pacific Community concept, although acknowledging Southeast Asia's strategic position in the grouping, prompted concern that ASEAN's identity would be lost in the much larger Pacific arena. However, the Pacific concept has continued to grow: When the ASEAN foreign ministers met in Jakarta in July 1984, they also met collectively for the third time with their counterparts from Australia, Canada, Japan, New Zealand, and the United States in what was later dubbed the "6+5." ASEAN's confidence in acting decisively within the new Pacific Community was important to both ASEAN and the larger community.

ASEAN and Security Issues

ASEAN's primary value, despite repeated statements to the contrary, has always appeared to be its strategic and security-related management of regional order. Very early, it was observed that "from the outset ASEAN helped provide an intangible yet quite significant security function by creating a sense of solidarity among like-minded governments keenly aware of their delicate internal power bases."[21] Although ASEAN member states felt economically vulnerable because of their varying degrees of underdevelopment, it was the potential for internal political manipulation of their underdevelopment by external forces that they feared most because the international environment was viewed as "predatory, hazardous, even brutish in nature."[22] Initially, the concept of security was articulated in terms of national and later regional resilience, meaning the development of levels of domestic stability sufficient to eliminate potential bases for communist or other insurgency. To enhance security, joint border patrols and information exchanges were begun on a bilateral basis. Particularly from the Indonesian perspective, China was the principal threat—not in terms of direct invasion but because of its willingness and ability to support internal insurgencies led by local communist groups. This view of China became an ASEAN version of the old, U.S. expounded domino theory.

Military security remains an area of indirect ASEAN involvement. Some member states, both before and since ASEAN's formation, have conducted joint military exercises and numerous joint border patrol operations, and many of these continue outside the ASEAN framework. ASEAN is not a formal military alliance, nor is it linked directly to an external alliance with the British through Malaysia or Singapore or with the United States through Thailand or the Philippines. Such security as it offered was initially derived from the collective strength gained from internal harmony and stability, thus precluding opportunities for external penetration and disruption. As ASEAN gained strength as an organization it added to the region's sense of security derived from the greater feelings of community among the member states, a kind of comfort and confidence in numbers, especially as individual states became willing to provide other members with assurances of support in critical conflict situations.

Although the formation of an ASEAN alliance remains highly unlikely, ASEAN has manifested some elements of a security organization because of the "shared sense of priorities of its somber governments"—even though its primary function was limited to giving "attention to apprehensions which they hold in common through displays of political solidarity and attempts at harmonization of policy as well as through economic cooperation."[23] In the first decades after its founding, security concerns among ASEAN states were focused primarily on internal subversion and instability. More recently, the members have given greater attention to security within a broader regional context. All of the ASEAN states except the Philippines have increased spending to upgrade their military capacities in order to "act in a regional setting."[24] Joint military training exercises, although bilateral, have continued, and Indonesia, Malaysia, and Singapore have signed agreements for joint undertakings to counter piracy in the Malacca Straits. In addition, all of the member states have some type of bilateral military support agreement with the United States to provide equipment, supplies, and training and to keep the United States in an "over-the-horizon" regional defensive position.

ASEAN and the Indochina Conflict

With the fall of South Vietnam and Cambodia to North Vietnamese control, ASEAN's security picture changed dramatically. Although views within ASEAN differed as to whether the principal threat to national and regional resilience was Vietnam or China, the organization demonstrated considerable skill in managing often divisive regional and global political aspects of its confrontation with Vietnam. Beginning in 1975, the ASEAN states confronted the reality of the U.S. retreat from Vietnam and the latter's unification, as well as the collapse of the conservative military government in Cambodia. Although not previously outspoken in support of U.S. involvement in Vietnam (despite participation in the war by two

ASEAN members), the group was initially unprepared to deal with a fully communist Indochina.

Vietnam's invasion of Cambodia and its installation of a client government there was met with unified ASEAN opposition. In the region the ASEAN governments were unable to use military force to challenge the invasion and could do little to undermine the growing Soviet support for Vietnam, but they succeeded at the global level. They were able to induce nearly unanimous rejection of Vietnam's actions—isolating Vietnam, for example, at the United Nations, where Vietnam sought to have its Cambodian client government recognized and seated. ASEAN lobbying at each annual UN session was successful in defeating recognition by substantial margins, and Vietnam eventually dropped its initiative to seat the Heng Samrin regime. ASEAN also successfully guided resolutions through the UN General Assembly that called on Vietnam to withdraw from Cambodia and to allow Cambodians to choose their own government. Finally, in an effort to head off waning support for the ASEAN position because it seemed to legitimize the vicious Khmer Rouge, ASEAN brought together the coalition of Cambodian opposition groups, which—although very weak—enabled ASEAN to dilute the focus on Khmer Rouge atrocities within a broad-based coalition group. The issue of Vietnam's control of Cambodia was important in and of itself, but the intricate political negotiations at both the regional and global levels demonstrated a maturity of purpose in ASEAN's policy initiatives that had previously been absent.

There were important differences among ASEAN members in their respective bilateral approaches to Vietnam. As expected, Thailand, as the frontline state confronting the expanded communist threat and with substantial ethnic linkages across its borders, reacted with the greatest concern. The Philippines, at the other end of the spectrum, saw the changed situation in Indochina as posing little threat. Indonesia and Malaysia, who still viewed China and the Chinese as the primary regional threat, were more conciliatory toward Vietnam than was Thailand. Indonesia, initially cautious in remembering its common revolutionary heritage with the Vietnamese but also distrusting their communist ideology, made serious bilateral overtures toward Vietnam seeking a solution outside of the ASEAN framework. By the mid-1980s, Indonesia was aggressively seeking a solution through bilateral action, although it did not reject the ASEAN strategy. Singapore supported the Thai position but raised concerns about the increasing bipolarization of the region. Although it recognized these different bilateral policies, ASEAN nonetheless was able to maintain a common regional policy in opposition to Vietnam.

As with most previous ASEAN ventures, its Indochina initiatives succeeded not because national goals were subordinated to a greater regional goal but because regional policy was shaped to take into account the critical needs of one state (in this case, Thailand) while leaving room for other states (Malaysia and Indonesia) to play out their own policy initiatives. The seriousness of the Cambodian crisis and its direct threat to Thai security made the entire Indochina crisis a formidable challenge for the ASEAN decisionmaking processes. The bilateral initiatives of ASEAN member states could not ignore Thai sensitivities without threatening the fabric of the organization. As the ASEAN position became caught up in global politics, however, the regional focus was more readily maintained through bilateral contacts. Although the strategy of mixing bilateral initiatives with the joint ASEAN approach was sometimes confusing and appeared weak in integrative terms, the reality for Southeast Asia and ASEAN was that the joint ASEAN position was sufficiently well-known, as were the special concerns of individual states, to allow separate bilateral initiatives without jeopardizing the fabric of regional cooperation.

Regional Cooperation in the Post–Cold War Era

The breakdown of the bipolar global system with its hallmark competition between the U.S. and the Soviet Union had tremendous implications for expanding ASEAN's latitude for independent action within the region and making possible for the first time significant action at the global level. (The fact that the change in the global system was external to Southeast Asia but had great import there confirms the subordinate status of the region because Southeast Asia itself had no control over the course of events at the global level.) It remains significant, however, that the states of Southeast Asia, particularly through ASEAN, were prepared for independent action and ready to take advantage of this or any other changes in the global system.

With the successful conclusion of the Cambodian crisis, ASEAN demonstrated its capacity to undertake complex and delicate negotiations. But having constrained Vietnam's imperial ambitions, the ASEAN states turned their attention to expanding ASEAN's regional grouping. Discussions were undertaken to bring Vietnam and Laos into contact with the ASEAN group as a first step toward membership. Vietnam began the formal application process by sending a delegation to the ASEAN secretariat in Jakarta in October 1994.[25] Burma continued to defer consideration of ASEAN membership, and Cambodia was reportedly eager to join but will wait until its internal situation stabilizes.

The end of the cold war and the Indochina conflict gave regional security a new complexion as China became the focus of attention. Responding to these changes, the ASEAN group defined three regional security strategies to include: (1) retaining the essential focus of each member state on its own national resilience and stability; (2) seeking assurance of an "over-the-horizon" U.S. presence for security matters; and (3) addressing regional security issues through diplomacy. The third component of this strategy led to an ASEAN declaration in July 1992 on security in the South China Sea, focused primarily on the disputed islands in the Spratley group. The declaration called for the peaceful resolution of all territorial claims to the islands, among other items. The South China Sea Declaration has been called a "bold departure from ASEAN's earlier practice of timidly muting regional security concerns."[26] The collective experience of the Southeast Asian states in dealing with external global powers—whether the EEC, Japan, the United States, Vietnam, or Cambodia—has raised their confidence levels even with respect to their age-old extraregional nemesis, China.

Somewhat ironically, although ASEAN has always rejected pressures to become a security alliance, it has de facto done so by the domestic strength—called national resilience in ASEAN parlance—that it has brought to its members. With superpower posturing ended in the region but China looming as a potentially more active participant in regional affairs, ASEAN's security focus has turned to stabilization of the regional environment—disputed territories, instabile borders, fishing rights, and control and supervision of international waterways. As for several millennia past, it is apparent that Southeast Asia must continue to operate as an essentially "open" subsystem, and the expectations of hostile penetration from outside, while perhaps diminished from the cold war period, have not been eliminated. Although most of the ASEAN states were critical of U.S. involvement in Vietnam, most now see a continued U.S. presence in Southeast Asia as essential for security and stability.

The 1992 Singapore summit was significant because it established (1) an ASEAN free trade agreement, (2) up-graded the ASEAN secretary-general to ministerial rank, (3) assigned a more prominent role to the ASEAN secretariat in promoting economic cooperation, (4) established a summit rotation plan on a three-year basis, and (5) undertook significant new discussions on topics in regional security.[27] Another challenge for ASEAN will be to maintain its separate identity within the wider Asia-Pacific context. Some have argued that ASEAN and Southeast Asia will "merge with a wider Asia-Pacific regionalism [that would] reduce the dilemmas that the ASEAN countries face in attempting to manage the negative consequences of great power actions."[28] It appears more likely, however, that the states of Southeast Asia, which have defined a clear and distinct regional identity for the first time in the region's history, will not quickly or easily trade that distinctiveness of identity for a minor role in the greater Pacific community. Southeast Asia will play an important role in the Pacific community, but it will use the strength of its newly defined regional identity to maximize its position and influence.

ASEAN's status in the global community has continued to grow as it has demonstrated its capacities to manage regional problems. After criticizing ASEAN as an "all talk—no action" organization for a decade, the world perhaps first recognized the importance of the Southeast Asian states and particularly of ASEAN when U.S. President Reagan visited Bali in 1986. Its regular meetings are now attended by a host of extraregional states. Twelve non-member states and organizations—including Japan, the United States, the EEC, Canada, Australia, New Zealand, South Korea, China, Russia, Vietnam, Laos, and Papua New Guinea—participated in the 1994 ASEAN foreign ministers meetings held in Bangkok.[29]

Responses to Regional Politics

Southeast Asia has been and will remain a subordinate region in the global system. It is subordinate to that global system because the global system and the primary actors in the global system have greater capacity for action and can influence events in the region more readily than can the region or its actors influence events in the global system. Southeast Asia has been a subordinate or dependent subsystem through successive international systems for the last two millennia, and this condition will not change. However, the contemporary states of Southeast Asia have taken a number of positive steps to minimize the degree of dependence on the global system by maximizing their abilities to act, individually and collectively, through regional cooperation in the global system. The collective approach to regional and global relations is new, having no precedent in either the traditional or colonial international systems.

ASEAN's viability has always been based on its indigenous approach to regional cooperation. It was not created as a security group, and it was not created with the Western model of regional integration in mind. Southeast Asian states, through ASEAN, continue to "strive to be, not a supranational community as envisaged by proponents of the European Community's Maastricht treaty, but a community of different nations and different peoples with their own identities."[30] Through this unique and indigenously defined strategy for regional cooperation, ASEAN has contributed greatly to the national strengths of its member states.

Regional cooperation in Southeast Asia, which during the early post–World War II years had occurred in response to outside leadership, increasingly followed indigenous initiatives. The Thais, sensing by the early 1960s that U.S. support would not last forever, first moved toward regional cooperation through ASA. The successive withdrawals of the French, the British, and the Americans left primary control of security in the hands of the regional states. With the temporary relaxation of global confrontation in Southeast Asia, the regional states focused more directly on their principal security concern—internal subversion.

Regional cooperation among Southeast Asian states can be divided into five periods: 1945 through 1959, when most political initiatives originated with powers outside the region; 1960 through 1967, when the states within the region began to experiment directly with regional organization; 1968 through 1976, when the member states of ASEAN engaged in serious exploratory discussions and experiments in the meanings and substance of regional cooperation; 1977 through 1988, when ASEAN began to demonstrate its capacities as a regional organization giving voice to national policy positions in concert; and 1989 to the present, when following the collapse of the Soviet Union and the concomitant demise of the bipolar global system, ASEAN became the principal organization for policy management in Southeast Asia and in the region's relations with its external environment. Parallel with this increasing regional cooperation were several other trends that have characterized regional politics since independence. First, there was a trend toward diminishing relationships with former colonial metropoles. Second, the limits of superpower intervention were defined, and the regional states themselves took a greater role in determining the agenda for regional politics. And third, this agenda has increasingly been defined by the regional states themselves in terms of the cultural and historical understandings of the region.

Once regional cooperation in Southeast Asia became more clearly focused on concepts of the exclusiveness of the region, it began to reflect the values and goals of the regional states themselves. All of the internally founded organizations—ASA, MAPHILINDO, and ASEAN— have accentuated the theme of Asian solidarity and the "Asian way" in the management of interstate relations. MAPHILINDO in particular had peculiarly racial and geographic connotations, given its ethnic Malay and archipelagic Southeast Asian composition. The concepts underlying this Asian way—such as ASEAN's consensus-style decisionmaking processes and the ability of the group to think in terms of regional cooperation to strengthen national rather than integrative capacities—remain somewhat obscure. All of the states have focused some of their regional exclusiveness on China and, to a lesser extent, on other extraregional powers. This exclusiveness has heightened regional consciousness. Although the concept of a *regional* culture seems an exaggeration, it is apparent that the commonality of culture throughout the region enhanced the development of a regional identity; to the extent that this identity developed, the likelihood of regional cooperation has been strengthened.

The decline of cold war bipolarity and the cuts in U.S. support may have given the regional states a broader range of foreign policy options and a greater measure of security. Although it may have been true that in the early, vulnerable years of independence "an increase in security almost always meant some loss of autonomy,"[31] time has shown that security and autonomy can be maintained through greater national resilience enhanced by modestly realistic regional cooperation. The breakdown of the U.S. alliance system in Southeast Asia did not stimulate new threats to the security of most of the regional states. Except for Thailand, the ASEAN states experienced a greater measure of stability, particularly in their relations with China.

Regional cooperation in Southeast Asia cannot ignore the context of the traditional regional system. No historical precedent for intense political cooperation existed, as the chronicles and oral traditions of the region give value to the aggrandizement of the individual state at the expense of neighbors. Further, the colonial experience provided no positive reinforcement for cooperative policies. Yet, also in the traditional style of the region, cooperation has been strengthened through personalized leadership, as shown in the decisional importance of summit diplomacy in the development of ASEAN. Also as exemplified by ASEAN's small secretariat staff, regional cooperation in ASEAN is still conceptualized in terms of *national resilience*, and its diplomacy is conducted by key national figures—primarily the foreign ministers.

Beginning from this base, the contemporary states of Southeast Asia have had to define the terms of cooperative politics, build a knowledge base of the interests and peculiarities of each participating state, and seek out strands of commonality among themselves. The fact that they have succeeded with an organization such as ASEAN is more than remarkable, given their individual problems of national identity and cohesion, the contemporary instability throughout the region, and the propensity for external penetration and interference.

NOTES

1. Richard Butwell, *Southeast Asia—Today and Tomorrow* (New York: Praeger Publishers, 1961), p. 163.
2. "Traveller's Tales," *Far Eastern Economic Review* (December 18, 1969), p. 593.

3. George Modelski, "Indonesia and the Malaysia Issue," *The Yearbook of World Affairs, 1964* (London: Sweet and Maxwell Stevens Journals, for the London Institute of World Affairs, 1965), p. 130.

4. Fred R. von der Mehden, "Southeast Asian Relations with Africa," *Asian Survey* 5 (July 1965), p. 341.

5. Guy J. Pauker, "Geographic Abstraction or Political Reality," in *Diversity and Development in Southeast Asia*, edited by Guy J. Pauker, Frank H. Golay, and Cynthia Enloe (New York: McGraw-Hill, 1977), p. 20.

6. H. Wriggins, "The Asian State System in the 1970s," in *Asia and the International System*, edited by Wayne Wilcox, Leo E. Rose, and Gavin Boyd (Cambridge, Mass.: Winthrop Publishers, 1972), p. 367, citing Ernest Haas, "The Challenge of Regionalism," in *Contemporary Theory in International Relations*, edited by Stanley Hoffman (Englewood Cliffs, N.J.: Prentice-Hall, 1961), p. 236.

7. Guy J. Pauker, "Indonesia in 1963: The Year of Wasted Opportunities," *Asian Survey* 4 (February 1964), p. 689.

8. Muhammad Yamin, "Unity of Our Country and Our People," in *Indonesian Political Thinking, 1945 to 1965*, edited by Herbert Feith and Lance Castles (Ithaca: Cornell University Press, 1970), p. 438.

9. Werner Levi, "The Future of Southeast Asia," *Asian Survey* 10 (April 1970), p. 350.

10. Mohamad Hatta, "One Indonesian View of the Malaysia Issue," *Asian Survey* 5 (March 1965), p. 140.

11. Russell H. Fifield, *National and Regional Interests in ASEAN: Competition and Cooperation in International Politics* (Singapore: Institute of Southeast Asian Studies, Occasional Paper no. 57, 1979), p. 7.

12. Ali Moertopo, *Indonesia in Regional and International Cooperation: Principles of Implementation and Construction* (Jakarta: Yayasan Proklamasi, 1973), p. 3.

13. Fuad Hassan, "Notes on the Prospects of Regionalism in Southeast Asia," in *Southeast Asia After the Vietnam War: Some Tentative Indonesian Views*, edited by Fuad Hassan (Jakarta: Institute of Strategic Studies, 1973), mimeographed, p. 13.

14. Frank H. Golay, "The Potential for Regionalism," in Pauker, Golay, and Enloe, *Diversity and Development in Southeast Asia*, p. 117.

15. Evelyn Colbert, "Southeast Asian Regional Politics: Toward a Regional Order," in *Dynamics of Regional Politics: Four Systems on the Indian Ocean Rim*, edited by W. Howard Wriggins (New York: Cambridge University Press, 1992), p. 236.

16. Fifield, *National and Regional Interests in ASEAN*, p. 7.

17. "Relationships," *Asia 1977 Yearbook* (Hong Kong: Far Eastern Economic Review, 1978), p. 57.

18. Sudarshan Chawla, Melvin Gurtov, and Alain-Gerard Marsot, "The View from Southeast Asia in the 1970s," in *Southeast Asia Under the New Balance of Power*, edited by Sudarshan Chawla, Melvin Gurtov, and Alain-Gerard Marsot (New York: Praeger Publishers, 1974), p. 114.

19. Stuart Harris and Brian Bridges, *European Interests in ASEAN* (London: Routledge and Kegan Paul, for the Royal Institute of International Affairs, 1983), p. 72. See also M. Rajendran, *ASEAN's Foreign Relations: The Shift to Collective Action* (Kuala Lumpur: Arenabuku, 1985), pp. 61–62, 147.

20. "Singapore: Foreign Relations," *Asia 1985 Yearbook* (Hong Kong: Far Eastern Economic Review, 1986), p. 235.

21. Charles E. Morrison and Astri Suhrke, "ASEAN in Regional Defense and Development," in *Changing Patterns of Security and Stability in Asia*, edited by Sudarshan Chawla and D. R. Sardesai (New York: Praeger Publishers, 1980), p. 201.

22. Arnfinn Jorgensen-Dahl, *Regional Organization and Order in South-East Asia* (London: Macmillan Press, 1982), p. 72.

23. Michael Leifer, "The Paradox of ASEAN, A Security Organization Without the Structure of an Alliance," *The Round Table*, 271 (July 1978), p. 264.

24. Sheldon W. Simon, "ASEAN Security in the 1990s," *Asian Survey* 29 (June 1989), p. 581.

25. "Vietnam Starts Talks on ASEAN Membership," *The Jakarta Post* (October 12, 1994), p. 11.

26. Rodney Tasker, "ASEAN; Facing Up to Security," *Far Eastern Economic Review* (August 6, 1992), p. 8.

27. Bilson Kurus, "Understanding ASEAN, Benefits and Raison d'Être," *Asian Survey* 33 (August 1993), pp. 830–831.

28. Leszek Buszynski, "Southeast Asia in the Post–Cold War Era; Regionalism and Security," *Asian Survey* 32 (September 1992), p. 847.

29. Rodney Tasker, Adam Schwarz, and Michael Vatikiotis, "ASEAN; Growing Pains," *Far Eastern Economic Review* (July 28, 1994), pp. 22–23.

30. Michael Richardson, "Vietnam and ASEAN Move to Strengthen Ties," *International Herald Tribune* (February 23, 1993), p. 5.

31. Marshall R. Singer, "The Foreign Policies of Small Developing States," in *World Politics*, edited by James N. Rosenau, Kenneth Thompson, and Gavin Boyd (New York: The Free Press, 1976), p. 289.

14

The Interstate System of Contemporary Southeast Asia

Whether Southeast Asia more closely resembles the rose or the unicorn may be debated for some years to come. What is less doubtful, however, is that the rose, the unicorn, or any point in between must be determined by focusing on how Southeast Asians define the region. In the past, Southeast Asian perceptions of the region and their common relationships within it were weak and sometimes nonexistent. However, the evidence is now clear that Southeast Asia can take its diversity in stride and can overcome problems and accomplish regional goals. Pointedly, this is a process of *self-definition* in which values, practices, and institutions will be constructed to fit indigenous needs rather than to conform to external, particularly Western, models.

Southeast Asia has been historically and will remain a subordinate state system. Nevertheless, its traditional cultures were vibrant and it is economically diverse; as the region has reestablished its identity in the contemporary global system, its traditional vibrancy, originality, and independence have reappeared despite its subordination to the global and greater Asian systems. At independence the states of Southeast Asia began a process of accommodation and adjustment to a global system constructed from values and institutions drawn from the Western or European regional systems. Early first-generation independence leaders often sought to accommodate or to copy organizational structures and practices from these Western models. At the same time, however, values and institutional concepts from the indigenous, traditional systems were reawakened and eventually reasserted. The states gained cohesion and strength internally as second-generation leaders—or sometimes first-generation leaders who survived long enough and who were skillful enough to capture these indigenizing trends—articulated these neotraditional values and reshaped institutions to better reflect local and traditional practices. Similarly, in the international field the Southeast Asian system has shown a growing measure of independence and creativity in responding to its subordinate position as its leaders have gained confidence in their neotraditional views and practices. These trends will continue. Although Southeast Asia has not lost its subordinate status, it has increased its effectiveness in dealing with and managing that status.

The foreign policies of the regional states in particular demonstrate the trend toward more effective relationships. During the 1950s and the early 1960s, the more influential first-generation regional leaders devoted much effort to the global politics of alignment and nonalignment. In the late 1960s and throughout the 1970s, however, the second generation of Southeast Asian political leaders began to focus instead on national cohesion and regional cooperation. Most Southeast Asian states were closely tied to former colonial powers in the early decades of independence, but by the 1970s the declining global status of those powers encouraged Southeast Asian leaders to reevaluate these linkages. Even the life-and-death ideological rhetoric of the cold war did not prevent the United States from downgrading its alliance relationships with Thailand and the Philippines when U.S. global interests so dictated. In this context, the regional states have grown to understand the vagaries of overcommitment to politics of the global system and, conversely, to value the greater continuity of regional interests.

While many of the principal objectives of the traditional Southeast Asian state—to control conflict, to manage international commerce and trade, and to optimize resource management, especially to extract as much possible from the population and from commerce—remain important for the contemporary states in Southeast Asia, the basic nature of the state and its relationships to its domestic and international environments have changed. The principal traditional responsibilities of the state—ritual roles as intermediary between this world and the supernatural—have vanished, although symbolic vestiges of some of the ritual practices have been mimicked by contemporary leaders as a means of demonstrating their stature as state leaders. However, the fundamental changes in the domestic and international environments in which these states operate have required that other goals and objectives of equal importance by added to the state's responsibilities.

The domestic environment in which the traditional state functioned enabled it to be largely extractive in that, despite collecting significant revenues from its mass peasant citizenry, the state was required to provide few social services in return. Fortunately, such costly activities as the traditional state's metaphysical ritual roles—especially temple construction or maintenance—are not part of contemporary government's recognized responsibilities and, therefore, do not consume much needed government resources (which is not to say that some contemporary leaders have not tried to build temples to themselves). However, no longer can the government presume that the autonomous village will provide sufficient economic opportunities or adequate social welfare. The economic and social disruption of Southeast Asian society during the colonial period broke down most traditional social relationships, especially at the village and clan levels, without providing alternative social or public-service philosophies. Both at independence and at present, the governments of Southeast Asia have found that they must deliver to their constituencies a range of programs and opportunities that have often been beyond the capacities and responsibilities of both contemporary and traditional Southeast Asian states. Neotraditional practices should enable the contemporary governments in Southeast Asia to respond more appropriately because (1) the messages are more effectively channeled through the bureaucracy, and (2) the language, symbols, and actions of officials are better understood by the people.

The international environment has similarly experienced fundamental changes. Since the 1500s, when the European states began their colonial expansion, the loosely connected group of regional subsystems that made up the global system were eliminated, at first economically and eventually politically, and the international system was transformed into a truly global system. Crucial to this transformation was the global acceptance of the concept of a multistate system of sovereign and equal states. The traditional Southeast Asian system, in contrast, was based on the primacy of a single state with subordinate vassal states arranged around the perimeter; the subordinate states' abilities to act independently roughly corresponded to their geographic distance from the primary state. It has become increasingly evident, however, that universal adoption of the Western European model has not been complete, given the weight of cultural difference and historical experience. A concept such as neo-traditionalization—usually applied to the bureaucratic, political, and economic behavior of individuals—also has explanatory power for interstate behavior. This is particularly true of Southeast Asia, where, as the newness of independence was worn away, traditional dimensions of state structures and behavior resurfaced.

The present Southeast Asian regional system differs in many fundamental ways from its traditional predecessor. Yet in other respects, traditional values and patterns of behavior, safely sheltered within the cultural totality that is Southeast Asia, have reemerged as the states of the region individually and collectively define their own unique identities with greater vigor and confidence. The process of neotraditionalization in interstate behavior has not meant the reassertion of precolonial behavior patterns in an original and unfettered form. Instead, political leaders, finding themselves participants in a multistate system based on Western international law, have pursued their own ends and sought to provide for the security of their own states through whatever means have been available. These leaders have been conditioned by the entire cultural and political experience of Southeast Asia—by the rules and behavior patterns of traditional Southeast Asia, as well as by the colonial and contemporary systems of government and international relations. Although in form the Western interstate system has been accepted globally, within Asia and particularly in Southeast Asia manifestations of the traditional system remain in the daily functioning of domestic and interstate relations. These elements of traditional behavior, many of which have been important for successful domestic political, economic, and social organization and policies, have given leaders in Southeast Asia a vigorous confidence in their values and abilities, which have carried over to the international system.

The states of Southeast Asia are members of the global multistate system and, in the main, follow its prescriptions for interactions. All maintain formal embassies in the leading capitals of the world. The volume and range of interstate contacts far exceed those of any previous period, given the degree to which diplomatic form is followed as well as the many educational, economic, sporting, and other exchanges that reinforce the concept of sovereign equality among states. The ways in which the states of Southeast Asia have adapted to this system while simultaneously restoring many of the familiar values and patterns of behavior of their traditional interstate system can be better understood when the region is again divided into subsystems.

Cultural and Religious Subsystems

In the traditional system, Indian religions and political concepts provided all of Southeast Asia, except for Vietnam, with a modicum of cultural homogeneity, particularly among the royal elites. These concepts formed the philosophical foundation for the political legitimacy of the king and were understood and accepted by the population as the rationale for the state and for life itself.

In the current system, when the states gained independence, however, no such homogeneity could be found. Government in the region, having lost its divinity, had difficulty finding a single, all encompassing, and uniform basis for its legitimacy. The Thai monarchy does play an important role in the maintenance of political legitimacy, but the bureaucratic polity in Thailand must also maintain legitimacy as the decisionmaking arm of the government.[1] Buddhism has been a factor in contemporary politics in Burma, Thailand, and—at times—Vietnam, but it has not provided a firm base for political legitimacy. As the premier of Burma, U Nu gave strong support to Buddhism and "became the link between the Burmese people, whose religious faith he shared and whose folk tales he knew, and the sophisticated Westernized Socialists who dominated much of the thinking" in the government.[2] Buddhist monks have been active in political protests in Vietnam but have not offered an organized alternative to communism there.

Islam also became a strong religious force in the traditional system, preceding the Europeans in the region and supplanting Indian kingship in most of the archipelagic states. However, even in the traditional period, Islam was adapted to the preexisting political concepts of Hinduism; names and terms were changed, but seldom were the substance and functions of royalty altered. Moreover, although Islam may have spread farther through archipelagic Southeast Asia in response to the Christianizing efforts of the Portuguese, it was unsuccessful politically in drawing the region's sultanates together to combat the European penetration.

As a force for political legitimacy in the contemporary period, Islam has played a similarly quixotic role. It has not been relevant, of course, for the mainland states, but even in the archipelago—the area of the region that has been largely Islamicized—only Brunei has made significant use of Islam for political legitimacy. The government in Malaysia by contrast for many years used Islam as a legitimizing force among ethnic Malays; however, in recent years and particularly since the revolution in Iran stimulated and reinvigorated Islam, it has been more difficult for the government to control. Now the government in Malaysia faces the delicate task of controlling Islam—essentially radical groups and radical ulamas—while trying to remain its official protector. Indonesia has had less difficulty but an equally fractious relationship with Islam. Confronted with a small but vocal group that espoused an Islamic state format for Indonesia, the more syncretic Javanese who control the government have curtailed Islamic influences, sometimes by force and other times with policies that limit Islamic activities. It is certain that Islam cannot form the basis for government legitimacy in Indonesia and probably not in Malaysia without seriously disrupting the multiracial balance of the present governments.

Other ideologies have been important only in Vietnam, which has adhered to communism, and Indonesia, which has adopted what it calls

Pancasila as a weak form of ideological legitimacy for the government. In Vietnam it is clear that communism has provided legitimacy in the quest for establishing a single government throughout Vietnam. At least at times, communism has had potent legitimizing force through the entire society, even reaching into the village with land-reforms and other restructuring. Indonesia's Pancasila ideology, on the other hand, is much less prescriptive of a political action agenda and provides essentially five vague tenets, which can be interpreted with great latitude, for fundamental social beliefs and organization.

Among all of the governments in the contemporary period, there has been one important and consistent change. In the present system, professions of support for democratic principles of government, in one form or another have replaced religion as the legitimizing force behind government. Imported Western democratic practices may have been no more real than was the traditional king's interaction with Siva, but even the most autocratic and dictatorial governments in Southeast Asia—whether right or left ideologically—govern in the name of the people. What has become significant in Southeast Asian political development has been the ways in which governments have adapted Western institutions, such as parliaments and political parties, to meet the needs and realities of their domestic political and social contexts.

The crucial question for future political development is whether the people understand the implications of democracy and this shift in the basis of legitimacy to the people. The generalized expectations of government responsiveness remain as they were under the traditional system. It appears (if we exclude the experience of some students and some of the urban elite) that expectations of governmental support and services have as yet changed very little, despite the radically different base for government legitimacy. Expressions of neotraditional values have provided a common mechanism for communication between the elite and the general population, but whether or how these values can be modified (adapted) to provide a new, popular base for legitimacy or whether these same values will be used to repress popular participation and insulate the elite (as was the practice in the traditional system) remains an evolving question.

The generally low level of popular expectations may have provided most Southeast Asian governments with a temporary respite from the more pervasive demands of a broadly participatory system, but this is undoubtedly a short-term reprieve. Expectations and demands for participation and services will continue to rise, and governments will have to accommodate these changing demands. This is not to imply that Western-style democracy will soon be demanded by the general populace anywhere in Southeast Asia. It is abundantly clear that other practices and forms will be accepted by most peoples, but, however structured, these governments will have to become more effective at *hearing* the concerns of the people and more efficient in *responding* to those concerns. These processes will benefit if the institutions of government more fully reflect traditional values and practices, but the governments themselves will have to adopt much more open and service-oriented postures to successfully meet these demands, an orientation that finds little precedent in traditional practice.

The Economic Subsystem

The current economic system has also changed from that of its traditional predecessors insofar as its dependence on the global economic system, which was great during the traditional period, is now more complete. The subsistence economic base of village agriculture has been destroyed, and the social fabric and independent welfare system of the village have been broken through economic change and disruption of landholding patterns, as well as by dramatic population growth and migration to cities. The remnants of village economic and social systems offer some measure of insulation for a declining percentage of Southeast Asia's population, but the village cannot provide a subsistence security base against fluctuations of the global economic system. Problems of an aging population group without the traditional support of the extended family and also with insufficient government or private-enterprise systems will become a major dilemma for all of the region's governments.

Other aspects of Southeast Asia's present economic system more nearly resemble the traditional system. Much of the commercial sector at all levels is controlled by foreigners, especially the Chinese, although Indians also play a significant role in some states. The distaste Southeast Asians, especially ethnic Malays, traditionally displayed for commerce remains prevalent. There is some evidence that during the traditional period indigenous Southeast Asians played an active role in commerce[3] and that these groups were eliminated during the colonial period. The historical situation may be in doubt, but in the contemporary system all of the region's economies have been influenced by nonindigenous ethnic groups. The Malaysian economy is largely controlled by Chinese and, to a lesser extent, by Indians, and government policies designed to assist ethnic Malays have produced increasing friction among ethnic groups while bringing only marginal improvements to Malays. These practices have taken on the appearances of an economic "pay-off" for the already politically dominant Malays. In Indonesia, the Chinese community represents a much smaller percentage of the population than that in

Malaysia, but the Chinese still hold substantial control of the economy, although in recent years the government and the army have taken a larger role. The most sophisticated economic entity in the region—Singapore—is almost entirely Chinese in character. Burma and, more recently, Vietnam have driven out many of the Chinese (as well as the Indians in Burma) business community, and the governments have taken control of most commercial activities. In Thailand and the Philippines, the Chinese business community has been more effectively assimilated, although Chinese businesspersons can still be the subject of discrimination and are often blamed for corruption.

The present economic system also resembles the traditional system in terms of the lack of clear separation of commercial and state activities. The traditional role of the wealthy merchant classes in supporting the kings of Southeast Asia where there was no separation between the person and the official position and wealth accruing to the position was part of the legitimate compensation of the person holding the position continues today. In the traditional system this accrued wealth was often the only compensation, whereas in the contemporary system there is a government paid salary that at least in theory provides full compensation to the officeholder. The traditional state's direct participation in commerce by collecting taxes and levies in-kind and marketing these surpluses also finds parallels in contemporary Southeast Asia. The close relationships between government officials and major commercial interests, interpreted as matters of corruption in Western eyes, find easy historical precedent in traditional Southeast Asia. Government participation in the economic sector has also been formalized in state monopolies such as the state petroleum organizations of Indonesia, Malaysia, Burma, the Philippines, and Thailand. There are other state-run economic organizations such as Burma's Agricultural Corporation, an appendage of the Ministry of Agriculture that plans, supervises, and markets major crops. More recently the military in most Southeast Asian countries has developed strong commercial interests, and retired general staff officers have moved in large numbers into the private sector as directors, consultants, or government lobbyists and liaison officers.

In the traditional economic system, government intervention was limited both by the weakness of the state's bureaucratic apparatus and by the power of the wealthy merchants to counter or flee from the power of the king. In the current system, both of these restraints have been curtailed. Bureaucratic effectiveness, however scant at independence, has improved in recent decades. A high level of governmental economic control also exists at present. Although wealthy merchants still have the ability to obtain favors and to influence policy, they cannot replace the government at their will.

Economic development has been quite rapid in most of Southeast Asia. Led by Singapore followed by Malaysia and Thailand with Indonesia as well performing impressively, growth rates have been very strong. Much of this growth has been in consumer products that can take advantage of low cost labor. However, each country in succession has experienced rising labor costs, which parallel the rising skill levels of its labor force. Labor exploitation is a problem of varying degrees in these countries, particularly for undocumented foreign workers and unskilled rural laborers who migrate to the urban industrial centers. Yet the patterns and linkages between economic development and political development are already clear; continuing economic development requires ever increasing skill levels in the labor force, but the education required to attain these higher skill levels also produces a population that is politically less apathetic and passive as compared with its more traditional, less educated predecessors. An educated population will not necessarily reject neotraditional political values outright but will demand that these values be adapted to provide more opportunities for mass participation.

With the possible exception of Singapore, even the recent impressive economic growth has not reached evenly throughout society. The educated and prosperous labor force remains very much a minority. Although the village subsistence economic structure has collapsed, no adequate alternative has been found. The core of the former peasant society has been separated from its social and economic base, but the economies of the states have developed insufficiently to sustain these people as producers-consumers. In an economic sense, large segments of the population in all of the states of Southeast Asia exist in economic limbo—somewhere between starvation and ad hoc subsistence. Governments have yet to develop the resource base or the social ethic to provide the welfare these people could have expected from the traditional village. In these evolving political systems, obvious disjunctions such as this remain because the general populace has not yet learned how to use the system to its fullest advantage and, more probably, remains convinced that government is incapable of providing for the general welfare even if such were demanded. Popular government is a two-way proposition—the people must demand and the government must respond, and neither of these aspects is fully developed in most Southeast Asian states.

Political and Diplomatic Subsystems

At independence, the states of Southeast Asia were brought into the global diplomatic system and into such international organizations as the United Nations. In this respect, the international system accepted and confirmed the sovereignty of each state, a status that was not universally accepted domestically for most of these states. The concept of a sovereign territorial state had no historical precedent in the region. Sovereignty in the traditional Southeast Asian state was held in the person of the ruler and was extended through space (i.e., territory) to a limit that, in effect, became the perimeter of the kingdom, which fluctuated over time as the relative power extended from the center toward the periphery shifting in search of an ever changing and elusive equilibrium in counterbalance to the power of another center extending from the opposite direction. The concept of territorial sovereignty was first imposed externally during the colonial period and did not represent, as territorial sovereignty had in Europe, a growing recognition of a national and territorial identity among the general population. Tan Sri Ghazali Shafie, Malaysian minister of home affairs, has said that "one of the unpleasant realities of Southeast Asia is that many of its states are mere territorial entities in search of national identities."[4] National identity will develop as the national governments improve their ability to communicate with their citizens, and this communication has improved as national elites have discovered the value of neotraditional symbols and practices. National identity will also grow stronger as national governments find more ways to meet the changing needs of their citizens.

Responses to their new sovereign status have differed among the regional states, depending on their experience in attaining independence, their longer-term relationships with the former colonial powers, and their national leaders' perceptions concerning the critical issues facing these new nations. One of the few relatively consistent positions among the new regional states was the propensity to ignore regional neighbors in favor of relations with former colonial powers, superpowers, and major economic and military benefactors and donors. By 1954 Thailand, the most experienced in foreign affairs among the Southeast Asian states, had established a full embassy within the region only in Burma and the Philippines, although Cambodia, Laos, Indonesia, and Vietnam were accredited with lower-level legations. In the same year, Indonesia had full embassies only in Burma and the Philippines, although it maintained embassies in fourteen countries outside the region, including such major countries as the United States and also a number of Islamic states. Burma and the Philippines did not establish relations until 1956, when they accredited their respective ambassadors who were already in place in Bangkok rather than establishing separate embassies in Rangoon and Manila.

For several states, diplomacy offered a way of enhancing weak domestic political legitimacy. Some Southeast Asian leaders defined themselves and their states as part of the vanguard of a new global system opposing the bipolar global system dominated by superpower politics. Burma and Cambodia used this policy in the Non-Aligned Movement, but it was Indonesia's Sukarno who skillfully and flamboyantly molded and manipulated antiglobal themes for national as well as international purposes creating the angry image of long-repressed peoples who—ignoring Sukarno's mismanagement and misguided domestic policies—were at last prepared to confront the real enemy—the industrialized West.

Given Burma's geographic vulnerability vis-à-vis China and Cambodia's location in the midst of a global dispute, somewhat passive forms of nonalignment became the only policy option that offered them some hope of continued independence. In terms at least of the maintenance of independence (a primary fear for small states that are in contention with global powers), this policy strategy has been relatively successful for Burma but, ultimately, not for Cambodia. Indonesia, on the other hand, sometimes undertook a more aggressive approach to its nonaligned policies in an attempt to minimize domestic criticism that it leaned too much to the left or the right, although Sukarno later aligned with Beijing and Hanoi.

Following independence, all of the states were involved with neighbors in defining and controlling disputed or otherwise uncertain borders because, as a corollary to their newly acquired territorial sovereignty, all of these states had some difficulty controlling border areas. Burma was among the most active states in seeking formal diplomatic resolutions for its border disputes, especially with China and India, although many of Burma's problems stemmed from ethnic divisions within the country itself. Thailand had similar border problems with Burma, Cambodia, and especially Laos, where Lao-speaking peoples have lived for centuries on both sides of the Mekong River. Historically, the Mekong had been an artery for communication and commerce rather than a border. The archipelagic states, too, had problems with ethnic minorities who historically had held separate and sovereign status. Because Southeast Asian statehood has most often been built around the values and the religion of a dominant ethnic group to the disadvantage of other ethnic groups that had equally distinctive historical experiences but that had been passed over during the colonial period, the sense of sovereign legitimacy gained from global recognition was critical for the newly independent states.

The rather schizophrenic focus on the global system level and the domestic level while virtually ignoring intermediate or regional relations did not begin to dissipate until the Southeast Asian states had gained experience in the international system and developed a more complete sense of their domestic status as independent states. In time, both the utility of the global system for providing political legitimacy and the need to rely on global mentors for security guarantees lessened. A new regional context emerged in which these states recognized that their own futures could be controlled internally and that external interference and manipulation could best be controlled through cooperative regional action. At about the same time, the global powers—particularly those in the West—perhaps began to understand that "assumptions concerning the possibility of transforming Southeast Asian states into some copy, or at least approximation, of nations in the West were illusory."[5] But more important, the ideological conflict of the cold war eventually diminished, and thus the likelihood of external interference in the internal development of these states also declined.

By the mid-1960s, diplomacy in Southeast Asia had entered a new phase in which regional relations were gradually strengthened. As the individual identities of the states solidified, the Southeast Asian region also took on its own image. As the residue of colonial influence and the pressures of the cold war diminished, it became more obvious that within Southeast Asia itself subregional areas of spheres of influence existed. One analyst concluded that the "Southeast Asian islands clearly represent a sphere of influence within which historical forces have contested for prominence,"[6] and events in Indochina created a second sphere controlled from Hanoi.

The continued weakening of the global system—first the expansion of detente between the superpowers and eventually the defeats of the United States in Vietnam and the Soviet Union in Afghanistan—gave the states of Southeast Asia sufficient room to begin to articulate regional policies substantively different from those advocated by the superpowers. However, the collapse of the Soviet Union in 1989 and the subsequent reduction of global spheres of influence, while exposing the degree to which Southeast Asia as a subordinate subsystem had been controlled by the global system, gave the states of Southeast Asia the greatest degree of freedom in regional policy formation that had ever been available to them. As the West retired from the field of political competition and shifted its focus primarily to economic relations with the region, China reemerged as the principal external power with longterm political interests in the region, a circumstance not greatly different from that of the traditional system of the first millennium of the Christian era.

The Military Subsystem: Security and Regional Conflict

In traditional times, the states of Southeast Asia clearly used force to good advantage. It is also clear that the role of military force is now radically different, not only in the obvious areas of modern equipment but, perhaps more important, in the military's value as an instrument of state power. In the traditional system, the power of the military depended on the continued loyalty and support of semi-independent chieftains, leaders, and lords; but following World War II and independence, the hierarchical command structure of the modern military as adopted in Southeast Asia has made it the most efficient and effective bureaucratic structure in these countries. From one perspective, "a military establishment comes as close as any human organization can to the ideal type for an industrialized and secularized enterprise."[7] In all of the countries of Southeast Asia, the military has played an important role in suppressing rebellions and insurgencies. In all of the countries except Vietnam, Malaysia, and Singapore, the military has extended that influence directly into the political sphere—at one time or another taking direct control of the government in Indonesia, Burma, Thailand, and Cambodia.

A lack of internal cohesion still characterizes most of the states in Southeast Asia. Challenges continue from ethnic minorities seeking greater autonomy or independence, from religious—particularly Islamic—groups seeking majority control of the government or greater minority autonomy, and from ideological competitors seeking revolutionary change, particularly communist revolutionary groups which continue insurgency movements in Burma, the Philippines, and Cambodia despite the collapse of the communist global system. Although support for insurgency movements was often part of the confrontation between the superpowers, since the breakdown of the U.S. containment policy and the collapse of the Soviet Union most of the violence in the region has been domestic as governments have tried to quash revolutionary insurgencies. The use of force in the traditional system was the primary tool for extending territorial limits and securing the periphery of the kingdom. In the present system, the territory of the state has been defined and, with very few exceptions, agreed upon by all actors in the international system, but force has remained a principal means for securing control—particularly among ethnic minority and other dissident and revolutionary groups residing at the figurative perimeter of the state.

Aside from border problems, which sometimes spilled over into neighboring states, interstate violence continued long after independence. Although the level of this violence declined after the 1960s, it was not eliminated as an acceptable means of interaction, and force remained a potent tool in the range of interstate contacts within Southeast Asia. Vietnam's occupation of Cambodia was the most conspicuous recent example, but others abound: Indonesia in Timor and earlier in the Irian and Malaysian campaigns, the Philippines in the Malaysia dispute and in conflict with its Islamic minorities, Malaysia and Thailand on their common border, and Burma in the border regions with China and Thailand. External powers have also been directly involved in regional conflicts: first, the Dutch and French attempted to reestablish colonial regimes; second, the United States took the French-Vietnam colonial conflict and converted it to a global struggle against communism; and third, China tried to assert its traditional suzerainty over Vietnam.

In the archipelago the traditional role of Southeast Asian states as masters of the international sea-lanes and providers of entrepôt services for international commerce has been reestablished with adjustments made for the contemporary global system. In a sense, Singapore still plays this role, although the naval complement no longer is the responsibility of a single state but is handled through agreements among Indonesia, Malaysia, and Singapore. As in the traditional system, piracy remains a problem in all the maritime regions of Southeast Asia. Despite the importance of maritime commerce in virtually every country in Southeast Asia it is the army that is paramount among the military services in both size and political influence.

Even under the pressure of continuing international conflicts, the states of Southeast Asia have offset their declining diplomatic concern for global strategizing with an increasing concern for issues of internal stability and security. China continues to be feared as a potential fomenter of insurgency, but the region's governments have realized that the best counter to such insurgencies is a strong, stabile, and growing domestic economy. Early paranoia associated with the departure of U.S. ground forces from the region gave way to more realistic planning, not only in the military field but also in such areas as rural development and agricultural production policies. Much of this common understanding has been derived from the shared experiences through ASEAN and from the states' individual and collective willingness to forthrightly and confidently articulate their own original ideas and turn them into practical policy prescriptions.

The states of Southeast Asia have continued to eschew formal military alliances among themselves, although some have maintained security agreements with extraregional powers. However, as the regional states have intensified bilateral relations since the mid-1960s, and as regional associations such as ASEAN have gained strength, they have found it easier to "talk frankly about collective security."[8] A wide variety of military interchanges such as joint maneuvers, training exchanges, intelligence exchanges, and joint planning exercises have been carried out bilaterally among ASEAN members. With the fundamental changes in the global system, especially the collapse of the Soviet Union and the rising interest of China in developing its deep-water naval capacity, ASEAN has increasingly taken a more aggressive stance on regional security, releasing a five-point declaration on the South China Sea aimed at defusing potential conflicts over the Spratley Islands, inviting Vietnam and Laos to participate in ASEAN, and urging the United States to maintain a military presence in the region.[9]

Extraregional Powers

As was true in the traditional Southeast Asian system, and as should be expected in any subordinate system, extraregional powers have been active in Southeast Asia throughout the post–World War II era. The configuration of powers has expanded and changed, moving from an initial period of near domination by the United States to a period of considerable U.S.-Soviet competition to a period when China's influence is expanding. Nevertheless, regional states have asserted their independence and taken more effective control of regional as well as national politics. Although this does not imply that Southeast Asia's subordinate status will end, it does suggest that external powers can be contained and that the regional states, as they develop greater international skills and broader regional resilience, will find more opportunities for independent action.

Traditional extraregional power roles have changed. India, which provided much of the cultural and philosophical underpinnings of the traditional system, has lost most of its influence, although Buddhism remains strong among the mainland Southeast Asian states, and Burma has maintained close relations with India. In the early years of independence, Jawaharlal Nehru was one of the truly global spokespersons for neutralism and nonalignment, and Sukarno, U Nu, and Sihanouk were closely associated with Nehru as leaders of the newly independent nations of Asia. But this collegial relationship failed to spread beyond the nonaligned movement, and in the modern era India has not played the leadership role ascribed to it by early scholars. Still other extraregional influences remain important as renewed interest in Islam has added an influential element to politics in several Southeast Asian states, and Western ideas and practices continue to provide an attractive model for many in Southeast Asia.

China's role as an extraregional power has very closely followed its traditional patterns, particularly with regard to political interaction. China's traditional economic role as the principal source for goods traveling through Southeast Asia has ended, although commerce between China and most Southeast Asian states is growing again in complexity and volume. Also, as a result of the great increase in the numbers of Chinese now residing in Southeast Asian countries, its current economic and political roles are less well understood. Throughout most of the cold war, China's political activities in the region were indirect, largely involving relations with fraternal communist parties. At different times, China maintained strong government-to-government relations with Indonesia (1960–1965), Cambodia (1975–1979), and Vietnam (until 1975). China's relations with Burma have been stabile and friendly but not intimate.

The Chinese approach to Southeast Asia has been low-key, much like its traditional foreign policy strategy. China made much of the hydraulic agrarian nature of its society in trying to assert its influence over communist ideological thought in Asia. The Chinese policy toward Southeast Asia as a regional entity was not always well formulated, although on the mainland the Chinese sought to limit Soviet involvement in Indochina and, failing that, expanded relations with Thailand and Burma in addition to providing support to Cambodian insurgents. At the same time, the Chinese military incursion into Vietnam could be considered a manifestation of the tradition of punishing an ungrateful vassal.

However, China has recognized that the nature of the global system places the present Southeast Asian system in a new position. No longer one of a series of loosely linked and semiautonomous regional systems, Southeast Asia instead became an area of direct global involvement and confrontation. The U.S. strategy of containment of the communist Asian heartland was challenged and broken on Southeast Asian soil. Moreover, China's opposition to Vietnam's control of Cambodia stemmed not from a fear of a powerful Vietnam but from the recognition that the Soviet alliance with Vietnam introduced a new form of containment with the Soviet Union militarily entrenched on China's southern flank. Now that the Soviet Union no longer exists and the United States has no permanent military bases in the region, China's traditional view that Southeast Asia is a special sphere in which China's influence among extraregional powers should be paramount has gained new significance for the region as well as the United States.

For the United States few vital issues pertaining to Southeast Asia appear to require direct intervention. The possibility of superpower confrontation in the region ended with the collapse of the Soviet Union, but the resulting ambiguity of policy goals and vital interests, especially for the United States, has left a power vacuum which China may choose to fill. The United States considers it important to protect the sea-lanes that connect Japan to Middle Eastern oil, but Southeast Asia cannot claim the same vital position that Europe, for example, holds for U.S. interests. China's primary interests in Southeast Asia—whether communist or noncommunist—remain strategically vital and will become increasingly vital in economic terms.

For the Chinese, economic competition in Southeast Asia will come not from the United States but from Japan. Through the end of the twentieth century, as Chinese economic capabilities expand, Southeast Asia will be important for raw materials and markets. In the meantime, the region will increase its productivity and seek Chinese markets. With Japanese technological and managerial leadership, the economic future should be bright, although conflict in the region could undermine this potential, especially conflicts involving extraregional powers.

Characteristics of the System

This study has outlined in broad terms the interstate system of Southeast Asia from its historical base to its present configuration. The level of generalization necessary for such an overview becomes both its strength and its weakness: The themes and generalizations used to describe the region systemically can often be challenged with specific examples that vary dramatically from the norms; yet it is the norms that provide the framework against which the exceptions can be most readily understood. The fact that the norms constitute a working and unique system appears beyond doubt; moreover, the system's unique characteristics have become more evident as individual state actors find in their contemporary policies that elusive mix of cultural interpretation and adaptation required to meet external challenges and threats, as these cultures have done so effectively for two millennia or more.

Institutional Strength

The current states of Southeast Asia continue to exhibit many of the same weaknesses as their traditional predecessors. These states did not evolve historically through common undertakings of the mass of the population, and the idea of a social contract between the governors and the governed remains weak. Government derives its authority from the acquiescence of the people rather than from their consent. The modern state has been unable to build broad-based support, particularly among religious and ethnic minorities, although economic growth may be creating a middle class group of important size with sufficient commitment to the status quo to insure support for incumbent governments in all but the most extreme situations. Even among states that experienced a common revolutionary struggle against former colonial masters, unity was lost once the common goal of expelling the colonial power was accomplished. This became immediately apparent after Indonesia gained its independence, and it explains in large part the failure of parliamentary democracy there. Similar problems overtook Vietnam, particularly as it tried to impose new policies in the south. Yet acquiescence has been an essential political ingredient in Southeast Asian political systems for millennia. It will be supplanted only very slowly and with rising education levels and increased political experience.

The centrist nature of the current Southeast Asian states also resembles that of their traditional predecessors. Revolutionary movements were led by Western-educated urban elites, many of whom demonstrated little understanding of the rural regions of their countries. Political parties have rarely been mass organizations and have more often been little more than small cliques of politicians. There have been exceptions, such as some of the region's communist parties, but most of the government-controlled organizations that have extended into rural areas, such as Indonesia's GOLKAR or the Burmese Socialist Program Party (BSPP) after 1981, remain tools for outward control from the urban center to the rural fringes. Although GOLKAR has widened its membership and the Indonesian government has made some efforts to broaden the base of participation in political and governmental institutions, few of these government-managed parties have had notable success in engendering strong political support among rural populations.

Although the boundaries of the Southeast Asian states were clearly demarcated at independence, except for a few interstate territorial disputes, most of these countries have had difficulty extending effective power throughout their territorial confines. Most fragmentation came not through territorial challenges from other states but from domestic ethnic or religious minorities or other revolutionary groups that refused to accept the authority of the state. This has been a problem in the archipelago, but separatist movements in Sumatra and in eastern Indonesia were suppressed, and the Muslim rebels in the Philippines have been unable to secure their autonomy. For years, Vietnam made free use of the border territories in Laos and Cambodia for military purposes. The Lao population on both sides of the Thai-Laotian border sees itself as a single people, and the Shan, Karen, and other areas technically within Burma are administered largely as independent states that primarily lacked international recognition. Border regions in Southeast Asia have tended to resemble the buffer zones that separated the traditional states. Not only have borders on land been difficult to protect; coastal shipping continues to suffer from the piracy that has escalated in recent years, despite formal agreements and coordinated naval action against pirates by Indonesia, Malaysia, Thailand, and Singapore.[10]

At independence, all of the states of Southeast Asia were plagued by severe weakness in political institutions, and some states continue to face serious problems. However, contemporary Southeast Asia resembles a continuum on a weakness-strength scale, with several states—notably Singapore and to a somewhat lesser extent Malaysia—having consolidated the institutions of government far more effectively than Burma or Cambodia. Among all states the degree of bureaucratic-military control of government has continued to grow. Neotraditionalization continues to influence the patterns of behavior within these bureaucratic governments. More than four decades of training and education (with much of the advanced training done internationally) have resulted in a greater capacity for planning, decisionmaking, and implementing government policy—although perhaps in a neotraditional style.

Interstate Exchange and System Recognition

Regional interstate relations have evolved through several different phases as regional states came to terms with their own independence and with the regional and global environments in which they found themselves. On the basis of their experiences before and during the colonial period, the newly independent states of Southeast Asia initially found little in common. At first they sought their closest political and economic relations outside the region, despite many public flourishes about the importance of good relations among their more immediate neighbors. Early foreign policies were responsive to the very hostile bipolar global system and took one of two forms: (1) alignment with a superpower, or a former colonial metropole that was aligned with a superpower; or (2) the "brave new world" approach to foreign policy that sought to challenge the established powers and wrest control of the global system away from the superpowers. By the mid-1960s, the nonaligned and Western-aligned states (except for Burma) discovered that there was a certain safety in numbers and that their similar developmental and political plights gave them much in common. Their capacities for cooperative interchange remained limited by a lack of resources, limited experience in regional cooperation, and the fragile nature of their political institutions. Nevertheless, cooperation among a significant group of regional states developed beyond anticipated levels, and Southeast Asia was "characterized by an imbalance of 'power,' which the region's governments, determined to control their own fate, may prefer to any balance system dominated by major military powers."[11] The principal product of this recognition of the value of regional cooperation was ASEAN.

Indonesia and Vietnam have been identified as two "core members" of the larger East Asian system and as "the two most important states of Southeast Asia, Indonesia for the insular archipelago and North Vietnam for the mainland."[12] At one time, with Vietnam allied with and supplied by the Soviet Union, as well as in control of Indochina, the region seemed poised for a period of bipolar conflict between the ASEAN group and the Indochina group. The regional multistate system took on the complexion of an imperial or a hegemonic system similar to the traditional Southeast Asian system which had held a strong preference for hegemonic relations between states. The propensity toward monopoly control of commercial sea-lanes, commodity ports, and entrepôt centers—especially in the archipelago—reinforced this unequal relational structure. Throughout traditional Southeast Asia, ethnic suspicions reinforced by Hindu-Buddhist and Confucian political concepts of state legitimized superior-vassal interstate relations within the regional system. Similar superior-vassal hegemonic relations appeared to have found contemporary expression in the bipolar division of the regional system: "From a security perspective, the past decade has witnessed the development of two Southeast Asias. One, [is] centered on the membership of the Association of Southeast Asian Nations . . . the other, centering on a Vietnamese-dominated Indochina."[13]

Although seeming to contradict the tenets of independence and self-determination, two leading regional powers—Vietnam and Indonesia—sought control beyond the full colonial territory from which they sprang. Aside from its annexation of Portuguese Timor, Indonesia had not made serious efforts to expand its territory, but since before independence there has been in Indonesian political thinking a vague concept of "greater Nusantara"—meaning Indonesian influence, control, or hegemony spread throughout the archipelago. Indonesia has been muted but firm in its leadership within ASEAN. Indonesia fought doggedly to claim all of the former Dutch territory despite a paucity of historical or cultural ties to such areas as West Irian, but although it has long harbored desires for regional leadership, it has had less success in imposing its will on any neighboring states. Sukarno's bombastic policies of confrontation gave way to more subdued positions, but—particularly since the formation of ASEAN—Indonesia has consolidated its influence within the archipelagic subregion of Southeast Asia. Some see Indonesia as the paramount, but not the dominant, state in the region.

With the consolidation of its hold on Indochina, Vietnam fulfilled an objective for the Indochinese Communist Party that had been stated at least as early as the 1930s. In addition, the process of Vietnamese expansionism dated back several hundred years. A paranoia regarding security, developed from decades of foreign hostility, may have increased the ideological resolve to consolidate Indochina, but Vietnam's apparent success engendered the expansion of major ethnic groups in a manner that was almost endemic to Southeast Asian history.

The unfolding of Vietnam's imperial power in Southeast Asia polarized the region, jeopardizing regional stability and increasing the possibilities for conflict by focusing for the first time nearly all of the region's power resources along the Thai borders with Laos and Cambodia. Yet as might be anticipated for conflict in such a subordinate system—particularly one reflecting the last trappings of control from the tight, ideologically aligned, bipolar global system—the impetus for ending the regional conflict came from outside the region when Vietnam's benefactor, the Soviet Union, reduced its support to Vietnam before the Soviet Union itself collapsed.

The brief interlude of the Vietnam-Indochina and Indonesia-ASEAN subsystems was suggestive of previous imperial systems of traditional Southeast Asia, although imperialism must be viewed less in J. A. Hobson's economic terms (i.e., as a function of expansion of excess capital) and more, as Joseph Schumpeter has argued, in terms of the inherent propensity of states to expand.[14] Nationalist, ethnic, and cultural motivations for Vietnamese and Indonesian expansion are plausible and have solid historical precedents. And to the extent that "regional organization corresponds to countries falling within that sphere, then the nature of a successful grouping will likely be hegemonical."[15] The obvious differences in the strategies and structures of the two hegemonic subsystems can be explained in terms of available, usable power in which security is perceived not "solely as a military matter in the conventional sense" but can be envisioned as including "sources of domestic instability—political, economic, social, cultural, and ideological."[16]

The realignment of the region which followed the collapse of the bipolar global system offered Southeast Asia an opportunity to strengthen regional identity and cooperative mechanisms as had never previously been possible. The suddenness of the transformation was nearly incomprehensible but much foundation work had been done previously to take advantage of the opportunity. For example, although the ASEAN group had successfully challenged Vietnam's policies in Cambodia, Indonesia particularly had been careful to try to maintain contacts and dialogue with Vietnam so that, when the opportunities arose the ASEAN group was ready to make the transformation from confrontation to communication quickly. Vietnam was invited to the 1992 ASEAN foreign ministers meetings in Manila to sign the ASEAN Treaty of Amity and Cooperation giving Vietnam observer status within ASEAN. Within a short period of time, Laos was also considering a formal relationship with the ASEAN group.

For the first time ever, regional relations have begun to encompass the entire region in principally cooperative activities. Perhaps one of the ironies of the situation is that China—the extraregional power with the longest history of interest and involvement in the region—is again emerging in a strong position. Much of the motivation underlying the quick and, apparently, easy accommodation between Vietnam and the other Southeast Asian states is a common fear of China, particularly given China's recent expressions of intent to greatly expand its naval capacities. At the 1992 ASEAN foreign ministers conference, a five-point program on the peaceful settlement of regional disputes was announced, and the primary focus of this declaration was China.

Regional relations remain far from perfect. The Philippines remains one of the weaker partners in the ASEAN group, and Burma has not moved to become part of the organization. The road ahead for Vietnam and ASEAN may not be smooth, particularly as Indonesia and Vietnam compete for leadership within the organization.

The value of regional cooperation for the states of Southeast Asia is beyond dispute. It will not undo the subordinate status of the region, but it has been shown to give the region a much more effective voice in the global system than the individual states could claim for themselves. Such cooperation in the traditional Southeast Asian system might have provided a very different story-line for Asia in the sixteenth through the early twentieth centuries, yet the common cultural experience of these earlier centuries for the contemporary states has been very important in strengthening cooperation. Nevertheless in contemporary economic relations, the ASEAN group has successfully negotiated agreements with most major powers and most other regional organizations, and in political matters ASEAN's successful handling of its Cambodian challenge of Vietnam was an example of very sophisticated diplomacy. Southeast Asia has clearly entered a new era of cooperation and regional strength.

System Dependence

As the Cambodian crisis so aptly demonstrated, a principal characteristic of any subordinate system is its relatively higher degree of dependence on some greater system rather than the reverse. This was true for the traditional Southeast Asian system, and it remains true today. Southeast Asia has demonstrated that under certain circumstances, it can influence and even overcome policy objectives of states in the dominant global system, as when nationalist movements defeated the returning colonial powers, when the North Vietnamese defeated the United States, and when the ASEAN states martialed UN support against the Soviet Union and Vietnam on issues regarding Cambodia. But despite these specific incidents, Southeast Asia as a subordinate, regional system remains limited in its ability to influence the global system.

Nonetheless, clear limits have also been found in the ability of global actors to influence the region. The United States was unable to achieve its goal in Vietnam; the Soviet Union was careful to remain aloof when China attacked its Vietnamese ally; and even the Chinese did not attempt a full-scale military intervention in Vietnam. Thailand, the Philippines, and others—fearing the worst when U.S. troops withdrew from the region—have found that alternative arrangements and linkages with regional neighbors may be more effective and dependable than fickle relationships with globally oriented superpowers. As the global system became less polarized and the superpowers concomitantly lost some of their ideological will and zeal for imposing their policy prescriptions on client and other subordinate states, the countries of Southeast Asia, individually and collectively, found greater policy latitude in regional and international affairs.

Consequently, Southeast Asia's dependence has lessened, and its regional states have opened new relations with former enemies and developed closer working relationships among themselves in an attempt to control and resolve regional conflicts before extraregional powers become involved. Some degree of perhaps issue-specific dependence will continue, but regional states will find more opportunities to shape the nature of global interventions to fit their own regional and national needs. Within the region, the collapse of the Soviet Union and declining U.S. interest in Southeast Asia left a power vacuum. However, whereas the United States will continue to play a role in regional affairs and China will seek to assert greater influence in the region, much of the vacuum has been filled by the regional states themselves. Southeast Asia has not lost its subordinate status, but the convergence of declining capacities at the global level and increasing strength at the regional level has given Southeast Asia a measure of autonomy and control of its destiny that has rarely been possible in the past.

Conclusion

Many have argued that Southeast Asia—like the unicorn—does not, in fact, exist as more than a geographic place that requires external molding to give it structure and to define its reality. Others—searching for a rose—have found social, political, economic, anthropological, biological, botanical, or other evidence to "prove" that the region exists. One critic has maintained that no group of states should be considered a true region unless the states show (1) a "common institutional structure," (2) some "common cementing experience," or (3) distinctive and intensive interstate actions.[17] The evidence reported in this book demonstrates that Southeast Asia has met these criteria, although the Southeast Asian system may not be as tidy as that of Europe or some other regions. It must also be acknowledged that Southeast Asia as a contemporary term and in its historical context is still in the definitional stages, but—both historically and currently—Southeast Asians have "abundantly demonstrated their capacity to absorb and, more important, to discriminate in what they absorb"[18] in the process of creating a system suitable to their circumstances. It is essential to understand that Southeast Asians have undertaken the task of defining themselves and their region—as they have for millennia—and that conformity to Western models or definitions is less important than it was in the years immediately following World War II when these states gained their independence. At the national and popular levels, Western political and social institutions have been rejected, not out of hand and categorically but with the qualification—as old as the region itself—that externally derived concepts and institutions will be blended with the indigenous (much of which was also previously imported) and fitted to local sensibilities and needs. Similarly, at the regional level the states of Southeast Asia have found a common bond, based on their unique national systems, that has given the region a unity and resilience to speak with a single voice, or even multiple voices in harmony, to better deal with regional problems and extraregional influences.

Southeast Asia's status as a subordinate system will not change. However, the latitude for independent action, as well as the capacity to undertake independent action, among the regional states has changed dramatically since World War II. It is hypothetically possible that this greater capacity could be reversed or, perhaps more likely, that actors from the global system will regain the will and the commitment to undertake more penetration and manipulation in the region. (Perhaps, for example, heightened global competition and confrontation between China and the United States would stimulate such involvement.) But such a reversal would require dealing with a group of states that is almost uniformly stronger internally, in both political and economic terms, than in decades past and that is substantially more committed to maintaining Southeast Asia as a discrete regional entity than at any time in the past.

At no time during the traditional or colonial eras was the sense of regional community as strong as it is today. The confidence and solidarity that are derived from that sense of community have provided a fertile environment for the cultivation of a regional "rose" unique in its social, cultural, political, and economic characteristics but, importantly, a rose of indigenous propagation derived from a core continuity of thought—of cultural, social, and political values—that has survived through the millennia. This body of thought was disrupted by the colonial intrusion, and some of its tenets were undoubtedly lost or altered in the process. It has also been challenged by the global pressures on the region from the contemporary international system, especially during the cold war, and from the general encroachment of Western thought and values. At independence, even the political elites accepted much of Western thought and attempted to organize independent states along Western lines. But this continuity of thought has been maintained not so much at the elite level as at the popular level—among farmers and villagers, transplanted urban laborers, petty bureaucrats, and private citizens. Slow to grasp Western ideas put forth by their own leaders, these groups have inexorably drawn their leaders toward the more familiar, safe, and understandable—toward the neotraditional concepts now being asserted throughout the region as the standard form for government and society.

NOTES

1. Fred W. Riggs, *Thailand: Modernization of a Bureaucratic Polity* (Honolulu: East-West Center Press, 1966), pp. 91–109.

2. John F. Cady, *A History of Modern Burma* (Ithaca: Cornell University Press, 1958), p. 597.

3. John K. Whitmore, "The Opening of Southeast Asia: Trading Patterns Through the Centuries," in *Economic Exchange and Social Interaction in Southeast Asia*, edited by Karl L. Hutter (Ann Arbor: Michigan Papers on South and Southeast Asia, no. 13, 1977), pp. 73–96.

4. "Malaysia; Foreign Affairs," *Asia 1975 Yearbook* (Hong Kong: Far Eastern Economic Review, 1975), p. 217.

5. Milton Osborne, *Region in Revolt: Focus on Southeast Asia* (Victoria: Penguin Books, 1971), p. 184.

6. Jon M. Reinhardt, *Foreign Policy and National Integration: The Case of Indonesia* (New Haven: Yale University, Southeast Asian Studies Monograph Series, no. 17, 1971), p. 149.

7. Lucian W. Pye, "Armies in the Process of Political Modernization," in *The Role of the Military in Underdeveloped Countries*, edited by John J. Johnson (Princeton: Princeton University Press, 1962), p. 75.

8. Werner Levi, "The Future of Southeast Asia," *Asian Survey* 10 (April 1970), p. 350.

9. Rodney Tasker, "ASEAN; Facing Up to Security," *Far Eastern Economic Review* (August 6, 1992), pp. 8–9.

10. "Malaysia, RI and S'pore Go On Fighting Piracy and Pollution," *Jakarta Post* (February 23, 1993), p. 5.

11. Melvin Gurtov, *China and Southeast Asia—The Politics of Survival* (Lexington, Mass.: Heath Lexington Books, 1971), p. 177.

12. Sheldon Simon, "East Asia," in *World Politics*, edited by James N. Rosenau, Kenneth Thompson, and Gavin Boyd (New York: The Free Press, 1976), p. 530.

13. Sheldon W. Simon, "The Two Southeast Asias and China: Security Perspectives," *Asian Survey* 24 (May 1984), p. 519.

14. J. A. Hobson, *Imperialism: A Study* (Ann Arbor: University of Michigan Press, 1965), pp. 3–27; and Joseph A. Schumpeter, "Imperialism and Social Classes," in *The Imperialism Reader*, edited by Louis L. Snyder (Princeton: D. Van Nostrand, 1962).

15. Reinhardt, *Foreign Policy and National Integration*, p. 149.

16. Peter Polomka, "Intra-Regional Dynamics: ASEAN and Indochina," in *International Security in Southeast Asia and the Southwest Pacific Region*, edited by T. B. Millar (St. Lucia: University of Queensland Press, 1983), p. 117, citing Jusuf Wanandi, "The International Implications of Third World Conflict: A Third World Perspective," in *Third World Conflict and International Security, Part I* (London: International Institute for Strategic Studies, Adelphi Papers no. 166, Summer 1981).

17. Peter Lyon, *War and Peace in South-East Asia* (London: Oxford University Press, 1969), p. 3.

18. Charles A. Fisher, *South-East Asia: A Social, Economic and Political Geography* (London: Methuen, 1964), p. 776.

About the Book and Author

Bridging the perceived gap between Southeast Asia's historical and contemporary situations, Donald McCloud focuses on continuities in the region's internal dynamics as well as its relationship to the greater global environment. The author challenges widely held views that diversity and fragmentation are the hallmarks of the region, identifying instead the commonalities that have bound the countries of Southeast Asia together through at least two millennia and have provided the basis for a unique regional dynamic.

It has only been since World War II that Southeast Asians, long influenced by the global environment, have defined and developed their own institutions, social structures, and communities. Turning away from inadequate and unadaptable Western institutions, they have begun to create structures more in tune with their own historical experiences. Particularly in the political sphere, many of these new structures seemed to be straightforward military dictatorships. However, time has shown them to be more complex, and many unique organizational practices have developed that may presage more open political systems—if not democracies by strict Western definitions.

With the expansion of regional cooperation through ASEAN and strong economic growth, confidence among Southeast Asian states has grown as well. The growing references to an "Asian way" of life have given verbal expression to a surge in neotraditional values and behavior that have always been part of the fabric of Asian life but that in the past were frowned upon as "nonwestern." This text traces the evolution of Southeast Asia and focuses for the first time on the neotraditional bases for contemporary, independent development of the region.

Donald G. McCloud is senior associate director of the Midwest Universities Consortium for International Activities (MUCIA).

Index